ADVANCES IN CONTROL NETWORKS AND LARGE-SCALE PARALLEL DISTRIBUTED PROCESSING MODELS

edited by

Martin D. Fraser

Department of Mathematics and Computer Science
Georgia State University
Atlanta, GA

ABLEX PUBLISHING CORPORATION
NORWOOD, NEW JERSEY

Printed in the United States of America

Library of Congress Cataloging-in-Publication Data

Advances in control networks and large-scale parallel distributed processing models / edited by Martin D. Fraser.
p. cm.
Includes bibliographical references and index.
ISBN 0-89391-647-1 (cl)
1. Parallel processing (Electronic computers) 2. Electronic data processing—Distributed processing. 3. Neural networks (Computer science) I. Fraser, Martin D.
QA76.58.A38 1990
004′.35—dc20 90-1192
CIP

Ablex Publishing Corporation
355 Chestnut Street
Norwood, New Jersey 07648

Contents

Series Editor's Preface

This is the first volume of a series concerned with state-of-the-art developments in modeling control and processing in distributed networks. Contributions from researchers and practitioners in universities, private industry, and government are included. This initial volume reports a broad range of advances in neurobiological, simulation, robotic, control, and mathematical modeling.

Recent interest in massively parallel computing has refreshed the efforts to determine the computational basis of biological information processing. Kammen and Yuille study the use of global modification and adaptation rules in biological systems, specifically visual cortex. They review the biological evidence for the "Hebb rule," describe a number of applications of Hebbian learning to computer vision algorithms, and give results on training and teaching motion-sensitive and velocity-tuned cells. Hartline points out recent research indicates neurons are not just passive network elements but have computational properties, which are modifiable by biochemically mediated reprogramming. He presents a model designed for neurophysiologically realistic simulation of small networks of real neurons. Further, he describes the biochemical elements of this model which allow nerve cells to be reprogrammed. Eilbert and Guez suggest that the success of animals on perceptual and common sense reasoning tasks far exceeds the best machine intelligence, which may be due to structural simplifications commonly made by modelers. They discuss the Hierarchical Neural Network project, whose goal is to produce a network capable of controlling an autonomous system. They develop a biological basis for the design by showing that a hierarchical structure occurs in the model similar to that in vertebrate brains.

Competitive activation, recently proposed by Reggia, is a new approach to producing competitive or inhibitory effects in connectionist models. Reggia, Sutton, and Cho present methodological concepts for deriving competitive interaction mechanisms and describe initial work on formulating learning methods which use this mechanism. The authors explore methodology needed to apply this mechanism in two large, complex networks: print-to-sound conversion, and diagnostic hypothesis generation. Besides connectionist models applications, there is growing interest in decentralized, or hostless, control for the allocation of scarce resources, such as in multiprocessing or multitasking computing environments. Gagliano and Schaefer develop a decentralized control model, the Challenge Ring, which is abstracted from a few, essential features of market processes. They study abstract agents which follow strategies leading to cooperation or defection in the context of past experience. The authors present simulations which indicate that, in busy systems, a hostless system can perform more effectively than a hosted system when agents cooperate.

Redundant manipulator systems are characterized by an excess of degrees of freedom with respect to the number of parameters required for a task. Mussa-Ivaldi, Morasso, Hogan, and Bizzi note that redundancy is attracting attention in robotics research because it appears to be the key to versatility in human movements. The authors study redundancy in both biological and artificial manipulator systems and use distributed processing models to represent control and planning processes. They exploit the notion of motor impedance and obtain a natural representation and regularization of kinematic redundancy. Another view of control is voting, which is not only a political process but is also a general systems technique. Windeknecht and Gagliano describe a voting model which provides a means for studying the dynamic stability and convergence of the global search process found in specific instances of voting. They use the stereotype approach to modeling and analyzing voting groups and present a theory of stability, convergence, and computation.

Networks of model neurons can be expected to find uses in future computing systems. Koikkalainen and Oja introduce a general purpose development environment for neural networks, CARELIA, implemented in Occam on a multi-Transputer processor network. The authors point out that such environments are the first step for more general uses of neural networks. The system level of CARELIA is built as a network of communicating layers, which are networks of communicating neurons. The authors have studied existing neural network architectures to design preprogrammed neural primitives. D'Autrechy and Reggia point to the resurgence of interest in developing neurobiologically motivated parallel processing models and to the great variety of approaches taken in developing these connectionist models. The authors describe the Maryland MIRRORS/II connectionist model simulation system, a general purpose software environment for developing and evaluating simulations. They characterize the system in terms of a high-level nonprocedural language, a general event handling mechanism, and an integrated library system. Cavallo, Baran, and Restorff point out that the size of model networks is restricted by the growth rate of the storage requirements for the synaptic weight matrix. They study accelerating the Glauber dynamics on local memory multiprocessor systems using simulations. A network is partitioned into subnets distributed among the parallel processors, which perform coordinated isolated updating.

Information systems in their most general form are systems for storing, manipulating, and retrieving data. Coleman proposes that a formal logic for describing the behavior of networks can provide information on the flow of processes and make the sense in which behavior can be shared between networks rigorous. He views network processes as generalized computations and describes and investigates the structure of the system with category theory. Dare and Zobrist point out that the amount of data needed to be processed by information systems, and the diversity of organizations using them, are increasing dramatically. They suggest that this increased expectation and use of information systems has produced a favorable environment for sharing research objectives and methods between artificial intelligence, neural network, and database systems.

The editor wishes to thank the contributing authors for making available the information contained in this book. Subsequent volumes will continue the focus of this volume:

- models and methodologies for distributed control and parallel distributed processing networks
- feedback and control, distributed control, and self-organization
- model performance evaluation
- testing of models and simulations
- learning and memory
- internodal communications and network flow
- information transmission and processing.

Researchers who wish to submit manuscripts for future editions of this Advance series should contact: Dr. Martin D. Fraser, Department of Mathematics and Computer Science, Georgia State University, Atlanta, GA 30303.

Martin D. Fraser
Atlanta, Georgia

1

Self-Organizing Neural Networks: Hebbian Learning in Development and Biological Computing*

Daniel M. Kammen
Division of Biology
and Division of Engineering and Applied Science
California Institute of Technology
Pasadena, CA

Alan L. Yuille
Division of Applied Science
Harvard University

1. INTRODUCTION

The recent interest in massively parallel computing has cast a new light on efforts to determine the computational basis of biological information processing. Computation in biological systems is interesting both in that the information processing appears to employ highly parallel architecture, at least at some stages, and in that the coordination of massive numbers of neurons requires sophisticated developmental and functional algorithms. From a theoretical, or systems analysis perspective, this investigation involves the integration of biological learning rules to both "wire up" the known cortical circuitry and to allow the adult organism sufficient flexibility to react and adapt to novel environmental conditions.

Among primate sensory modalities none has received such intensive anatomical and physiological scrutiny as has the visual system. Of the 10^{11} or 10^{12} neurons and more than 10^{15} synapses in the human brain, perhaps one third are involved in the processing of visual information. The visual system thus presents a particularly intriguing environment for the study of systems development and

* A.L.Y. would like to thank the Brown, Harvard, and M.I.T. Center for Intelligent Control Systems for an United States Army Research Office grant number DAAL03-86-C-0171. D.M.K. is the recipient of a Weizmann Postdoctoral Fellowship. We would also like to thank Roger Brockett for his support. Conversations with Jim Clark, John Daugman, Dan Kersten, Graeme Mitchison, and Norberto Grzywacz were extremely useful. Some of the work reported here was completed with D. Cohen and W. Softky.

adaptation, in that techniques to simulate and integrate large numbers of processing units as well as large amounts of input information are necessary. In addition, studies of prenatal animals have revealed that, while the circuitry and function of individual cells is altered by the environment, much of the system develops prior to exposure to the visual world.

Precisely because of the scale, complexity, and inherent developmental capability of the system, we have selected it to illustrate the use of global modification and adaptation rules in biological systems. To begin with, we will present a brief summary of the physiology and developmental history of the visual cortex. We shall see that the internal structures of individual cell types in the mammalian visual cortex, as well as the basic connectivity patterns present between neurons in the striate (visual) cortex, are well predicted by the maturation of a population of cells under the influence of a set of remarkably simple developmental principles. We will then explore a biophysically motivated synaptic modification scheme, the "Hebb rule," that has been demonstrated to take place in a number of neural cell types and is particularly useful from a computational perspective. Hebbian, or activity dependent, modification schemes are interesting from a systems analysis perspective in that they lead to unsupervised "self-organization" of the network into a computationally useful structure without the need for detailed task specification or supervision (i.e., a "teacher"). We will then describe a number of applications of Hebbian learning to computer vision algorithms, and the genesis of networks that perform useful object recognition and data compression of input visual images.

The organization of this chapter is as follows. After briefly reviewing the biological evidence for Hebbian learning, we describe several theoretical scenarios for the development of orientation selective cells in the visual cortex (section 2). We consider the effect of using structured data (section 3) and then show that similar ideas, supplemented with training by example, can be used to model the development of motion and velocity sensitive cells (section 4).

1.1. Biological Evidence for Hebbian Learning

In 1949 Donald Hebb postulated that a *sensible* synaptic plasticity scheme would be one whereby correlated activity in neurons resulted in enhanced efficacy, or strength, of the synaptic connection. Given a presynaptic cell, A, and a postsynaptic cell, C, Hebb suggested that correlated activity in cell A and in the postsynaptic cell C would lead to an enhancement in the strength of the connection, or synapse, from A to C. Among the natural modifications of this scheme is the addition of collective activity, such as a second presynaptic cell, B, that must also exhibit enhanced activity in order to generate an increase in the strength between cells A and C, and the introduction of anti-Hebbian learning, or the reduction in the synaptic strength between two cells when their activity is anticorrelated.

Since Hebb's initial statement of the learning rule a number of experiments have been performed to test the hypothesis in a number of organisms and several mammalian cortical areas. Carew et al. (1984) have found that a version of the Hebb-rule involving a second presynaptic cell, B, in conjunction with cell A does result in modification of the A to C synaptic strength. These experiments were performed on neurons involved in a motor response: the defensive withdrawal reflex. In addition, a series of experiments by Brown (Kelso, Ganong, & Brown, 1986; Brown, Chaug, Ganong, Keenan, & Kelso, 1988) and his collaborators, as well as Stanton and Senjowski (1989), have revealed that CA3 pyramidal cell pairs in rat hippocampus, the cortical area commonly associated with associative memory, do exhibit Hebbian synapse modification.

In the visual cortex recent experiments have also revealed Hebb-type synapse modification. In experiments on binocular cells in kittens deprivation of input from one eye has resulted in the postsynaptic cell that receives input from both eyes responding exclusively to the cells leading up from the open eye (Rauschecker & Singer, 1979), even though the deprived eye and visual pathway remain functional.

2. QUADRATURE AND ORIENTATION SELECTIVE CELLS

Our first example is a Hebbian model for the development of orientation selective cells in the visual cortex (Yuille, Kammen, & Cohen, 1989). After a survey of the basic properties of cortical neurons we describe the mechanics of the model in detail, both as a necessary lead-in to future sections that will build on the basic model and as a simple example of the workings of a Hebbian modification scheme.

Linsker (1986a,b,c) has described a self-organizing model using a linear feed-forward layered network of cells which develop center-surround receptive fields and orientation selectivity. This orientation selectivity develops even though the system is symmetric and depends only on the form of the correlation function of the activities of the cells of the previous layer. Kammen and Yuille (1988) and Softky and Kammen (1990) showed that the development of orientation selectivity could be explained in terms of spontaneous symmetry breaking of an energy function which governs the maturation of the receptive fields. The key point is that, although the minima of the energy function are distributed symmetrically, the system can only go to one minimum, and the specific choice (which is determined by arbitrarily small noise fluctuations) breaks the symmetry. These models produce receptive field profiles that resemble those measured experimentally (Jones & Palmer, 1987) in cat striate cortex, although our simulations of the symmetry-breaking model have only produced cells with symmetric center/surround receptive fields (see Figure 1.1).

Experiments have been performed on cats and monkeys which suggest that the orientation selectivity in regions of the cortex is correlated with the orientation tuning in the corresponding regions of the retina (Schall, Perry, & Leventhal, 1986a; Schall, Vitek, & Leventhal, 1986b; Schall & Leventhal, 1987). A "wave of maturation," or progression of developmental activity (Schall et al., 1986a) may be responsible for this selectivity by sequentially biasing the dendritic fields of retinal ganglion cells from circularly symmetric to slightly elliptical in an orderly fashion across the retina. Systematic inhomogenieties in the initial dendritic fields, therefore, could serve to bias the maturation of the cortical mosaic of cells, and by the presence of a "pattern" or "seed" much like the activity of a boiling chip in a beaker of heated water (Kammen, 1988). Linsker (personal communication, June 1988) reports that small asymmetries in the correlation function (which could arise naturally from geometric asymmetries) do not affect his results significantly.

In the following sections we will present a new model, with a theoretically motivated version of the Hebb rule, in which orientation selectivity occurs due to amplification of small asymmetries in the correlation function, rather than by spontaneous symmetry breaking. At this point a natural connection between the maturation of cells designed to filter input signals and optimal algorithms from information theory presents itself. Oja (1982, 1989; see also Cooper, Liberman, & Oja, 1979, and Linsker, 1988) has shown that some versions of the Hebb rule naturally extract the principal, or most significant, components from an input message, given that the network must preserve this incident information with a finite number of channels (neurons). In the extension to the symmetry-breaking model (section 2.2.1) presented below, the introduction of biologically observed lateral connections between neurons in the same layer of the network results in an array of cells that perform principal component analysis and exhibit quadrature, or "spatial phase-opponent" receptive field structure as observed by Pollen and Ronner (1981) in cat cortical cells. Lateral inhibitory connections are critically important for orientation selectivity (Sillito, 1987). Linsker (1986c) has used excitatory connections to generate neighboring cells with identical orientation selectivity, while in our model this effect is achieved by the (small) asymmetry of the correlation function.

Moreover, with the addition of inhibitory terms between cells at the same layer, this model leads naturally to the development of quadrature pairs (adjacent cells with the same orientation tuning but 90 degree spatial phase differences; see Figure 1.1) of orientation selective cells. The phenomena of quadrature is an intriguing experimental and theoretical question. It was first reported by Pollen and Ronner (1981), and more recently Jones and Palmer (1987) have shown that receptive fields of both types exist. Daugman (1985) has shown that cosine and sine Gabor functions (which correspond to a quadrature pair) are good approximations to the receptive field profiles. He also points out that Gabor functions are, in a certain mathematical sense, optimal for information transmission (Gabor, 1946). Thus, the phenomenon of quadrature seems closely related to

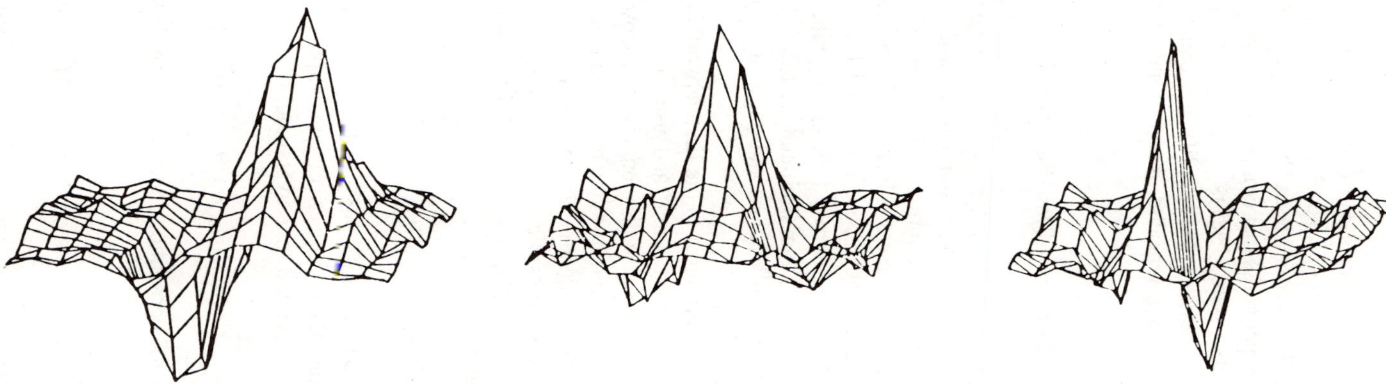

Figure 1.1. Receptive field profiles of orientation selective cortical cells in the cat. The spontaneous symmetry breaking model only generates "symmetric" receptive fields of type (b). Our new model generates receptive fields of all three kinds. The experimental results of Pollen and Ronner suggest that "symmetric" and "asymmetric" cells occur in quadrature pairs. From Daugman (1985): the profiles were recorded by Drs. Palmer and Jones at the University of Pennsylvania Medical School.

information processing ideas. Some theories of motion measurement (Heeger, 1987; Grzywacz & Yuille, 1989) also make use of Gabor functions on computational grounds. Quadrature cells have also been shown to develop in one-dimensional, backpropagation-based networks that compress the signal by squeezing it through a layer of hidden units (Spiro, 1987).

Finally, some remarks on notation. To simplify the equations we use the summation convention; if an index is repeated, then it is automatically summed; i.e., $f_i F_{ij} \equiv \Sigma_i f_i F_{ij}$.

2.1. Brief Description of the Symmetry-Breaking Model

This section gives a brief description of the symmetry-breaking model. We outline the mathematical construction here; a complete description of the symmetry-breaking scenario can be found in Kammen and Yuille (1988) and Kammen (1988). The model is essentially the same as Linsker's (1986a,b,c) but differs in two respects: (a) Our model does not impose upper and lower bounds on the strength of synapses, but instead uses terms in the energy function to keep the strengths finite; (b) We take the continuum limit and treat the synaptic strengths as a field $\phi(x,y)$. The network is purely linear, and our analysis depends on this fact.

The basic model assumes random input to the first network layer (we assume the continuum limit for ease of calculation) and uses a modified Hebb-type learning rule. The feedforward geometric distribution of synapses is assumed to be a two-dimensional Gaussian, $G(x,y)$, from the neuron in layer i to a neuron in layer $(i + 1)$. The feedforward network structure (which will only have inhibition between neighboring elements when explicitly stated) is depicted in Figure 1.2. Representing synapse strengths by $\phi(x,y)$ and the input to a layer by $I(x,y)$, we then use the linear output rule:

$$O(x,y) = \int G(x - w,y - z)\phi(x - w,y - z)I(w,z)dwdz, \tag{1}$$

where $\phi(x,y)$ is the receptive field profile of a cell and is the quantity that we expect to develop into an orientation selective, bandwidth limited, structure. Multiplying equation (1) by $I(r,s)$ and time averaging:

$$\langle O(x,y)I(r,s)\rangle = \int G(x - w,y - z)\phi(x - w,y - z)\langle I(w,z)I(r,s)\rangle dwdz. \tag{2}$$

The quantity $\langle I(w,z)I(r,s)\rangle$ is the correlation function for the ith layer, which we represent as $D_i(w - r,z - s)$. Equation (2) thus becomes:

$$\langle O(x,y)I(r,s)\rangle = \int G(x - w,y - z)\phi(x - w,y - z)D(w - r,z - s)dwdz, \tag{3}$$

which we use as the increment for Hebb-type learning. We assume that the time scale of the random fluctuations of the inputs is much smaller than the time scale

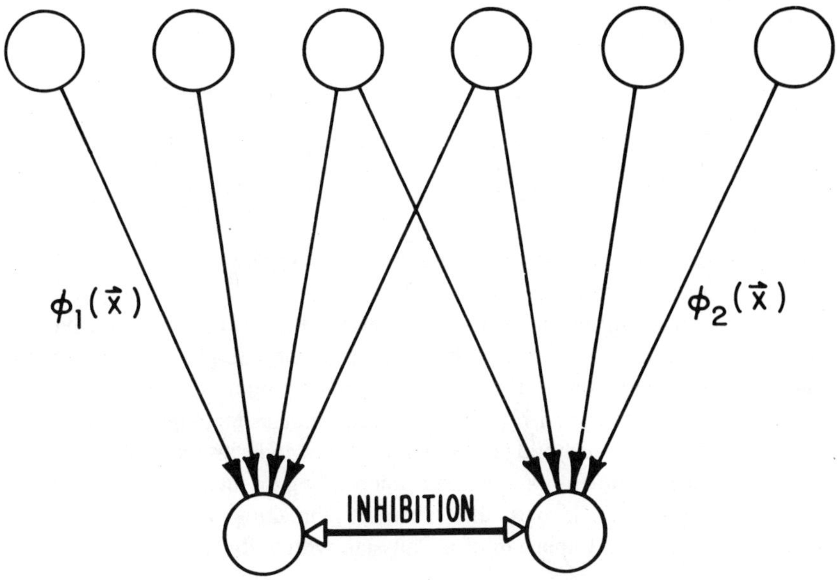

Figure 1.2. The structure of a feedforward network. The elements of the layer at the top of the figure feed into the elements of the bottom layer. Inhibition between elements in the same layer will only occur if explicitly mentioned.

for learning. This means that we can replace terms like $I(w,z)I(r,s)$ in the learning rule by their time average, $D_i(w - r, z - s)$.

The synapse modification rule used in the symmetry-breaking model is a simple continuum case of the Hebb rule:

$$\frac{d\phi(x,y)}{dt} = -A - 2B\phi(x,y) - 4C\phi(x,y)^3 + 2\int D(x - w, y - z)\phi(w,z)G(w,z)dwdz, \tag{4}$$

where the first and fourth terms in equation (4) are standard for Hebb-type learning and correspond to a general inhibition and a positive correlation for neighboring synapses, respectively. The second and third terms maintain synapse strengths in a bounded range, accomplished in other models by either setting fixed bounds (Linsker, 1986a,b,c) or using a strong saturation rule (Hopfield, 1984). The learning rule (equation 4) is related to the minimum of an energy function by the update rule popularized by Hopfield (1984):

$$\frac{d\phi(x,y)}{dt} = -\frac{\partial E[\phi(x,y)]}{\partial \phi}. \tag{5}$$

The resulting energy function:

$$E[\phi(x,y)] = A\int \phi(x,y)G(x,y)dxdy + B\int \phi(x,y)^2G(x,y)dxdy$$
$$+ C\int \phi(x,y)^4G(x,y)dxdy$$
$$- \int\int \phi(x,y)G(x,y)D(x - w,y - z)\phi(w,z)G(w,z)dxdydwdz, \quad (6)$$

exhibits spontaneous symmetry breaking, as studied in physical (Coleman, 1985) and mathematical (Sattinger, 1979) systems.

Symmetry breaking occurs when the energy function is symmetric but the individual minima are not. While the minima of the energy function are distributed symmetrically, the system can only go to one minimum, and the specific choice (which is determined by small stochastic noise fluctuations) breaks the symmetry. Kammen and Yuille (1988) demonstrated that symmetry breaking can occur for the energy function (equation 6), depending on the specific form of the correlation function, D. In particular, symmetry breaking will occur if the correlation function is the Laplacian of a Gaussian with sufficiently small standard deviation.

In this model the input $I(x,y)$ to the first layer is assumed to be uncorrelated white noise with correlation function $D_1(x,y) = N\delta(x,y)$, where N is a positive number (representing the amplitude of the noise) and $\delta(x,y)$ is the Dirac delta function. The synapses from the first to the second layer are then trained by applying the modification rule of equation 1. After these synapses have been trained, we can calculate the input to layer two again by equation 1. We can repeat this procedure by using these inputs to train the synapses from layer two to layer three (still assuming white noise as the input to the first layer). To follow the development of receptive fields in this model, only a knowledge of he variation of $D_i(x - r,y - s)$ from layer to layer is necessary. The correlation function, D, can be calculated in general from the auto-convolution of equation (1). The details can be found in Kammen and Yuille (1988), with the result that:

$$D_{i+1} = G\phi_{i,i+1} * D_i * G\phi_{i,i+1} \quad (7)$$

where $\phi_{i,i+1}$ represent the synapses from layer i to $i + 1$. The correlation function in the first layer is simply a Dirac δ-function because the input signal is assumed to be white noise. The interaction term, D_i, is therefore determined for the entire multi-layer system. Symmetry breaking depends on the form of D. For early layers D remains roughly Gaussian, and no symmetry breaking is observed. As D develops into $-\nabla^2G(x,y)$ symmetry breaking will occur, and orientation selectivity results.

2.2. The Principal Component Analysis

Unlike the approach taken previous studies (Linsker, 1986a,b,c; Kammen & Yuille, 1988), we will not consider the development of all the layers, but will concentrate only on the layer at which orientation selectivity occurs. The development of center/surround receptive fields (Mexican-hat profiles) is simple to generate within any model employing Gaussian filters of various sizes (e.g., Kammen & Yuille, 1988), and this will be assumed to have occurred in the prior development of the neurons in the network.

We can now show that a model which uses a Hebb rule that extracts the principal component of the input signal will also give rise to orientation selectivity by a mechanism different from, but related to, symmetry breaking.

Suppose we have a system of N vectors f_i^μ, where μ labels the vectors and i labels their components. The Karhunen-Loeve matrix is defined to be F_{ij}, where

$$F_{ij} = \frac{1}{N} \sum_{\mu=1}^{N} f_i^\mu f_j^\mu. \tag{8}$$

The eigenvectors of this matrix correspond to the principal components. The eigenvectors with the biggest eigenvalues carry the most important information. Karhunen-Loeve eigenvector analysis (or principal component analysis, PCA) is an efficient scheme for data reduction and, as the vectors are orthogonal, provides a complete basis set for the data which can be rank ordered (by the modulus of the eigenvalue).

2.2.1. Using Hebb Rules to Extract the Principal Components

Oja (1982, 1989; see also Cooper et al., 1979) developed a version of the Hebb rule that, he showed, led to a matched filter which extracted the eigenvector of the Karhunen-Loeve matrix of inputs with the largest eigenvalue. This result is very interesting and shows that the system extracts the principal component of the signal.

Oja's rule is given by

$$\frac{d\phi_i(t)}{dt} = O(t)[I_i(t) - O(t)\phi_i(t)], \tag{9}$$

where $O(t)$ is the output, $I_i(t)$ are the inputs, and $\phi_i(t)$ are the synaptic strengths. These are related by

$$O(t) = \sum_j \phi_j(t) I_j(t). \tag{10}$$

Suppose we have input generated by some stochastic process in time. Again we assume that the time scale of the random fluctuations of the inputs is much smaller than the time scale for learning. Then the Karhunen-Loeve matrix is equivalent to the correlation function of the input

$$F_{ij} = \langle I_i(t) I_j(t) \rangle \tag{11}$$

Taking the expectation value of equation (10) and using (9), we obtain (using the summation convention):

$$\frac{d\phi_i(t)}{dt} = \phi_j(t) F_{ij} - \phi_i(t)\phi_j(t)\phi_k(t) F_{jk}. \tag{12}$$

It is clear that the only steady state solutions of this equation occur at eigenvectors of the Karhunen-Loeve matrix $F_{ij}\phi_j = \lambda\phi_i$, or at $\phi_i = 0$. It is also intuitive, and Oja quotes just such a theorem, that the most stable state is the largest eigenvalue of the Karhunen-Loeve matrix.

We now modify Oja's result to obtain a Hebb rule that minimizes a cost function and extracts the principal component. This simplifies the analysis of convergence and, in particular, provides a simple proof that the only stable solution corresponds to the eigenvector with biggest positive eigenvalue, or to $\phi_i = 0$, if no positive eigenvalue exists.

We define a cost function $E(\phi_i)$ by

$$E(\phi_i) = -\frac{1}{2} F_{ij}\phi_i\phi_j + \frac{k}{4} (\phi_i\phi_i)^2, \tag{13}$$

where k is a positive constant.

Performing steepest descent on this function gives an update rule

$$\frac{d\phi_i}{dt} = F_{ij}\phi_j - k\phi_i(\phi_j\phi_j). \tag{14}$$

The first term on the right-hand side of equation 14 is a standard Hebb rule (the expectation value of the correlation between the input and the output), and the second term provides a mechanism to limit the strength of the synapses. From (14) we see that extrema of the cost function are either eigenvectors of the Karhunen-Loeve matrix $F_{ij}\phi_j = \lambda\phi_i$ with $|\phi_i| = \sqrt{(\lambda/k)}$ (this means only eigenvectors with positive eigenvalues correspond to extrema), or are $\phi_i = 0$. The stability of these extrema can be found by computing the Hessian H_{ij}:

$$H_{ij} = \frac{\partial^2 E}{\partial\phi_i \partial\phi_j} = -F_{ij} + k(\phi_k\phi_k)\delta_{ij} + 2k\phi_i\phi_j. \tag{15}$$

Hence, the extremum $\phi_i = 0$ is a minimum if, and only if, F_{ij} is negative definite (which is impossible if F_{ij} is a Karhunen-Loeve matrix).

To investigate the stability at the other points, we first observe that the eigenvectors of the Hessian evaluated at these extrema are just the eigenvectors of the Karhunen-Loeve matrix. Thus we can diagonalize the Hessian using these eigenvectors. To determine the stability of an extremum at an eigenvector ϕ_i with eigenvalue λ, we need only to compute the products $H_{ij}\psi_i\psi_j$ for all eigenvectors ψ_i. The extremum will be stable if, and only if, all these products are positive. For an eigenvector ψ_i (of unit norm) with eigenvalue μ we find

$$H_{ij}\psi_i\psi_j = (\lambda - \mu), \tag{16}$$

for $\psi_i \neq \phi_i$, and

$$H_{ij}\psi_i\psi_j = 2\lambda, \tag{17}$$

for $\psi = \phi$. This will be positive definite for all (ψ_i, μ) if, and only if, λ is the biggest positive eigenvalue of F_{ij}.

To summarize:

(1) if F_{ij} is negative definite (which is impossible for a Karhunen-Loeve matrix), then the only minimum of the cost function is $\phi_i = 0$,

(2) if F_{ij} has positive eigenvalues, then the only minimum is the biggest positive eigenvalue.

2.2.2. The Continuum Limit

The analysis of the eigenvectors for our system is simplified by taking the continuum limit. In this limit the Karhunen-Loeve matrix becomes the correlation matrix of the inputs $F_{ij} \rightarrow D(\vec{x} - \vec{y})$, assuming that the input is translation invariant. The eigenvectors $f(\vec{x})$ obey the equation

$$\int D(\vec{x} - \vec{y})f(\vec{y})d\vec{y} = \lambda f(\vec{x}). \tag{18}$$

Applying the convolution theorem, we find that (for all $\vec{w}$)

$$\bar{D}(\vec{w})\bar{f}(\vec{w}) = \lambda\bar{f}(\vec{w}), \tag{19}$$

where $\bar{f}(\vec{w})$ and $\bar{D}(\vec{w})$ are the Fourier Transforms of $f(\vec{x})$ and $D(\vec{x})$. Note that $\bar{D}(\vec{w})$ is the power spectrum of the signal. If follows that, unless $D(\vec{x})$ is a delta function (and hence $\bar{D}(\vec{w})$ is constant), the Fourier Transforms of $f(\vec{x})$ must be delta functions. Thus the eigenvectors are of form $f(\vec{x}) = sin(\vec{w}_0 \cdot \vec{x} + a)$, and the eigenvalues are $\lambda = \bar{D}(\vec{w}_0)$ for any choice of $\vec{w}_0$.

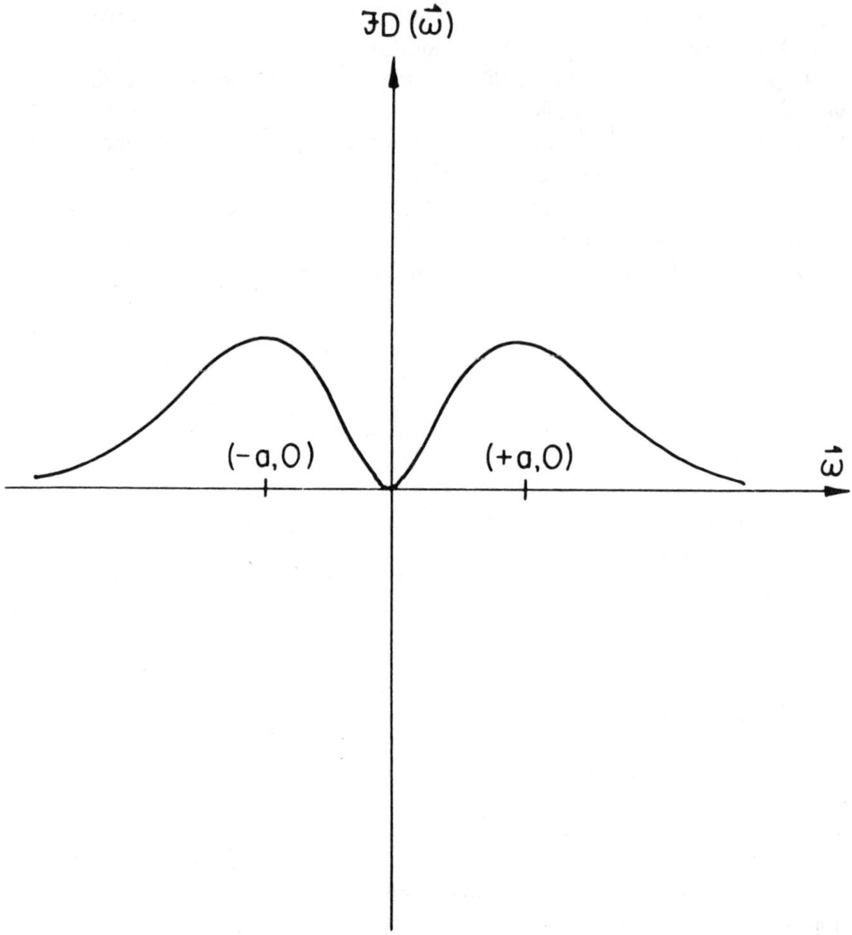

Figure 1.3. The Fourier Transforms of the correlation function. The Fourier Transform of the negative Laplacian of a Gaussian, shown in (a), is $|\vec{w}|^2 \exp\{-|\vec{w}|^2\sigma^2/2\}$ and has a positive maxima on a circle $|\vec{w}| = \sqrt{2/\sigma}$. We show a contour plot of this function in (b). The space of biggest (positive) eigevectors is degenerate and symmetry breaking need not occur in this situation. In the contour plot (c) we show that a small asymmetry in the Laplacian of a Gaussian (with eccentricity $e = \sigma_x/\sigma_y = 0.95$) reduces the degeneracy of the eigenspace, and leads to strong orientation selectivity.

This analysis gives insight into the genesis of orientation selectivity. If the maximum of $\tilde{D}(\vec{w})$ is at the origin then the biggest eigenvalue corresponds to $\vec{w} = 0$ and the eigenvector is symmetric. If, however, the maximum of $\tilde{D}(\vec{w})$ is away from the origin, for example if $D(\vec{x})$ is the negative of a Laplacian of a Gaussian (or a band-pass filter), then the biggest eigenvalues will have $|\vec{w}| = \sqrt{2}/\sigma$ and the

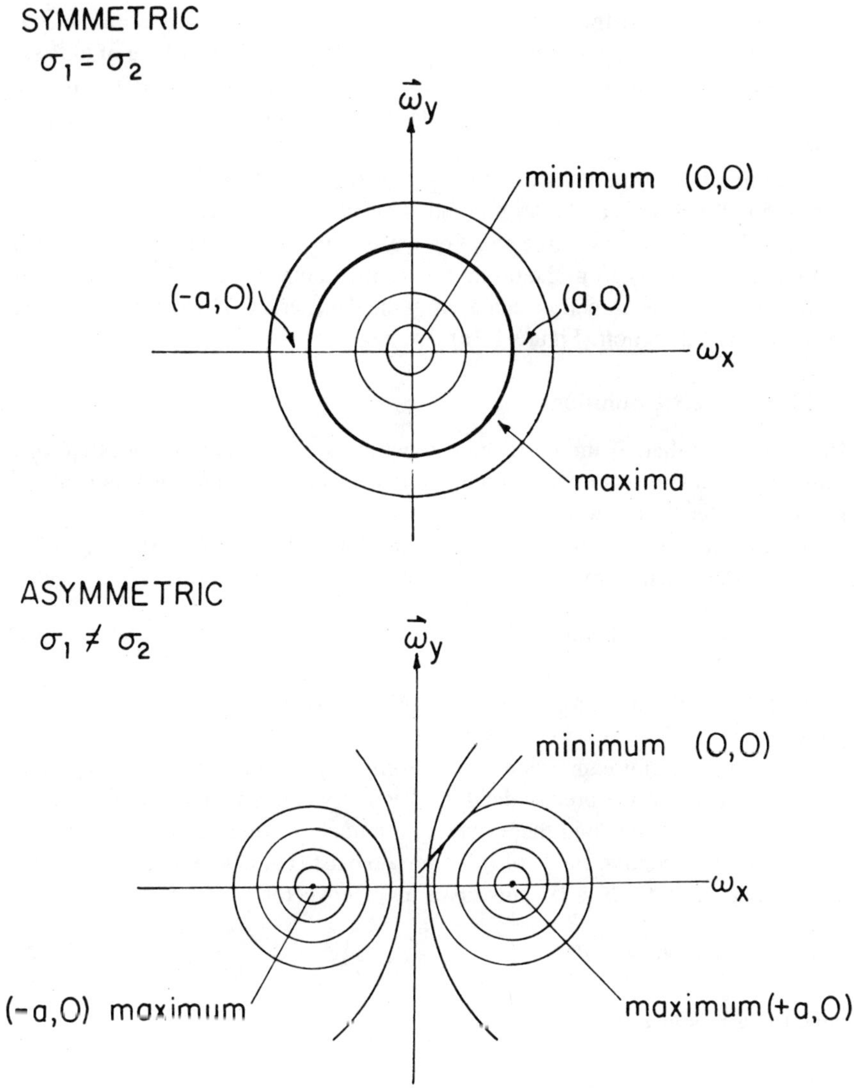

Figure 1.3. (continued)

eigenvector will have a preferred direction (see Figures 1.3a, 1.3b). However, there will be many degenerate eigenvectors with this eigenvalue, and the system will settle into a linear combination of them. By taking suitable linear combinations, it is possible to obtain a symmetric receptive field in the form of a zeroth order Bessel function (see section 2.2.3). Other combinations of eigenvectors will correspond to more complicated receptive field structures.

The degeneracy of the ground state is destroyed if there is any asymmetry in $D(\vec{w})$. For example, suppose we choose it to be the second derivative of a biased Gaussian (with unequal standard deviations in the x and y directions). This will give just two maxima, corresponding to a unique preferred direction (Figure 1.3c).

The important point is that, if the largest value of the Fourier Transform of the correlation function is at the origin (and is positive), then small asymmetries are unimportant and will have little effect on the system. If the smallest values form a symmetric ring away from the origin (as for the Laplacian of a Gaussian, Figure 1.3b), then small asymmetries can destroy the degeneracy of the system and lead to a preferred direction (Figure 1.3c).

2.2.3. Symmetric Solutions

Here we show that, if the correlation function is taken to be the negative of a Laplacian of a Gaussian, linear combinations of minimal eigenvectors can give rise to symmetric solutions.

Suppose the largest (positive) eigenvalue for $D(\vec{w})$ occurs on the ring $|\vec{w}| = w_0$. Then the eigenvectors with this eigenvalue are of the form

$$f(\vec{x}) = \sum_{\theta,\phi} a_{\theta,\phi} cos(rw_0\{cos\theta\} + \phi), \tag{20}$$

where θ labels the direction of angle of orientation in Fourier Space and ϕ is a phase angle.

Theoretically, any expression of this form might occur as a receptive field. Naturally, however, the precise dendritic geometry is likely to break the degeneracy of the eigenvalues and there may be a unique maximal eigenvector.

Symmetric receptive fields of this form do exist. For example, let $\phi = 0$ and $a_{\theta,0} = 1$, $a_{\theta,\phi} = 0$, $\phi \neq 0$. This gives an eigenvector

$$g(\vec{x}) = \int cos(rw_0\{cos\theta\})\, d\theta, \tag{21}$$

which is a Bessel function or zeroth order.

2.3. The Geometrical Distribution of Synapses

The preceding analysis assumes that the geometric distribution of synapses from one layer to the next is flat. A more realistic assumption is that the distribution of synapses falls off with distance and has a single peak. A Gaussian distribution is therefore a reasonable approximation of the synaptic distribution function. In our simulations we also consider a flat distribution with a finite cutoff. The form of the geometric distribution helps determine the spatial fall off of the receptive field profiles.

We now modify our model to take this geometry into account. We send $\phi_i \rightarrow G(\vec{x})\phi(\vec{x})$, taking the continuum limit. $G(\vec{x})$ and $\phi(\vec{x})$ correspond to the geometrical distribution of the synapses and their strengths. With this notation we can modify the energy function to be

$$E_{cell}(\vec{\phi}) = -\frac{k}{2}\int\int G(\vec{x})\phi(\vec{x})D(\vec{x} - \vec{y})G(\vec{y})\phi(\vec{y})\, d\vec{x}\, d\vec{y} + \frac{1}{4}\left(\int G(\vec{x})\phi(\vec{x})^2\, d\vec{x}\right)^2, \tag{22}$$

where $F_{ij} \rightarrow D(\vec{x} - \vec{y})$ is the correlation function. The Hebb rule is found by performing steepest descent on the energy function. This leads to (after factoring out a $G(\vec{x})$ term):

$$\frac{d\phi(\vec{x})}{dt} = k\int G(\vec{z})\phi(\vec{z})D(\vec{x} - \vec{z})d\vec{z} - \phi(\vec{x})\int G(\vec{z})\phi(\vec{z})^2 d\vec{z}. \tag{23}$$

The effect of geometry, and the need for asymmetry needed in $D(\vec{x})$, can be investigated by simulating these equations. This is described in section 2.5 below.

2.4. Quadrature

We first review the experimental and theoretical work on quadrature. Then we show that a simple modification of the model described in the previous section, by introducing inhibition between neighboring cells in the same layer (see Figure 1.2), will cause quadrature cells to develop.

Pollen and Ronner (1981) surveyed 12 pairs of adjacent simple cells in the visual cortex of the cat. In every case both cells were tuned to the same orientation and direction (to within 10°) and were tuned to the same spatial frequency (to within one-fourth octave). All pairs of cells exhibited intrapair phase shifts (see Figure 1.1) in response to a drifting grating of between 82° and 105°, with a mean value of 92.5° ± 6.5°.

Although the precise function of these cell pairs is not yet understood, the quadrature relationship is highly suggestive of some sort of signal processing application such as image decomposition by primitive basis sets (Gabor, 1946) or maximum information transmission (Barlow, 1981).

Daugman (1985) suggests that the receptive fields of pairs of cells are of the form $sin(\vec{w}\cdot\vec{x})\exp(-\|\vec{x}\|^2/2\sigma^2)$ and $cos(\vec{w}\cdot\vec{x})\exp(-\|\vec{x}\|^2/2\sigma^2)$, corresponding to sin and cos Gabor functions. Hence, the receptive fields may be a product of two mutually orthogonal terms (the sine and cosine functions) which could be generated by the PCA mechanism described in section 2.2.1, and a function (the Gaussian) which provides a spatial fall off and which might be due to the geometry of the dendritic fields. We now develop a mechanism based on inhibition to ensure that the parts of the receptive field due to the PCA mechanism are mutually orthogonal.

We assume that neighboring cells in one layer have synapses to the corresponding cells in the previous layer, and hence the correlation function is approximately the same for both cells. We now write an energy function for the system.

$$E(\phi_1(\vec{x}),\phi_2(\vec{x})) = E_{cell}(\phi_1(\vec{x})) + E_{cell}(\phi_2(\vec{x})) + E_{INT}(\phi_1(\vec{x}),\phi_2(\vec{x})), \tag{24}$$

where $\phi_1(\vec{x})$ and $\phi_2(\vec{x})$ are the synaptic strengths of the cells, E_{cell} is given by equation (22), and the interaction term E_{INT} is given by

$$E_{INT}(\phi_1(\vec{x}),\phi_2(\vec{x})) = \frac{c}{2}\left(\int\int G(\vec{x})\phi_1(\vec{x})D(\vec{x}-\vec{y})G(\vec{y})\phi_2(\vec{y})\, d\vec{x}\, d\vec{y}\right)^2. \tag{25}$$

This interaction corresponds to an inhibitory term, which, if the geometric distribution is flat ($G(\vec{x}) = 1$), forces the receptive fields of neighboring cells to be orthogonal. To see this, observe that, without interactions, the ϕ fields would converge roughly to eigenvectors of $D(\vec{x})$ with the same eigenvalue (this convergence is exact since there are no geometric terms). The interaction energy will therefore be proportional to the product of the receptive field profiles with the L^2 norm, and hence will bias neighboring cells to be orthogonal. If the geometric distribution is not flat, then the cells will only be approximately orthogonal in the L^2 sense (in agreement with experiment). Cells can be orthogonal by:

(a) having the same spatial direction but a phase shift of ninety degrees (quadrature pairs),
(b) being orthogonal in the spatial domain, or
(c) differing by some complex combination of phase shift and spatial direction.

We now minimize $E(\phi_1(\vec{x}),\phi_2(\vec{x}))$ as a function of ϕ_1 and ϕ_2 by steepest descent. This gives rise to equations

$$\frac{d\phi_1(\vec{x})}{dt} = k\int G(\vec{z})\phi_1(\vec{z})D(\vec{x}-\vec{z})d\vec{z} - \phi_1(\vec{x})\int G(\vec{z})\phi_1(\vec{z})^2 d\vec{z}$$
$$- c\int D(\vec{x}-\vec{y})G(\vec{y})\phi_2(\vec{y})\, d\vec{y}\int\int G(\vec{z})\phi_1(\vec{z})D(\vec{z}-\vec{y})G(\vec{y})\phi_2(\vec{y})\, d\vec{z}\, d\vec{y} \tag{26}$$

$$\frac{d\phi_2(\vec{x})}{dt} = k\int G(\vec{z})\phi_2(\vec{z})D(\vec{x}-\vec{z})d\vec{z} - \phi_2(\vec{x})\int G(\vec{z})\phi_2(\vec{z})^2 d\vec{z}$$
$$- c\int D(\vec{x}-\vec{y})G(\vec{y})\phi_1(\vec{y})\, d\vec{y}\int\int G(\vec{z})\phi_1(\vec{z})D(\vec{z}-\vec{y})G(\vec{y})\phi_2(\vec{y})\, d\vec{z}\, d\vec{y}. \tag{27}$$

In equations (26) and (27), the first term corresponds to a standard Hebb rule; it is the correlation between the input activity $I(\vec{x})$ to a given synapse and the output O. The second term prevents the strength of any synapse from becoming too large. Note that it requires that the overall sum of the squares of the synaptic strengths can be computed by the neuron. The third term is a standard Hebbs term weighted by the expected correlation between the activities of the two outputs. It is shown in the next section that the first and third terms follow from a standard Hebb rule after allowing for inhibition between the outputs of the two cells. This interaction is akin to shunting inhibition.

Our model of the genesis of cortical cells produces cells in quadrature spatial phase relationship. Moreover, unlike previous symmetry breaking mechanisms, we will start to get quadrature effects (symmetric and antisymmetric cells) using inhibition between cells in the same layer. This causes the receptive fields of cells to be orthogonal. If they have the same orientation tuning (which will arise from local biases in the D term), then this forces them to be ninety degrees out of phase. Intralayer inhibitory effects have been demonstrated by Vidyasagar and Urbas (1982) and Sillito (1987) in a series of impressive experiments in which the receptive field profiles of simple cortical cells were radically altered by the addition of bicuculine, a drug that is thought to destroy the normal communication between cells by blocking GABA transmission.

2.4.1. Inhibition Between Cells

We now show how the first and third terms in the update rules in equations (26) and (27) can arise from a standard Hebb rule using inhibition between the two cells. For simplicity we will assume the geometry is flat but will not take the continuum limit.

If the cells were uncoupled, their outputs would be $O_1 = \phi_i^1 I_i$ and $O_2 = \phi_j^2 I_j$. We propose a form of inhibition which couples the two cells altering their outputs to

$$\bar{O}_1 = O_1 - < O_1 O_2 > O_2 \tag{28}$$

and

$$\bar{O}_2 = O_2 - < O_1 O_2 > O_1. \tag{29}$$

This can be thought of an approximation to shunting inhibition,

$$\hat{O}_1 = \frac{O_1}{1 + O_2^2}. \tag{30}$$

The updating is now done using the Hebb rule on $\bar{O}_1$ and $\bar{O}_2$. This gives rise to two contributions for each cell: (a) the standard Hebb term (as for the single cell), and (b) a term which is the gradient of the interaction energy.

The outputs of neighboring cells can be put in form

$$\bar{O}_1 = \phi_i^1 I_i - \langle(\phi_i^1 I_i)(\phi_j^2 I_j)\rangle\, \phi_k^2 I_k. \tag{31}$$

$$\bar{O}_2 = \phi_i^2 I_i - \langle(\phi_i^1 I_i)(\phi_j^2 I_j)\rangle\, \phi_k^1 I_k. \tag{32}$$

Equations (31) and (32) can now be cast as standard Hebb rules by forming the Input-Output products:

$$\langle O_1 I_i\rangle = \phi_j^1 F_{ij} - \phi_l^I \phi_m^2 F_{lm} F_{ij} \phi_j^2, \tag{33}$$

$$\langle O_2 I_i\rangle = \phi_j^1 F_{ij} - \phi_l^1 \phi_m^2 F_{lm} F_{ij} \phi_j^1. \tag{34}$$

The interaction between the two cells is inhibitory, since it forces the cells to have orthogonal receptive strengths and therefore they do not respond equally to the same input pattern.

2.5. Experimental Results

We performed computer simulations to confirm our theoretical results and to observe the effect of different dendritic geometries the correlation functions. The simulations fell into two classes: (a) single cell experiments to investigate orientation selectivity, and (b) paired cells with inhibitory interactions to investigate quadrature.

In both cases we only investigated the layers at which symmetry breaking took place. We assumed that the correlation function takes the form (possibly asymmetric) of a Laplacian of a Gaussian. Previous simulations (Linsker, 1986a,b,c; Kammen & Yuille, 1988) showed that correlation functions of this form could be generated by the early layers from white noise inputs to the first layer. The results of section 3.1 show that the precise form of a Laplacian of a Gaussian is, however, unimportant for these results. The main point is that the Fourier Transform of the correlation function has its largest positive eigenvalues away from the origin.

2.5.1. Single Cell Experiments

We performed simulations for single cells with two types of dendritic arborization patterns: (a) a Gaussian, and (b) a square box. The correlation function was the negative of a Laplacian of a Gaussian with a variable eccentricity e - σ_x/σ_y, where σ_x and σ_y are the standard deviations in the x and y directions. The update was performed by equation (21).

For the purpose of simulation the ϕ field was represented as a 31 by 31 grid. The correlation function, $-\nabla^2 G$, was defined on a 17 by 17 grid with $\sigma_x = 2.0$

and $\sigma_y = e\sigma_x$ with $0.8 < e < 1.0$. We fixed the boundary conditions for the convolution by padding the ϕ field with zeros.

Initially, each element of ϕ was set to a random value in the range -2.0 to 2.0. The field was then allowed to develop according to equation (20), with $\delta t = dt$ regulated to maximize the rate of descent while avoiding unbounded energy oscillations. The two terms contributing to the update were found to be of the same order when k was 50,000. Typically the cells stabilized after about 200 iterations.

Two synaptic distributions were used; one with a Gaussian distribution with $\sigma = 5.0$, and the other with a square feed-forward window of 15 by 15 grid units. The square was normalized to have the same volume (namely, 1) as the Gaussian. These factors are illustrated in Figure 1.4a.

Sample results are displayed in Figure 1.4. For eccentricities less than 0.95, oriented selective cells are generated for either geometry along the preferred direction (see Figure 1.4b). These cells have varying phases and their receptive field strengths fall off with distance, the fall off being faster for the Gaussian dendritic geometry. For eccentricities above 0.95 the different geometries start having significant effects. For the Gaussian geometry the receptive field become increasing symmetric, although some orientation bias can be found even for the unbiased case with $e = 1$. Although symmetric fields can be found for the square box geometry, oriented cells with arbitrary orientations can be generated even with $e = 1$. Moreover, trilobed cells with the centers of the three regions approximately located on the corners of the equilateral triangle occur (see Figure 1.4c). These field profiles may be similar to cells reported by Linsker (personal communication, June 1988). Trilobed cells are interesting as they might correspond to feature detectors, and are unusual in the symmetry-breaking scenario. Simultaneous symmetry breaking in multiple directions is unusual.

These results are consistent with our theoretical arguments. An asymmetric correlation function will give a strong bias to the orientation selectivity of the cell until the eccentricity is close to 1. As the eccentricity nears 1, the receptive field will become a superposition of sinusoids at different orientations. This could account for the trilobed cells. A more plausible explanation, however, is that they correspond to approximate minima of the energy function and can be described as $sin(wx)$ for $y \geq 0$, and $-sin(wx)$ for $y \leq 0$ (see next section). The Gaussian geometry would tend to make the receptive field more symmetric, and we have not observed trilobed cells for this geometry.

In summary, a small bias in D is sufficient to break the degeneracy of the space of minimal eigenvalues and generate strong orientation preference.

2.5.2. Trilobed Cells

We now mention an explanation for the occurrence of trilobed cells based on states which are not minimal eigenvectors, but which have energy only slightly

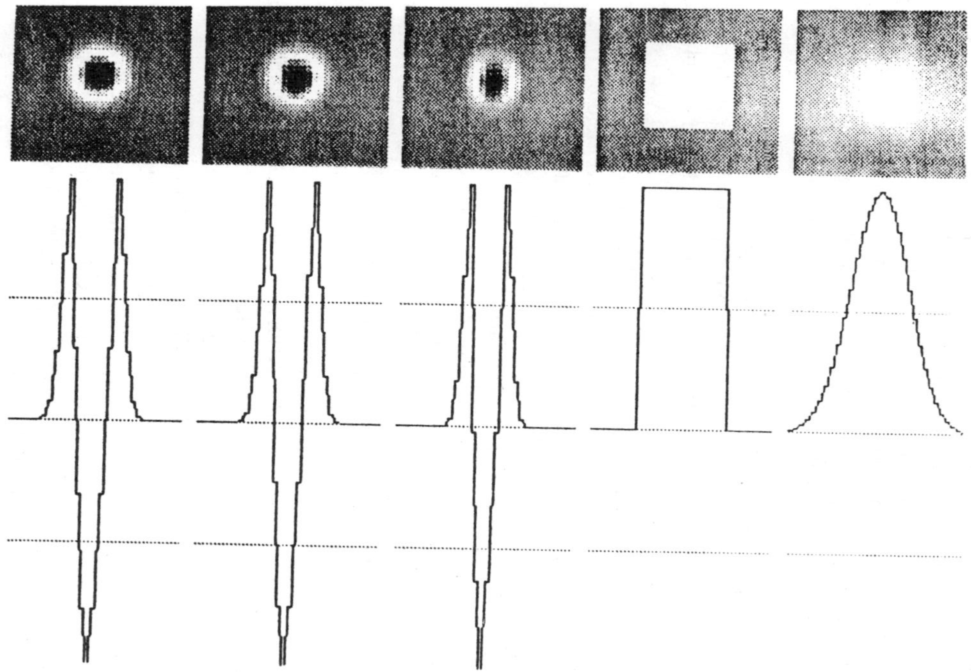

Figure 1.4. Single Cells. (a) The correlation functions and the dendritic geometry. From left to right we have three Laplacians of a Gaussian with $(\sigma,e) = (2.0,1.0)$, $(\sigma,e) = (2.0,0.95)$, and $(\sigma,e) = (2.0,0.80)$, a square window with 15 by 15 grid, and a Gaussian with $\sigma = 5.0$. In the upper pictures the intensity codes the height (white is positive, black is negative). The lower pictures give 1-dimensional slices of the corresponding upper picture. (b) The development of a cell with the square geometry and eccentricity $e = 0.8$. It develops, from left to right and top to bottom, into a sine wave receptive field. (c) Trilobed cells occur for $e = 1$ with the square geometry. The bottom left cell was given an initial value of $H(y) \sin x$ ($H(y) = sign(y)$, see section 2.5.2) and only changed by a negligible amount during the development stage. It is very similar to the other three cells which developed from an initial random state.

Figure 1.4. (continued)

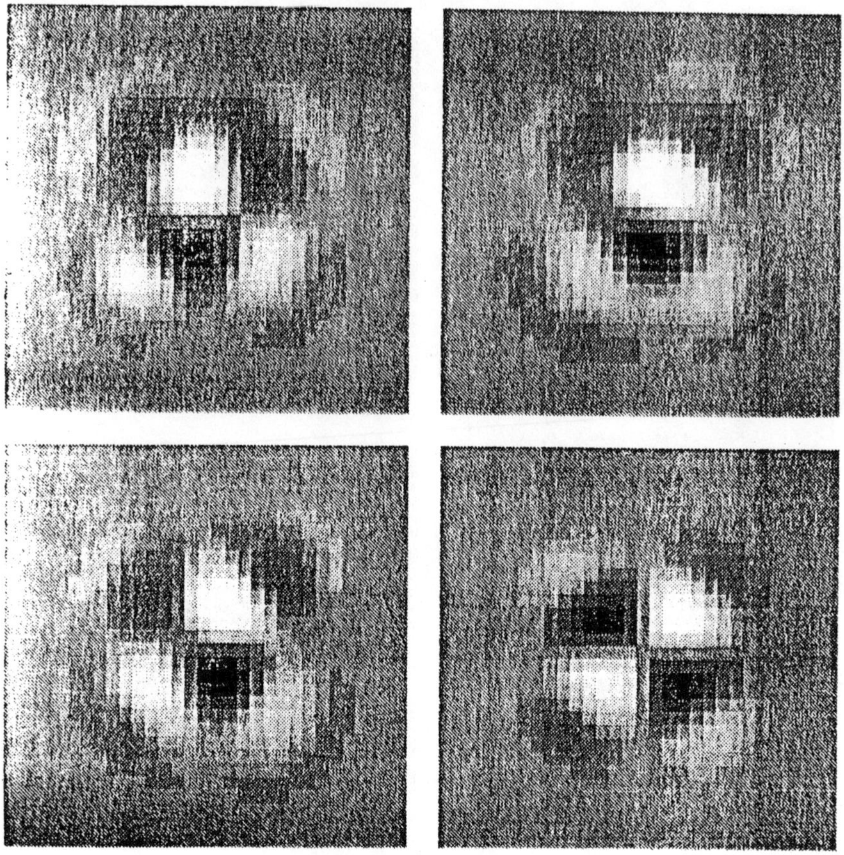

Figure 1.4. (continued)

higher than such eigenvectors. An explanation for some trilobed cells is evident in terms of an approximate minima of the energy function. Most of our trilobed cells are of form

$$f(\vec{x}) = H(y) sin(wx) \tag{35}$$

(i.e., rectified sinusoids) where $H(y) = +1$, $y \leq 0$ and $H(y) = -1$, $y \geq 0$. This will have similar energy to a cell with receptive field $g(x,y) = sinwx$, an eigenvector with the maximal eigenvalue. To see this, first observe that the overall norm is identical, $f(x,y)^2 = g(x,y)^2 = sin^2wx$, so the second term of (22) will be the same. The first term of (22) will depend on the product of $\nabla^2 G(x,y) * f(\vec{x})$ with $f(\vec{x})$. We find that

$$\nabla^2 G(x,y) * f(\vec{x}) = \frac{\partial^2}{\partial x^2}\{G(x) * sin(wx)\}\{G(y) * H(y)\}$$

$$+ \{G(x) * sin(wx)\} \frac{\partial^2}{\partial y^2}\{G(y) * H(y)\}. \tag{36}$$

Note that this has the form of a product of a *sin* function of x with a function of y. Therefore, this will be orthogonal to a cell with receptive field $cos(wx)$, so the interactive energy will be zero.

Finally, the first term of equation (22) will be very similar to that for $g(x,y)$. This can be seen from the consolution,

$$f(x,y)\nabla^2 G(x,y) * f(x,y) = sin(wx)H(y) \frac{\partial^2}{\partial x^2}\{G(x) * sin(wx)\}\{G(y) * H(y)\}$$

$$+ sin(wx)H(y)\{G(x) * sin(wx)\} \frac{\partial^2}{\partial y^2}\{G(y) * H(y)\}. \tag{37}$$

Since $G(y) * H(y) \approx H(y)$, except near the origin, the y contribution to the first term of equation (37) is essentially 1. The first term is practically the same as it would be for $g(x,y)$. Since $\frac{\partial^2}{\partial y^2}\{G(y) * H(y)\} \approx 0$ (except near the origin) the second term of (37) is essentially zero. This implys that the first term of (22) will be essentially the same for $f(x,y)$.

Thus $f(x,y)$ will have essentially the same energy as a true minimum. Computer simulations show that the energy differences is less than a half a percent. Further simulations (see Figure 1.4c) show that cells with an initial state of $H(y) sinwx$ change by a negligible amount during development, and are very similar to trilobed cells that develop from random initial inputs.

2.5.2. Quadrature Pairs

We also performed simulations for a pair of cells with similar inputs and inhibition between cells. Again we varied the geometry and the eccentricity of the correlation function. The update was implemented by incrementing equations (26) and (27).

The details of the simulations for cell pairs was essentially the same as for the single cell case. Both cells were assumed to have identical correlation functions and dendritic geometries. This situation is developmentally plausible where neighboring cells receive similar input.

Good results were obtained for eccentricities lower than 0.95. It was necessary to keep the interaction term small for the first part of the simulation. This allowed the cells to develop the preferred orientation, but usually not the same phase, before the interactions became significant. Once the receptive fields were

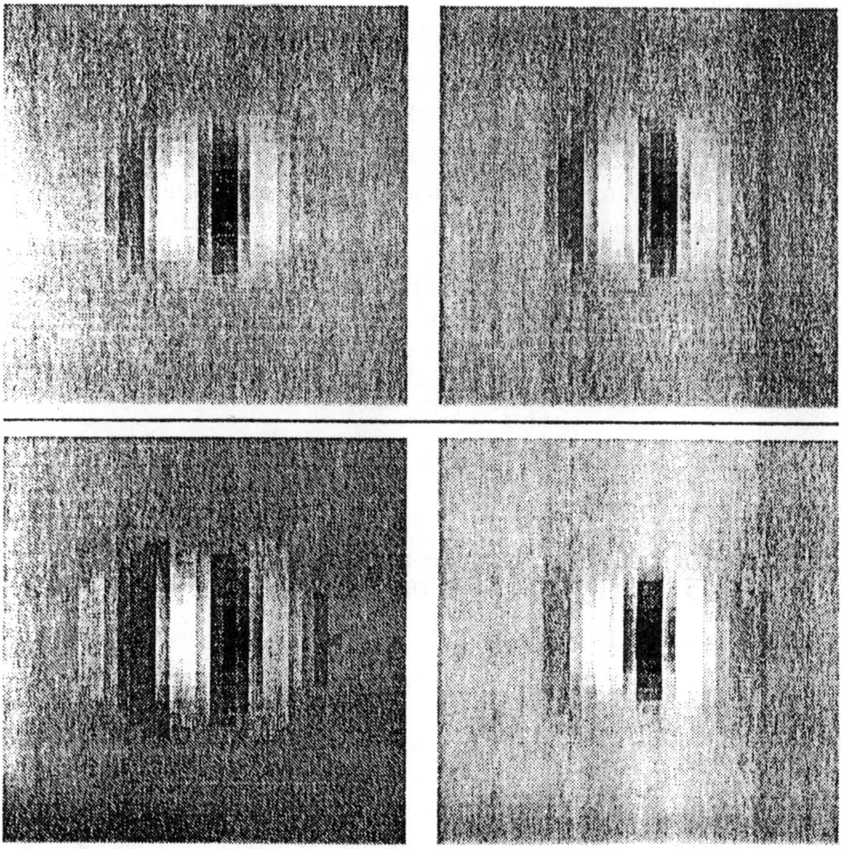

Figure 1.5. Quadrature Pairs. (a) A pair of cells before (upper pictures) and after (lower pictures) the interaction. The geometry is Gaussian with $\sigma = 5.0$ and $e = 0.8$. Observe that the cells form a sine-sine pair before the interaction and develop into a sine-cos pair. (b) Cross sections of the cells shown in (i) demonstrating the quadrature relationship. The leftmost two pictures show the cells before the interactions (when they are in phase). The rightmost two pictures show that the interaction has produced quadrature pairs (the cells are 90 degrees out of phase). (c) The upper two pictures show a sine-cos pair for the square geometry with $e = 0.8$. The lower pictures show that, with the same parameter values, the interaction can sometimes force neighbouring cells to have different preffered directions.

nearly settled, the coefficient c of the first term in equations (26) and (27) was linearly increased to 500,000,000 over a period of 140 iterations. The large value of c was used to make the interaction the dominant term in the period of cell interaction. The interaction then altered the relative phase difference until it was 90 degrees, thereby giving quadrature pairs (see Figures 1.5a,1.5b). In some

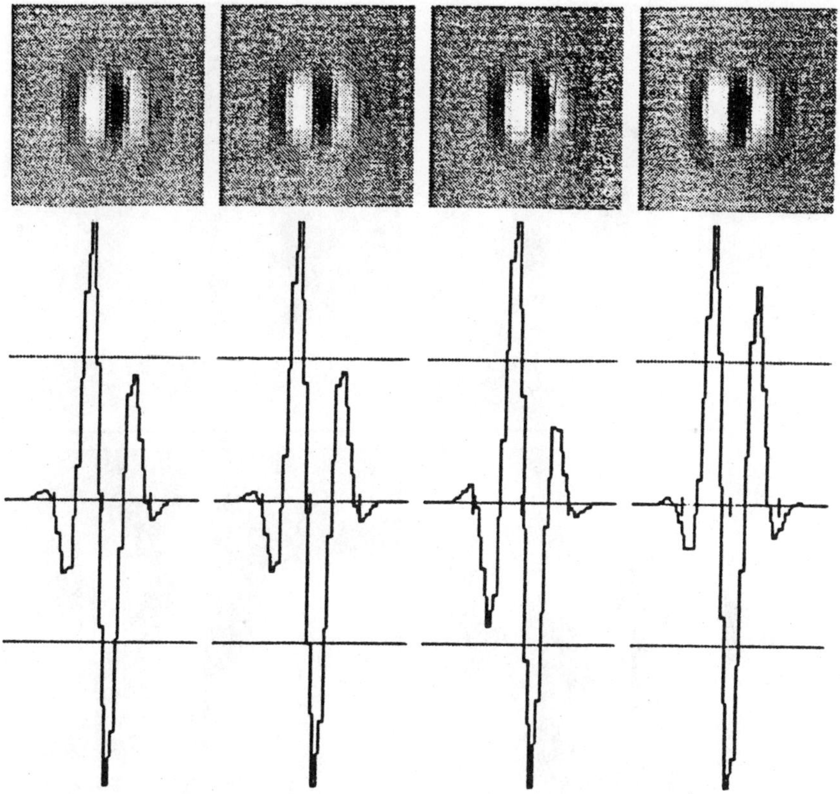

Figure 1.5b. (continued)

cases, when the eccentricities neared 1, the orientations of the cells actually changed (see Figure 1.5c).

It is important to emphasize that, in our simulations, orientation selectivity develops individually for each cell, and *then* the cell–cell interaction is increased to a point where it significantly alters the receptive fields. The orthogonality (or psuedoorthogonality with the Gaussian geometry) then forces the phases to differ by ninety (or thereabouts) degrees. If the cells have no preferred orientation there are several ways in which they could be orthogonal (in space, phase, or in some combination of the two), and spatial quadrature pairs therefore do not develop. If the asymmetry of the correlation function is small, then changing the relative orientations of the cells is another way to obtain orthogonality in (25). This might provide a mechanism to help generate the sharp discontinuities in the orientation preference of neighboring cells that are experimentally observed (Swindale, Matsubara, & Cynader, 1987).

It is interesting that, if the interaction terms were initially large, the receptive

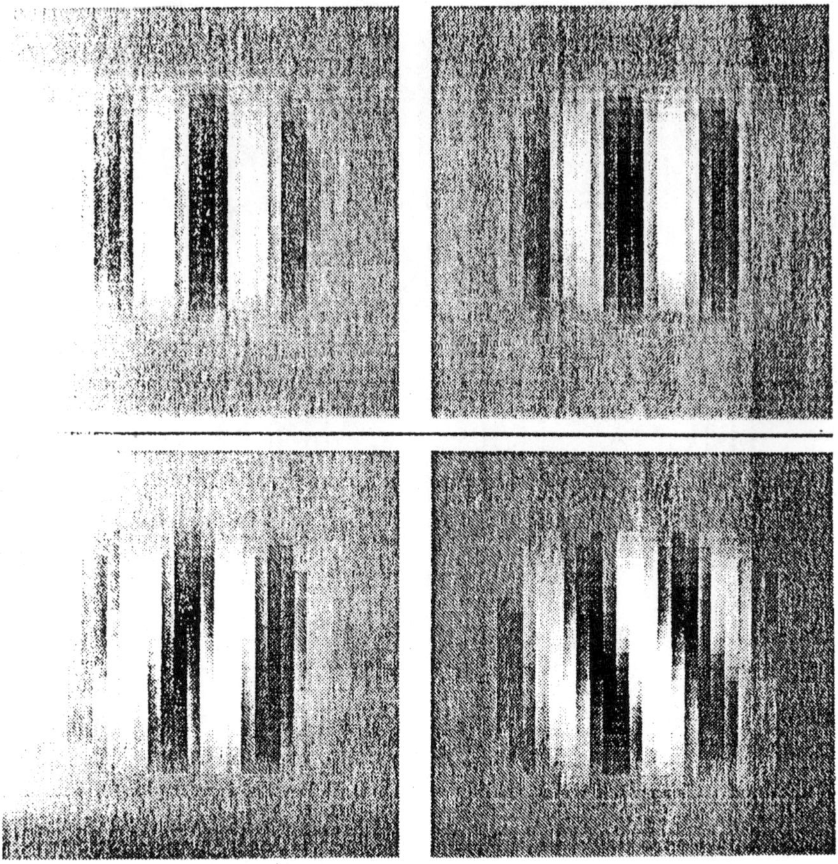

Figure 1.5c. (continued)

fields became unstructured in some of our simulations. This sensitivity to the interactions between cells in the same layer suggests a connection with Sillito's (1987) results of strong intralayer interaction effects in the orientation selectivity of cortical simple cells.

2.6. Comparisons to a Backpropagation Network

It is interesting to contrast these results for a feedforward network with a Hebb rule to those obtained using a backpropagation network (see Figure 1.6a) in one dimension (Spiro, 1987; Kersten, personal communication, April 1988).

In the backpropagation approach the network is trained by "squeezing" data through a smaller number of intermediate, or "hidden," units than the data was

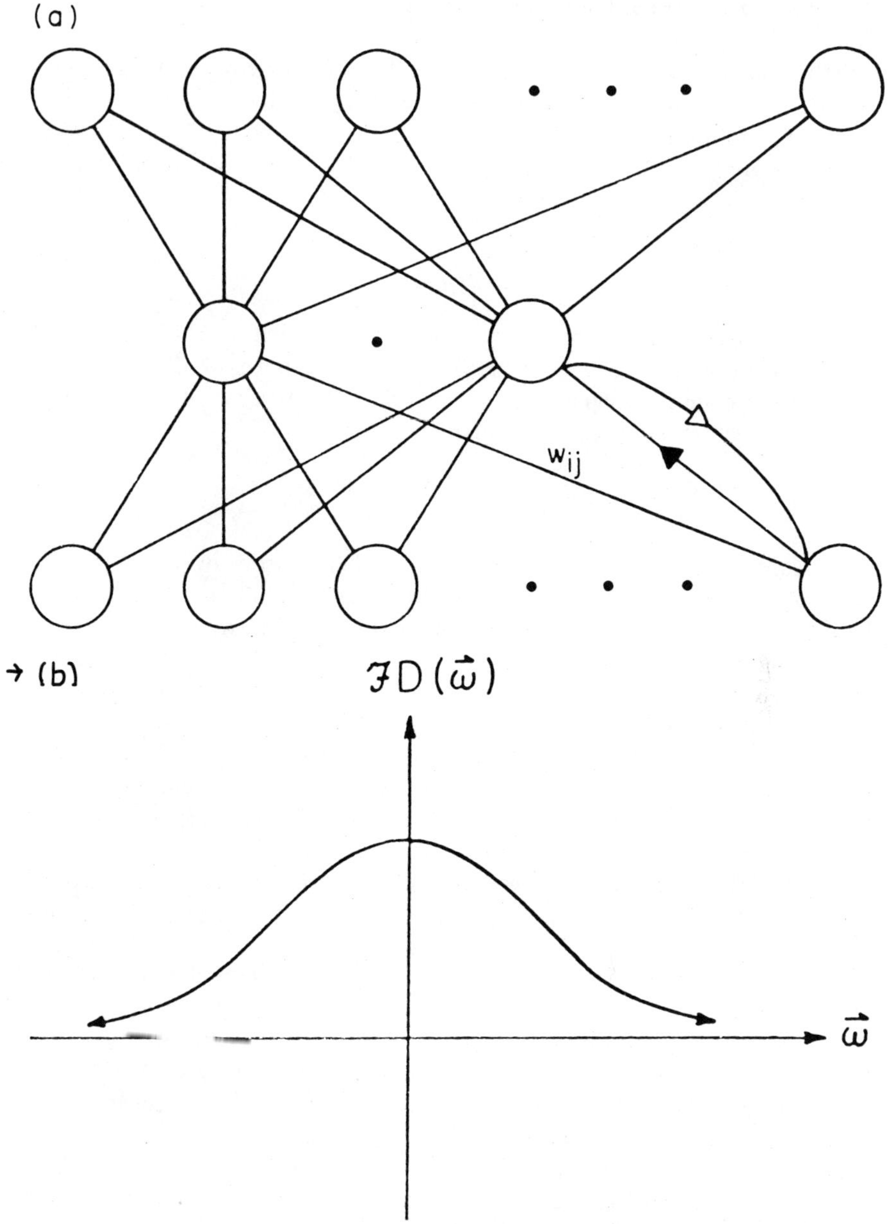

Figure 1.6. (a) A backpropagation network. The input units (at top of picture) are connected to the output units (at bottom) only by the hidden units (in the center). The numbers of input and output units are equal and is greater than the number of hidden units. (b) The Fourier Transform of the correlation function for fractal inputs will be peaked at $\vec{w} = 0$. The system will attempt to preserve most of the eigenvectors with small $|\vec{w}|$. The receptive fields of the hidden units will correspond to *sin* and *cos* waves with these frequencies (and arbitrary phase).

initially input to the network. Let $\{I_k\}$, $\{H_j\}$, and $\{O_i\}$ be the activities of the input, hidden, and output units, respectively. These are related by

$$O_i = \sum_j \Omega_{ij} H_j, \tag{38}$$

$$H_j = \sum_k w_{jk} I_k, \tag{39}$$

where $\{\Omega_{ij}\}$ and $\{w_{jk}\}$ are the synaptic strengths from the hidden units to the outputs, and from the inputs to the hidden units. The number of hidden units is less than the number of input (and output) units. The network attempts to preserve the structure of the input by minimizing

$$E(\Omega_{ij}, w_{jk}) = \sum_\mu \sum_i (O_i^\mu - I_i^\mu)^2 \tag{40}$$

as a function of the $\{\Omega_{ij}\}$ and $\{w_{jk}\}$, where μ labels a series of input vectors.

It can be shown that the global minimum of equation (40) is achieved when the hidden units select the biggest eigenvectors of the Karhunen-Loeve matrix (the number of eigenvectors encoded, or passed, equals the number of hidden units). Spiro (1987) used fractal inputs, so, by an argument similar to the one in section (3.2), the largest eigenvalues correspond to sinusoid function with small periods (see Figure 1.6b). Restricting the connections in equations (26) and (27) to be local yields receptive fields similar to Gabor functions (Kammen, 1988) that also exhibit quadrature (Spiro, 1987). This is consistent with our analysis (see Kammen, 1988, for more details).

The backpropagation network works by selecting the principal components of the input. This leads naturally to quadrature, since the principle components come with an arbitrary phase and the network will be most efficient if both sine and cosine terms are present. Our analysis also suggests that orientation selectivity will occur for two-dimensional networks.

It is interesting that both the backpropagation and the feedforward networks essentially work by extracting the principal components. There is, however, a critical difference: the feedforward network is highly local (minimizing cost function that relates only to neighboring cells), while the backpropagation network, though locally connected, is minimizing a global cost function. Feedforward Hebbian networks are therefore regarded as more faithful representations of developing biological networks.

2.7. Summary of Section 2

We have demonstrated a method for obtaining orientation selective cells by using a different form of Hebb rule from those used in previous work (Linsker,

1986a,b,c; Kammen & Yuille, 1988). Orientation selectivity occurs due to the sensitivity of the system to small asymmetries in the correlation function, rather than by a symmetry-breaking mechanism. These asymmetries may be due to asymmetries in the dendritic geometry (Schall et al., 1986a,b). Inhibition between cells leads to quadrature pairs developing (cells with the same orientation selectivity, but ninety degrees out of phase), as observed experimentally (Pollen & Ronner, 1981). The periods of the cells are related to the positions of the (positive) maximum of the Fourier Transform of the correlation function.

In this theory the development of orientation selectivity and the formation of isoorientation domains is caused by small local asymmetries in the correlation function. Neighboring cells are likely to have inputs from the previous layer with similar correlation functions, and so will develop with similar orientations. In contrast, Linsker (1986c) used local excitations between neighboring cells in the same layer to bias cells to have similar orientations. Our theory uses local inhibition to obtain the quadrature effect. This local inhibitory mechanism might also help generate the sharp discontinuities in the orientation preference of neighboring cells that are experimentally observed (see Figure 1.5c).

The construction of this theory has been strongly dependent on ideas of information processing. In particular, it has emphasized the importance of extracting the leading principal component of the signal (Oja, 1982, 1989; Linsker, 1988) by a Hebb rule.

Our work also has connections to the work of Sanger (1988). He also used a Hebb-type rule to extract the principal components of an image. Unlike as in our theory, however (which only extracts the leading principal component), he obtains receptive fields corresponding to several of the principal components. The receptive fields due to these other components, for images consisting of (smoothed) white noise, are of oriented, trilobed, or multilobed form. This seems consistent with our theoretical results in Section 3. The Fourier Transform of the correlation function for smoothed white noise will be peaked at the origin, so the leading principal component will give a symmetric receptive field. The other components, however, will tend to be asymmetric, although symmetric receptive fields should still be possible due to the degeneracy of the eigenspace.

3. HEBBIAN LEARNING IN A STRUCTURED ENVIRONMENT

The models discussed so far address the development of cortical cells in an unstructured (prenatal) visual environment. A critical test and extension of the Hebbian developmental picture is the role of visual information (structured input) in the *further,* postnatal, development of the visual system.

In the mammalian visual cortex, orientation-selective 'simple cells' which detect straight lines may be adapted to detect curved lines instead. We have explored the hypothesis that a biologically plausible single-neuron model, which learns oriented receptive fields upon exposure to unstructured input and maintains orientation selectivity upon exposure to edges or bars of all orientations and positions, can also learn arc-shaped receptive fields upon exposure to an environment of only circles. These results suggest several simple neurobiological experiments (Softky & Kammen, 1990; Softky, 1989).

In the mammalian visual cortex, orientation-selective cells (simple cells) can develop even in the absence of structured input. However, a restricted visual environment (stripe-rearing) may be able to alter the population ratios of their different orientations (see Singer, 1976; Hirsch, Leventhal, McCall, & Tieman, 1983).

Because only populations (rather than single cells) have been studied, and only in environments spanning a very restricted subset of the natural environment, little is known about whether an individual cell can alter its receptive field (RF) shape based on environmental effects (Stryker, Sherk, Leventhal, & Hirsch, 1978).

We explore this question by testing whether such a change is theoretically possible.

3.1. Mathematical Model

There are three important features of this model. One is that it uses a visual environment of structured input (bars, edges, or circles) rather than stochastic input. The input is Laplace filtered to simulate the retinal processing stage, and all connections are excitatory, like direct afferent input to simple cells.

The visual environment consists of a set of N 60 × 60 pixel pictures (e.g., various orientations of a black bar centered on a white background), with a fixed contrast. The environment seen by the neuron is a set of N 50 × 50 arrays of nonnegative integers; each integer is the positive output of a spatial-opponent filter of radius 5, forming an array of interleaved on-center and off-center excitatory filters on a checkerboard pattern.

The neuron's input synapses cover a circle of radius 10 within a 20 × 20 array. A single exposure to the environment overlaps one of the N filtered images (chosen at random), shifting it by a random vector (S_x, S_y) subject to

$$\sqrt{S_x^2 + S_y^2} < 15 \tag{41}$$

and

$$S_x + S_y = \text{even} \tag{42}$$

This overlap pairs each synapse with an input from a like-polarity filter (see Figure 1.7).

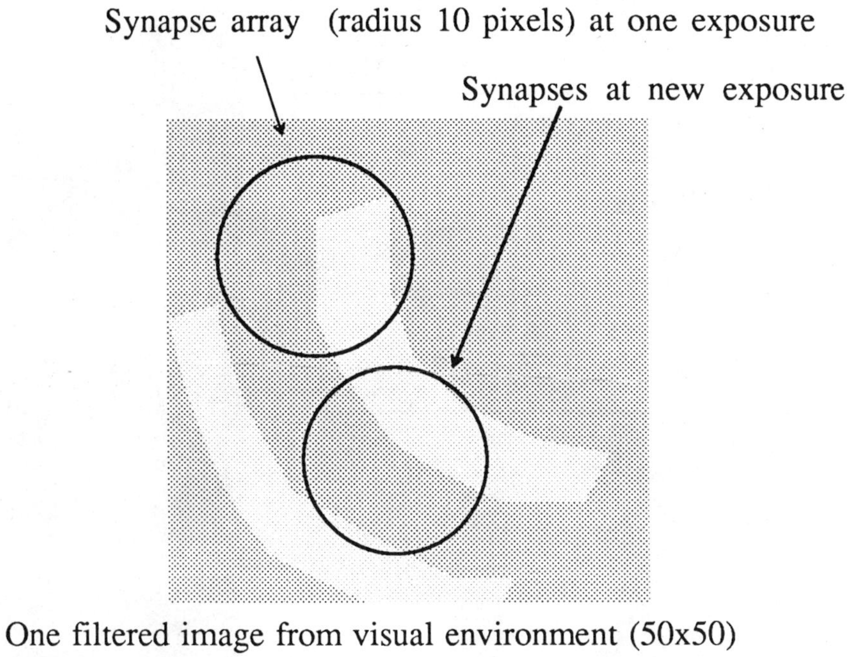

Figure 1.7. Exposure to Environment: Circles represent possible positions of the synapse array relative to the input filtered image.

A typical run involves perhaps 10^6 exposures. There is no time variable, so that motion and time-correlations between images are entirely absent. During each exposure synapses are adjusted according to the cell output and the current input value according to a Hebb rule (see below). After synapse maturation, the filtering process is inverted to obtain a picture of the resulting RF (see Figure 1.8).

All synapse values were initialized in the interval [0,5], and a pattern was considered mature only if most of the synapses reached their extreme limits at 0.5 or 10.0.

During each exposure to filtered-image inputs in_i, synapses syn_i were adjusted according to the following type of hard-limited Hebb rule.

$$out = \sum_{syn} syn_i \times in_i \qquad (43)$$

And if $(out - thresh) > 0$:

$$\Delta syn_i = (out - thresh)^n \times in_i \times growth \quad \text{if } in_i > 0 \text{ and } syn_i < 10 \qquad (44)$$

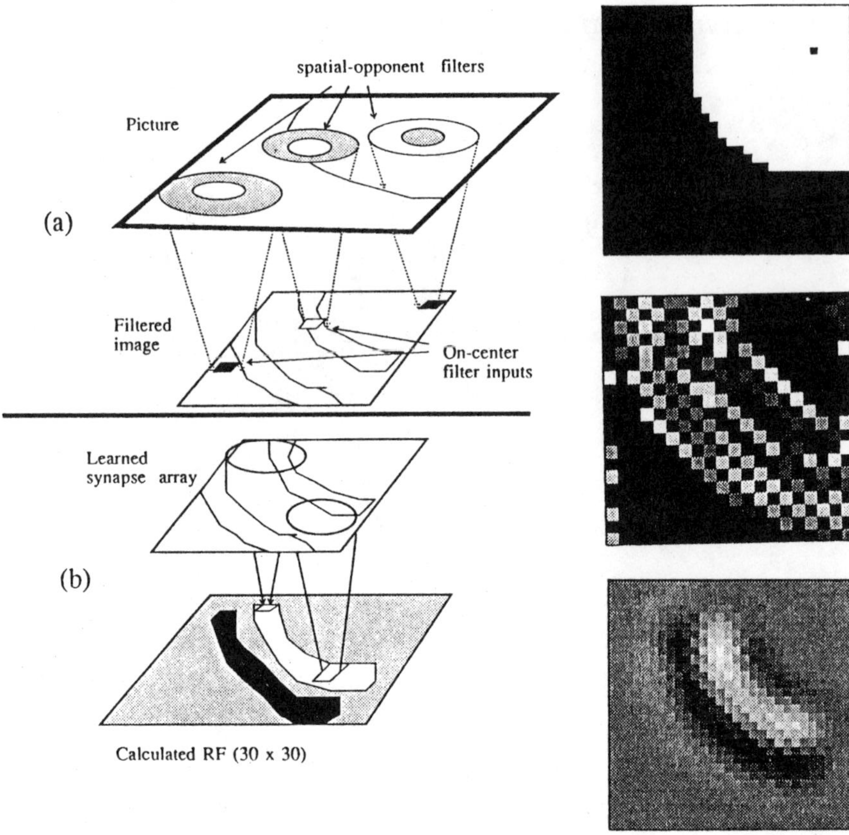

Figure 1.8. Schematic of the (a) center-surrounded filtering and (b) inverse filtering processes. Sample outputs (a picture with corresponding filtered image and calculated RF) are stacked on the right.

$$\Delta syn_i = -(out - thresh)^n \times decay \quad \text{if } in_i = 0 \text{ and } syn_i > 0.5 \tag{45}$$

$$\Delta syn_i = 0 \text{ otherwise} \tag{46}$$

The constants *growth* and *decay* are positive, and n is at least one. The two types of threshold both depend on the neuron's recent output history: either the average of the previous 200 outputs, or one half the maximum previous output (decaying by .9995 each exposure until a new $\frac{max}{2}$ exceeds it).

In the special case of arbitrary binary inputs following a binomial distribution, a pattern with x '1' bits out of N makes the Hebb potential the same as the excess

Shannon information above the mean information for the parameter values $n = 2$ and $thresh = \langle x \rangle$:

$$H_{excess} = H(x) - H(\langle x \rangle) \quad (47)$$

$$= \frac{(x - \langle x \rangle)^2}{NP_1P_0} \quad (48)$$

$$\text{where } \langle x \rangle = NP_1 \quad (49)$$

The threshold $thresh = \frac{max}{2}$ is usually higher and thus gives a more selective Hebb rule than $thresh = \langle out \rangle$. When $\frac{max}{2}$ is used as a cell-output threshold, cells have the well-known "rectified A.C." rcsponse to drifting gratings (De Valois, Albrecht, & Thorell, 1982).

Most simulations used $n = 1,2,3$ with both thresholds. The simulation results are summarized in Table 1.1 and Figure 1.9.

3.2. Discussion of Learning with Correlated Input

The production of oriented RFs during exposure to unstructured input confirms previous results by Linsker (1986b) and Kammen and Yuille (1988), but with some important differences. Like those models, this neuron learns an oriented stripe-pattern as a lowest energy configuration upon exposure to spatially correlated inputs. But unlike those models, this model does not use inhibitory connections or synapses, synaptic-density gradient, global conservation of synapse strength, or adjustable free parameters, which can yield differently-shaped RFs.

This model predicts spatial-frequency resonance effects for stripe-rearing (Softy & Kammen, 1990). Assuming that intracortical inhibition is weak enough to allow the single-neuron effects described above to influence neuron population ratios, an animal reared viewing vertical stripes of spatial frequency f (chosen to be intermediate in the range of normal RF frequencies) should exhibit (a) a larger-than-normal population of cells tuned to f for vertical stripes, (b) a smaller population tuned to frequencies adjacent to f than to f for vertical stripes, (c) a higher population ratio $\frac{vertical}{horizontal}$ at f than at other frequencies, and (d) possibly a higher ratio at $3f$, which is the next Fourier-expansion term of a square wave stripe pattern. These results are summarized in Table 1.1.

These results also suggest that animals which see only circles of a certain scale during the critical period may develop RFs (Barrow, 1987) which differ qualitatively from those observed by such experiments as Jones and Palmer's (1987), who report seeing no curved contours in their point-by-point mappings of kitten RFs.

Table 1.1

VISUAL ENVIRONMENT	DESCRIPTION	STARTING SYNAPTIC WEIGHTS	PARAMETERS n	$thresh$	LEARNED PROPERTIES of R.F.
Unstructured	200 pictures of random pixels	random	1, 2, 3 1, 3	$max/2$ avg	Straight or slightly curved stripes of period $P_{natural} = 1.8R_{filt} = 9$ pixels
Edges	Centered straight border at 32 orientations over 360°	noise-reared stripes	1, 2, 3 1	$max/2$ avg	Oriented edge-like RF
Edges	(same)	(same)	3	avg	Circular dot
Single Bars	Centered straight bar of width 5 pixels at 16 orientations over 180°	Noise-reared stripes	1, 2, 3 1, 3	$max/2$ avg	Oriented bar-like RF
Vertical Stripes	Three orientations (0° and ±11°) of square-wave stripes of period P	Noise-reared stripes	1 3	avg $max/2$	Vertical stripes of period $P < P_{learned} < P_{natural}$ if $0.7P_{natural} < P \leq P_{natural}$
					Vertical stripes of period $P_{natural} < P_{learned} < P$ if $P_{natural} < P < 2P_{natural}$
					A single vertical bar of period $P_{natural}$ if $P = 0.33P_{natural}$
					Disordered or no learning for other periods
Cells of natural spatial frequency near the exposed frequency 'convert' to detect stripes nearer the exposed frequency.					
Circles	A single annular circle of mean diameter $< R_{circ} >$	Noise-reared stripes	1, 2, 3 1, 3	$max/2$ avg	Centered arc-shaped RF of curvature 45° if $< R_{circ} >= 15$
					Less curved RF at border of synapse array as R_{circ} decreases
The circles giving the clearest arcs had dimensions in the range $< R_{circ} >= (2.5 - 3.0) \times$ Annular Width					
Most results above for unstructured environment, stripes, edges, and circles were reproduced when synpase upper-limits had a gaussian distribution with $\sigma \approx$(radius of synapse array).					

This model does not attempt to explain curve-detection in a normal visual system. We already know that simple cells are not tuned for curves, and there are credible theories of normal curve-detection (e.g., by the difference between end-stopped complex cells). Rather, this model proposes looking for a RF property which is distinctly unnatural, in order to better understand the rules by which normal visual properties emerge.

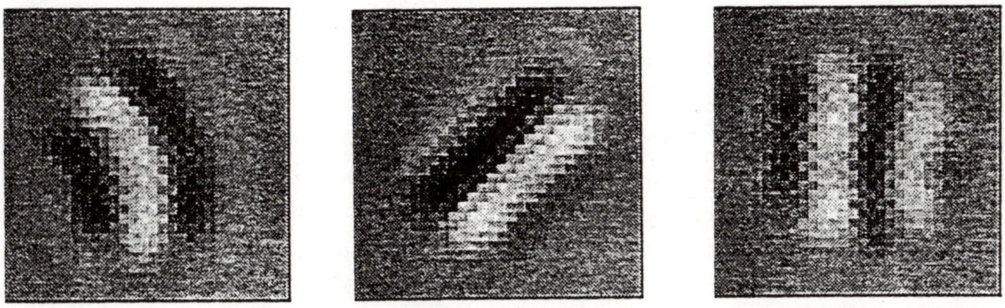

Figure 1.9. Learned receptive fields. (left) Stripes learned from noise, (center) RF learned from edges, (right) arc learned from circle.

4. MOTION AND VELOCITY SENSITIVE CELLS

This section (Yuille & Cohen, 1989) extends the previous developmental results to training and teaching motion-sensitive and velocity-tuned cells. The motion-sensitive cells in the primary visual cortex are tuned to the spatio-temporal frequency components of the signals rather than directly to their velocities (for reviews, see Nakayama, 1985; Hildreth & Koch, 1987; Anderson & Siegel, 1989). Later pattern cells in the middle temporal cortex are tuned to the velocities (Newsome, Gizzi, & Movshon, 1983).

There have been several theories using motion energy filters and correlation models to measure motion (Hassenstein & Reichardt, 1956; Poggio & Reichardt, 1973; Daugman, 1985; Adelson & Bergen, 1985; Watson & Ahumada, 1985; van Santen & Sperling, 1985; Heeger, 1987; Bulthoff, Little, & Poggio, 1989). A recent paper (Grzywacz & Yuille, 1990) analyzes the problem mathematically and proposes a method to determine the velocity of motion from the output of frequency-sensitive cells. It discusses a possible neuronal implementation of such a theory and shows that it is quantitatively in agreement with electrophysiological recordings for some experiments. This section attempts to show that such theories can be learned using Hebb rules.

Our strategy is to first use self-organization to develop the motion-sensitive cells (which roughly resemble Gabor functions in space-time, although the temporal behaviour looks more like a log Gabor). Mathematically, this corresponds to generalizing the results of Yuille et al. (1989) to include the time dimension. As in previous work the training is done on random stimuli and does not need structured input.

After a set of motion-sensitive cells has been developed, the velocity-sensitive cells can be trained on the output of these cells using structured examples with a teacher. The use of a teacher is justified, since the visual system can use a head–eye tracking mechanism to determine whether it has estimated the correct velocity. Such a teacher was used by Zipser and Anderson (1988) in their work on the different, but related, problem of invariance under eye movements. Our network, however, does not require hidden units and is therefore more neuronally plausible than backpropagation schemes.

Our model is related to the interesting work of Sanger (1989a) on self-organization for stereo. The critical difference is our use of a teaching stage to obtain velocity-sensitive cells. Although Sanger's model, which is based purely on self-organization, does develop receptive fields sensitive to disparity (the analogue to velocity for his system), they are not specifically tuned to disparity, and it would seem difficult to obtain this tuning without a teacher. The use of a teacher makes our work somewhat similar to other models of learning for vision (Kersten et al., 1987; Hurlbert & Poggio, 1988; Lehky & Sejnowski, 1988) which, however, do not involve a self-organization stage. It is interesting to speculate on thc relative effectiveness of self-organization and learning with a teacher as strategies for training systems and the tradeoffs involved.

Section 4.1 briefly describes a two-stage model of motion perception, the type of model we wish our system to learn. In section 4.2 we discuss the theory for the development of motion sensitive cells by self-organization. Section 4.3 describes computer simulations of this theory. In section 4.4 we use learning by example to train velocity sensitive cells from the outputs of the motion sensitive cells.

4.1. Motion Measurement

A number of recent models have suggested that motion is measured using a set of motion energy filters tuned to spacetime frequencies rather than directly to velocity. One such model (Grzywacz & Yuille, 1989) uses spacetime Gabor filters and proposes that cells correspond to nonlinear filters

$$N(\vec{\Omega},\Omega_t:\vec{x},t) = f_1^2(\vec{\Omega},\Omega_t:\vec{x},t) + f_2^2(\vec{\Omega},\Omega_t:\vec{x},t) \tag{50}$$

where

$$f_1(\vec{\Omega},\Omega_t:\vec{x},t) = \cos(\vec{\Omega}\cdot\vec{x} + \Omega_t t)e^{-|\vec{x}|^2/2\sigma^2}\, e^{-t^2/2\sigma_t^2} * I(\vec{x},t) \tag{51}$$

$$f_1(\vec{\Omega},\Omega_t:\vec{x},t) = \sin(\vec{\Omega}\cdot\vec{x} + \Omega_t t)e^{-|\vec{x}|^2/2\sigma^2}\, e^{-t^2/2\sigma_t^2} * I(\vec{x},t) \tag{52}$$

The cells are tuned to spacetime fourier frequencies $\vec{\Omega},\Omega_t$. For each point $\vec{x}$ on the image plane there are many such cells.

The velocity of the stimulus can be computed from the outputs of these frequency tuned cells (Figure 1.10). It can be shown (Daugman, 1985) that, if an image is translating rigidly with velocity $\vec{v}$, then the power spectrum of the image lies on the plane $\vec{v}\cdot\vec{\Omega} + \Omega_t = 0$. Only cells tuned to frequencies near this plane will fire so the plane, and hence the velocity can be deduced.

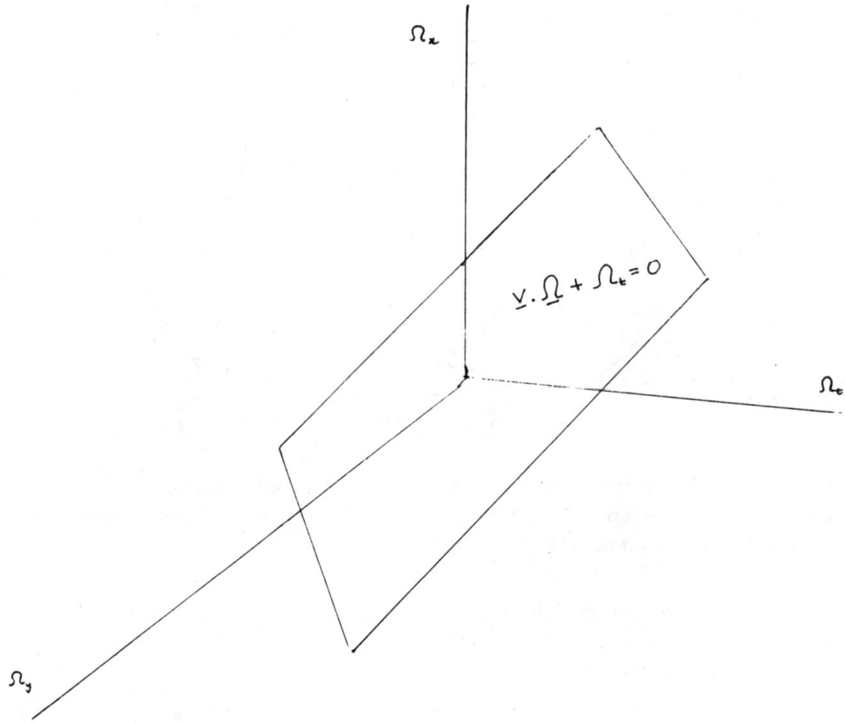

Figure 1.10. The Fourier coefficients of an image translating with velocity $\vec{v}$ lie on a plane $\vec{v}\cdot\vec{w} + w_t = 0$.

4.2. Theory for the Development of Motion-Sensitive Cells

We first show how the receptive fields of the frequency cells can be developed by self-organization without a trainer using Hebb update rules and a single layer linear feedforward network with lateral inhibition.

Although it is known that the strength of synapses can be modified, there is little reason to believe that their time dependencies can be. To generate time-dependent receptive fields, we propose that, for every spatial position, there are several synapses with different time dependencies—usually time delays. The network is shown in Figure 1.11.

Initially we will ignore the lateral interaction. Then, with a linear network, the output is

$$O(t) = \sum_{i,\lambda} \phi_i^{\lambda} I_i(t - \lambda\delta t), \tag{53}$$

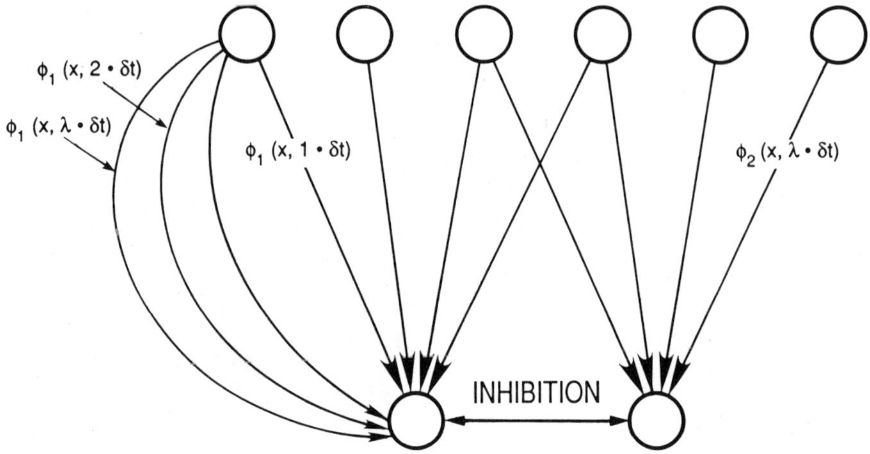

Figure 1.11. The single layer network with time delayed synapses and inhibition between output elements. The continuous, dotted and dashed lines represent synapses with different amounts of time delay.

where ϕ_i^λ is the receptive field of the λ'th time channel of the ith cell and $\lambda\delta t$ is the time delay of the λth time channel.

We can rewrite this as

$$O(t) = \sum_{i,\mu} \phi_{i\mu} I_{i\mu}, \tag{54}$$

where the time label μ can now be treated as another spatial dimension.

We now want to show that we can generate cells that behave roughly like Gabor functions. We assume that the inputs are generated spontaneously and are possibly filtered through several layers (Linsker, 1986a,b,c). These inputs can be spatially homogeneous, and the only property we require is that the correlation functions are shift invariant and that the power spectrum is not peaked at the origin. This may be achieved by assuming random input noise at the first layer, using self-organization, developing the right form of correlation function.

For single cells we choose an update rule of form

$$\frac{d\phi_{i\mu}}{dt} = \langle O(t) I_{i\mu} \rangle - \lambda(\phi_{j\nu}\phi_{j\nu})\phi_{i\mu}, \tag{55}$$

The first term correpsonds to a standard Hebb update term, while the second term is imposed to put bounds on the synapse strengths. After using (54) to substitute for $O(t)$, we obtain

$$\frac{d\phi_{i\mu}}{dt} = F_{ij\mu\nu}\phi_{j\nu} - \lambda(\phi_{j\nu}\phi_{j\nu})\phi_{i\mu}, \tag{56}$$

where $F_{ij\mu\nu} = \langle I_{i\mu} I_{j\nu} \rangle$ is the spatiotemporal correlation function. This update rule corresponds to minimizing an energy (Lyapunov) function

$$E[\phi_{i\mu}] = \frac{-1}{2} F_{ij\mu\nu} \phi_{i\mu} \phi_{j\nu} + \frac{1}{4} \lambda (\phi_{j\nu} \phi_{j\nu})^2. \qquad (57)$$

The energy function gives rise to symmetry breaking (F is positive definite), since it has a negative quadratic term and a positive quartic term.

By our previous analysis (see section 2.2) we know that $E[\phi_{i\mu}]$ has no local minima and that the global minimum occurs when $\phi_{i\mu}$ is the eigenvector of $F_{ij\mu\nu}$ with biggest eigenvalue. If the biggest eigenvalue is degenerate, then the global minimum corresponds to a line not a point.

Again by our previous analysis (see section 2.2) we know that, if the correlation function F is shift invariant, then, as we take the continuum limit, the maximum eigenvalue corresponds to the maximum value of the fourier transform of F (the power spectrum of the input). Moreover, the eigenfunctions correspond to sinusoids with arbitrary phase. In particular, if the maximum of the power spectrum occurs at frequency $w = w_0$, then the eigenfunction with biggest eigenvalue is of form $\sin(\vec{w}_0 \cdot \vec{x} - \alpha)$ (thus there are two orthogonal eigenfunctions with this eigenvalue). If the correlation function is rotationally symmetric (i.e., assuming homogeneity in space), then the maximum of the power spectrum will occur on a circle with radius $|w| = |w_0|$, and the ground state of eigenfunctions will be degenerate, and there will be no preferred direction. However, a slight bias in F due to noise fluctuations will destroy this symmetry (by genericity arguments) and will give a unique maximum eigenvalue and hence a preferred direction $\vec{w}_0$.

Thus, if the correlation function has the fourier transform shown in Figure 1.12, then small fluctuations in the correlation function will give rise to symmetry breaking, and cells with preferred directions of their receptive fields will develop.

There is still the degeneracy of the eigenfunctions due to phase. We now show how, using lateral inhibition (thereby enforcing orthogonality in the receptive fields), this can explain the development of quadrature pairs of cells with receptive fields out of phase by approximately 90 degrees.

We assume a form of lateral inhibition in which the outputs O_1, O_2 of two adjacent cells are modified to $\bar{O}_1$, $\bar{O}_2$ where

$$\bar{O}_1 = O_1 - \langle O_1 O_2 \rangle \, O_2, \qquad (58)$$

$$\bar{O}_2 = O_2 - \langle O_1 O_2 \rangle \, O_1, \qquad (59)$$

this can be thought of an approximation to shunting inhibition.

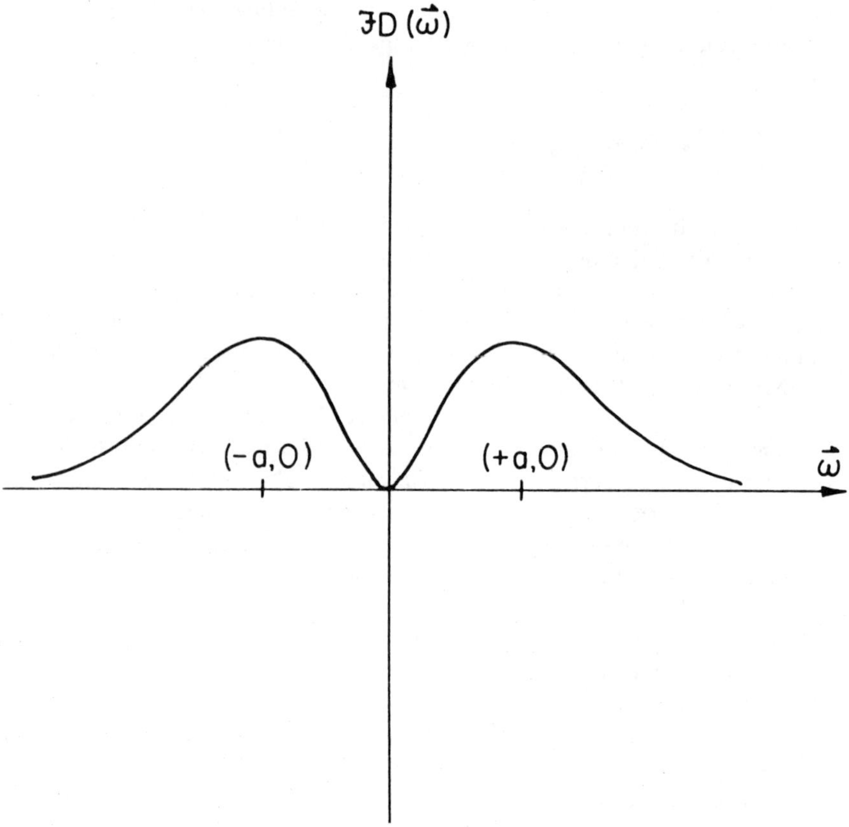

Figure 1.12. The Fourier Transforms of the correlation function. The Fourier Transform of the correlation function (a), has a positive maxima on a sphere. We show a contour plot of this function in (b) suppressing the w_t direction. The space of biggest (positive) eigevectors is degenerate and symmetry breaking need not occur in this situation. In the contour plot (c) we show that a small asymmetry in the correlation function reduces the degeneracy of the eigenspace, and leads to strong orientation selectivity.

We now modify the update, equation (55), replacing O_1, O_2 by $\bar{O}_1$, $\bar{O}_2$ to obtain

$$\frac{d\phi^{I}_{i\mu}}{dt} = \langle \bar{O}^1(t) I_{i\mu} \rangle - \lambda(\phi^1_{j\nu}\phi^1_{j\nu})\phi^1_{i\mu}, \tag{60}$$

and

$$\frac{d\phi^2_{i\mu}}{dt} = \langle \bar{O}^2(t) I_{i\mu} \rangle - \lambda(\phi^2_{j\nu}\phi^2_{j\nu})\phi^2_{i\mu}, \tag{61}$$

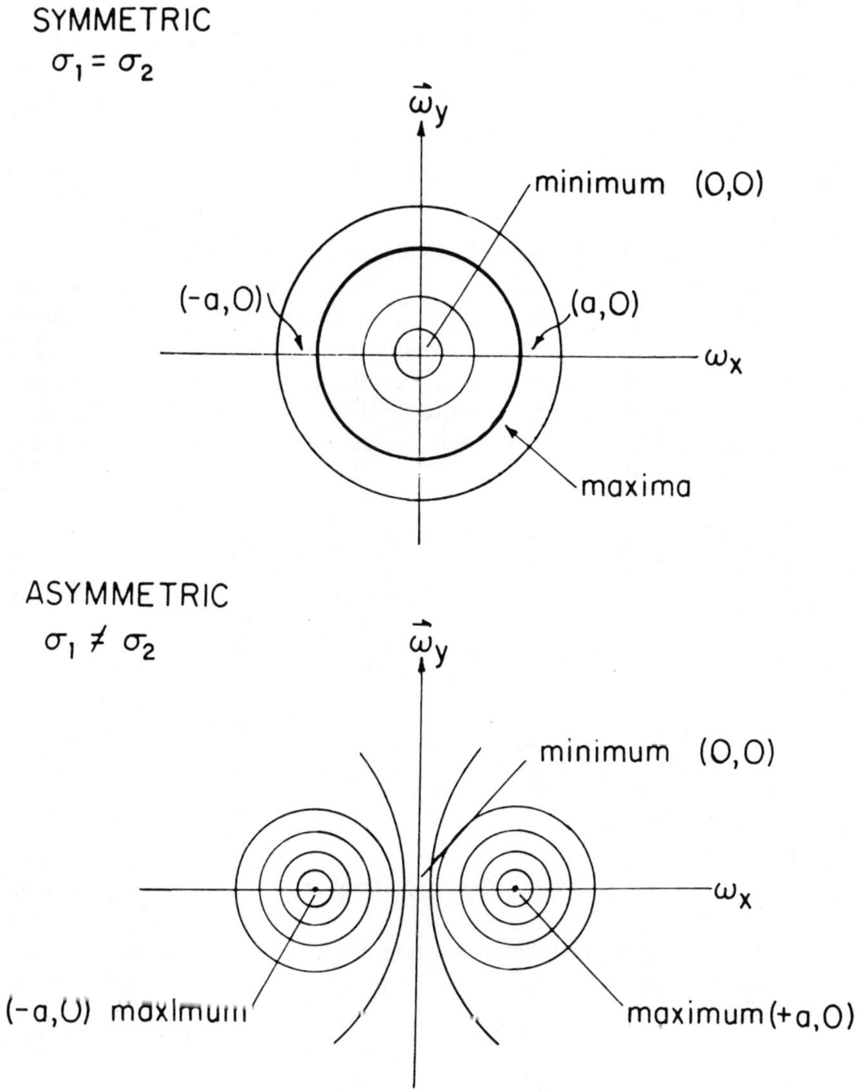

Figure 1.12. (continued)

where $\phi^1_{i\mu}$ and $\phi^2_{i\mu}$ are the receptive fields of the two cells. Substituting for $\bar{O}_1$ and $\bar{O}_2$, using (58) and (59), gives

$$\frac{d\phi^1_{i\mu}}{dt} = F_{ij\mu\nu}\phi^1_{j\nu} - (\phi^1_{k\tau}F_{kj\tau\sigma}\phi^2_{j\sigma})\, F_{ij\mu\rho}\phi^2_{l\rho} - (\phi^1_{j\nu}\phi^1_{j\nu})\, \phi^1_{i\mu}, \tag{62}$$

and similarly for $\phi^2_{i\mu}$.

This minimizes an energy (Lyapunov) function

$$E[\phi^1,\phi^2] = -\frac{1}{2} F_{ij\mu\nu}\phi^1_{i\mu}\phi^1_{j\nu} - \frac{1}{2} F_{ij\mu\nu}\phi^2_{i\mu}\phi^2_{j\nu} + \frac{1}{2} (F_{ij\mu\nu}\phi^1_{i\mu}\phi^2_{j\nu})^2$$
$$+\frac{1}{4} (\phi^1_{j\nu}\phi^1_{j\nu})^2 + \frac{1}{4} (\phi^2_{j\nu}\phi^2_{j\nu})^2. \tag{63}$$

This energy function is the sum of two functions for individual cells, see (57), and an interaction term (the third term on the right-hand side of (63)). The interaction term forces the cells to be orthogonal and hence ninety degrees out of phase. Thus we obtain quadrature pairs of cells.

The above analysis has assumed that the distribution of synapses is homogeneous. A more realistic assumption is that the distribution is given by a Gaussian function. To take this into account we go to the continuum limit and modify the energy function to be

$$E[\phi^1(\vec{x}),\phi^2(\vec{x})] = E_{cell}[\phi^1(\vec{x})] + E_{cell}[\phi^2(\vec{x})] + E_{int}[\phi^1(\vec{x}),\phi^2(\vec{x})], \tag{64}$$

where

$$E_{cell}(\phi(\vec{x})] = \frac{-k}{2} \int\int G(\vec{x})\phi(\vec{x})D(\vec{x} - \vec{y})G(\vec{y})\phi(\vec{y})\, d\vec{x}\, d\vec{y}$$
$$+\frac{1}{4}\left\{\int G(\vec{x})\phi^2(\vec{x})\, d\vec{x}\right\}^2, \tag{65}$$

and

$$E_{int} = c\left\{\int\int G(\vec{x})\phi^1(\vec{x})D(\vec{x} - \vec{y})G(\vec{y})\phi^2(\vec{y})\, d\vec{x}\, d\vec{y}\right\}^2, \tag{66}$$

where $D(\vec{x} - \vec{y})$ is the correlation function and $G(\vec{x})$ is a Gaussian function.

The self-organization corresponds to steepest descent of this energy function using the update equations

$$\frac{d\phi_1(\vec{x})}{dt} = \frac{-1}{G(\vec{x})}\frac{\partial E[\phi^1,\phi^2]}{\partial\phi^1(\vec{x})}, \tag{67}$$

$$\frac{d\phi_2(\vec{x})}{dt} = \frac{-1}{G(\vec{x})}\frac{\partial E[\phi^1,\phi^2]}{\partial\phi^2(\vec{x})}. \tag{68}$$

4.3. Simulations of Motion Sensitive Cells

We now describe the results of computer simulations for the development of motion-sensitive cells.

The size of the receptive field was set at 25 × 25 × 25, with the third dimension being time. In order to speed the convolution, the correlation function D was taken to be a Gabor cosine function, which is separable, rather than the inseparable laplacian of a Gaussian previously used (see section 2). The size of the kernel used in the convolution was 11 × 11 × 11, so the resulting increase in speed due to the use of the separable function was of order $11^3 \div (3 \times 11)$, or a factor of about 40.

We assume a Gaussian distribution for synapses with $\sigma = 4.0$ in all of the simulations. For the correlation function, $\sigma = 2.0$ and $w_x = 1.0$. w_y and w_t were zero. The update equations, from (64), (67), and (68), are

$$\frac{d\phi_1(\vec{x})}{dt} = k \int G(\vec{z})\phi_1(\vec{z})D(\vec{x} - \vec{z})d\vec{z} - \phi_1(\vec{x}) \int G(\vec{z})\phi_1(\vec{z})^2 d\vec{z}$$
$$-c \int D(\vec{x} - (\vec{y})G(\vec{y})\phi_2(\vec{y})\, d\vec{y} \int\int G(\vec{z})\phi_1(\vec{z})D(\vec{z} - \vec{y})G(\vec{y})\phi_2(\vec{y})\, d\vec{z}\, d\vec{y}$$
$$\frac{d\phi_2(\vec{x})}{dt} = k \int G(\vec{z})\phi_2(\vec{z})D(\vec{x} - \vec{z})d\vec{z} - \phi_2(\vec{x}) \int G(\vec{z})\phi_2(\vec{z})^2 d\vec{z}$$
$$-c \int D(\vec{x} - \vec{y})G(\vec{y})\phi_1(\vec{y})\, d\vec{y} \int\int G(\vec{z})\phi_1(\vec{z})D(\vec{z} - \vec{y})G(\vec{y})\phi_2(\vec{y})\, d\vec{z}\, d\vec{y}$$

The constant k was chosen to be 50,000, and c was set to zero while the two cells developed independently, and then linearly increased from zero to 10 million over a period of 60 iterations. The procedure was halted as soon as the energy ceased to decrease significantly after C had risen to full value. The value of dt was chosen so that the most rapidly changing element of the receptive field changed by .35 per iteration. The initial values for the receptive fields were chosen to be random numbers between −2.0 and 2.0.

Typically, the first stage in which the cells developed independently took 70 iterations. Sixty iterations were then devoted to raising the constant c of the interaction term to full value. The energy was usually stable within five iterations after this.

Figure 1.13 shows the results of such a simulation. The resulting receptive field is of the form of a sinusoid with a spatial cutoff due to the dendridic geometry and is reminiscent of a Gabor function.

4.3.1. Sampling Frequency Space

By giving different (small) biases to the correlation function, we can generate receptive fields with arbitrary spatiotemporal frequency tuning. In practice we used the receptive field derived above and rotated it in spacetime to generate 39 receptive fields.

These frequencies were chosen to sample the frequency space fairly evenly. We "placed" the cells at these positions by hand, we hope in forthcoming work to develop self-organizing patterns to generate groups of quadrature pairs spanning the frequency space.

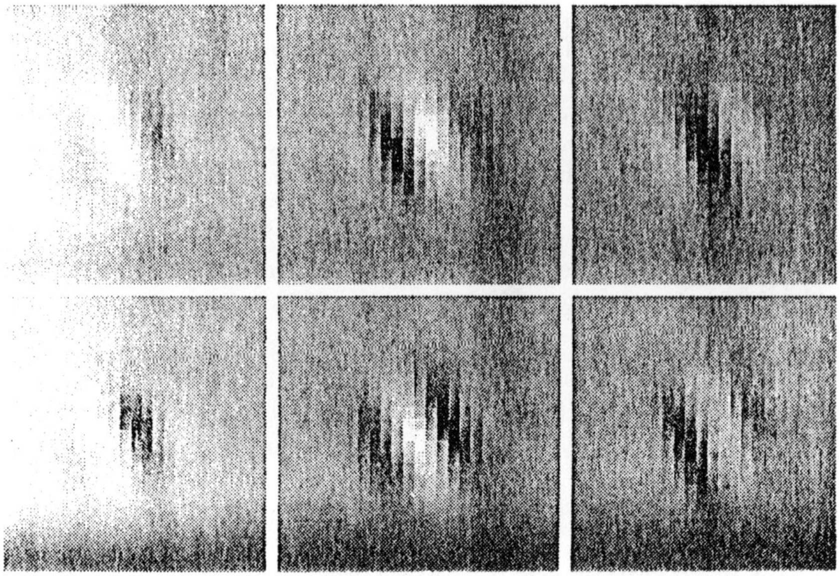

Figure 1.13. One dimensional slices of the receptive field of a cell developed using self-organisation.

The frequency layer consisted of 39 quadrature pairs of cells connected to every frequency cell. The frequency cells were distributed on three half spheres in frequency space, 13 on each sphere, and had the following coordinates:

	Sphere 1			Sphere 2			Sphere 3		
Cell	w_x	w_y	w_t	w_x	w_y	w_t	w_x	w_y	w_t
1.	0.31	0.81	−0.50	0.46	1.21	−0.75	0.62	1.62	−1.00
2.	0.31	0.81	0.50	0.46	1.21	0.75	0.62	1.62	1.00
3.	0.31	−0.81	−0.50	0.46	−1.21	−0.75	0.62	−1.62	−1.00
4.	0.31	−0.81	0.50	0.46	−1.21	0.75	0.62	−1.62	1.00
5.	0.81	0.50	−0.31	1.21	0.75	−0.46	1.62	1.00	−0.62
6.	0.81	0.50	0.31	1.21	0.75	0.46	1.62	1.00	0.62
7.	0.81	−0.50	−0.31	1.21	−0.75	−0.46	1.62	−1.00	−0.62
8.	0.81	−0.50	0.31	1.21	−0.75	0.46	1.62	−1.00	0.62
9.	0.50	0.31	−0.81	0.75	0.46	−1.21	1.00	0.62	−1.62
10.	0.50	0.31	0.81	0.75	0.46	1.21	1.00	0.62	1.62
11.	0.50	−0.31	−0.81	0.75	−0.46	−1.21	1.00	−0.62	−1.62
12.	0.50	−0.31	0.81	0.75	−0.46	1.21	1.00	−0.62	1.62
13.	1.00	0.00	0.00	1.50	0.00	0.00	2.00	0.00	0.00

where w_x, w_y, and w_t are the frequencies in the x, y, and t directions.

These particular frequencies were chosen by taking the midpoints between the vertices of a dodecahedron. The two cells with $w_x = w_y = 0$, $w_t = \pm 1$ obtained by this means were discarded, as they correspond to no real velocities. Each of the three spheres of frequency cells was constructed by taking a single cell with $w_x = 1.0$, 1.5, or 2.0, and $w_y = w_t = 0$, and rotating it into the 13 desired positions.

4.4. Velocity Sensitive Cells

The previous computer simulations have generated a set of quadrature pairs of motion-sensitive cells each tuned to a specific spatiotemporal frequency $\vec{\Omega}$, Ω_t. Following the models described in section 4.1, we assume that, for each quadrature pair, the outputs are summed and added.

We now show that we can train a network of velocity sensitive cells to estimate the correct velocity from the response of the population of frequency sensitive cells. The input to the frequency cells is a set of real images travelling with a fixed velocity.

The system is assumed to train itself by using knowledge of the velocities, training by a teacher. The system might obtain this knowledge by using its tracking system to check whether it has computed the correct velocity. A similar assumption was used by Zipser and Anderson (1988).

4.4.1. The Velocity Layer

Since the velocity cells should respond most strongly to frequency cells lying on the plane $w_xV_x + w_yV_y + w_t = 0$ in frequency space, the velocity cells which will respond to a particular frequency cell lie on the line

$$V_y = \frac{(w_t + w_xV_x)}{w_y} \tag{69}$$

in velocity space.

In order to maximize the information available to each velocity cell, the coordinates (V_x, V_y) were chosen to lie at the intersections of two or more of the lines given by the equation above (see Figure 1.14). Presumably, in the cortex there would be so many frequency cells that every velocity cell would lie near the lines corresponding to several frequency cells. There were 24 such intersections:

Cell No.	V_x	V_y	Cell No.	V_x	V_y	Cell No.	V_x	V_y
1.	0.00	0.62	9.	0.00	2.62	17.	0.62	0.38
2.	0.00	−0.62	10.	0.00	−2.62	18.	0.62	−0.38
3.	1.62	0.00	11.	0.62	1.62	19.	−0.62	0.38
4.	−1.62	0.00	12.	0.62	−1.62	20.	−0.62	0.38
5.	1.00	1.00	13.	−0.62	1.62	21.	2.62	1.62
6.	1.00	−1.00	14.	−0.62	−1.62	22.	2.62	−1.62
7.	−1.00	1.00	15.	0.38	0.00	23.	−2.62	1.62
8.	−1.00	−1.00	16.	−0.38	0.00	24.	−2.62	−1.62

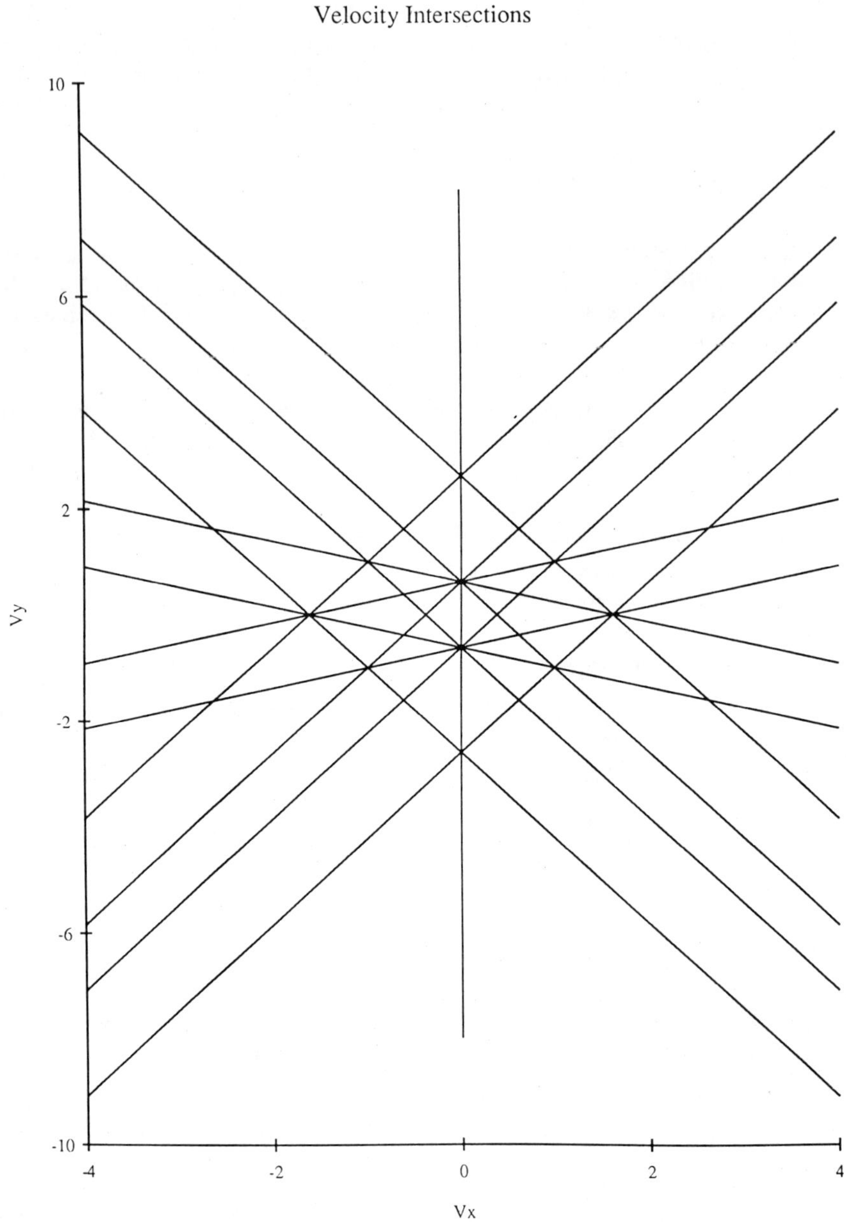

Figure 1.14. The velocity cells are chosen to lie near the intersections of the lines $\vec{\Omega}\cdot\vec{v} + \Omega_t = 0$ where the $(\vec{\Omega},\Omega_t)$ are the frequencies of the frequency tuned cells.

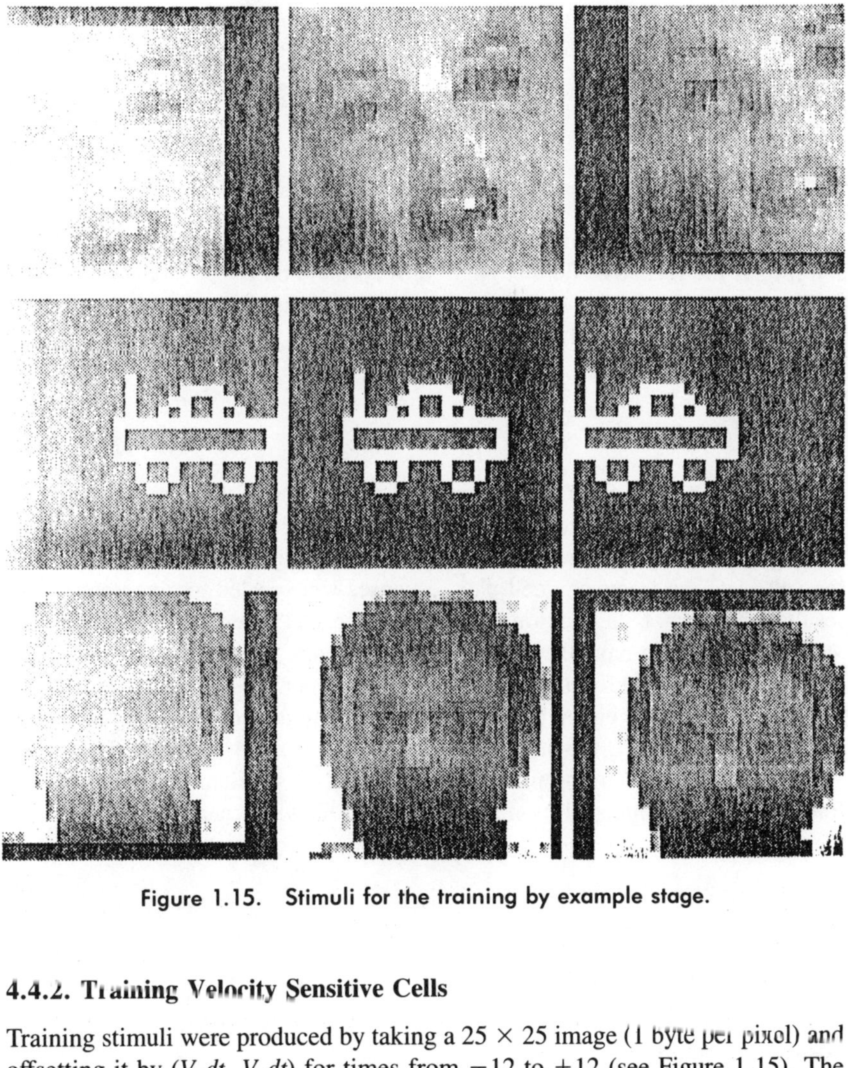

Figure 1.15. Stimuli for the training by example stage.

4.4.2. Training Velocity Sensitive Cells

Training stimuli were produced by taking a 25 × 25 image (1 byte per pixel) and offsetting it by ($V_x dt$, $V_y dt$) for times from −12 to +12 (see Figure 1.15). The result resembled a movie with 25 frames. Thus each stimulus could be represented as a 25 × 25 × 25 array with the two space dimensions and one time dimension. Since there were 24 velocities corresponding to cells, each image was used to produce 24 stimuli, each of which matched the preferred velocity of exactly one of the velocity cells.

Before beginning to train the network on a set of stimuli, the response of each of the 39 frequency cell pairs to each stimulus in the set was computed. The output was considered to be the sum of the squares of the outputs of the two individual cells making up the quadrature pair. Thus the response should be independent of the phase of the component being measured. These individual outputs were computed simply by multiplying the value at each point (in space and time) of the cell's receptive field by the intensity of the image at that point, and summing the results, i.e.,

$$R_f = I_{ijk}\Phi_{ijk} \tag{70}$$

(using the summation convention), where I_{ijk} is the image intensity at (i, j, k), and Φ_{ijk} is the receptive field strength at the same point.

The output of the velocity cells was defined to be sigmoid, with a range of 0.0 to 1.0. The exact formula used was:

$$R^{\mu}(\vec{v}:w_{f\vec{v}}) = \frac{1}{1 + e^{-\alpha\Sigma_f I_f^{\mu} w_{f\vec{v}}}}\,. \tag{71}$$

where I_f^{μ} is the input from frequency pair f responding to the stimulus μ, $w_{f\vec{v}}$ is the synaptic weight between frequency cell f and velocity cell $\vec{v}$, $R^{\mu}(\vec{v}:w_{f\vec{v}})$ is the response of the cell tuned to velocity $\vec{v}$ for stimulus μ, and $\alpha = 1$. Note that the values of the frequency cell pair responses were scaled to give appropriate results when $\alpha = 1$. In addition, the outputs of each "sphere" of frequency cells were normalized to have the same average response.

Given the sigmoid form for the velocity cell response, the "desired output" of a cell was defined as either 1.0, for a stimulus with a velocity corresponding to that of the cell, or 0.0 for others.

Two methods of training were employed. In the "simultaneous" method, the training was accomplished by minimizing the following energy equation:

$$E[w_{f\vec{v}}] = \frac{1}{2}\sum_{\mu} A_{\vec{v}\mu}(D_{\vec{v}}^{\mu} - \mathrm{R}^{\mu}(\vec{v}:w_{f\vec{v}}))^2, \tag{72}$$

where D_v^{μ} is the correct response for the cell tuned to velocity $\vec{v}$ for stimuli μ (i.e., 0 or 1). The constants $A_{\vec{v},\mu}$ are chosen to give heavier weightings for positive examples.

This leads to the update equation:

$$\frac{dw_{f\vec{v}}}{dt} = \alpha\sum_{\mu} A_{\vec{v},\mu}(D_{\vec{v}}^{\mu} - R_{\vec{v}}^{\mu})(R_{\vec{v}}^{\mu})^2 I_f^{\mu} e^{(-\alpha\Sigma_f I_f^{\mu} w_{f\vec{v}})} \tag{73}$$

A higher weighting of the update terms due to positive stimuli was helpful in preventing the more numerous negative stimuli from causing all, or too many, of the weights to go negative (this effect was achieved in practice by setting the term $(R_{\vec{v}}^{\mu})^2$ in the update equation to 1.0 for every positive example).

In the sequential approach we minimize a cost function for each input. Suppose that, before the μth input, the weights are given by $w_{f,\vec{v}}^{\mu-1}$. After the μth input the weights are chosen to minimize

$$E[w_{f\vec{v}}^{\mu}] = \frac{1}{2} \sum_{\vec{v}} (D_{\vec{v}}^{\mu} - R^{\mu}(\vec{v} : w_{f\vec{v}}^{\mu}))^2 + \frac{1}{2} \sum_{f\vec{v}} m_{\vec{v}}^{\mu} (w_{f\vec{v}}^{\mu} - w_{f\vec{v}}^{\mu-1})^2, \tag{74}$$

where the second term gives "inertia" and prevents the weights from changing too fast for a new stimulus. The m_{v}^{μ}'s are chosen to give more inertia for negative examples ($m = 0.1$ for negative examples and $m = 0.01$ for positive examples). This was again done to make it easier for the heavily outnumbered positive examples to influence the synaptic weights, and harder for the negative examples to change the weights once they had been pulled up by the positive ones. This gives the update equation:

$$\frac{dw_{fv}}{dt} = \alpha(D_{\vec{v}}^{\mu} - R_{\vec{v}}^{\mu})(R_{\vec{v}}^{\mu})^2 I_f^{\mu} e(-\alpha \sum_f I_f^{\mu} w_{f\vec{v}}^{\mu}) + m(w_{f\vec{v}}^{\mu-1} - w_{f\vec{v}}^{\mu}) \tag{75}$$

Weights were initially set to 0.0 or to a random value in the range −2.0 to 2.0. The value of *dt* was chosen so that the most rapidly changing weight would have its value increased or decreased by 0.2 at each iteration. The energy descent was halted when the energy showed no significant decline over a period of 100 iterations, or in any case after 10,000 iterations (this condition probably never actually occurred). A few hundred iterations were usually required for the cases discussed here. The descent was also halted when the energy dropped below 0.005, i.e., when the output of a cell was, at worst, within 0.1 of the desired response for every stimulus. This condition was the principal means of halting the descent in the simultaneous case; in the sequential case, the energy generally leveled off long before the outputs reached this level of accuracy (see Figure 1.16).

The accuracy of the sequential case was found to be significantly improved by presenting the same stimuli repeatedly. The results here are for simulations in which the complete set of stimuli was presented fives times in succession (during sequential learning only) (see Figure 1.17).

For the case of 13 (×24) = 312 training stimuli (that is, 13 images, each moving in 24 different directions, or 312 actual stimuli), sequential training took on the order of two hours on the Sun4. Simultaneous learning took longer, ~8 hours.

With 29 (×24) = 696 stimuli, sequential learning took ~5 hours; simultaneous took ~36 hours. The sequential learning is faster, because it is allowed to forget. Each time a new example is learned, the energy function is minimized with a momentum term which prevents radical change of the synaptic weights, but allowing a partial destruction of previously learned information, or causing

Sequential training on 1 (x24) Stimuli

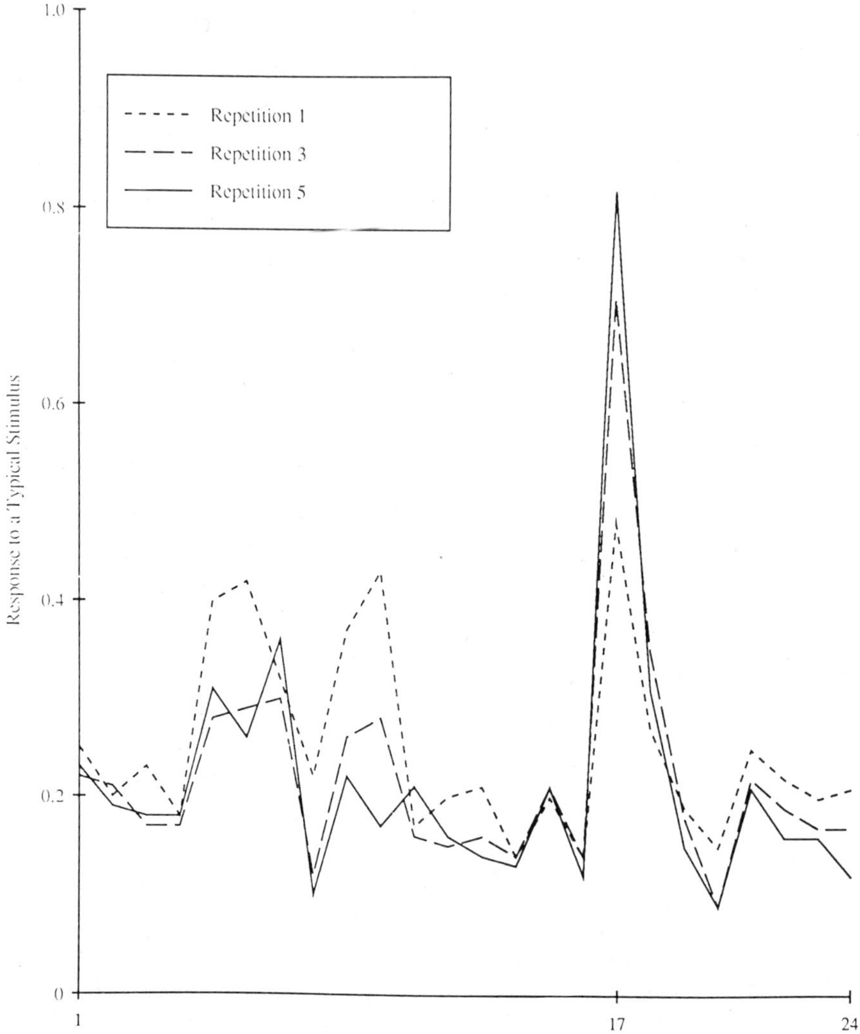

Figure 1.16. For sequential training the strength of the correct response increases with the number of repetitions of the stimuli.

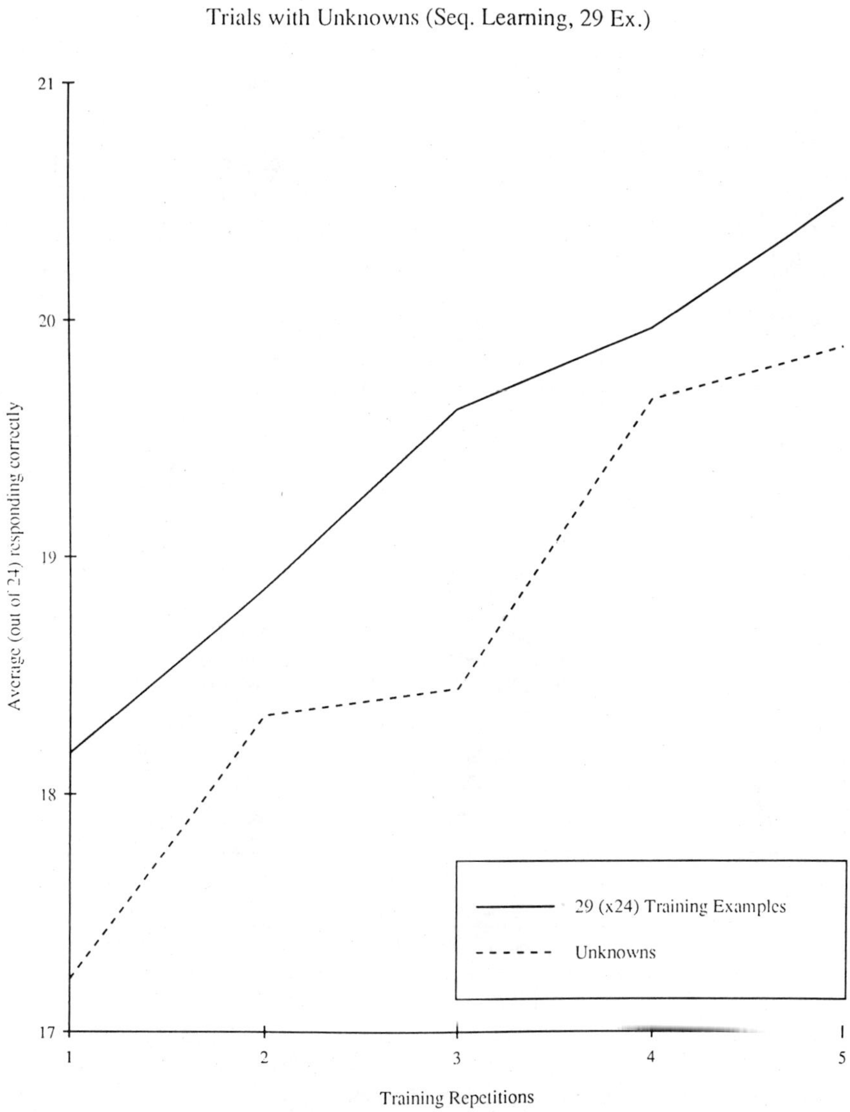

Figure 1.17. For sequential training the proportion of correct responses on both known and unknown stimuli increases with the number of repetitions.

only partial learning of the new information at the time the energy function, is minimized.

With 1 (×24) = 24 stimuli, sequential learning took ~10 minutes, as opposed to ~3 minutes for simultaneous. Thus, at very small numbers of stimuli, the simultaneous method is not only more accurate but faster as well. The reverse seems to be true for large numbers of stimuli (see below).

4.4.3. Results of Velocity Training

In the charts below, a "correct" response for a velocity cell means that for a certain image presented to the cell (shown in 24 versions, each with a different velocity), the strongest response was for that velocity which was the same as the one the cell had been trained to pick out.

Sequential Training, 29 (×24) stimuli:

Repetition	Av. correct responses (of 24) for examples used in training	Av. correct responses (of 24) for 9 unknowns
1.	18.172	17.222
2.	18.862	18.333
3.	19.621	18.444
4.	19.966	19.667
5.	20.517	19.889

Sequential Training, 13 (×24) stimuli:

Repetition	Av. correct responses (of 24) for examples used in training	Av. correct responses (of 24) for 9 unknowns
1.	12.231	12.444
2.	14.769	15.111
3.	16.306	15.444
4.	16.692	15.333
5.	16.923	16.111

Simultaneous Training, 29 (×24) stimuli:

Av. correct responses (of 24) for examples used in training	Av. correct responses (of 24) for 9 unknowns
16.207	15.333

Simultaneous Training, 13 (×24) stimuli:

Av. correct responses (of 24) for examples used in training	Av. correct responses (of 24) for 9 unknowns
20.462	15.556

Surprisingly, the simultaneous training, which took much longer, also turned out to be less accurate than sequential learning, with the difference increasing as the number of training stimuli increased. Note that the performance of the simultaneous method actually worsened as more stimuli were presented. For small numbers of stimuli, however, the simultaneous method was able to learn with near perfect accuracy. The explanation for this seems to lie in the sequential network's ability to disregard individual examples of data with little effect on the learning of the other examples. If one presents to the sequential network a stimulus which contains information contradictory to what it has already learned, the momentum term of the energy will prevent the synaptic weights from changing much, and the new data will not be learned, while the old data will remain basically unaltered. On the other hand, contradictory information presented to the simultaneous network will cause the convergence of the energy function to halt before any of the data has necessarily been learned. The cost is paid by making the response to every stimulus somewhat less accurate, rather than by throwing out the worst cases altogether. It seems, then, that there is really no advantage to the simultaneous method, at least as it is defined here. It is not only less plausible biologically, but less accurate and significantly slower for any reasonable number of training stimuli.

It is interesting that, for sequential learning, performance on unknowns seems to be about as good as performance for stimuli on which training has occurred.

Earlier trials were made with 13 and 26 frequency cells (i.e., lying on one and two spheres), and it was apparent that increasing the number of frequency cells brought about an increase in accuracy. Since reasonable results were achieved here with only 39 frequency cells, one would expect the human visual system to perform quite well with its far larger number of such cells.

Increasing the number of training stimuli also resulted in greater and greater accuracy in the trained network.

4.5. Summary of Section 4

From these results we see that the system can claim to have learned to detect velocity, since the proportion of correct answers is high even for stimuli that the system has not been trained on. The proportion of correct responses rises with the number of examples and repetitions. Thus we argue that increasing the number of examples and increasing the number of frequency cells should give a system which can be trained to arbitrary high accuracy. Moreover the errors in velocity estimation were almost always small and usually corresponded to choosing neighboring velocity cells.

The combination of self-organization and training by example gives a system that is capable of performing well on real data. It is interesting to speculate on the relative effectiveness of these two methods as strategies for training systems and the tradeoffs involved.

5. CONCLUSION

This chapter has described three models using self-organization with Hebb rules. It is very encouraging that such simple models, using biologically plausible learning rules, can generate the types of structures predicted by computational theories of vision. The next step in the development of models that realistically and comprehensibly capture the salient features of neurobiological maturation is a more realistic treatment of the interconnection schemes found in local cortical circuits.

REFERENCES

Adelson, E. H., & Bergen, J. (1985). Spatiotemporal energy models for the perception of motion. *Journal of the Optical Society of America, A, 2,* 284–299.

Anderson, R. A., & Siegel, R. M. (1989). Motion processing in primate cortex. In G. M. Edelman, W. E. Gall, & W. M. Cowan (Eds.), *Signal and sense: Local and global order in perceptual maps.* New York: Wiley.

Barlow, H. (1981). Critical limiting factors in the design of the eye and visual cortex. *Prowlings of the Royal Society, B, 212,* 1–34.

Barrow, H. (1987). Learning receptive fields. *First I.E.E.E. Conference on Neural Networks, IV,* 115–121.

Brown, T. H., Chang, V. C., Ganong, A. H., Keenan, C. L., & Kelso, S. R. (1988). Biophysical properties of dendrites and spines that may control the induction and expression of long-term synaptic potentiation. In *From biophysics to behavior* (pp. 201–264). New York: Alan R. Liss, Inc.

Bulthoff, H., Little J., & Poggio, T. (1989). A parallel algorithm for real-time computation of optical flow. *Nature, 337,* 549–553.

Carew, T. J., Hawkins, R. D., Abrams, T. W., & Kandel, E. R. (1984). A test of Hebb's postulate at identified synapses which mediate classical conditioning in *Aplysia. Journal of Neuroscience, 4,* 1217–1224.

Coleman, S. (1985). *Aspects of symmetry.* Cambridge, UK: Cambridge University Press.

Cooper, L. N., Liberman, F., & Oja, E. (1979). A theory for the acquisition and loss of neuron specificity in visual cortex. *Biological Cybernetics, 33,* 9–28.

Daugman, J. G. (1985). Uncertainty relation for resolution in space, spatial frequency, and orientation optimized by two dimensional visual cortical filters. *Journal of the Optical Society of America, A, 2,* 1160–1169.

De Valois R., Albrecht D., & Thorell, L. (1982). Spatial frequency selectivity of cells in Macaque visual cortex. *Vision Research, 22,* 545–559.

Gabor, D. (1946). Theory of communication. *Journal of Instruments and Electronics, 93,* 429–457.

Hassenstein, B., & Riechardt, W. E. (1956). Systemtheoretische analyse der zeitreihenfolgen- und vorzeichenauswertung bei der bewegungsperzeption des russelkafers *chlorophanus. Z. Naturforsch, 11b,* 513–524.

Hebb, D. O. (1949). *The organization of behavior.* New York: Wiley.

Heeger, D. (1987). Model for the extraction of image flow. *Journal of the Optical Society of America, A, 4,* 1455–1471.

Hildreth, E. C., & Koch, C. (1987). The analysis of visual motion: From computational theory to neuronal mechanisms. In W. M. Cowan, E. M. Shooter, C. F. Stevens, & R. F. Thompson (Eds.), *Annual Review of Neuroscience* (Vol. 10, pp. 477–533). Palo Alto, CA: Annual Reviews.

Hirsch, H., Leventhal, A., McCall, M., & Tieman, D. (1983). Effects of exposure to lines of one or two orientations on different cell types in striate cortex of cat. *Journal of Physiology, 337,* 241–255.

Hopfield, J. J. (1984). Neurons with graded response have collected computational properties like those of two-state neurons. *Proceedings of the National Academy of Sciences USA, 81,* 3088–3092.

Hubel, D. H., & Wiesel, T. N. (1974). Sequence regularity and geometry of orientation selectivity and binocularity in the monkey striate cortex. *Journal of Comparative Neurology, 158,* 267–294.

Hurlbert, A. C., & Poggio, T. A. (1988). Synthesizing a color algorithm from examples. *Science, 239,* 482–485.

Jones, J., & Palmer, L. (1987). The two-dimensional spatial structure of simple receptive fields in cat striate cortex. *Journal of Neurophysiology, 58,* 1233–1258.

Kammen, D. M. (1988). *Self-organization in neural networks.* Unpublished doctoral dissertation, Harvard University, Cambridge, MA.

Kammen, D. M., & Yuille, A. L. (1988). Spontaneous symmetry-breaking energy functions of orientation selective cortical cells. *Biological Cybernetics, 59,* 23–31.

Kelso, S. R., Ganong, A. H., & Brown, T. H. (1986). Hebbian synapses in hippocampus. *Proceedings of the National Academy of Sciences, USA, 83,* 5326–5330.

Kersten, D., O'Toole, A. J., Sereno, M. E., Knill, D. C., & Anderson, J. A. (1987). Associative learning of scene parameters from images. *Applied Optics, 26,* 4999–5006.

Lehky, S. R., & Sejnowski, T. J. (1988). Network model of shape from shading: neural function arises from both receptive and projective fields. *Nature, 333,* 452–454.

Linsker, R. (1986a). From basic network principles to neural architecture: Emergence of spatial-opponent cells. *Proceedings of the National Academy of Sciences, USA, 83,* 508–7512.

Linsker, R. (1986b). From basic network principles to neural architecture: Emergence of orientation-selective cells. *Proceedings of the National Academy of Sciences, USA, 83,* 8390–8394.

Linsker, R. (1986c). From basic network principles to neural architecture: Emergence of orientation columns. *Proceedings of the National Academy of Sciences, USA, 83,* 8779–9783.

Linsker, R. (1988, March). Self-organization in a perceptual network. *Computer,* pp. 105–117.

Nakayama, K. (1985). Biological motion processing: A review. *Vision Research, 25,* 625–660.

Newsome, W. T., Gizzi, M. S., & Movshon, J. A. (1983). Spatial and temporal properties of neurons in macaque MT. *Investigations in Ophthalmology and Vision Science, 24,* 106.

Oja, E. (1982). A simplified neuron model as a principal component analyzer. *Journal of Mathematical Biology, 15,* 267–273.

Oja, E. (1989). Neural networks: principal components and subspaces. Submitted to *International Journal of Neural Systems.*

Poggio, T., & Reichardt, W. E. (1973). Considerations on models of movement detection. *Kybernetics, 13,* 223–227.

Pollen, D., & Ronner, S. (1981). Phase relationships between adjacent simple cells in the visual cortex. *Science, 212,* 1409–1411.

Sanger, T. (1988). Stereo disparity computation using Gabor filters. *Biological Cybernetics, 59,* 405–418.

Sanger, T. (1989a). Optimal unsupervised learning in a single-layer linear feedforward network. *Neural Networks.*

Sanger, T. (1989b). An optimality principle for unsupervised learning. In D. Touretzky (Ed.), *Advances in neural information processing systems* (p. 11). San Mateo, CA: Morgan Kaufmann.

Sattinger, D. H. (1979). *Group theoretic methods in bifurcation theory* (Lecture Notes in Math. 762). Berlin, Heidelberg, & New York: Springer.

Schall, J. D., Perry, V. H., & Leventhal, A. G. (1986a). Retinal ganglion cell dendritic fields in Old-World monkeys are oriented radially. *Brain Research, 368,* 18–23.

Schall, J. D., Vitek, D. J., & Leventhal, A. G. (1986b). Retinal constraints on orientation specificity in cat visual cortex. *Journal of Neuroscience, 6,* 823–836.

Schall, J. D., & Leventhal, A. G. (1987). Relationships between ganglion cell dendritic structure and retinal topography in the cat. *Journal of Computational Neurology, 257,* 149–159.

Sillito, A. M. (1987). Synaptic processes and neurotransmitters operating in the central visual system: A systems approach. In G. Edelman, E. Gall, & M. Cowan (Eds.), *Synaptic function* (pp. 328–371). New York: Wiley Interscience.

Singer, W. (1976). Modification of orientation and direction selectivity of cortical cells in kittens with monocular vision. *Brain Research, 118,* 460–468.

Softky, W. R., & Kammen, D. M. (1990). Can simple cells learn curves? A Hebbian model in a structured environment. *Advances in Neural Information Processing Systems 2.* San Mateo, CA: Morgan Kaufmann.

Spiro, P. (1987). *Receptive field shape as a function of dimensionality reduction and image statistics.* Unpublished bachelor's thesis, Brown University, Providence, RI.

Stanton, P. K., & Senjowski, T. J. (1989). Associative long-term depression in the hippocampus induced by hebbian covariance. *Nature, 339,* 215–218.

Stryker, M., Sherk, H., Leventhal, A., & Hirsch, H. (1978). Physiological consequences for the cat's visual cortex of effectively restricting early visual experience with oriented contours. *Journal of Neurophysiology, 41,* 896–909.

Swindale, N. V., Matsubara, J. A., & Cynader, M. S. (1987). Surface organization of orientation and direction selectivity in cat area 18. *Journal of Neuroscience, 7,* 1414–1427.

van Santen, J. P. H., & Sperling, G. (1985). A temporal covariance model of motion perception. *Journal of the Optical Society of America, A, 1,* 451–473.

Vidyasagar, T. R., & Urbas, J. V. (1982). Orientation sensitivity of cat LGN neurons with and without inputs from visual cortical areas. *Experimental Brain Research, 46,* 157–169.

Watson, A. B., & Ahumada, A. J. (1985). Model of human visual-motion sensing *Journal of the Optical Society of America, A, 2,* 322–341.

Yuille, A. L., & Cohen, D. S. (1989). *The development and training of motion and velocity sensitive cortical cells by Hebb rules* (Tech. Rep. No. 89–9). Cambridge, MA: Harvard Robotics Laboratory.

Yuille, A. L., Kammen, D., & Cohen, D. (1989). Quadrature and the Development of Orientation Selective Cortical Cells by Hebb Rules. *Biological Cybernetics, 61,* 183–194.

Zipser, D., & Anderson, R. A. (1988). A back-propagation programmed network that stimulates response properties of a subset of posterior parietal neurons. *Nature, 331,* 679–684.

2

The Neuron as a Reprogrammable Computing Element in Neural Networks*

Daniel K. Hartline
Békésy Laboratory
University of Hawaii
Honolulu, HI

1. INTRODUCTION

The neuron as a component of a network was long viewed by theorists as an invariant passive computing element, summing inputs and giving an output (e.g., a spike) when the sum exceeds a threshold (e.g., McCullogh & Pitts, 1943; Farley & Clark, 1961; Little, 1974; Harth, Lewis, & Csermely, 1975; Hopfield, 1982). This view, based on early neurophysiological findings, was slowly replaced by one based on more recent physiological results which give the neurons themselves computational properties that modify the inputs they receive. Network models have been developed in which component neurons exhibit adaptation (Lange, Hartline, & Ratliff, 1966), postinhibitory rebound (Perkel, 1964, 1976), synaptic kinetics (Perkel, 1964), and slow regenerative active responses (Hartline, 1979). However, physiological research has continued to change the rules on which modelers must base their work, and the last 15 years have seen yet another revolution in our understanding of the way neurons operate. This one is based on the finding that the computational programs executed by neurons are not fixed, but can be radically modified by biochemically mediated reprogramming.

An example of this reprogramming is shown in Figure 2.1, taken from a small neural network of 30 neurons found in crustacean nervous system and known as the *stomatogastric ganglion* (STG). Figure 2.1a shows an intracellular recording from a "passive" motor neuron from this ganglion, known as the *LP* cell. The cell at rest does not fire impulses; although it is periodically inhibited by synaptic barrages from another motorneuron in the ganglion, the endogenously bursting *PD* cell (the periodic dips in intracellular voltage seen in the LP trace correspond-

* Supported by NIH grant NS15314. I am indebted to M. Andres, N. Nakata, and B. Tomiyasu for technical assistance and help making up figures, and to R. Sanborn for assistance with computer operations.

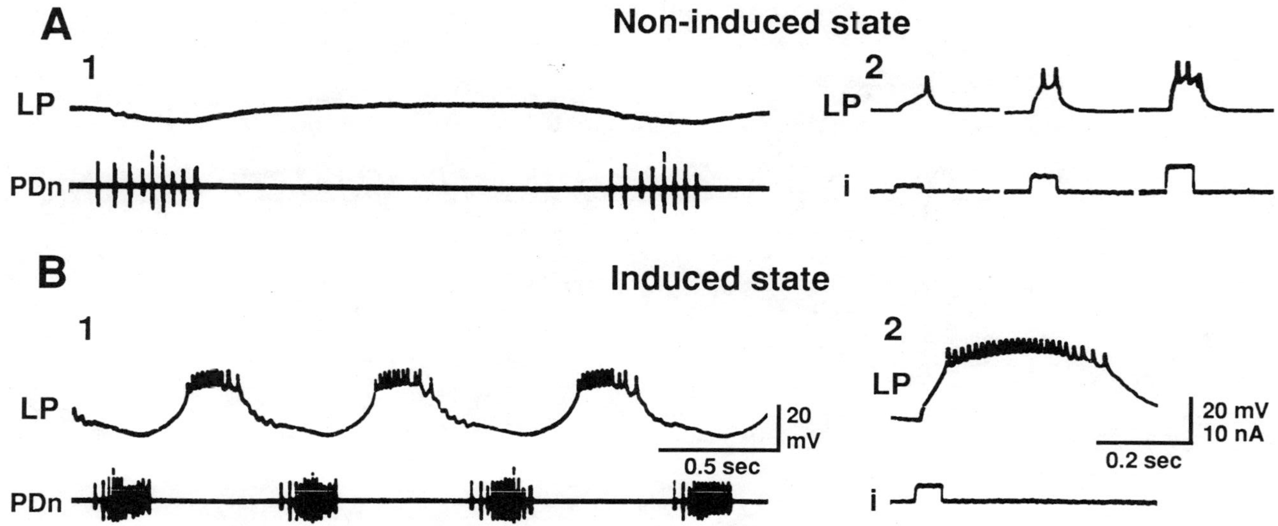

Figure 2.1. Induction of plateau properties by cellular reprogramming. Intracellular recordings from a lateral pyloric (LP) neuron of the stomatogastric ganglion of the spiny lobster *Panulirus interruptus*. a. Activity in a ganglion isolated from CNS input with a pool of isotonic sucrose placed on the main input nerve (stomatogastric nerve: stn) to block nerve impulse traffic entering the ganglion. b. Activity in a ganglion with the sucrose block removed. In both a and b, panel 1 is a record of spontaneous activity, and shows as well an extracellular recording trace (PDn) from a nerve containing two axons from endogenously bursting network-driver neurons. Panel 2 shows the effects of 50 msec duration depolarizing current pulses of various magnitudes on the firing behavior of the LP. In b2, a hyperpolarizing offset current of 5 nA prevents the cell from firing spontaneously, and the current pulse is timed to follow the period of inhibition from the PD cells (modified from Hartline et al., 1988 [G3]†.

† Codes in brackets refer to author's experimental designations for this and all other figure captions in this chapter.

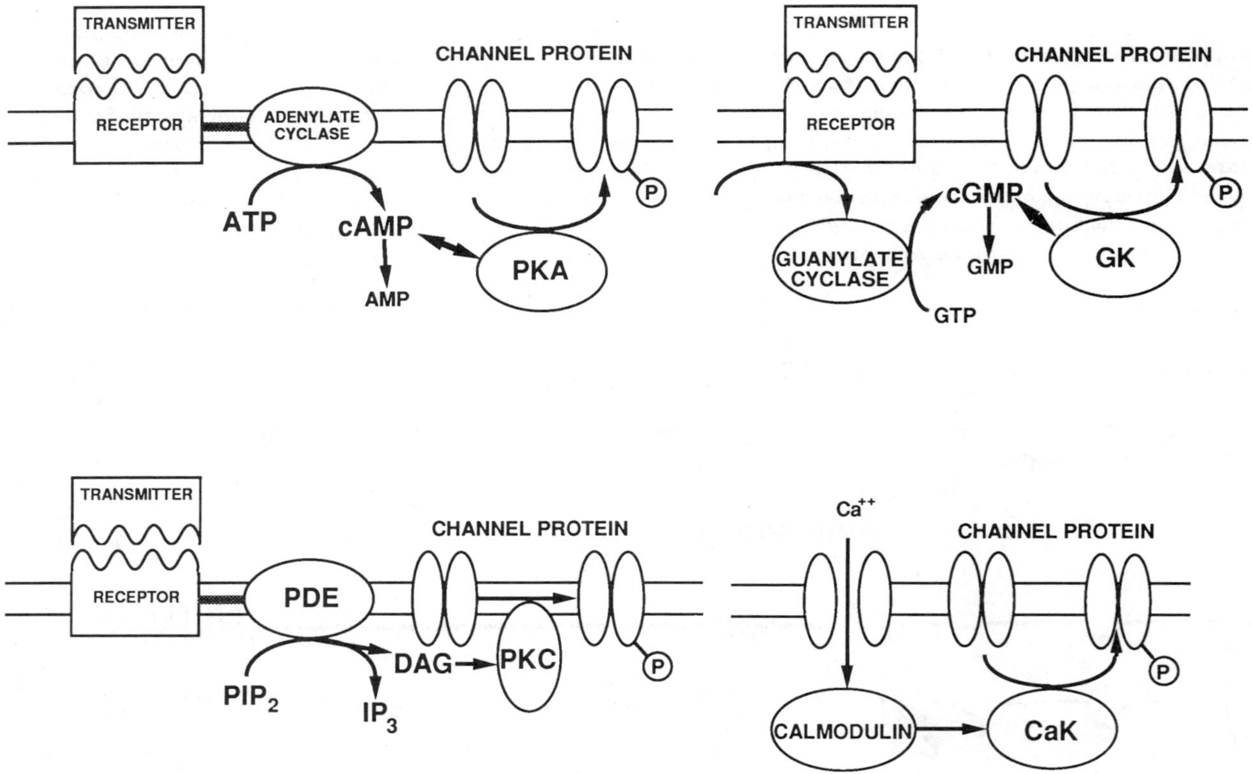

Figure 2.1. (continued)

ing to impulse bursts in the PDn trace of Figure 2.1a1). The LP, if excited by passing a depolarizing current, only fires impulses while the current is flowing, as shown by its reaction to current pulses of various sizes in Figure 2.1a2. In this state, it performs a moderately linear transformation on incoming information, producing a train of spikes proportional in frequency to the sum of impinging inputs (although it also produces modifications from its own cellular properties, including adaptation and postinhibitory rebound). This picture changes dramatically if certain inputs from the central nervous system (CNS) are permitted to activate the cell, as shown in Figure 2.1b. Now the LP cell fires vigorous bursts of impulses between periods of inhibition from the PD and other cells (Figure 2.1b1). These bursts result from an induced nonlinear membrane property in the LP cell, which is revealed in its responses to the same current pulses which produced only linear behavior before (Figure 2.1b2). Such pulses now elicit prolonged bursts of impulses which far outlast the triggering current itself. The transform on incoming information which is now performed is highly nonlinear. Not only is there a tendency for the cell to switch between a silent "off" state and an "on" state with high frequency firing, but the temporal relations between an input and output are greatly distorted compared to the noninduced state (Russell & Hartline, 1978; Hartline, Russell, Raper, & Graubard, 1988). The LP neuron has been reprogrammed from a basically linear device into a highly nonlinear one.

The way such reprogramming is understood to occur in most cases is through receptor-mediated biochemical cascades within neurons, which usually end up

---

Figure 2.2. Simplified diagrams of various second messenger systems for cellular reprogramming. a. Cyclic adenosine monophosphate (cAMP) system. Binding of transmitter to receptor activates the membrane-bound enzyme adenylate cyclase which produces cAMP from ATP. This in turn activates cAMP-dependent protein kinase (PKA) which phosphorylates a target protein (shown here as an ion channel protein, for diagrammatic purposes; phosphorylation of intermediate modulator proteins is also possible). b. Cyclic guanosine monophosphate (cGMP) system. This has a schema similar to that for the cAMP system. cGMP activates cGMP-dependent protein kinase (GK). c. Inositol phosphate system. Transmitter binding activates the receptor-linked enzyme phosphodiesterase (PDE) which cleaves membrane-bound phosphatidylinositol 4,5-bisphosphate (PIP_2) to produce cytoplasmic inositol 1,4,5-trisphosphate (IP_3) and membrane-bound diacylglycerol (DAG). The DAG in turn activates membrane-bound protein-kinase-C to phosphorylate membrane proteins. IP_3 also acts as a second messenger for other reactions, in particular, mobilization of calcium from intracellular stores. d. Calcium entry *via* voltage-dependent channels (or other means) binds to the calcium-binding protein calmodulin, which activates a calcium-calmodulin-dependent protein kinase (CaK) which phosphorylates proteins. In other cases, Ca^{++} can act more directly on channel proteins to alter their properties. The reaction systems are significantly more complex in detail than diagrammed (in part after Kaczmarek & Levitan, 1987b).

modifying physiologically important proteins such as those forming ion channels in the membrane. Several different biochemical pathways producing such effects have been identified so far, some of the more important of which are diagrammed in Figure 2.2. A neurotransmitter molecule binds to an externally exposed receptor molecule, which activates the enzymatic production of a second messenger. Cyclic AMP (cAMP), cyclic GMP (cGMP), and the two products of phosphatidylinositol 4,5 bisphosphate breakdown (inositol 1,4,5 trisphosphate, IP_3, and diacylglycerol, DAG) serve as second messengers in various systems. In a variation on this theme, Ca^{++}, entering through voltage-activated channels or released from internal stores, can also serve as a second messenger. The second messenger in turn activates other processes. The examples shown in the figure involve the activation of protein kinases, enzymes that phosphorylate various proteins, potentially including ion channel proteins (as shown in the figure, for diagrammatic purposes). Other internal chemistries can be modified by the second messengers, including processes involved in the synthesis or release of neurotransmitter, or the growth or developmental modification of neurons (Miller, 1985; Kaczmarek & Levitan, 1987a).

The specific way in which the LP neuron of Figure 2.1 is reprogrammed has not yet been elucidated, but it should be apparent that if any of the three receptor-mediated processes diagrammed in Figure 2.2 were to convert an inactive (blocked) channel selective for ions carrying inward current (e.g., for Na^+ or Ca^{++} ions to enter the cell) to an active voltage-dependent channel, it could have the potential for producing active depolarizations. This is because voltage-dependent inward currents in most biological membranes tend to be inherently unstable or regenerative. The inward current causes positive feedback through depolarization of the membrane, which in turn increases the conductance for that current. Such a mechanism could produce highly nonlinear membrane voltage behavior and might drive bursts of nerve impulses at the neuronal trigger zone. An equally reasonable mechanism for enhancing regenerative properties of membrane would be for the second messenger system to cause a block of voltage-dependent outward current mechanisms that are antagonistic to regenerative inward currents. Both types of mechanism have been described (e.g., Reuter, 1979; Siegelbaum, 1987). The challenge for network modelers, then, is to incorporate the new information on second messenger biochemistry into model neurons and to explore the implications of these properties on real as well as theoretical networks.

In this chapter, a brief review will be given first of some of the classical electrical properties of nerve cells, indicating how these are handled in the model SYNETSIM-3 (version 3.2), the most recent version of a series of models designed for physiologically realistic simulation of small networks of real neurons. Next, the biochemical elements of this model which allow nerve cells to be reprogrammed will be described, and several examples given.

2. SYNETSIM CHEMO-ELECTRICAL PROPERTIES

The operation of SYNETSIM-3 can be conveniently broken into two segments (see Figure 2.3): the chemoelectrical properties (i.e., the classical neuron properties, including chemically mediated conductance changes in postsynaptic membrane) and the biochemical properties (the inductive or modulatory processes). The chemoelectrical properties of nerve cells which are integratively important can in turn be classified into several categories:

2.1. Electrotonic Spread

The basic element for computing electrical integrative events in SYNETSIM-3 is the compartment. As with other compartmental models of branching dendritic trees (e.g., Rall, 1964), SYNETSIM-3 compartments consist of a capacitance, a leak conductance, and a leak battery (Figure 2.3, top). In addition, each compartment may possess any number of chemoelectrical "branches," simulating synaptic effects, voltage-dependent mechanisms, and repetitive firing processes. For the most part, these are represented by variable conductances in series with fixed ionic batteries. Any of these are readily "wired" into a compartment by adding a parameter line to the parameter file which serves as model input (Figure 2.3, middle). Compartments are interconnected with ohmic resistors to represent the various geometrical regions of a nerve cell—the soma, dendrites, axons, etc. Calculations for such compartments are almost as straightforward as for passive compartmental models, the main caveat being that, to assure accuracy, the effects of increased conductances on length and time constants must be kept in mind, so that more compartments must be used to represent a given neuron with active conductances than for the same one with fixed conductances. In general SYNETSIM-3 utilizes the simpler of several computational alternatives (e.g., spherical instead of cylindrical compartments, Euler integration of time instead of higher-order methods), which makes it slower and more wasteful of memory than it might otherwise be, but easier to program and to modify.

Electrotonic interactions among different neurons are easily produced by resistively coupling compartments belonging to different cells. Rectifying electrical connections among cells can also be simulated, by specifying a different coupling conductance depending on the direction of current flow between two compartments. In the matrix of coupling conductances, g_{ij} is used for computing current flow if $V_i < V_j$, whereas g_{ij} is used if $V_i > V_j$. Note that some inaccuracy is present in this representation since in physiological cases the transition in coupling conductance in the region $V_i \sim V_j$ is not abrupt (Furshpan & Potter, 1959; Graubard & Hartline, 1987).

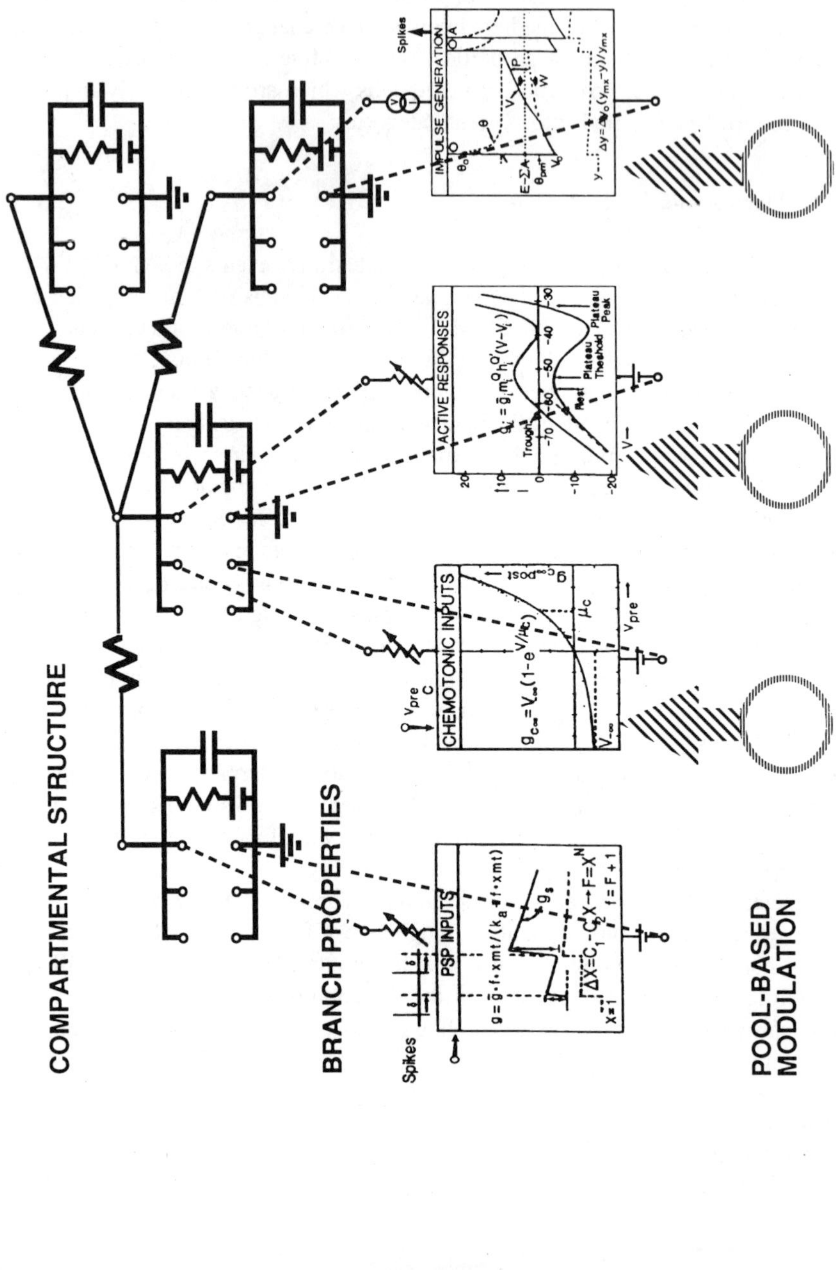
COMPARTMENTAL STRUCTURE
BRANCH PROPERTIES
POOL-BASED MODULATION
Spikes
PSP INPUTS
CHEMOTONIC INPUTS
ACTIVE RESPONSES
IMPULSE GENERATION
Spikes

2.2. Repetitive Firing

Hodgkin-Huxley (HH) formulations can be used in SYNETSIM-3 to simulate repetitive firing, following approaches developed by Connor and Stevens (1971) and Partridge and Stevens (1976) (see Active Responses, below). Three voltage and time-dependent HH mechanisms (I_{Na}, I_K, and I_A) are required for repetitive firing, and at least one for adaptation, each having 14 to 24 parameters. Also, very short time increments (10 μsec) must be used. Thus employing such a model is a major drain on computing time.

An alternative approach that was developed in earlier versions of SYNETSIM (Hartline, 1976a,b) and is still used in SYNETSIM-3 represents the kinetics of repetitive firing using a total of 16 parameters, plus 4 parameters for each adaptation component. It gets by on a time-step of 1 msec. This "TRIGR" section of the model produces a repetitive train in response to sustained excitation with an increase of firing frequency as a function of excitation. The relation between frequency and excitation, the pacemaker response relation (PMR), is nearly linear over a wide range of frequencies above rhythmic threshold. Following an increase in excitation, firing frequency decreases with time, owing to the developing of adaptation, which can be of two types, refractory (spike-dependent) or accommodative (excitation dependent). Postinhibitory rebound may be treated as a form of disadaptation, or it may be treated as a special active cellular property. An important feature of real repetitively firing neurons which is handled appropriately by TRIGR (Hartline, 1976a) is their phase-dependent responses to perturbation (antidromic spikes or changes in excitation: Perkel, Schulman, Bullock, Moore, & Segundo, 1964; Fohlmeister, Poppele, & Purple, 1974) including phase locking to periodic stimuli (e.g., Fohlmeister et al., 1974; Knight, 1972).

2.3. Active Responses

Several special properties neurons possess (in addition to spikes) can be traced to voltage-dependent active responses in the membrane. In recent versions of SYNETSIM, these are represented by various forms of the Hodgkin-Huxley equations (Hodgkin & Huxley, 1952). For such processes, current generated by the

---

Figure 2.3. Organizational diagram for SYNETSIM-3. Modular compartment design permits electrical compartments to be interconnected resistively or with diodes; a variety of electrical branches containing variable conductances in series with fixed ionic batteries can be added to each compartment; key parameters in each branch can be the target of modulatory effects mediated by chemical pools (for additional details, see also Hartline, 1989).

process (I) is equal to the product of the ionic conductance for a particular ionic mechanism and the net driving voltage on the ion:

$$I = \bar{g}MH(V - V_{rev}) \tag{1}$$

where the conductance is the product of a maximum conductance, $\bar{g}$ with time and voltage-dependent activation (M) and deinactivation (H) variables, and the driving voltage is the difference between membrane potential and the reversal potential for the mechanism. This equation is accurate only for ohmic conductances. Although the sodium and potassium mechanisms of squid axon are remarkably ohmic, several important channels show substantial rectification in their V(I) curves, and are more accurately modeled with a relationship such as the Goldman-Hodgkin-Katz (GHK) equation (Hodgkin & Katz, 1949). Nevertheless, the HH formulation of SYNETSIM can be used to simulate many important physiological mechanisms:

1. *Plateau potentials* (regenerative depolarizations: Russell & Hartline, 1978; Figure 2.1b2), *driver potentials* (self-terminating plateaus: Tazaki & Cooke, 1979) and *endogenous bursting* (in some cases, at least, produced by repetitive driver potentials: Strumwasser, 1968) can be produced with a slowly or noninactivating voltage-dependent inward current mechanism with a sigmoidal dependence of steady state activation on membrane voltage. In cases in which activation time constants are short compared with the timecourse of development of the active response, activation kinetics can be omitted, simplifying the simulation. Voltage-dependent restoring mechanisms which cause termination of the regenerative depolarization and, in endogenously bursting cells, pacemaker activity bringing the membrane to threshold for the next burst, can be represented by HH formulations with long time constants. The representation of Ca^{++}-activated mechanisms (e.g., potassium conductances: $g_{K(Ca)}$), which have been assigned roles in some endogenously bursting cells (Thompson, 1976; Smith, 1978; Kramer & Zucker, 1985), requires the chemical simulation capabilities described in a later section.

2. *Delaying mechanisms,* which slow a neuron's recovery from preceding hyperpolarizations (Byrne, 1980; Hartline, 1979) are readily simulated with an A-current mechanism using the HH formulation developed by Connor and Stevens (1971).

3. *Postinhibitory rebound* (PIR), which produces transient firing (or increases above ongoing levels) following release of a hyperpolarization can be simulated as the reverse of an adaptation process. Adaptation can in turn be simulated as a slow voltage-dependent outward current obeying HH kinetics (Partridge & Stevens, 1976). Simulations of adaptation involving $g_{K(Ca)}$ require the second-messenger formulations developed below. Other possible mechanisms for PIR such as hyperpolarization-activation of a slowly decaying inward current might be simulated with a HH formulation.

4. *Example:* Figure 2.4 shows how the electrotonic interactions and the endogenous burst mechanisms interact to synchronize oscillations in a network. Figure 2.4a shows intracellular recordings from two coupled endogenously bursting neurons in STG. The measured strength of coupling is such as to produce a voltage attenuation factor of ca. 0.2. Figure 2.4b shows a SYNETSIM simulation of this situation, representing the two cells as single compartments (which limits the validity of the model) with input impedances of 5 Mohms each, coupling resistance 20 Mohms (giving an attenuation factor of 0.2), and active response parameters which produce endogenous bursting (Hartline, 1987). The burst parameters have been adjusted so that the PD neuron naturally bursts at a slower rate than the AB (for which there is physiological evidence), as shown in Figure 2.4c with the cells decoupled. The coupling is sufficient to cause synchronization in the model cells, and in fact, if bursting, these two cells are virtually never observed out of synchronization in physiological preparations.

2.4. Synaptic Interactions

Two types of chemically mediated synaptic interactions are represented by SYNETSIM, spike-mediated and chemotonic (nonspiking). These simulate the release of a chemical neurotransmitter from a presynaptic neuron, and its effect on the conductance of a postsynaptic neuron. Such changes in postsynaptic conductance lead to voltage changes in the postsynaptic cell (known as *postsynaptic potentials,* or PSPs), which in turn affect the output of the cell:

2.4.1. Spike-Mediated PSPs

The more general of two options for simulating synaptic potentials uses a tabulated time course of transmitter release which is summed with transmitter released by earlier spikes in the same presynaptic unit. Synaptic conductances, g_s are related to synaptic transmitter concentration, S(t), by a simple binding equation:

$$g_s = \bar{g}_s \, S(t)/(K_{ds} = S(t)) \tag{2}$$

where $\bar{g}_s$ is the maximum conductance at infinite transmitter concentration, and K_{ds} is the dissociation constant for transmitter binding. The simulation treats transmitter concentrations at the postsynaptic membrane as simply additive, which is acceptable if they are low compared with transmitter concentration in the synaptic vesicles, and if the geometry of the synaptic region does not change.

Following a spike in the presynaptic cell, a synaptic delay may be specified; then the tabulated release kinetics, scaled by an amplitude factor, is added into the array representing transmitter concentration. The amplitude factor is in turn the product of an intrinsic synaptic strength with a history-dependent facilitation factor. For each synapse, an arbitrary number of "facilitation pools" may be

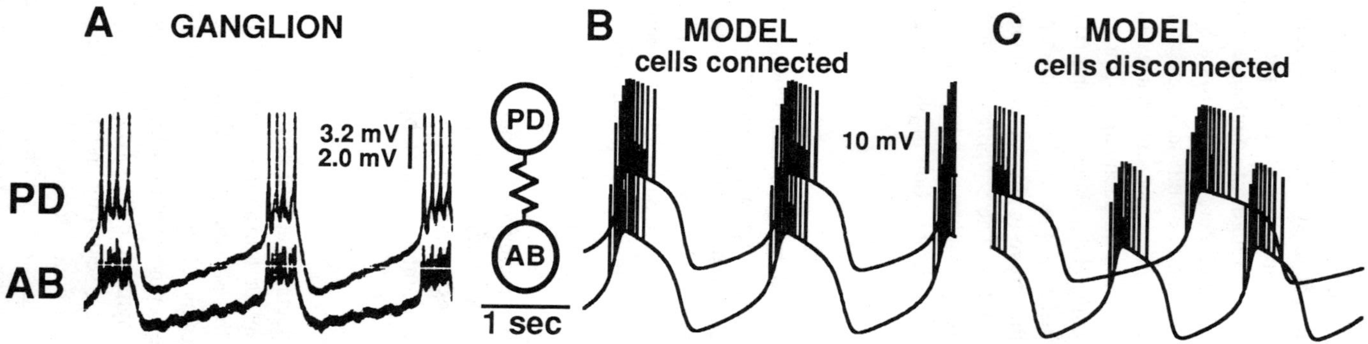

Figure 2.4. Electrotonic coupling between endogenously bursting neurons. a. Intracellular recording from two of the three electrically coupled network driver cells from the pyloric subsystem of STG. The other driver neuron is a PD (pyloric dilator) cell virtually indistinguishable from the one shown. The AB (anterior burster) is an interneuron with axon projecting to the CNS. Spontaneous activity in isolated ganglion [E76]. b,c. Simulations of PD-AB pair by SYNETSIM 3.2. In b, an electrotonic coupling conductance of 0.05 μmho suffices to synchronize oscillations. c shows that, without this coupling, the natural burst rates of the two cells differ substantially.

specified. The value of each pool parameter, X, raised to a specified power, relative to the resting level X = 1, represents the contribution of that pool to the facilitation factor that augments the basic PSP amplitude. The facilitation pools mimic the kinetic balance between an "active" and an "inactive" form of a regulating substance (e.g., internal Ca^{++}). This gives multiple exponential kinetics, which are sufficient to simulate the simpler types of facilitation and antifacilitation (Mallart & Martin, 1967; Zucker, 1985) but fail to suffice for certain complex examples (e.g., Friesen, 1975; Magleby & Zengel, 1982; Gingrich & Byrne, 1985; Parnas, Dudel, & Parnas, 1986).

As an option that avoids the necessity of tabulating synaptic release, a simple computed transmitter time course with an abrupt rise and exponential decay is also available.

2.4.2. Chemotonic Interactions

For the direct release of transmitter as a graded function of presynaptic depolarization, transmitter concentration (S) is represented as an exponential function of presynaptic voltage (V_{pre}):

$$S = S_o \exp(V_{pre}/\mu_c) \tag{3}$$

where S_o is the level of transmitter when presynaptic membrane potential = 0, and μ_c is the characteristic voltage for the exponential function. Conductances are calculated from equation 2. This conforms to studies by Graubard, Raper, and Hartline (1989). An example of the application of a related model is shown in Figure 2.5. This shows a simulation of an oscillating network of three cells coupled by chemotonic inhibitory interactions, as shown in the diagram in Figure 2.5c. Physiological recordings (obtained by Raper, 1979) from two of the cells are shown in Figure 2.5a. The network produces coordinated oscillations even in the absence of nerve impulses (which in this preparation have been blocked by tetrodotoxin) owing to the endogenous burst properties of the network driver cells (PD) and the plateau properties and chemotonic interactions in the rest of the network. The model (arranged as diagrammed in Figure 2.5d) shows a similar pattern of oscillation, in which, every time a presynaptic neuron depolarizes (see diagram at right), the neurons postsynaptic to it through chemotonic pathways hyperpolarize (Figure 2.5b).

3. SYNETSIM BIOCHEMICAL PROPERTIES

Like the electrical properties, the basis for simulation of biochemical properties is a set of compartments, termed *pools,* which are interconnected by first-order rate constants. Pools can be used to simulate either diffusion of substances

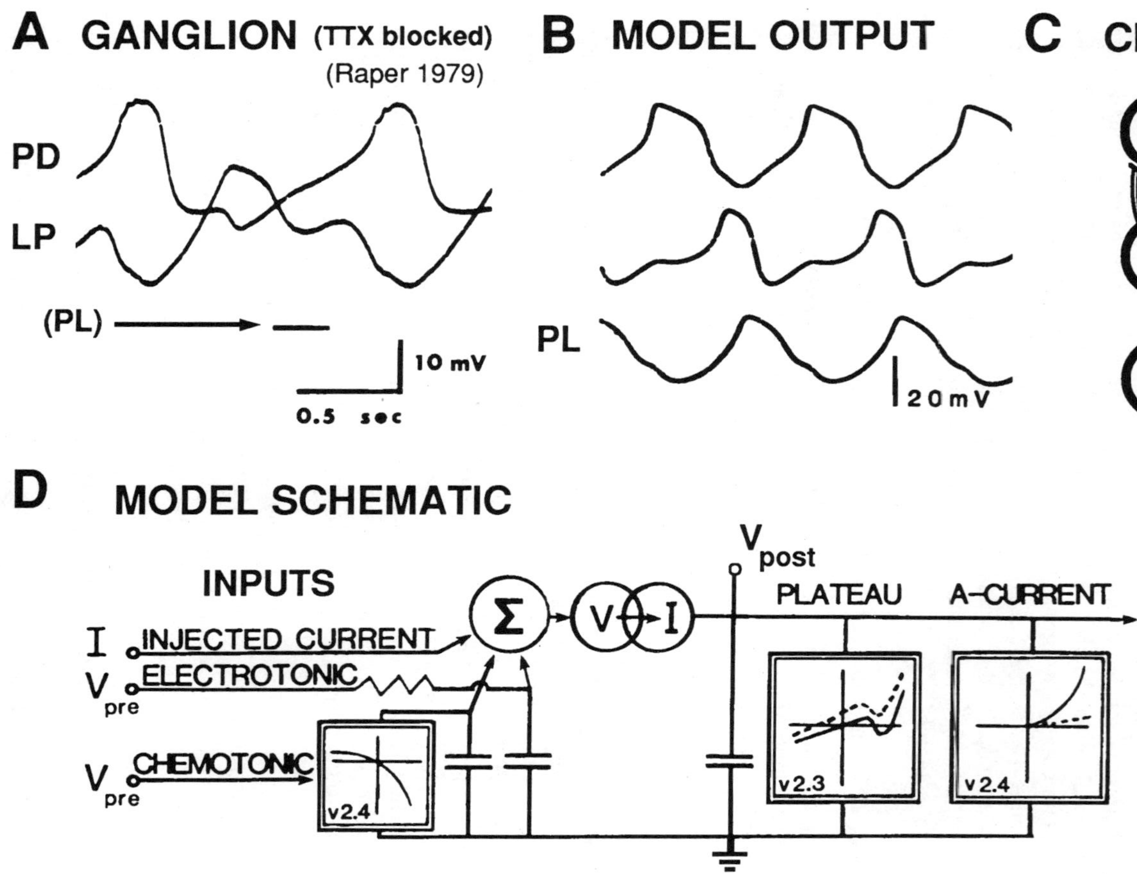
A GANGLION (TTX blocked)
(Raper 1979)
PD
LP
(PL)
10 mV
0.5 sec
B MODEL OUTPUT
PL
20 mV
C CIRCUIT
PD
LP
PL
D MODEL SCHEMATIC
INPUTS
I INJECTED CURRENT
V pre ELECTROTONIC
V pre CHEMOTONIC
v2.4
Σ
V I
V post
PLATEAU
A-CURRENT
v2.3
v2.4

between different regions of a cell or first-order reaction chains of the sort A↔B↔C.

3.1. Pool Types

Four pool types are differentiated according to the process being simulated (Figure 2.6; "c" in each equation is a scaling constant, in general different for each pool):

3.1.1. Type 1

Pool level (P) is proportional to the amount of bound transmitter at a specified synapse. The synapse must be one of the spike-mediated ones. The binding parameters may in general be different from those used by the electrical computations. This is consistent with suggestions that the receptors for the immediate synaptic conductance change may be different from those for the second-messenger-activated cascades (e.g., Russell & Hartline, 1981). This pool shows no kinetics, but it can be used to simulate relatively rapid processes, such as the cyclase activated by bound transmitter.

3.1.2. Type 2

The *filling* of the pool (i.e., dP/dt) is proportional to bound transmitter. This can be used to represent the production of second messenger by a transmitter-activated enzyme. The pool is emptied by first-order kinetics, which can represent the inactivation of second messenger by other biochemical processes, or its diffusion away from the compartment of origin. The rate-constant, k, for this and the remaining pool types, governs this decay.

3.1.3. Type 3

The filling rate of the pool is proportional to ionic current, with first-order decay. This type of pool can be used to represent entry to calcium ions through one of the electrical branches of the model, and its sequestration by first-order processes.

Figure 2.5. Coordination of network oscillations by chemotonic interactions (modified from Hartline, 1987). a. Intracellular recordings from PD and LP neurons with axonal spikes blocked by local application of tetrodotoxin (TTX) leaving plateau-inducing central input intact. Bar below LP trace, corresponding to dip in LP trajectory, indicates where depolarization of PL cell occurred (modified from Raper, 1979). b. Simulation of the situation in A with the circuit in C. c. Chemotonic "wiring diagram" of basic STG pyloric system. d. Diagram of model (SYNETSIM 2.4) used for simulation.

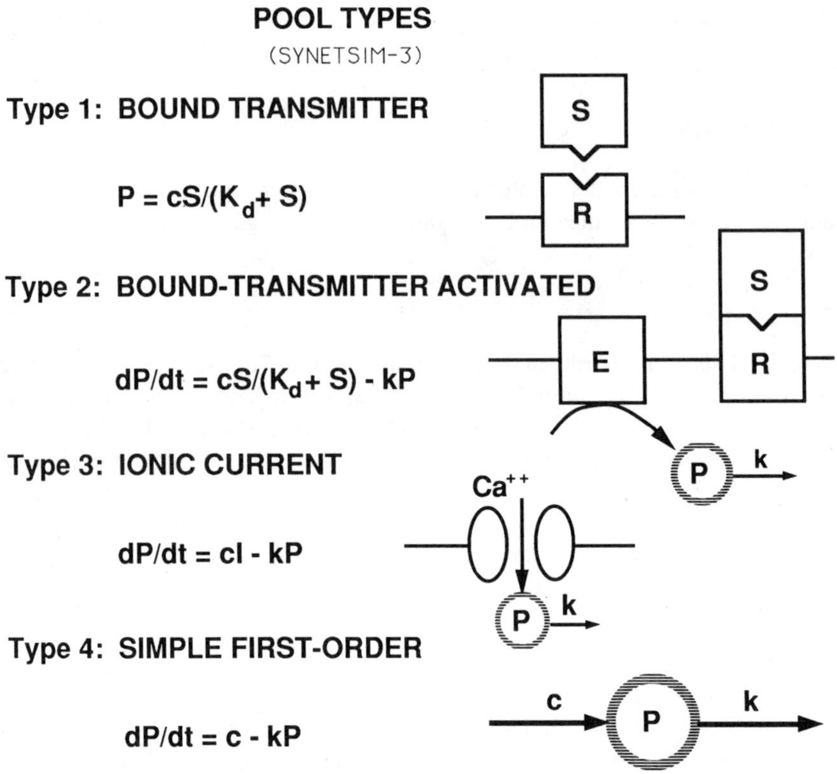

Figure 2.6. Diagrams of SYNETSIM pool types. Pools in figures are indicated by horizontally hatched circles.

3.1.4. Type 4

The filling rate of the pool is constant, with first-order decay. This can be used to simulate a substance which is synthesized and degraded, rates for which can then be modulated by other pools, e.g., enzymatic regulation of synthesis and degradation.

3.2. Pool Interactions

The full power of the pool representation is realized through *pool interactions*. In these, pool levels can be used to modulate (i.e., control) virtually every parameter in the model, including other pool parameters. This permits pool levels to completely reprogram the model, as well as allowing simulation of much more complex biochemical reactions than the simple first-order pool properties would by themselves allow. For example, any of the conductances, voltage-dependent or synaptic, can be made dependent on pool levels, allowing pools filled by transmitter binding (types 1 and 2) to simulate the modulation of voltage-dependent or transmitter-dependent conductances by synaptic or hormonal input. Alternatively, a type 3 pool can be used to simulate calcium-dependent conductances.

There are seven types of pool interactions (Figure 2.7).

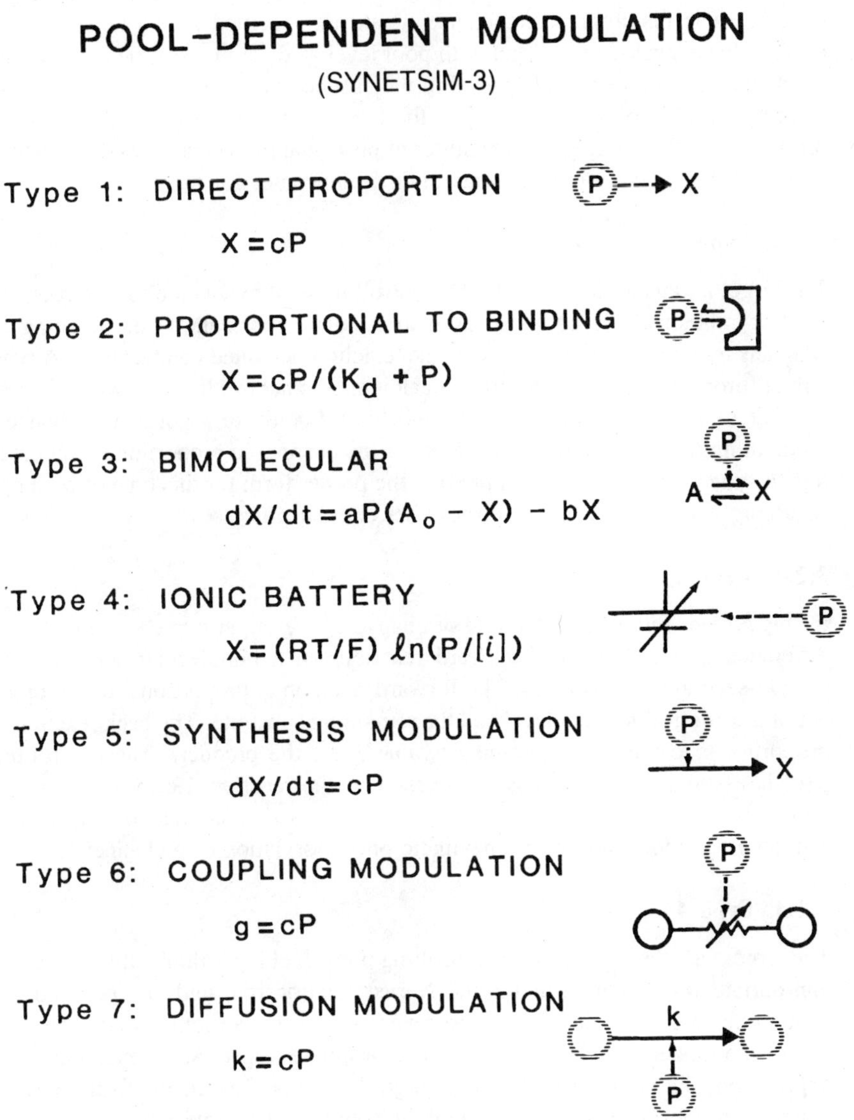

Figure 2.7. Diagrams of SYNETSIM pool interactions.

3.2.1. Type 1

The target parameter is directly proportional to the controlling-pool level. This is the simplest way of modulating a model parameter. Thus to place the maximum conductance of a voltage-dependent ion channel of a particular compartment under modulatory control of a synaptic input, one could use a type 1 controlling pool, the level of which is proportional to bound transmitter from an input synapse. The maximum conductance would be specified as the target for the pool. A base level for the target with pool level = 0 can be specified to give the conductance a nonzero resting level in the absence of modulatory input. A train of presynaptic impulses which raises the level of the type 1 controlling pool in proportion to the binding of transmitter at postsynaptic receptors would produce a proportional elevation of the maximum conductance for the channel.

3.2.2. Type 2

The target parameter is related to the controlling pool by an equilibrium receptor binding relation. This could be used to simulate for example the opening of channels by internal calcium ions, as in a calcium-activated conductance. A type 3 pool, proportional to current from a calcium channel mechanism, would represent internal Ca^{++}. This Ca^{++} would bind directly to a potassium channel, modulating the maximum conductance for the channel in proportion to the binding. A type 2 interaction would provide the proper form for this type of binding, assuming it is fast in comparison to other cellular processes.

3.2.3. Type 3

In this type of interaction, the rate of change of the target is proportional to the difference in forward and backward reactions in a bimolecular scheme with pseudo-second-order kinetics. The forward reaction is proportional to the product of the controlling pool level and the remaining substrate. The back reaction is proportional to the target parameter value (i.e., the product). The controlling pool is assumed not to change as a result of the reaction; i.e., the reactant it represents is present in great excess. This can be used to simulate the kinetics of saturable receptor binding, or enzymatic phosphorylation of a channel.

3.2.4. Type 4

The target value is related to the controlling pool level logarithmically. This is the appropriate functional form for the Nernst relationship, and can be used for simulating ionic batteries. Thus, the reversal level for an ionic conductance in one of the model branches would be an appropriate target. As an example of an application, the pool controlling this might be a type 3 pool, the filling rate of which is proportional to ionic current. It could be the same ionic current that flows through the target conductance. This will simulate the trapping of the ions flowing through the conductance by a diffusionally restricted space, such as the Frankenhaeuser-Hodgkin (1956) space of squid axon.

3.2.5. Type 5

The rate of change of the target is proportional to the controlling pool value. The controlling pool in this case acts like an enzyme level, catalyzing the first-order conversion of a substrate present in infinite supply. This can be used to simulate the enzymatically limited synthesis of a compound from a large substrate pool.

Figure 2.8 shows an example of an application. In Figure 2.8a, an experiment is shown (again in STG) in which an inactive (noninduced) PD neuron is activated by electrical stimulation of the main input nerve from the CNS. In addition to conventional synaptic potentials which drive the cell during stimulation, there is a prolonged period of endogenous bursting that follows the stimulation period. As with the LP neuron shown in Figure 2.1, the induction of endogenous bursting (due to induction of plateau properties and possibly other cellular properties: Russell & Hartline, 1978) is thought to be due to an increase in relative dominance of voltage-dependent inward over outward current mechanisms through release of modulatory transmitter. In the simulation below, the transmitter is represented by a type 1 pool (level proportional to transmitter binding) which exerts a type 5 interaction on pool 2, representing a second messenger. Thus the synthesis rate of this pool is proportional to transmitter binding at the synapse. Pool 2 in turn exerts a type 1 interaction on the maximum conductance for the voltage-dependent inward current of a plateau mechanism, making the maximum conductance directly proportional to second messenger (pool 2) level. Pool 2 decays with long time-constant, simulating a slowly decaying second messenger level. Stimulation of the synaptic input, in addition to driving spikes 1:1 (via a conventional excitatory synapse), leaves the plateau mechanism in an induced high state, leading (through interaction with restoring conductances also programmed into the cell) to a prolonged train of endogenously produced bursts.

3.2.6. Type 6

The coupling conductance is the target of modulation, being proportional to the controlling pool. This can be used to simulate the modulation of electrotonic coupling in a network of interconnected cells by transmitters or second messengers.

3.2.7. Type 7

The diffusion rate constant between two pools is the target of modulation, being proportional to the controlling pool. This can be used to simulate the effect of changing enzyme concentrations on the rates of first-order reactions.

This type of interaction can be used for a more realistic simulation of the same

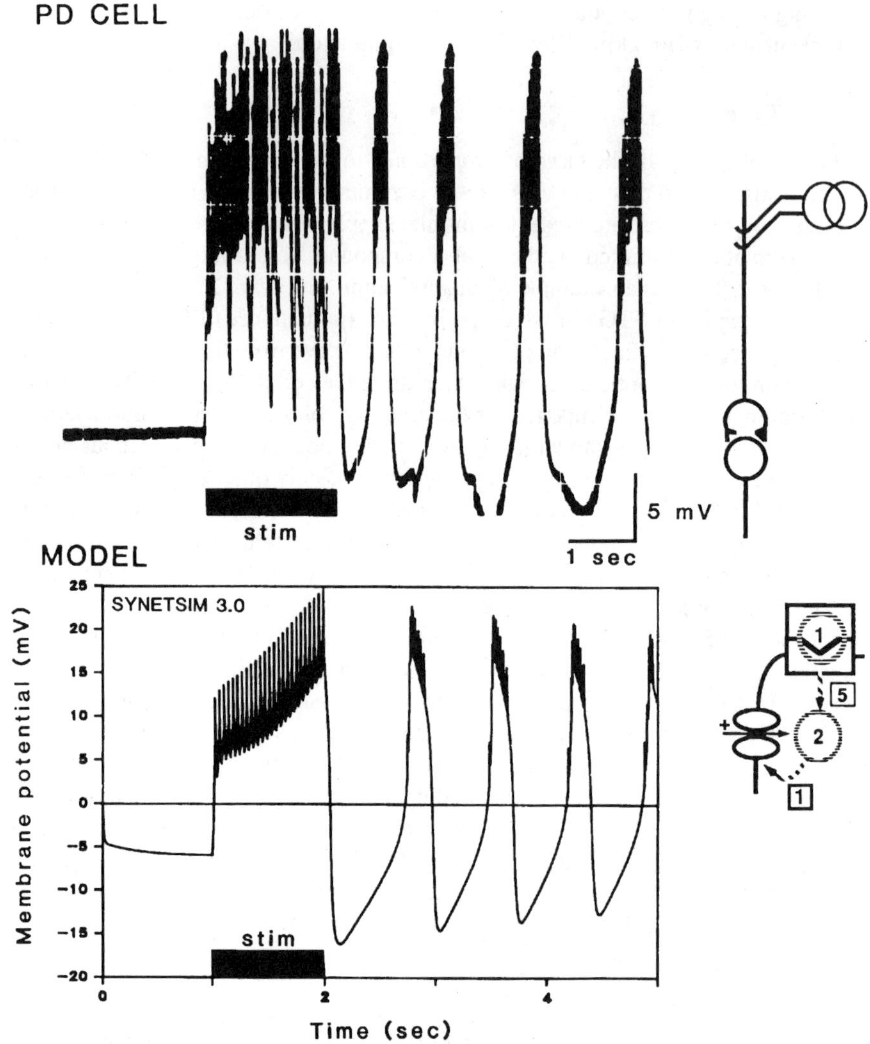

Figure 2.8. Induction of endogenous bursting by a Type 5 pool interaction. a. Intracellular recording from PD cell in isolated ganglion from *P. marginatus*. Input nerve (Stn) stimulated at 10 Hz for 2 sec [L1]. b. Simulation of a similar experiment. Inducing input places both conventional synapse and modulatory one on target cell.

type of burst-induction process illustrated just previously. The schema is shown in Figure 2.9. The cell has a constant number of channels of a voltage-dependent inward current mechanism (not in the diagram), but is kept from showing bursting properties by a voltage-dependent outward current mechanism (here figured as potassium) having the same voltage-dependence as the inward current. The

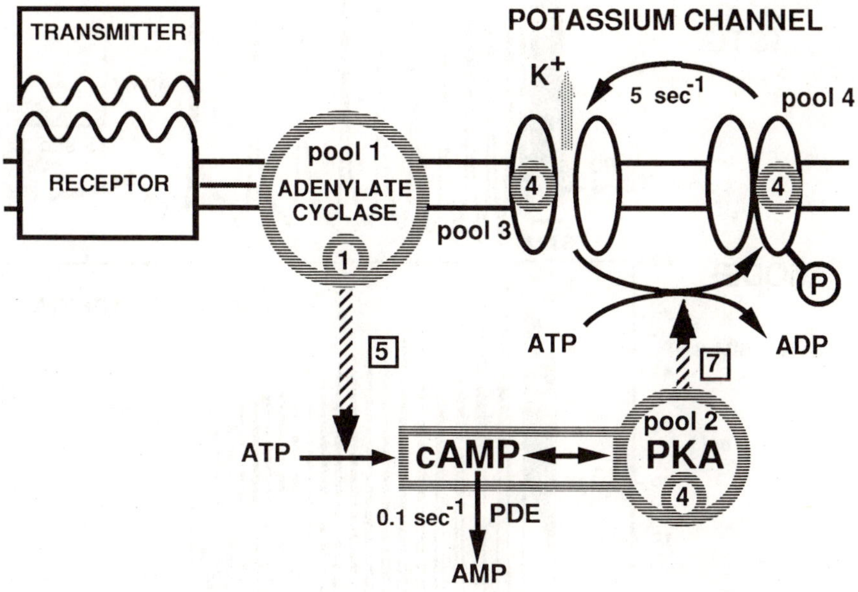

Figure 2.9. Diagram of second-messenger-mediated K-channel closing.

potassium channel has two forms, represented by two type 4 pools with zero synthesis and zero decay (i.e., conservation of total channel number). The "active" channel type is represented as a nonphosphorylated form (represented by pool 3 acting *via* a type 1 interaction on the maximum conductance parameter for voltage-dependent potassium) which is capable of opening when the membrane depolarizes. The "inactive" or blocked channel type is represented as the phosphorylated form (pool 4) and cannot open. The two forms are interconvertible through the first order "diffusion" kinetics of the pools. At rest, the rate constant for conversion from active to inactive form (pool 3 to 4) is zero, while that from inactive to active is a fixed positive number. Thus, all channels are initially in an active form and will conduct current if the membrane is depolarized, hence counteracting any tendency of the inward current mechanism to depolarize the membrane. Binding of transmitter, represented by a type 1 pool (pool 1), causes synthesis of a second messenger (pool 2; cAMP as represented here) and a protein kinase (PKA) by a type 5 interaction, representing an enzyme-mediated (adenylate-cyclase) conversion similar to the example of Figure 2.8. The simulation would be more realistic if the production of cAMP and its reaction with PKA to form an activated protein-kinase were simulated as separate steps, but the assumption is made here that this step is rapid compared with other events. Pool 2 (PKA) in turn catalyzes the phosphorylation of the potassium channel (conversion of pool 3 into pool 4) by modulating the rate constant for interpool "diffusion" (= first-order conversion) by a type 7 interaction.

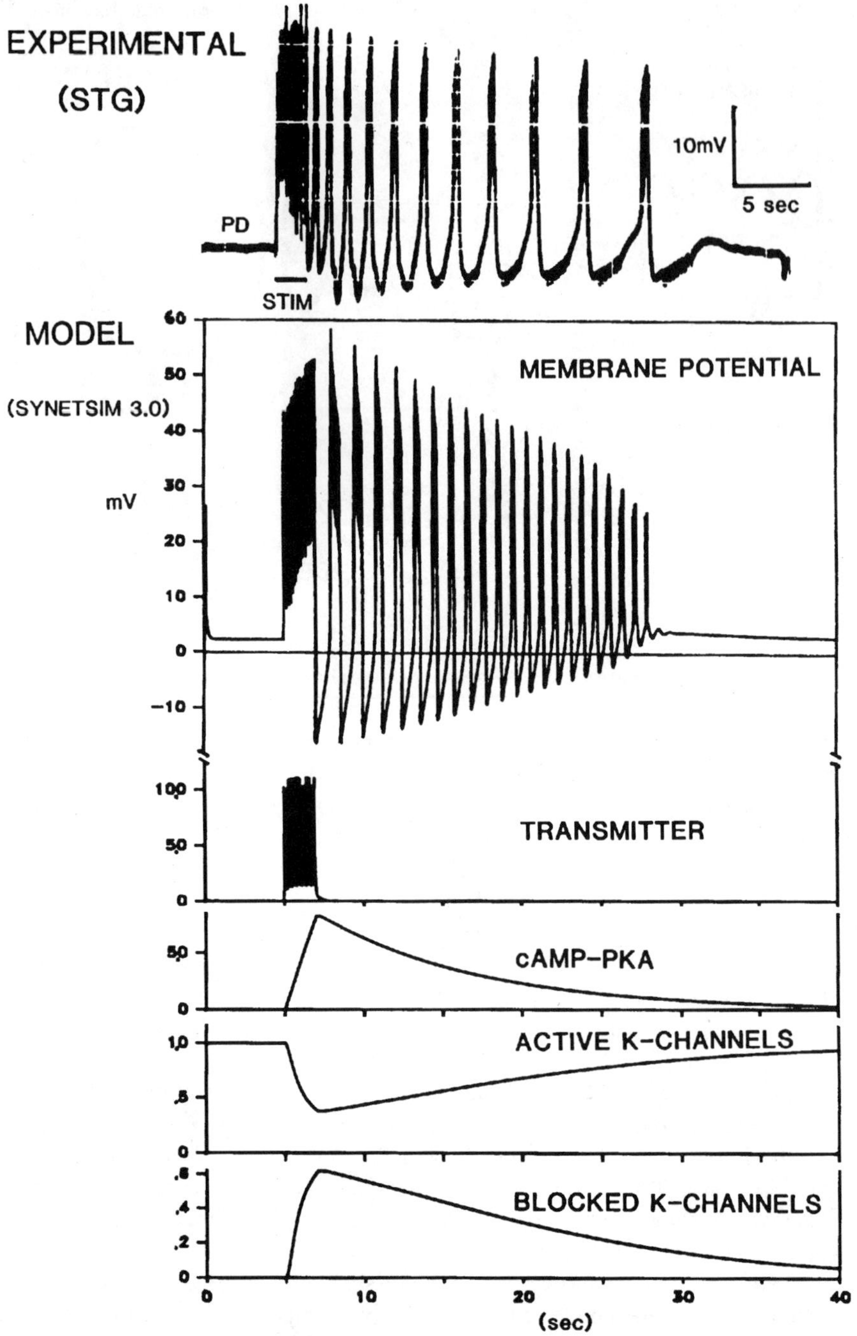

Figure 2.10. Induction of endogenous bursting by K-channel closing. a. Intracellular recording from PD cell in isolated ganglion of *P. marginatus*, with input stimulation (Stn) of 10 Hz for 2 sec [L1]. b. Similar experiment using the model diagrammed in Figure 9.

The results of a simulation similar to that of Figure 2.8, but using this more refined model for burst induction, is shown in Figure 2.10. At top is an experimental run, at slow sweep, showing the burst activation by a brief period of input nerve stimulation (bar labeled "STIM"). Bursting is intense just following the stimulation, and weakens with time over the next several tens of seconds. Note that the peak-to-trough amplitude of the bursts (which, however, includes spikes and an inter-burst barrage of IPSPs from another cell) decreases progressively as the bursting weakens. In addition, the interval between bursts lengthens significantly, typical effects seen in real oscillatory neural networks. The simulation below exhibits similar induction of bursting behavior, followed by weakening of the burst and a (rather larger) decrease in peak-to-trough oscillation amplitude. Note, however, that the burst rate does not progressively slow. This is a significant discrepancy from the physiology. The graphs below show first transmitter (pool 1) level, which oscillates over a sizable range due to its decay between presynaptic impulses. It decays rapidly after the cessation of stimulation. The level of conversion enzyme (pool 2: cAMP-PKA) rises steadily during the stimulation and then decays exponentially (owing to a drain rate constant of 0.1 sec^{-1}). Under the influence of the rising conversion enzyme levels, active K-channels (pool 3) are converted into blocked K-channels (pool 4) during stimulation. Because the dephosphorylation of K-channels is assumed to be rapid in this example, the peak in blocked K-channels occurs immediately after stimulus cessation, and active channels are regenerated as cAMP-PKA decays. Endogenous bursting generated by the blockage of K-channels continues until around 80% of the channels are restored to an active (dephosphorylated) state.

4. CONCLUSIONS

The SYNETSIM model does a fair (though not perfect) job of simulating much of what is presently known about cellular reprogramming brought about by second messenger biochemistry. Certain improvements, in particular, the ability to accommodate second and higher-order chemical reactions, would increase its physiological accuracy. However at present, so little is known about appropriate parameters for many of these systems in individual neurons that valid values would be hard to come by. The model represents a first attempt to deal with the complexities of what will undoubtedly become an even more complex biochemical picture of profound importance to the understanding of computational properties of neural networks.

SYNETSIM-3 is written in Microsoft BASIC for IBM-PC compatible computers. A copy of the current version with documentation is available from the author.

REFERENCES

Byrne, J. H. (1980). Quantitative aspects of ionic conductance mechanisms contributing to firing pattern of motor cells mediating inking behavior in *Aplysia californica*. *Journal of Neurophysiology, 43,* 651–668.

Connor, J. A., & Stevens, C. F. (1971). Prediction of repetitive firing behaviour from voltage clamp data on an isolated neurone soma. *Journal of Physiology* (*London*), *213,* 31–53.

Farley, B. G., & Clark, W. A. (1961). Activity in networks of neuron-like elements. In C. Cherry (Ed.), *Information theory* (pp. 242–251). New York: Academic Press.

Fohlmeister, J. F., Poppele, R. E., & Purple, R. L. (1974). Repetitive firing: Dynamic behavior of sensory neurons reconciled with a quantitative model. *Journal of Neurophysiology, 37,* 1213–1227.

Friesen, W. O. (1975). Antifacilitation and facilitation in the cardiac ganglion of the spiny lobster *Panulirus interruptus*. *Journal of Comparative Physiology, 101,* 207–224.

Frankenheuser, B., & Hodgkin, A. L. (1956). The after-effects of impulses in the giant nerve fibres of *Loligo*. *Journal of Physiology* (*London*), *131,* 341–375.

Furshpan, E. J., & Potter, D. D. (1959). Transmission at the giant motor synapses of the crayfish. *Journal of Physiology* (*London*), *145,* 289–325.

Gingrich, K. J., & Byrne, J. H. (1985). Simulation of synaptic depression, posttetanic potentiation, and presynaptic facilitation of synaptic potentials from sensory neurons mediating gill-withdrawal reflex in *Aplysia*. *Journal of Neurophysiology, 53,* 652–669.

Graubard, K., & Hartline, D. K. (1987). Full-wave rectification from a mixed electrical-chemical synapse. *Science, 237,* 535–537.

Graubard, K., Raper, J. A., & Hartline, D. K. (1989). Quantitative analysis of non-spiking synaptic transmission between spiking stomatogastric neurons. *Society for Neuroscience Abstracts, 15,* 1047.

Harth, E., Lewis, N. S., & Csermley, T. J. (1975). The escape of *Tritonia*. Dynamics of a neuromuscular control mechanism. *The Journal of Theoretical Biology, 55,* 201–208.

Hartline, D. K. (1976a). Simulation of phase-dependent pattern changes to perturbations of regular firing in crayfish stretch receptor. *Brain Research, 110,* 245–257.

Hartline, D. K. (1976b). SNAX: a language for interactive neuronal modeling and data processing. In P. B. Brown (Ed.), *Computer technology in neuroscience* (pp. 41–65). Washington, DC: Hemisphere Press.

Hartline, D. K. (1979). Pattern generation in the lobster (*Panulirus*) stomatogastric ganglion. II. Pyloric network simulation. *Biological Cybernetics, 33,* 223–236.

Hartline, D. K. (1987). Modeling stomatogastric ganglion. In A. I. Selverston & M. Moulins (Eds.), *The crustacean stomatogastric system* (pp. 181–197). Berlin: Springer-Verlag.

Hartline, D. K. (1989). Simulation of restricted neural networks with reprogrammable neurons. *IEEE Transactions on Circuits and Systems, 36,* 653–660.

Hartline, D. K., Russell, D. F., Raper, J. A., & Graubard, K. (1988). Special cellular and synaptic mechanisms in motor pattern generation. *Comparative Biochemistry and Physiology, 91C,* 115–131.

Hodgkin, A. L., & Huxley, A. F. (1952). A quantitative description of membrane current and its application to conduction and excitation in nerve. *Journal of Physiology, 117,* 500–544.

Hodgkin, A. L., & Katz, B. (1949). The effect of sodium ions on the electrical activity of the giant axon of the squid. *Journal of Physiology, 108,* 37–77.

Hopfield, J. J. (1982). Neural networks and physical systems with emergent collective computational abilities. *Proceedings of the National Academy of Sciences, USA, 79,* 2554–2558.

Kaczmarek, L. K., & Levitan, I. B. (1987a). *Neuromodulation.* Oxford, England: Oxford University Press.

Kaczmarek, L. K., & Levitan, I. B. (1987b). What is neuromodulation? In L. K. Kaczmarek & I. B. Levitan (Eds.), *Neuromodulation* (pp. 3–17). Oxford, England: Oxford University Press.

Knight, B. W. (1972). Dynamics of encoding in a population of neurons. *The Journal of General Physiology, 59,* 734–766.

Kramer, R., & Zucker, R. (1985). Calcium-dependent inward current in *Aplysia* bursting pace-maker neurones. *Journal of Physiology (London), 362,* 107–130.

Lange, G. D., Hartline, H. K., & Ratliff, F. (1966). The dynamics of lateral inhibition in the compound eye of *Limulus.* II. In C. G. Bernhard (Ed.), *The functional organization of the compound eye* (pp. 425–449). London: Pergamon.

Little, W. A. (1974). The existence of persistent states in the brain. *Mathematical Biosciences, 19,* 101–120.

Magleby, K. L., & Zengel, J. E. (1982). A quantitative description of stimulation-induced changes in transmitter release at the frog neuromuscular junction. *The Journal of General Physiology, 80,* 613–638.

Mallart, A., & Martin, A. R. (1967). An analysis of facilitation of transmitter release at the neuromuscular junction of the frog. *The Journal of Physiology, 193,* 679–694.

McCullogh, W. S., & Pitts, W. (1943). A logical calculus of ideas imminent in nervous activity. *Bulletin of Mathematical Biophysics, 5,* 115–133.

Miller, R. J. (1985). Second messengers, phosphorylation and neurotransmitter release. *Trends in Neuroscience, 8,* 463–465.

Parnas, H., Dudel, J., & Parnas, I. (1986). Neurotransmitter release and its facilitation in crayfish: VII. Another voltage dependent process beside Ca entry controls the time course in phasic release. *Pflügers Archiv, 406,* 121–130.

Partridge, L. D., & Stevens, C. D. (1976). A mechanism for spike frequency adaptation. *Journal of Physiology, 256,* 315–332.

Perkel, D. H. (1964). *A digital-computer model of nerve-cell functioning* (Memorandum RM-4132-NIH). Santa Monica, CA: Rand Corp.

Perkel, D. H. (1976). A computer program for simulating a network of interacting neurons. I. Organization and physiological assumptions. *Computers in Biomedical Research, 9,* 31–44.

Perkel, D. H., Schulman, J., Bullock, T. H., Moore, G., & Segundo, J. (1964). Pacemaker neurons: effects of regularly spaced synaptic input. *Science, 145,* 61–63.

Rall, W. (1964). Theoretical significance of dendritic trees for neuronal input-output relations. In R. F. Reiss (Ed.), *Neural theory and modeling* (pp. 73–97). Palo Alto, CA: Stanford University Press.

Raper, J. A. (1979). *Non-impulse mediated synaptic transmission in the stomatogastric ganglion of the spiny lobster*. Unpublished doctoral dissertation, University of California, San Diego (Neuroscience).

Reuter, H. (1979). Properties of two inward membrane currents in the heart. *Annual Review of Physiology, 41,* 413–424.

Russell, D. F., & Hartline, D. K. (1978). Bursting neural networks: a reexamination. *Science, 200,* 453–456.

Russell, D. F., & Hartline, D. K. (1981). A multiaction synapse evoking both EPSPs and enhancement of endogenous bursting. *Brain Research, 223,* 19–38.

Siegelbaum, S. A. (1987). The S-current: a background potassium current. In L. K. Kaczmarek & I. B. Levitan (Eds.), *Neuromodulation* (pp. 187–205). Oxford, England: Oxford University Press.

Smith, S. J. (1978). *The mechanisms of bursting pacemaker activity in neurons of the mollusc* Tritonia diomedia. Unpublished doctoral dissertation, University of Washington, Seattle.

Strumwasser, F. (1968). Membrane and intracellular mechanisms governing endogenous activity in neurons. In F. D. Carlson (Ed.), *Physiological and biochemical aspects of nervous integration* (pp. 329–341). Englewood Cliffs, NJ: Prentice-Hall.

Tazaki, K., & Cooke, I. (1979). Isolation and characterization of slow, depolarizing responses of cardiac ganglion neurons in the crab, *Portunus sanguinolentus. Journal of Neurophysiology, 42,* 1000–1021.

Thompson, S. H. (1976). *Membrane currents underlying bursting in molluscan pacemaker neurons.* Unpublished doctoral dissertation, University of Washington, Seattle.

Zucker, R. S. (1985). Synaptic facilitation and residual calcium. In A. I. Selverston (Ed.), *Model neural networks and behavior* (pp. 461–475). New York: Plenum.

3

Synergistic Interactions Among Distinct Populations of Neurons

James L. Eilbert
Grumman CRC
Bethpage, NY

Allon Guez
Drexel University
Philadelphia, PA

1. INTRODUCTION

Animals perform amazingly well on perceptual and common-sense reasoning tasks. Even simple animals surpass the capabilities of the best machine intelligence systems. The attempts to duplicate animal performance with NN models of whole nervous systems have at best been partially successful (Selverston, 1985). This is almost certainly because, in making the structural simplifications necessary for mathematical tractability, modelers have thrown away critical information. At this point, it is not clear whether the important information is contained in the current neuroanatomical, electrophysiological, and autoradiography data, or whether it is still missing from our databases. Examples of known information that have been ignored in NN models are processing levels below the single neuron level, and differences in the connection patterns among neurons.

To choose idealizations that capture the real information-processing capabilities of the brain, the characteristics of the model must be constrained by secondary sources of information. For biologically based NNs, this is best done by testing the model against sets of psychological data that characterize the role of the original system. Lynch (Lynch, 1985; Lynch, Granger, Larson, & Baudry, 1988) developed a surprisingly successful model based on the neuroanatomy of the olfactory cortex. Their model exhibited unexpected temporal processing capabilities which agreed with the behavior of the neural system on which the model was based.

Grossberg (1987) has made idealizations of neuroanatomical data based on the biological solutions to dilemmas (i.e., situations where a cognitive system is faced with competing objectives). A NN that does pattern recognition must suppress noise yet not saturate in response to strong signals, i.e., solve the noise vs. saturation dilemma. It must also retain sensitivity to small changes in input while responding over a large range of input strengths, i.e., solve the sensitivity vs. dynamic range dilemma. Grossberg's solution to these dilemma's was to modify the response function, f, of the individual 'simulated neurons' (throughout the chapter *neurons* refer to biological neurons, while *Sneurons* refer to the units in a simulation) in a basic recurrent NN model

$$\frac{dx_j}{dt} = -A_j x_j + f(\sum_k w_{jk} x_k) + E_j$$

Neurons in the brain may be classified into three main populations, based on differences in the spatial distribution of their axon terminations and the nonlinear characteristics of their input-output transformations. Neural Network (NN) models with multiple populations potentially have greater storage and processing capabilities than single population NNs of comparable size. These improvements result when the effects of one population on a second one creates modules of the optimal size for storing particular types of information or changes the steady state topology of the second population. Multiple neural populations are only advantageous if their interactions are stable. In the models we examine, the stability of the individual populations is sufficient to insure the global stability to the entire network. In general, global stability is not satisfied by pairs of neural populations. The patterns of activity supported by the individual populations, and by combinations of the populations are also studied in this chapter.

Several results concerning population interaction are presented:

1. It is shown that these three populations generate a hierarchy of functional units: single neurons, columns, and broadcast nodes.
2. The steady states of slowly evolving populations subdivide the faster populations into distinct functional modules that encompass both processing and learning. This modularization can serve as a model of selective attention.
3. Structured representations are needed to direct selective attention. It is argued that the natural form of structured representation for the HNN has the characteristics associated with cognitive maps. Complex representation in a NN is an intriguing idea, since the lack of this capability has prevented NN research from interfacing with the best ideas developed in Artificial Intelligence.

The model to be discussed in this chapter is a many-population model called the *hierarchical neural network* (HNN) (Eilbert, 1988, 1980). The overall goal of the HNN project is to produce a NN capable of controlling an autonomous system in a natural environment. To accomplish this goal, the HNN is modular with respect to tasks, and hierarchical within the modules. This type of design allows one to extract components of the model for neurocomputing applications.

The first three sections of this chapter give a design specification for an autonomous NN. We begin with a list of roles that current NNs can perform. Next, there is a discussion of several attentional or modularizing roles that we would like the HNN architecture to be able to perform. The discussion then moves to the type of psychological data that the model tries to explain, i.e., work on attention, cognitive maps, and mental models. The next two sections present a mathematical description of the HNN architecture. The discussion concentrates on the mathematical properties of the model that allow it to do modularization. Finally, we point out that the properties of the HNN make it a reasonable candidate for a cognitive map model (Kaplan & Kaplan, 1982).

2. NN ROLES

2.1. Categorization

Categorization can be done in a number of ways, as discussed in the next two sections. The simplest technique is to define a set of critical sensory features for each category and a range of values for each feature. A member of a multiple range category is then any object with the acceptable values in each dimension. A second method of categorizing involves dividing feature space into a set of decision regions corresponding to the various categories. Any input falling in the decision region is labeled a member of the category. Alternatively, it is possible to replace the label with an action. This implies that every behavior can be defined by linking a decision surface in feature space to an action. Thus, categorization is important for autonomous systems, since it is a prerequisite for sensory-guided behavior (Edelman, 1987). Feedforward NNs, such as perceptrons (Rosenblatt, 1961), least mean square (LMS) (Stearns & Widrow, 1985), back-propagation (Rumelhart, Hinton, & Williams, 1986), and Nestor (1987) are all examples of the decision region approach to categorization.

2.2. Associative Retrieval and Optimization

Associative retrieval is essentially recalling a prototype vector in feature space, when the system is presented with a vector that is sufficiently similar to the prototype. In most NN architectures that perform associative retrieval, a prototype is a steady state of a recurrent NN, and *sufficiently similar* means that a vector falls in the basin of attraction of the prototype. Although any steady state can be thought of as a prototype, the operation that is performed during the approach to the steady state depends on how the connections between simulated neurons (Sneurons) are selected. Typical operations include associative recall (Anderson, 1983), filling-in (Grossberg & Mingolla, 1985), short-term storage of activity patterns (Grossberg, 1987), optimization (Hopfield & Tank, 1985), or fuzzy cognitive mapping (Kosko, 1986). For optimization, filling-in, and fuzzy cognitive map, the selection of connection strengths is based on the characteristics or the constraints of the problem to be solved by the NN (Hopfield & Tank, 1985). For the associative retrieval and short term storage, connections strengths are selected in order to position stable states of the network. Clearly, the ability to do associative retrieval and filling-in are required by any system that must interpret noisy or partial information from the environment.

Associative retrieval can also be considered a third method of categorization. A member of a prototype category is then an instance which falls within the basin of attraction of the prototype. Note that, when an input is categorized in this way, the form of the prototype is retrieved as well as its label. Note also that the accuracy of the categorization made depends on the similarity metric selected or learned.

Another version of associative retrieval, which can be considered a fourth method of categorization, involves storing a set of examplars for each category. An instance is a member of an examplar category, if there is an examplar whose metric distance from the instance is less than its threshold associated with that examplar. Biological evidence supports categorization by examplars (Smith & Medin, 1981), or perhaps by prototypes (Knapp & Anderson, 1984), rather than by decision surfaces.

2.3. Spatial Transformations

A third NN role is performing global transformations of activity. These transforms are the result of a spatial pattern of activity moving from one layer to another. For example, Schwartz (1980) pointed out that the electrophysiological data from the LGN and Area 17 were consistent with a log polar transform. Pribram, Nuwer, and Baron (1974) have examined the effects of local Fourier transforms that also appear in the electrophysiological data. Such transformations may play an important role in the creation of invariant features (Linsker, 1988).

2.4. Learning

A fourth NN role among current systems is learning or adaptation. Learning involves permanent, local weight changes. All NN learning algorithms are incremental, as opposed to most machine learning algorithms, which are not. They make weight changes, ∂w_{ij}, proportional to the product of the input, x_i, and the difference between the real, y_j, and the desired, t_j, or expected output.

$$\partial w_{ij} \propto x_i * (t_j - y_j)$$

To compute weight changes, the system needs real stimulus–response pairs, plus expected stimulus–response pairs. In addition, as Grossberg (1978) points out, autonomous systems need a signal indicating that it is time to learn.

Learning algorithms treat training data in different ways. ART (Carpenter & Grossberg, 1986) treats every new input as a new prototype. Nestor (1987) treats new input as either a new examplar of a known category or a counterexample that reduces category size. ASE networks (Barto & Sutton, 1981) use inputs to generate responses that affect the environment in ways that can increase or decrease drive satisfaction. Finally, inputs act as drivers for gradient descent in Adaline (Widrow & Stearns, 1985), perception (Rosenblatt, 1961), backpropagation (Rumelhart, Hinton, & Williams, 1986), or Brain-State-in-a-Box (Anderson, 1983) systems.

The performance criteria for a learning algorithm include convergence, finding the right decision surface or basin of attraction, the number of Sneurons required to learn a given concept, and the time to converge (both in terms of computation and number of training trials). Grossberg's learning algorithms for feedback networks converge quickly in terms of trails, but they cannot guarantee convergence nor control the shape of the basin of attraction around a prototype (although see Bell & Eilbert, 1988). However, if there are only a few examplars in each category, the arbitrary boundaries produced are generally acceptable. Feedforward algorithms need many trials but can guarantee convergence to correct decision surfaces in some cases (e.g., linearly separable surfaces). Restricted Coulomb energy (Nestor, 1987) networks converge to the right decision surface up to a given resolution on all cases, but they must expand their number of nodes and may require a tremendous number of training trials to do it. In summary, the choice of learning algorithm currently depends on which performance criteria you consider most important.

Learning will always be an important aspect of autonomous behavior, because the ongoing generation of novel objects and situations in a natural environment makes it impossible to store complete information in advance. However, the number of types of learning required, and how to initialize learning systems, must still be determined. We believe that three distinct types of learning seen in mammals are in fact required for an autonomous mobile system. These include plasticity, skill acquisition, and learning using models or cognitive maps.

Plasticity fine-tunes the genetically specified set of sensation and action primitives available to the system. It is primarily a mirror of experience (Hirsch & Spinelli, 1971; Spinelli, 1979). Cats are born with cortical neurons sensitive to orientation, motion, spatial frequency, etc. (Hubel & Wiesel, 1977). However, these features are untuned or very broadly tuned, and must be tuned through interactions with the environment.

Skill acquisition refers to the transformation that changes a sequence of behavior primitives that are frequently used together, then, into a single automatic behavior. This can be modelled by dropping the unnecessary initial sensations of the intermediate behavior primitives. At the same time redundant features are dropped from the set of sensations that trigger the behaviors (Neves & Anderson, 1981; Greeno, 1983).

The skill learning is required to reduce the processing of sensory input associated with selecting behaviors. The longer the sequence of actions a system can perform in response to single sensation, the smaller the information-processing load (DeJong, 1986). However, the length of the sequence must be compatible with the predictability of the environment, or the system may take action based on conditions that no longer exist. Extended practice is needed to guarantee that environmental variation is really small over the behavior (Shiffern & Dumais, 1981; Newell & Rosenbloom, 1981).

Modification of internal models allows complex context information to be brought to bear on decision making problems. In higher animals, this type of learning seems to be supported by a special behavior mode called *exploration*. Exploration can be used to learn sensory features, action sequences, or plans. In each case, animals explore using a different set of stereotyped actions. In the case of sensory features, a larger set of features is examined in the exploratory mode than in the search mode. There is also a broader field of view, and longer dwell times between eye movements, during exploration (O'Keefe & Nadel, 1978). The exploratory sequence allows the animal to limit its attention to the subset of features whose combination distinguishes the object. In the case of motor commands, one tests a simple set of movements that isolate different muscle groups or the effects of external forces. An example of exploration tailored to learn an action sequence is hefting a tool before you use it. Exploration, in the case of plans, involves generating 'what if' scenarios. In each type of exploration, more features are examined for a longer time, and the attention channels are larger and less numerous than in other behavior modes (Eilbert & Guez, 1987).

Most of the learning algorithms proposed in the neural network literature would fall into the conditioning category, where information and rewards from the environment replace the internal model. These include the Hebb (1949) rule; the perceptron learning algorithm (Rosenblatt, 1961); Barto and Sutton's (1981) associative search elements, which use goal information to direct an unsupervised learning algorithm; and the higher order networks of Maxwell, Giles, Lee, and Chen (1986). In each case, there is a stimulus pool and a response pool; and the learning algorithm attempts to find the 'best' sensation–action primitive pairings for a particular task.

The NN approach to learning internal models starts with the assumption that there are certain sensation primitives (that may be tuned somewhat by plasticity), action primitives, exploratory behaviors, reflexes, and drives. The representation that is used to classify a sensation is based on features which are complex combinations of the sensation primitives. These features are learned during goal-driven exploration of the environment. On the other hand, most AI approaches start their analysis by assuming the system can detect a specialized set of features, based on the designer's knowledge of the inputs and the goals of the system.

3. THE NEED FOR ATTENTIONAL MECHANISMS

In addition to the roles for NNs listed in the previous section, biological NNs control sensory processing and learning with a variety of attentional mechanisms. These mechanisms include:

Low level: 1—arousal
2—orienting
High level: 3—the allocation of selective attention to sets of features, actions, internal models, or exploratory routines (Eilbert, 1988)
4—behavior mode switching.

This section discusses why these mechanisms are needed by autonomous systems with limited storage capacity.

3.1. The Need for Behavior Modes

Beginning with the premise that learning plays a central role in cognitive behavior, the following argument shows the need for distinct behavior models, i.e., groups of sensation/action pairs appropriate to a single task or goal. Finite resources imply that not all sensory input can be recorded. Therefore, the system must make a decision about whether or not to record any particular sensation/action pair. This forces the system to have at least two distinct modes of behavior, an exploratory mode and a search mode, one notable exception being animals with amnesiac syndrome, which do not exhibit exploratory behavior (O'Keefe & Nadel, 1978).

The finite storage available poses two additional pairs of competing objectives or dilemmas. The plasticity vs. stability dilemma (Grossberg, 1978) is the question of how a NN can learn everything that it needs to and yet avoid overwriting previously learned information when it is in the learning mode. This question cannot be answered locally, since it involves a decision about whether a global pattern has been seen before. Therefore, the adaptive resonance theory (ART) architecture adds an orienting subsystem to previously considered competitive NNs (which in ART is called *the attentional subsystem*). The new subsystem switches on the learning mode, while the old system performs input to stored category matches, generates expectations, and determines when learning should end. The incorporation of this solution into the architecture of the ART model leads directly to the category size vs. novelty detection dilemma. This is the question of how to make a category's area in feature space large enough to include a many members, but small enough so that similar objects requiring significantly different behaviors can be recognized as novel. Carpenter and Grossberg (1986) include a vigilance parameter in the ART model to control this trade off. However, this one parameter criteria for controlling category size only works when there are a small number of features and a small amount of noise in the measurement of each feature.

Further evidence of behavior modes occurs in fight vs. flight situations, where the selection of a set of drives radically changes an animal's pattern of response to inputs. Thus, both information capacity and psychological data argue for a cognitive system being able to switch between one behavior model and another.

If a system uses multiple behavior modes, one must postulate a method and sensory criteria for switching between them. The two characteristics of a sensation needed to initiate the learning mode are newness and biological significance (Kahneman, 1973). An arousal system is required to alert a NN that a biologically significant event has occurred. An orienting system is required to direct a system's attentional capacity toward a strong and/or novel sensation. Novelty is one of those intuitive notions that is easy to invoke but hard to define. In addition to newness, novelty implies a difference between real sensory input and expected sensory input. The problem is explaining how expectations are generated and compared to sensory input.

3.2. The Need for Selective Attention and Structured Representations

We claim that cognitive systems need to build complex, structured representations to generate the expectations which direct the allocation of attention. Structured representations would include concepts such as frames, schemas, mental models, or cognitive maps. In addition to being needed for generating expectations, we claim that structured representations are also needed to explain the difference between one-trial learning and slower learning (e.g., conditioning or skill acquisition) (Shiffern & Dumais, 1981; LaBarge, 1983; Kahneman & Treisman, 1984).

3.2.1. Sensory Expressiveness vs. Good Categorization

Novel inputs are those that fall outside of existing categories. The ability to detect novel stimuli is in direct competition with having large categories in a feature space of fixed size. However, there is an additional competition in selecting the number of features that belong in feature space, sensory expressiveness vs. useful categories.

A NN has full sensory expressiveness if it can distinguish between any pair of distinct objects that may appear in its environment. The NN does not know in advance what set of examples will be used or which features will be critical. The human ability to learn new categories and to subdivide old ones requires a large number of feature dimensions, i.e., a high degree of sensory expressiveness. If a very large number of feature dimensions are used, noise becomes a major problem in either the prototype or examplar theory. When a classification is being made by a single Sneuron which sums a large number of uncorrelated inputs, the smallest change that is detectable depends on the variance of its sum of inputs. This implies that the minimal detectable change grows with the number of inputs. Of course, if there are a large number of neural classifiers and a category can be defined in terms of the common activity of many Sneurons, then the size of the smallest detectable change depends on the $\max_i(\text{var}_i)$ over all inputs. It should be noted that the inputs to a neuron in the visual cortex receives a large number of correlated inputs. In fact, mammals go to a lot of trouble to insure that visual stimulation from the one object reaches the same cortical neuron by maintaining a comfortable viewing distance from an object.

In addition to increases in the minimal detectable difference, a large number of inputs requires that the system adjust a large number of parameters during learning. Thus, sensory expressiveness is in competition with achieving a useful balance between categorization and novelty detection.

3.2.2. Plan Selection vs. Detecting Plan Failure

Problems analogous to those in recognition exist in the motor control domain as well. Selecting a plan that will achieve a goal can be thought of as a type of categorization over sequences of actions rather than sensory features (Lee, 1984). When the system realizes that none of its plans will achieve the desired goal (i.e., failure is detected), the learning mode and exploratory behavior are switched on. However, in this case the system explores the space of action sequences rather than the space of sensory features.

A NN has full motor expressiveness if it can generate any sequence of action primitives. It should be able to build a sequence from either action primitives or composite actions. To respond to the myriad of unknown situations that may occur, humans must have access to a very large number of short actions. Having adequate motor expressiveness means that the number of action sequences that can be formed is huge, and this makes searching a computationally intensive task that people do not seem able to do in parallel. Thus, motor expressiveness is in competition with finding good plans.

The solution to these dilemmas involving expressiveness (sensory or motor) vs. accurate categories is to reduce the number of dimensions examined at any time through modularization based on attentional mechanisms. Given a small feature space, a NN can build categories with a simple parameter, i.e., vigilance.

There is strong evidence that people make heavy use of modularization of sensory processing. For example, one can only answer questions about a small portion of the visual field (Sperling, 1963). In addition, the evidence about making value judgments implies that only a small subspace of the space of meaningful sensations in the spatial focus of attention is actually examined at any point in time (Kahneman & Miller, 1986). The next section discusses a form of structured representation suited to do the modularization associated with selective attention.

4. COGNITIVE MAPS AND MENTAL MODELS

Many authors have argued that people use structured representations, such as schema (Rumelhardt, Smolensky, McClelland, & Hinton, 1986; Arbib, 1985) and cognitive maps (Kaplan & Kaplan, 1982), in most of their cognitive processing. The representation that we try to model with the HNN is based on data on cognitive maps which represent both declarative and procedural information. For a system engaged in autonomous activity, any useful representation must combine these types of information. We also argue that systems operating in a complex environment must create internal simulations of external events in order to guide their behavior and learning. As other authors have argued, some representation capable of organizing the large set of behavioral algorithms and concepts available to a human into modules is necessary for intelligence (Tolman, 1948; Lynch, 1960; Kaplan & Kaplan, 1982).

The characteristics of cognitive maps and mental models we wish to model are discussed next. Cognitive maps correspond to the standard psychological definition, based on 'landmarks,' given by Kaplan and Kaplan (1982), while the mental models are used to create visualizations. These two forms of internal representation allow the system to operate in two distinct modes, *throwness* and *reflection*. In Hiedigger's (Winograd & Flores, 1986) terminology, throwness occurs in situations where one is caught up in the affairs of the moment and must simply act. Cognitive maps can be used in situations where complete processing of an input is impossible, let alone extensive reflection. Reflection occurs when one has time to ask 'what if' questions, and there is no immediate need to make decisions about acting. Mental models are utilized in the reflection mode.

Winograd and Flores (1986) considered the difference between these two modes of performance and central issue limiting the utility of computer science and artificial intelligence (AI). The need for two representations has not been understood by the AI community. The AI establishment has argued that a reflective mode alone is sufficient, since it is possible to build a reflective system that carries out any particular task. However, the need for the two modes occurs only in large-scale systems with real-time constraints, which AI research has shied away from.

4.1. Cognitive Maps

For our purpose, a *cognitive map* is a set of landmarks linked by behaviors. Each landmark corresponds to one or more vectors of sensation features or prototypes. Multiple vectors are required to represent very different views of three-dimensional objects. Associated with each landmark is a 'bag of behaviors' that allows the system to reach a subset of the other landmarks in the cognitive map, as shown in Figure 3.1. Of the detectable features associated with a real object, only a subset is actually noticed when recognizing the landmark (Gould & Gould, 1985). The noticed features should be selected on the basis of their relevance to the 'bag of behaviors' associated with that landmark, and the current goals. (Note there is a direct connection between Gibson's, 1979, concept of *affordances* and the noticed features in our version of a cognitive map.) In addition to the functional linkage of landmarks by behaviors, there is a structural linkage between landmarks that share a large number of detectable features.

A mathematical specification of a cognitive map can be given as follows. The maps can be considered hyperplanes on the hyperspace of detectable features or sensory primitives. The landmarks that make up the cognitive map are defined by a vector(s) of noticed features, and a basin of attraction surrounding the vector(s) which lies in the hyperplane of the cognitive map. Ideally, each behavior or plan can be considered an mapping between a pair of landmarks in the same cognitive map. If the unnoticed and undetectable features relative to the cognitive map are essentially constant, then the behavioral mapping is essentially one-to-one in the noticed features. If the unnoticed features in the domain of the mapping vary, then the behavior may only map between landmarks with a certain probability. In other words, behaviors are generally fuzzy mappings between landmarks.

4.2. Mental Models

The nodes in the mental models are idealized behaviors, or *plans*. A plan consists of localized feature-vector descriptions of initial and final states, plus a list of actions that should move the system between them. The initial and final states of the plan are sufficiently detailed to associatively retrieve landmarks in the corresponding cognitive map, and they can be modified by an action. However, they are not generally adequate for direct matching with sensory input. The source of the final states is the current goal or task, while the initial state can either be derived from a sensation or a semantic process (Kahneman & Miller, 1986). A *visualization* is the process of testing a plan by instantiating the initial state of the system and mapping it through the list of actions and seeing if the desired final state is achieved. We intend visualization to be broad enough to include processes without specific image manipulation. Thus, a visualization can be considered a map between plans (as shown in Figure 3.1).

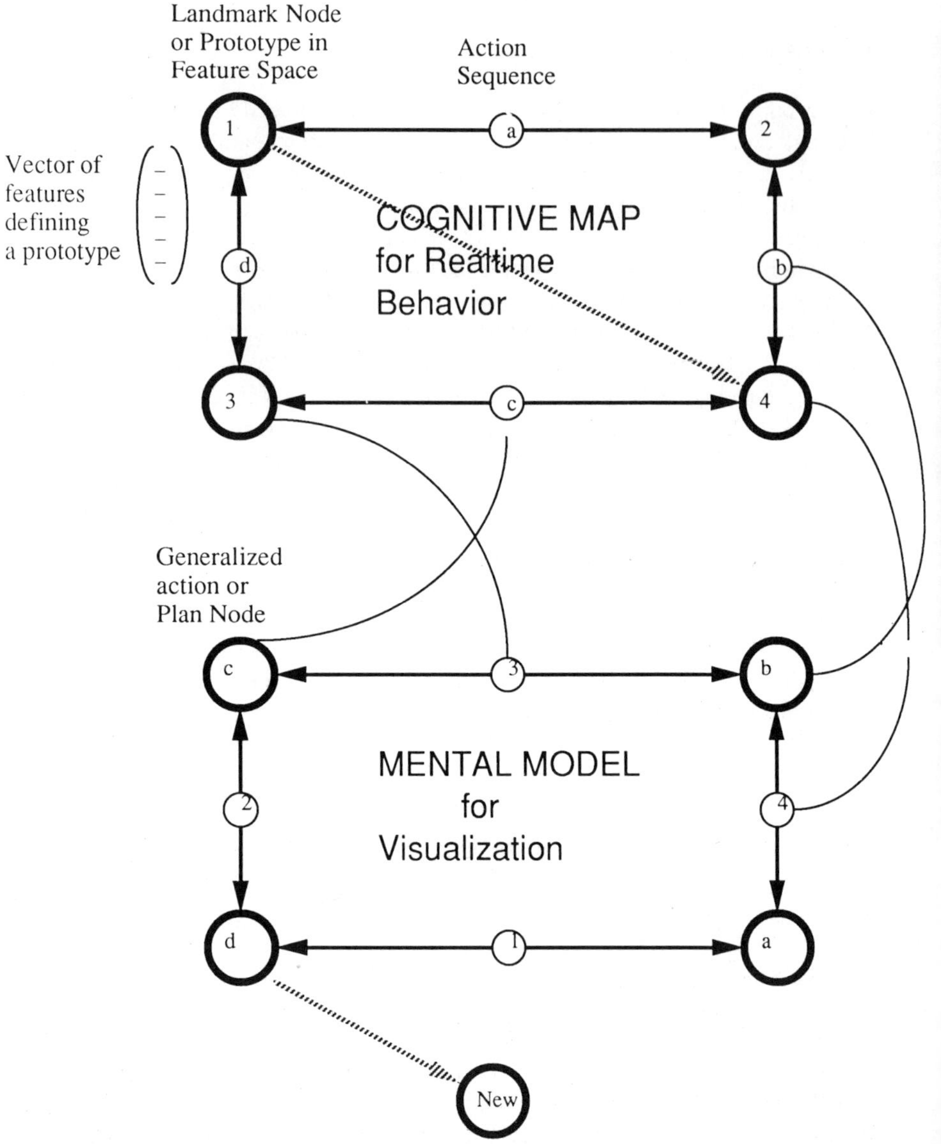

Figure 3.1. A proposed model of a cognitive map which consists of a set of landmark nodes and the behavioral algorithms links between them, and its corresponding mental model which consists of a set of plan nodes and the visualizations that link them. In the HNN, a landmark node is represented by a stable state in the column level of the system, while the behavioral algorithms are triggered by activity at the short range level and transmitted through association areas to motor areas. The plan nodes are also column stable states, but in the motor areas. The output of the short range level is transmitted back to the sensory region and induces visualization.

The real power of cognitive maps and the mental models comes from the ways in which they interact with each other. The actions that can be used in the plans for the mental model should be restricted to the action components of behaviors that already exist in cognitive maps. Thus, every mental model should be linked to a cognitive map in the way shown in Figure 3.1. Mental models should be related to each other to allow plan nodes to be expanded into complete mental models. Essentially, this would be an associative retrieval problem of using links to components to retrieve them and the visualizations that map between them. On the other hand, it should be possible to compress complete mental models into single nodes of more extensive mental models. In addition, detailed mental models should be linked to more abstract ones, so that generic plans can be specialized to particular cases and particular cases should generalize to form generic plans.

Modification of a cognitive map is a slow process compared to modification of a mental model, where stable learning may be achieved in just a few trials. Learning can affect several different aspects of a cognitive map, including:

1. recording new landmarks when they are explored,
2. replacing the landmark trigger for a behavior sequence,
3. reindexing components of a landmark to create new landmarks in the map.

The first modification technique allows the creation of new landmarks. The second technique allows links to be built between different cognitive maps. The third technique keeps the nodes of the cognitive map from becoming too specialized and allows the model of the environment to be upgraded through the recognition of novelty or errors. Mental models, by analogy, can be modified by adding new plan nodes, by exchanging plans in a plan sequence, or by dividing a single plan into several separate ones.

Why is learning in the context of cognitive maps and mental models necessary? If the landmark that a system uses to find its way home is removed, a new landmark must be learned in what amounts to a single trial (Tinbergen, 1958). In general, the appearance of a novel stimulus in a well-known environment should draw attention and be recorded in association with the rest of the environment. A short exploratory sequence should lead to linking a new landmark to a modified action sequence. This is done before the testing a system needs to commit to a fixed action pattern could be done. Thus, fast learning is worthwhile if, and only if, one can restrict the learning to one behavior mode and the context of one cognitive map.

5. NETWORKS OF INTERACTING NEURAL POPULATIONS

In the previous sections, the reasons for building a NN with the ability to model selective attention and behavior mode shifts were discussed, as well as the characteristics of the internal representations that would be needed. These abilities would allow a system to perform appropriate modularization. This in turn makes it possible to simultaneously maintain expressiveness and useful categories. In addition, modularization is needed for one-trial learning and the use of analogies. In this section, we propose a preliminary NN model for these attentional mechanisms, and the biological motivation for that model.

A *neural network* (NN) is a computing structure based on the anatomical and electrophysiological properties of biological networks of neurons. The activity of each element or Sneuron in the NN is a nonlinear function of the prior activities of the Sneurons in the network and of the external sources from which it receives input. The dynamics of a NN can be represented as a system of difference, differential, or integral equations. These equations depend on the following properties of the individual Sneurons: the distribution of connections among the Sneurons, the function which combines the current inputs to each Sneuron into a single overall potential, the response curve (i.e., the transformation that relates the overall potential to the firing rate), and the decay rate of the overall potential. A neural population will be defined to be a set of Sneurons in a NN whose equations of motion have the same form and whose architectural parameters come from the same distribution (Geman, 1982; Eilbert, 1988).

A neural population should also be identified by a number of functional characteristics. First, we note that steady states supported by different populations should have qualitatively different spatial distributions. Otherwise, one is essentially working with a larger single population. Second, the average time for evolution to a steady state should be different for different populations. This provides a basis for simultaneously modeling events with different time scales in the model. From a technical standpoint, it makes it possible to use singular perturbation techniques that simplify the stability analysis. Third, the global stability of the network should only depend at worst on the stability of the individual populations. Empirical evidence indicates that sets of interacting neural populations with global stability are rare. Fourth, the steady states of slow evolving populations should subdivide the faster populations into distinct functional modules. We will argue that arbitrarily large resonance patterns are of little use in information processing. However, most dynamic connection schemes allow the effects of a single pattern to spread throughout an entire population. We will show that interactions between populations in the HNN can not only localize processing, but can also select specific areas and features to be processed.

The brain is made up of many intermixed, interacting populations of neurons. Members of different neural populations differ in their distributions of input and output connections, neurotransmitters, intrinsic firing rates, and spatial and temporal resolution. In neural modeling, researchers have rarely used more than one population of neurons, Cohen and Grossberg's (1983) binocular/monocular system and Amari and Arbib's (1982) excitatory and inhibitory system being exceptions. Even in these cases, the response to a few specific input patterns was considered without elucidating the general properties of the interaction. Geman (1982) proved a general result about when interacting populations can be treated as a individual functional units, and Eilbert (1988) extended this result and applied it to biologically realistic neural populations. However, the details of the actual behavior were left open, even in the case where whole populations could be treated as individual units. In this section, we attempt to say more about the character of this interaction.

A model (Eilbert, 1988) called the *hierarchical neural model* (HNN) has been proposed which distinguishes Sneuron populations by their distribution of output connections (i.e., axon terminations) and by their effects on the target Sneurons (i.e., neurotransmitter effect). The HNN is a three-level hierarchical NN based on the concept of multinode functional units (MFUs). It is a true structural hierarchy in which a single MFU on one level of the system can contain a whole population of simpler nodes or simpler MFUs. The levels of the HNN operate on different spatial and temporal scales and, in the current model, subserve different cognitive tasks.

5.1. Biological Basis for the HNN

Each population is based on the connections of a different basic type of neuron. In the coarsest classification of neural types, one distinguishes interneurons whose axons remain within the nucleus where they originate, and relay cells whose axons leave the nucleus where they originate (Shepherd, 1984). The relay cells can be further subdivided into those whose axon terminations are concentrated in 0.5 mm in diameter cortical columns (Mountcastle, 1979; Szenthagothai, 1978), and those with diffuse terminations (Shepherd, 1984). To take axon shape into account, a model with short-range (ShR), long-range-columnar (LRC), and long-range-diffuse (LRD) nodes was proposed (see Figure 3.2; Eilbert, 1988). These nodes correspond to neurons classified as interneurons, columnar relay cells, and diffuse relay cells. Neurons were further classified by physiologial effects on their targets, which can be excitatory, inhibitory, or long lasting. Of the nine combinations of axon shape and transmitter effect possible, the five found in the nervous system have been included in the proposed neural model: excitatory and inhibitory ShR, excitatory and inhibitory LRC, and long-lasting LRD.

A theorem was proved showing that the proposed 5-node-type model contains groups of LRC nodes that work together as multinode functional units (MFUs), i.e., groups of nodes whose activities are so closely coordinated that they can be considered distinct functional units (Eilbert, 1988). In particular, it was shown that there are groups of LRC nodes in which every node follows the same trajectory to the same steady state value. The theorem required constant or steady state activity on the ShR nodes, and independent and identically distributed

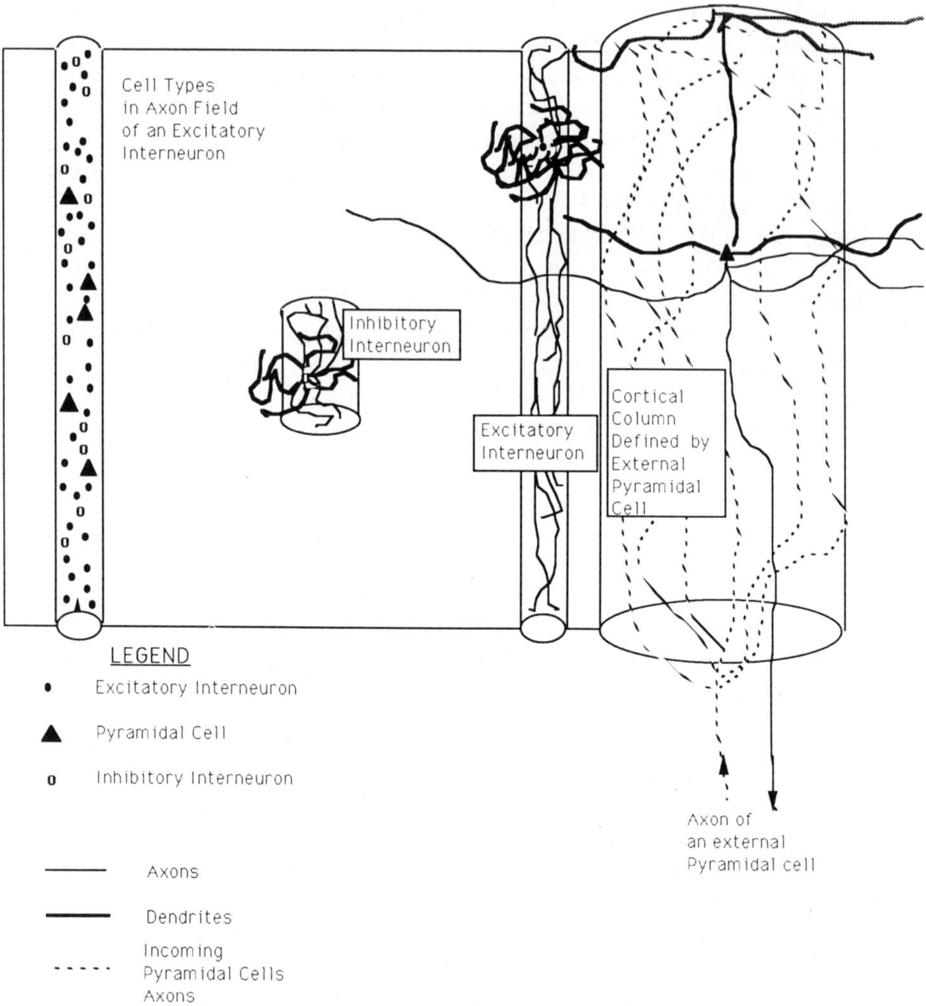

Figure 3.2. The spatial distribution of connections for the major cell types found in the visual cortex. Shown are the dendrites and axons of the excitatory and inhibitory interneurons. The distribution of relay (pyramidal) cell connections is also shown.

(i.i.d.) connection strengths among the LRC nodes forming a functional grouping. The smallest MFU corresponded directly to the set of relay cells in a single column defined by the termination of a columnar relay cell. Hereafter, a *column* will refer to a single unit made up of LRC neurons which have similar dynamics in the absence of local input. The *column population* is the set of all columns in the system. It was also shown that there are larger functional groups of LRC nodes designated coherent populations, which consist of sets of widely scattered columns. The existence of MFUs imposes a three-level hierarchical structure on the model, as shown in Figures 3.3 and 3.4. It was observed that physiological and behavioral evidence support the existence of a similar three-level hierarchy in vertebrate brains (Kahneman, 1973). The HNN model discussed in this chapter is a generalization and idealization of this previously proposed hierarchical model.

Evidence associates the midbrain and hypothalamus (sites of large concentrations of real LRD neurons) to behavior mode shifts. Lesions in these areas lead to changes in sleeping, eating, drinking, and aggression behaviors (Luria, 1973). Behavior modes may be maintained over extended periods (i.e., minutes to hours) by periodic activity within the LRD regions. Even longer lasting effects must rely on the permanent structural changes associated with long-term memory.

5.2. The Local or Diffusion Level of the HNN

In order to formulate the HNN mathematically, the meaning of activity must be specified for nodes at each level of the hierarchy. At the lowest level, the activity of a node, in analogy with a neuron, can be represented by its potential at the axon hillock or by its instantaneous firing rate. The potential, at a single point in time, contains more complete information than the firing rate. However, firing rate is the functional output for other nodes and has computational advantages in NN models (Guez, Kam, & Eilbert, 1988). Here, the governing equations of the HNN are given in terms of potential (conversion to firing rate is straightforward).

The nodes on the first level are based on interneurons, and are shown in Figure 3.2. They have shorter temporal and spatial scales than the nodes at the two higher levels, and a circularly symmetric distribution of outputs (Shepherd, 1984). The output of one ShR node can have either an excitatory or an inhibitory effect on its targets. The input to ShR nodes comes from other ShR nodes, from long-range-directional (LRC) nodes, and from remote external or sensory sources. The firing rates are computed using a nonlinear (sigmoidal) transform of the potential of the input nodes. A mathematical model for the set of ShR nodes contained in a single column-level node is a weighted sum of the firing rates it receives from internal and external sources, minus its decay. The details of the equations are given in Appendix 1.

5.3. The Columnar Level of the HNN

As shown in Figure 3.2, the LRC Sneurons in a column receive input from a subset of ShR nodes contained within the column, and from LRC nodes in other columns. They also receive control signals coming from the LRD nodes, which are the same over large sets of columns. It is assumed that columns do not overlap (see Figure 3.2). This means that all terminations from a single LRC

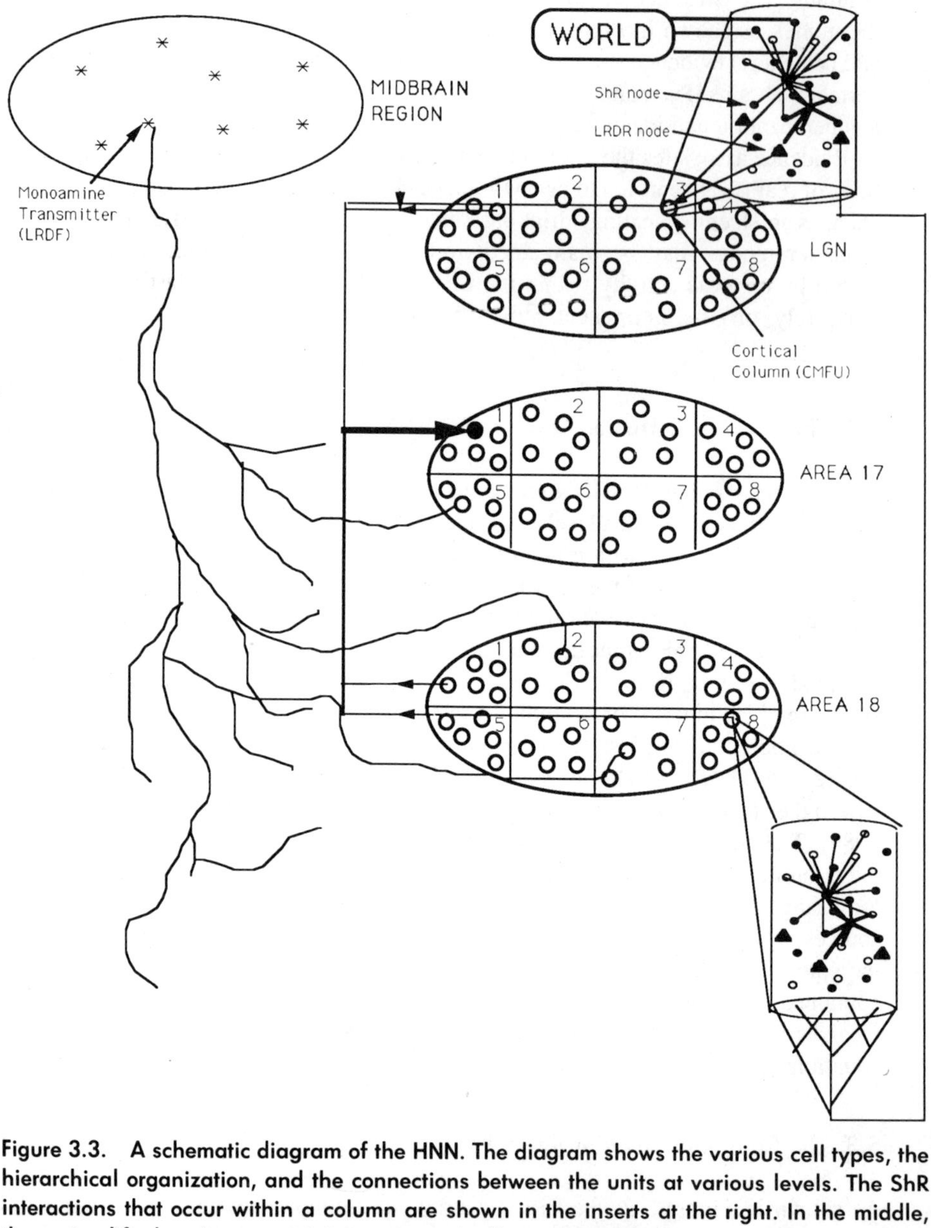

Figure 3.3. A schematic diagram of the HNN. The diagram shows the various cell types, the hierarchical organization, and the connections between the units at various levels. The ShR interactions that occur within a column are shown in the inserts at the right. In the middle, three simplified regions containing retinotopically organized columns are shown, and the connections to and from one column. (Inputs are the darker lines.)

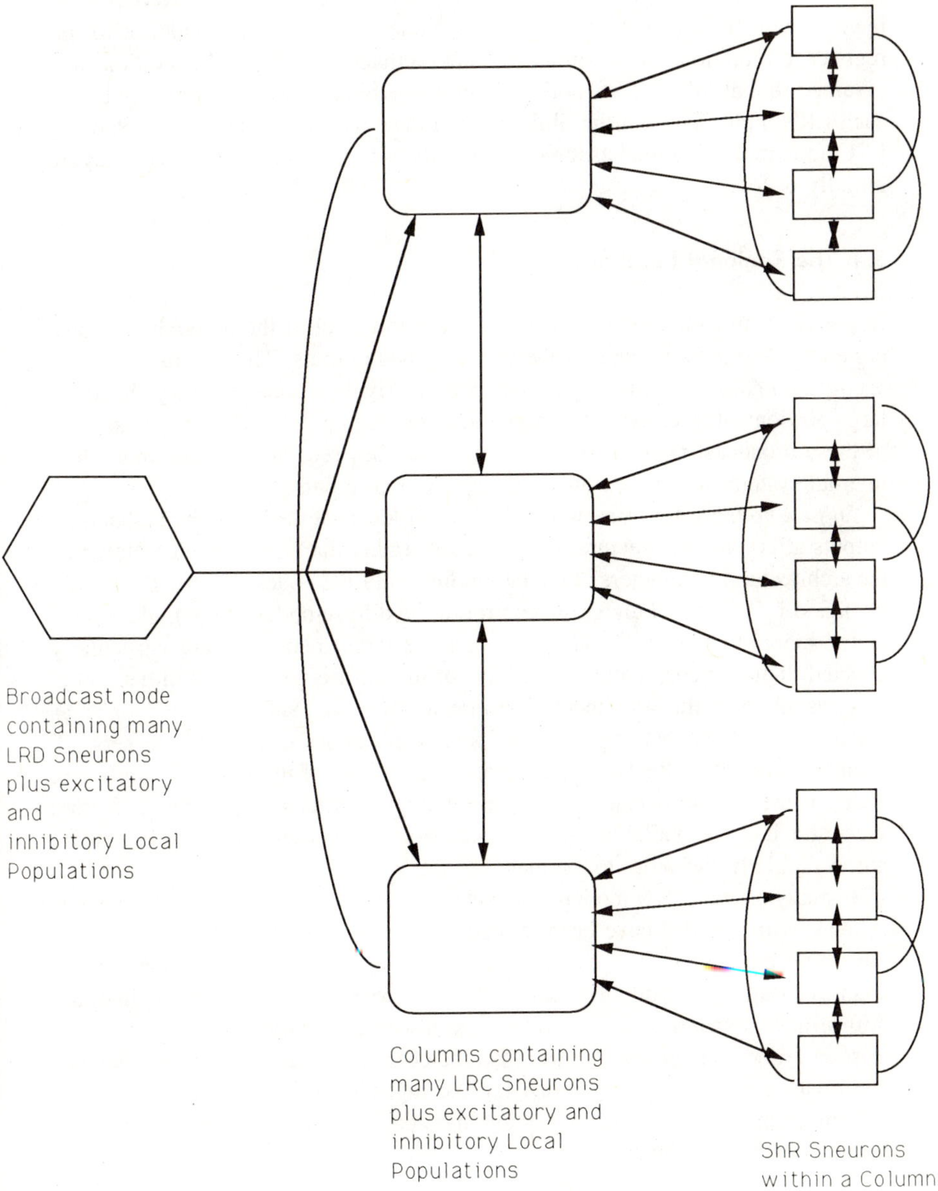

Figure 3.4. A block diagram of the HNN.

node end in a single column in a region, and that the terminations of all other LRC nodes in that region are either disjoint or in-register (i.e., overlap completely) with the terminations of the first node. There is some evidence for in-register terminations of pyramidal cells (Szenthagothai, 1978). In addition, it is assumed that all of the LRC nodes within a column receive the same input from each LRC input. Thus, if the ShR nodes in the column have zero activity, every LRC node in the column has the same activity as $t \to \infty$, even if their activities are initially different.

5.4. The Regional Level of the HNN

In the HNN model, the LRD neurons at the top level of the hierarchy are also organized into MFUs, which have vector-valued outputs. These units are called *broadcast nodes,* because they are not particularly directional and they can affect large portions of a region at the same time (see Figure 3.3 and 3.4). The activity of these broadcast nodes depends on the input they receive from columns, their internal system of interneurons, and any external inputs.

Diffuse nodes differ from units on the lower levels of the hierarchy in that their outputs affect the architecture of their targets rather than their activity. Note that the architectural parameters of the target ShR and LRC nodes, A^i, B^i, T^i, V^i, W^i, $g^i(.)$, and $h_i(Y)$, are all under the control of the diffuse nodes of the highest level of the hierarchy, while the activities of these target nodes are not particularly affected. Thus, incorporating the effects of the diffuse nodes units in the model requires treating the architectural parameters for the ShR and LRC units as dynamic variables. Having dynamic parameters under control of the network itself has dramatic effects on the storage capabilities of the network. Sufficient shifts in the variables can change the topology of the steady states in feature space. Each of the available topologies can store its own set of prototypes that are not available in the other topologies.

In many previous NN models, the connection weights associated with changes in long term memory have been treated as dynamic variables. Here, equations governing parameter changes can also be applied to temporary changes in the cognitive state, including behavior modes and arousal. The temporal scale of the diffuse node dynamics, and therefore the lower-level parameter changes, is at least an order of magnitude slower than the changes in column activity. Singular perturbation analysis of equations for the highest level of the HNN, and its influence on lower levels, is beyond the scope of this chapter and will be communicated elsewhere.

6. RESONANCE PATTERNS

The real reason for distinguishing neural populations is that the patterns of activity supported by one population can be dramatically different from the patterns supported by another. For example, a population with feedback can support stable states, periodic behaviors, or chaotic behaviors that are not available to networks with just feedforward connections. A feedforward network has an upper-triangular connection matrix with zeros on its main diagonal. Thus, activity will eventually reach the zero state in the absence of input. If it is symmetric, then the system will eventually evolve to some nonzero stable state (Cohen & Grossberg, 1983). The main subject of this section is the effects of the ShR and LRC populations on each other.

Like many other neural networks, the HNN model stores information in its stable states (Carpenter & Grossberg, 1986; Hopfield, 1984; Ackley, Hinton, & Sejnowski, 1985). However, the HNN has stable states in both the local and column populations, (Eilbert & Salter, 1986). Information transfer from the ShR to the LRC populations must take into account the fact that the time scale of interactions among the ShR nodes is an order of magnitude faster than among LRC nodes (Shepherd, 1984). Therefore, the classification decision made by the ShR populations must be presented to the LRC Sneurons at a rate they can track. Resonance patterns (i.e., either steady states or periodic activity) are the only mechanism in a NN that can maintain rapidly changing sensory input or classification decisions exactly. A set of ShR nodes in a stable state can store and transfer detailed activity patterns to LRC populations. Other storage mechanisms (habituation, sensitization, and conditioning) leave a trace in the connection weights that can affect future responses, but they do not retain the details of the sensation which caused them (Hawkins & Kandel, 1984). Thus, the processing ability of a NN with many populations operating at different time scales depends on the resonance patterns that its recurrent pathways can support.

We next consider the types of resonance patterns that can be supported by the various populations in the HNN, the interactions between these patterns, and the rules these patterns play in processing information. The resonance patterns, or *languages,* of each neural population will be discussed individually. It will be shown that information processing capability of each neural population is greatly enhanced through interactions with the other populations in the HNN. This enhanced information processing depends on the ability of LRC neurons to divide the ShR population into independent processing modules, and of the LRD neurons to divide the LRC population.

6.1. The Local Population

The circular connection pattern found in the ShR (see Figure 3.3) is perhaps the simplest type possible for neurons laid out on a 2-D sheet. More precisely, we consider a sheet with both excitatory and inhibitory nodes, where the average distance from cell body to output connection is greater for the inhibitory nodes than for the excitatory nodes. This pattern of connection is found, not only among the interneurons of the brain, but in the communication of diseases among animals, and the diffusion of dyes.

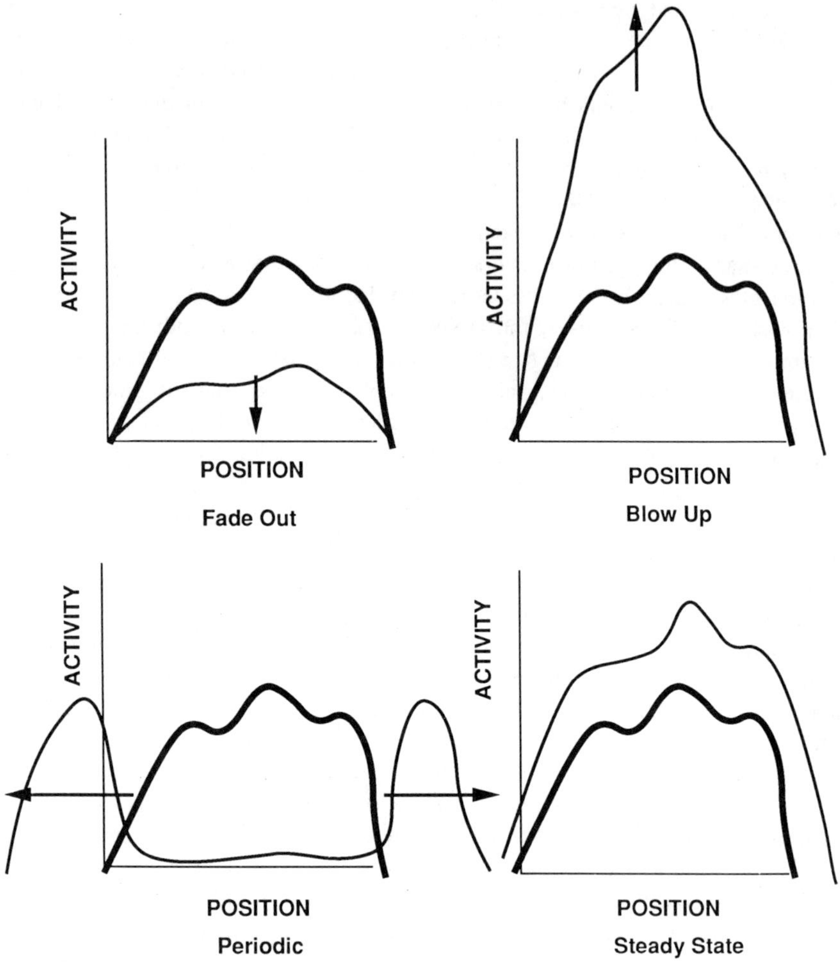

Figure 3.5. Activity patterns supported by the local population. The four patterns are all responses to impulse inputs: (A) Fade-Out and (B) Blow-Up are transient patterns, while (C) Periodic and (D) Steady State are sustained patterns.

A circular population can make four qualitatively different responses to a short, spatially localized input pattern (see Figure 3.5). Each of the four responses starts with the same initial activity pattern in space, shown as the dark lines. The lighter line shows what the initial pattern has evolved to a short time later, and the arrows show the direction in which the pattern will move after the later time. Two of the responses are transient: *fade out* (a response that shrinks to nothing when the input ends, or *blow-up* (a massive response that spreads out and then dies away). The other two responses are sustained: *periodic waves* (the interaction between the excitatory and inhibitory populations can lead to oscillation), or *steady state* (a spatial pattern, similar to the input can remain unchanged indefinitely).

The sustained modes are of greater interest in the following analysis. The steady state modes can clearly store specific 2-D spatial input patterns. However, any temporal and absolute magnitude information about the input that caused the steady state is lost. On the other hand, temporal (e.g., duration of input) and absolute magnitude information can be stored in the frequency and amplitude of the periodic mode. However, this temporal variation at each point prevents any relative spatial magnitude information from being stored in the periodic mode. Thus, 'complete' information about a stimulus can be stored if it gives rise to both a steady state and a periodic response. Note that there is a minimum resolution to any type of information stored in the resonance patterns of a circular population. Spatial resolution depends on the smallest group of neurons that can be self-sustaining, which is controlled by the average connection length of the excitatory connections. The temporal resolution is limited by the time course of the PSP. Thus, both the temporal and spatial resolution are limited by genetically determined factors.

Thus, populations with a circular distribution of axon connections can be dedicated to the storage of particular types of spatial or temporal data. For example, in vision individual Area 17 neurons seem to be sensitive to all of the following (Hubel & Wiesel, 1977):

- Spatial information
  - Intensity, Line or edge orientation, Edge length, Color, Disparity, Spatial frequency.
- Temporal information
  - Motion, Duration.

Only two transform dimensions can be represented on any patch of circularly connected tissue. However, additional types of information can be multiplexed into the activity of the individual neurons. In Area 17, local position is only a reliable indicator of orientation and spatial frequency (Hubel & Wiesel, 1977).

When the activity distribution in one region is transformed or recombined in going to another region, the multiplexed information can be reorganized so that other dimensions can be represented by position in the new region. This leads to the expectation that there are multiple retinotopic representations in the brain to take advantage of the many types of transformed information. In fact, more than a dozen retinotopic representations have been reported (Zeki, 1974).

What is the minimum diameter of a circular population with sufficient resolution to represent local spatial and temporal information adequately (i.e., how many distinguishable values are there in the various transform dimensions?)? In Area 17, a single cortical hypercolumn supports ($5^6 \approx 15{,}000$) states, which is sufficient to support five values for each of six variables, such as orientation, disparity, velocity, etc. The ability to discriminate any more variables or values would require functional units an order of magnitude greater. Any increase in the visual angle dealt with by a column would require a proportional increase in the number of values in orientation and spatial frequency values in the column. Since column size is similar throughout the brain (Shepherd, 1984), the ability to resolve 5–8 values/variable may hold everywhere in the cortex. If the spatial resolution of a variable is low, then few columns are needed to build its retinotopic map compared to high resolution features. To use the circular populations in Area 17 with maximum efficiency, the populations should be modularized into isolated patches about the size of hypercolumns, with each patch supporting distinct resonance patterns. The next section will show how the columnar population could do this.

6.2. The Columnar Population

While the local populations seem to work as extraction and storage systems, a columnar population must work as both a categorization and an attentional focusing system. The categorization is the result of feedforward interactions among columns, while attention depends on the interaction of columnar steady states and local populations. This suggests that the trajectory by which a column population approaches stability is more important than the form of the stable state. In fact, a blow-up followed by a slow fade-out may be a very useful response mode for the column populations.

The Columnar connection pattern is far more complicated than the circular one, as shown in Figure 3.3. By its nature, the column population is organized into a number of distinct regions. Within a region, we assume that a column is self-excitatory and inhibits all other columns in the same region, where the strength of the inhibition falls off exponentially. Columns excite all of the columns (and all of their Sneurons) they reach in other regions. Cohen and Grossberg (1983) have shown that columnar connections are stable if they have symmetric connections. If inhibition spreads equally through a region, such a system has a stable state with a single winner in each region. If inhibition within a single region falls off exponentially with distance, a stable activity pattern can contain several isolated columns per region (Eilbert, 1988). The spatial variations of an input are reflected in the exact members in the columnar steady state. Periodic oscillation in the input can be tracked by the column population. Note, however, that most of the detailed information must be stored in the local population.

Turning to the interaction between the local and columnar populations, let us make the following assumptions. There are N regions with ShR and LRC Sneurons. LRC nodes do not connect to ShR nodes. ShR nodes in a region communicate only with other nodes in that region. Any node can receive constant external input. Vidyasagar (1980) describes the algebraic manipulation that will convert equations for the regions into lower block diagonal form, where the whole LRC population is one block and the ShR nodes in each region are the others. Assuming the response function for the nodes obey reasonable continuity assumptions that any sigmoidal function would obey.

Theorem 1. A sufficient condition that a system including ShR and LRC neurons is globally asymptotically stable is that the ShR nodes in the individual regions and LRC nodes are each globally asymptotically stable.

Proof. Equation 1 for the ShR nodes is the equation for a simple additive net which is known to satisfy the criteria for the Cohen-Grossberg stability theorem (Cohen & Grossberg, 1983). Equation 2 with the ShR input at equilibrium reduces to a special case of the masking field networks discussed by Cohen and Grossberg (1986). A Lyapunov function exists for equations of this form (Cohen & Grossberg, 1983; Grossberg, 1987). Then by Theorem 4 of Hirsch (1989) or more generally by Theorem 3.4 of Vidyasagar (1980), the entire system is globally asymptotically stable.

The theorem does not address necessary conditions for stability, and there is the following argument for quasi-stability even when there are connections from the LRC to the ShR nodes. Consider a stable pattern of ShR nodes contained entirely within a single column. This would elicit a slow change in the LRC population. The LRC changes should cause a sequence of new stable states in the ShR nodes. If the sequence of changes between ShR stable stables approached zero, then the whole system should approach stability.

While this theorem addresses the existence of stability of the interaction between populations, it does not address the form of the joint stability. We note that steady states of the ShR Sneurons are not affected by the variation of the LRC Sneurons in the same column, since there are no inputs from LRC to ShR Sneurons in the same column in the current model. Input from external columns to the local population in a region is basically constant over a circle. Recall that the maximum inhibition and excitation at each location in the local population should cancel each other but the inhibitory connections go farther on the average than the excitatory ones. Grossberg and Cohen noted that this arrangement generally leads to minimal changes inside the circle, but creates a Mach-band-like ring around the circle, with the inner part of the band excitatory and the outer part of the band inhibitory. In addition to the excitatory part of the outer band, there are generally small excitatory regions arranged periodically within the circle. The spacing of these excitatory 'beats' depends on the length of the excitatory and inhibitory connections of the local population. Therefore, when external inputs reach a local population in a region, they are interacting with populations that already have an intricate spatial pattern of activity. Input that lands in an active column tends to be contained, since the outer inhibitory band acts as an absorbing layer. Input that activates local populations outside of the active columns will tend to cause spreading effects that interfere with other local population activity not contained in active columns. Periodic oscillations in the local population would cause even more interference than a steady state.

The local population within an active column is more likely to transmit its information to other regions for two reasons: the inhibitory ring around it allows less interference from other parts of the local population, and the activity of the columnar populations biases the responsiveness of the columns participating in a columnar resonance pattern, making it easier to transmit their information. This means that mutually supporting columns are a good candidate for directing selective attention. The complex representations that direct selective attention should provide the basis for forming resonance patterns among the columns. Since the modularization of the column population is controlled by the LRD Sneurons, the broadcast population should control the characteristics of the representation.

6.3. Broadcast Populations

The members of any self-stimulating set of columns are dispersed widely over the brain. Thus, it is not possible to localize an active sets of columns by building an inhibitory wall around them as is done for the Sneurons of the local population. In order to keep a columnar sustained state from moving into a region, it is necessary to either inhibit the whole region or change the shape of the column response curve over the whole region. Therefore, the best way to control the shape of a steady state in the column system is to prevent or promote the activation of Sneurons on a region by region basis. The second messenger effects of the LRD population, i.e., the alteration of structural parameters by transmitters, provide exactly this type of control. In addition, the second messenger effects endure over time periods at least an order of magnitude longer than it takes to establish steady states in the column population.

7. MODELING ATTENTIONAL CONTROL OF BEHAVIOR

This section describes a simple implementation of attention allocation and behavior mode switching in an HNN model. It also addresses the question of how cognitive maps tightly linked to mental models could emerge in an HNN. The dependence of both types of representation on innate exploratory behaviors is also considered.

7.1. Modeling Attention Shifts in the HNN

In an HNN with fixed architecture, a sensation-driven shift from one stable state in the column network to another models a shift in the attention channel, or, equivalently, a shift between cognitive maps. Changes in arousal or behavior mode are modeled by architectural changes in the HNN which can alter the number and size of its stable states.

To see how column stable states can represent attention channels or cognitive maps, the dual purpose served by each column must be considered (see Figure 3.3). On one hand, the components of a column's input and output vectors represent a collection or bag of allowable sensation–action pairs. On the other hand, a column acts as one element contributing to the maintenance of a stable state among the whole population of columns. This double role of the column manifests itself when an external input, I_{ij}, arrives at the Sneuron. The same external input which can shift the population of columns from one stable state to another can also differentially affect the output of each vector component of the column.

A very simple version of an external input shifting the focus of attention and eliciting a response is next modeled in a neural network with two columns, and no ShR level. This study of the computational power of the HNN utilizes a recent design algorithm for placing steady states in the state space of a neural model (Guez, 1987; Guez, Protopopescu, & Barhen, 1987). This design algorithm is more flexible than the 'outer product' design technique used by Anderson, Silverman, Ritz, and Jones (1977), Cooper, Liberman, and Oja (1979), or Hopfield (1982). Using this new algorithm, one can find a range of architectures that will ensure the stability of a particular point in state space. In the following example, two stable states were placed in a two Sneuron network.

Let N = 2; the response function, $g_i(x_i) = \tan^{-1}(x_i)$; and the stable states, $x_{e1} = (1, 0)^T$, $x_{e2} = (-1, 0)^T$. The equations governing this model are

$$d/dt\,(x_1) = -x_1 + (4/\pi)\tan^{-1}(x_1)$$

$$d/dt\,(x_2) = -x_1 + (2/\pi)\tan^{-1}(x_2) \qquad (3)$$

For this architecture, there are three equilibrium points (shown in Figure 3.6), since from Equation 3:

$$0 = -x_1 + (4/\pi)\tan^{-1}(x_1)$$

$$0 = -x_2 + (2/\pi)\tan^{-1}(x_2)$$

or $\{(x_1, x_2) \mid x_1 = 0, -1, +1;\ x_2 = 0\}$. Among these equilibria only two are stable $\{(-1, 0), (1, 0)\}$.

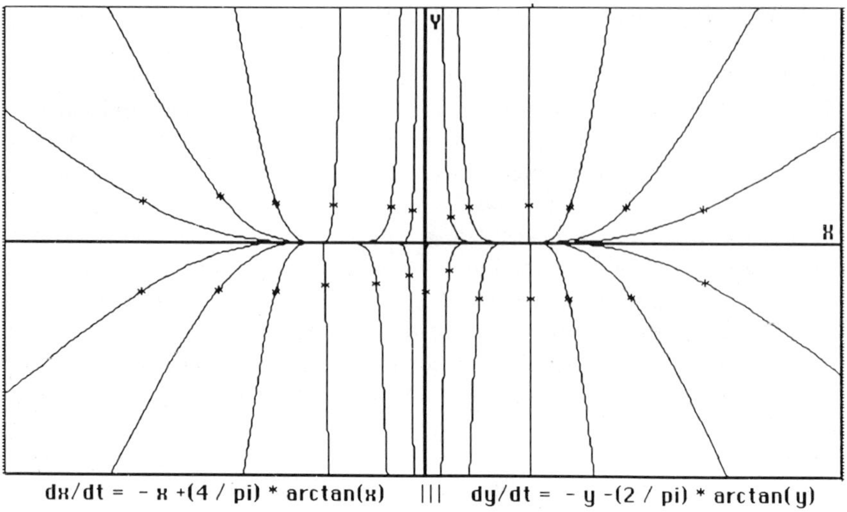

Figure 3.6. The state space diagram of Equation 3. It shows the stable points at (1, 0), −1, 0) and an unstable equilibrium at (0, 0).

An external input in the form of an impulse, with amplitude −3 and duration 2 in the x-direction, and amplitude 0 and duration 2 in the y-direction, moves the system from the stable point (1, 0) to (−1, 0) (see Figure 3.6). Thus, the system can model an attentional shift driven by external inputs. Note that larger amplitude and duration inputs in other directions may not change the stable state.

7.2. Modeling Behavior Mode Shifts in the HNN

The second mechanism that we wish to model is a change in the behavior mode. In particular, we wish to model the change in going from search to exploration. This change could be controlled by midbrain monoamine neurotransmitters (Bloom, 1979). Therefore, an HNN behavior mode change is an architectural change which is caused by the output of Diffuse Sneurons, which alter some combination of the decay rate, response function shape, or connection strength values.

Note that, in previous neural models, architectural changes have been associated with learning rather than attentional shifts. While the HNN model distinguishes learning from changes in arousal and behavior mode, the difference is more a matter of degree. One such difference is that the time interval needed to switch attention channels must be much shorter than the interval needed to make architectural changes associated with learning. A second difference is that a behavior mode or a degree of arousal should be temporary, whereas learning is generally assumed to be permanent. A third difference is that different architectural parameters are associated with the different processes. The HNN associates changes in connection strength with learning, as do most previous models. However, the HNN also allows changes in decay rate and response shape, and it is these that alter arousal level and behavior mode. In many cases, the Guez design algorithm can create the same stable state by adjusting decay rates and response shape, rather than connection weights. Thus, in the HNN, learning and behavior mode change can have the same effects on the performance of the system.

On biological and computational grounds, changes in response function shape seem best suited for shifting behavior modes. A change in the response functions of neurons over a large volume of the brain could be initiated by midbrain transmitters (Inversen, 1984). Computationally, the shape of $g_i(x_i)$ can alter the number of stable equilibria that the system can support in a predictable way (Guez et al., 1987).

Changes in the number and size of stable states have also been modeled in the simple two-column Sneuron case. By changing the architecture given in Equation 3 to

$$d/dt\ (x_1) = -2\pi\ x_1 + 10 \tan^{-1}(x_1) + 2 \tan^{-1}(x_2)$$

$$d/dt\ (x_2) = -4\pi\ x_2 + \tan^{-1}(x_1) + 17 \tan^{-1}(x_2) \qquad (4)$$

a completely different stable state topography was created. In this case, the weights were changed, but the same stable state topography could be achieved by differentially changing the response curves, $g_i(.)$. The stable states are $(-1, 1)$, $(1, -1)$, $(-2.086, -1.353)$, and $(2.086, 1.353)$; $(0, 0)$ is unstable; and there are four saddle points, all of which are shown in Figure 3.7.

7.3. Modeling Cognitive Maps and Mental Models in the HNN

The basic hypothesis for building complex representations in the HNN is that stable states in the columnar system represent both cognitive maps and mental models, and that much of their neural substrate is shared. The difference between the two types of representations lies in the regions that participate in each and the type of input that drives them. A cognitive map responds quickly to sensory-driven changes in the stable states of the local population. The movement between nodes of the cognitive map corresponds to the feedforward transient mode in the column system discussed above. It sets up a sensory expectation. A mental model responds to changes in goals or drives mediated by the broadcast system. It compares predictions about the results of behaviors to goals. Transitions between stable states in the column population correspond to switches between cognitive maps, while second messenger effects that change the stable state topology correspond to changes in behavior modes.

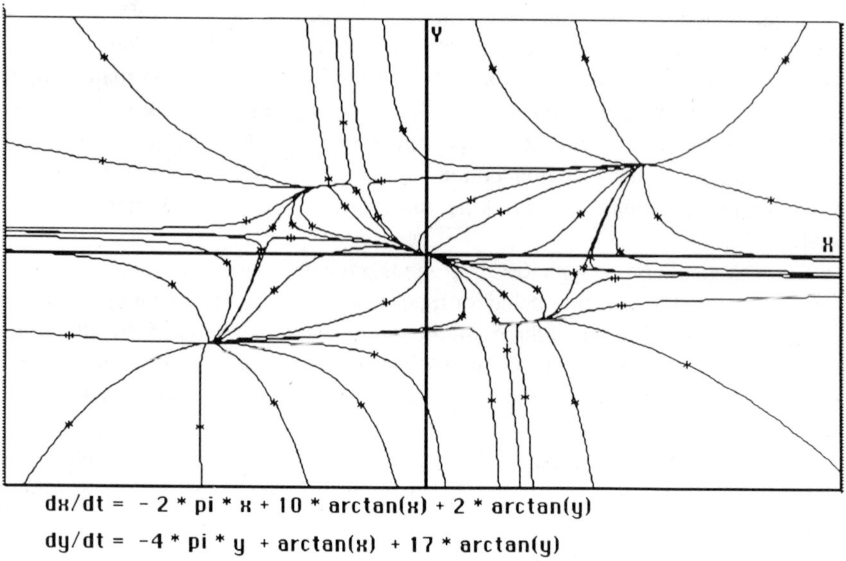

Figure 3.7. The state space diagram of Equation 4. It shows the four stable points at $\{(-1, 1), (1, -1), (-2.086, -1.353), (2.086, 1.353)\}$; the four saddle points, and an unstable equilibrium at (0, 0).

As stated above, the nodes of the cognitive map must be linked to other nodes both by structural similarity and functional relations. The structural similarity of two map nodes can be equated to the number of shared LRC neurons that they share. The functional relation between nodes should be based on mutually excitatory columns in different regions. The more difficult question is how the behaviors to be linked to a mode are selected. We propose that there are standard exploratory routines that are applied during the process of constructing a cognitive map node. The exploratory routines associated with a spatial cognitive map find objects in various directions that can become nodes in the cognitive map. Thus, an action, such as 'going east' until an object is found and classified, would be learned during the exploration that creates the node.

8. CONCLUSION

In this chapter, a number of mechanisms used by higher animals to achieve autonomous behavior have been explored from a modeling point of view. It was proposed that modularization of neural processing and learning is an important aspect of behavior. In addition, it was claimed that selective attention and behavior mode shifts are the major mechanisms of modularization, and that they depend on the difference in spatial and temporal scales of different neural populations.

The use of selective attention in modularization requires models and complex representations (Koch & Ullman, 1985). A cognitive map is one type of internal representation that is well documented in the literature. In basic form, it consists of set of landmark nodes and the behaviors that link them. In order to limit the type of behaviors that can be associated with a node, a variety of innate exploratory routine are used during the learning that builds a cognitive map.

There are many open issues in the HNN model. We must show that exploratory routines can indeed form the appropriate maps. We must specify how to recognize novelty, and how this recognition should trigger behavior mode switches. We must specify which conditions lead to activating different cognitive maps or other parts of a large cognitive map. Finally, we must show that the whole system can work together (Hofstadter, 1985). From the mathematical point of view, there is the question of which population types are stable together, which populations can modularize other populations, and which structural parameters should modified during behavior mode shifts to ensure new steady state topology with loss of information.

Interactions between processes operating on different spatial and temporal scales can be applied to a number of systems. In fact, Guez, Eilbert, and Kam (1988) have used this ideas in the construction of an adaptive controller based on the interaction of a NN and a standard controller.

9. REFERENCES

Ackley, D. H., Hinton, G. E., & Sejnowski, T. J. (1985). A learning algorithm for Boltzman machines. *Cognitive Science, 9*(1), 147–169.

Amari, S., & Arbib, M. A. (1977). Competition and cooperation in neural networks. In J. Metzler (Ed.), *Systems neuroscience* (pp. 119–165). San Diego, CA: Academic Press.

Anderson, J. A. (1983). Cognitive and psychological computation with neural models. *IEEE Transactions on Systems, Man, & Cybernetics, 13*(5), 799–814.

Anderson, J. A., Silverstein, J. W., Ritz, S. A., & Jones, R. S. (1977). Distinctive features, categorical perception, and probability learning: Some applications of a neural model. *Psychological Review, 84*, 413–451.

Arbib, M. A. (1985). Brain theory and cooperative computation. *Human Neurobiology, 4*, 201–218.

Barto, A. G., & Sutton, R. S. (1981). Landmark learning: an illustration of associative search. *Biological Cybernetics, 42*, 1–8.

Bell, B., & Eilbert, J. L. (1988). *Controlling basins of attraction in a Neural Network-Based telemetry monitor*. Paper presented at the 4th Annual Conference on AI for Space Applications.

Bloom, F. E. (1979). Chemical integrative processes in the central nervous system. In F.

O. Schmitt & F. G. Worden (Eds.), *The neurosciences: Fourth study program* (pp. 51–58). Cambridge, MA: MIT Press.

Carpenter, G. A., & Grossberg, S. (1986). A massively parallel architecture for a self-organizing neural pattern recognition machine. *Computer Vision, Graphics, and Image Processing, 37,* 54–113.

Cohen, M. A., & Grossberg, S. (1983). Absolute stability of global pattern formation and parallel memory storage by competitive neural networks. *IEEE Transactions on Man, Cybernetics, 13*(5), 815–825.

Cohen, M. A., & Grossberg, S. (1986). Neural dynamics of speech and language coding: development programs, perceptual grouping, and competition for short-term memory. *Human Neurobiol., 5*(1), 1–22.

Cooper, L. N., Liberman, F., & Oja, E. (1979). A theory for the acquisition and loss of neuron specificity in the visual cortex. *Biological Cybernetics, 33,* 9–28.

DeJong, G. (1986). An approach to learning from observation. In R. S. Michalski, J. G. Carbonell, & T. M. Mitchell (Eds.), *Machine learning II* (pp. 571–589). Los Altos, CA: Morgan Kaufmann.

Edelman, G. (1987). *Neural darwinism.* New York: Basic Books.

Eilbert, J. L. (1980). *A hierarchical model of visual perception.* Unpublished dissertation, NCSU.

Eilbert, J. L. (1988). Axon shape as a basis for multinode functional units in a hierarchical neural model. *Journal of Theoretical Biology, 130,* 95–122.

Eilbert, J. L., & Salter, R. M. (1986). Modeling neural networks in Scheme. *Simulation, 46*(5), 193–199.

Eilbert, J. L., & Guez, A. (1987, June). Attentional states and behavior modes in a hierarchical neural network. *Proceedings of the First IEEE Conference on Neural Networks, VIII,* 121–130.

Geman, S. (1982). Almost sure stable oscillations in a large system of randomly coupled equations. *SIAM Journal of Applied Mathematics, 42*(4), 695–704.

Geschwind, N. (1982). Disorders of attention: a frontier in neurophysiology. *Philosophical Transactions by the Royal Society of London, B, 298,* 173–185.

Gibson, J. J. (1979). *The ecological approach to visual perception.* Boston, MA: Houghton-Mifflin.

Gould, J. L., & Gould, C. G. (1985). An animal's education. *The Sciences, 25*(4), 24–31.

Greeno, J. G. (1983). Conceptual entities. In D. Gentner & A. L. Stevens (Eds.), *Mental models* (pp. 227–252). Hillsdale, NJ: Erlbaum.

Grossberg, S. (1978). A theory of human memory: Self-organization and performance of motor codes, maps, and plans. In R. Rosen & F. M. Snell (Eds.), *Progress in theoretical biology* (pp. 235–374). New York: Academic Press.

Grossberg, S. (1987). *The adaptive brain.* Amsterdam: Elsevier/North-Holland.

Grossberg, S., & Mingolla, E. (1985). Neural dynamics of perceptual grouping: Textures, boundaries, and emergent segmentations. *Perception and Psychophysics, 38,* 141–171.

Guez, A. (1987, January). Neural networks can design neural networks. *Proceedings of the IEEE Conference on Intelligent Control.* Philadelphia, PA.

Guez, A., Eilbert, J. L., & Kam, M. (1988). Neuromorphic architecture for adaptive robot control. *IEEE Control Sys Mag., 8*(2), 22–25.

Guez, A., Kam, M., & Eilbert, J. L. (1989). Natural variables for the nodes of a neural network. *IEEE Transaction on Man, Systems, & Cybernetics, 19*(2), 409–414.

Guez, A., Protopopescu, V., & Barhen, J. (1987). On the stability, storage capacity and design of nonlinear continuous neural networks. *IEEE Man, Systems, & Cybernetics.*

Hawkins, R. D., & Kandel, E. R. (1984). Is there a cell-biological alphabet for simple forms of learning? *Psychological Review, 91,* 375–391.

Hebb, D. O. (1949). *The organization of behavior.* New York: Wiley.

Hirsch, M. W. (1989, June). Convergence in cascades of neural networks. *Proceedings of the International Joint Conference on Neural Networks* (pp. 207–208). Washington, DC.

Hirsch, H. V. B. & Spinelli, D. N. (1971). Modification of the distribution of receptive field orientation in cats by selective visual exposure during development. *Experimental Brain Research, 12,* 509–537.

Hofstadter, D. R. (1985). Who shoves whom around inside the careenium? In D. R. Hofstadter (Ed), *Metamagical themas.* New York: Basic.

Hopfield, J. J. (1982). Neural networks and physical systems with emergent collective computational abilities. *Proceedings of the National Academy of Sciences, USA, 79,* 2554–2558.

Hopfield, J. J. (1984). Neurons with graded response have collective computational properties like those of two-state neurons. *Proceedings of the National Academy of Sciences, USA, 81,* 3088–3092.

Hopfield, J. J., & Tank, D. W. (1985). 'Neural' computation of decision optimization problems. *Biological Cybernetics, 52,* 1–12.

Hubel, D. H., & Wiesel, T. W. (1977). Functional architecture of macque monkey visual cortex, *Proceedings of the Royal Society of London, B, 198,* 1–59.

Inversen, L. L. (1984). Amino acids and peptides: fast and slow chemical signals in the nervous system? *Proceedings of the Royal Society of London, B, 221,* 245–260.

Kahneman, D. (1973). *Attention and effort.* Englewood Cliffs, NJ: Prentice-Hall.

Kahneman, D., & Miller, D. T. (1986). Norm theory: Comparing reality to its alternatives. *Psychological Review, 93*(2), 136–153.

Kahneman, D., & Treisman, A. (1984). Changing views of automaticity and attention. In R. Parasuraman, R. Davies, & J. Beatty (Eds.), *Varieties of attention* (pp. 29–52). New York: Academic Press.

Kaplan, S., & Kaplan, R. (1982). *Cognition and the environment.* New York: Praeger.

Knapp, A. G., & Anderson, J. A. (1984). Theory of categorization based on distributed memory storage. *Journal of Experimental Psychology, 10*(4), 616–637.

Koch, C., & Ullman, S. (1985). Shifts in selective attention: Towards the underlying neural circuitry. *Human Neurobiology 4,* 219–227.

Kosko, B. (1986). Fuzzy cognitive maps. *International Journal of Man-Machine Studies, 24,* 65–75.

LaBarge, D. (1983). Automatic information processing: a review. In S. Dormic (Ed.), *Attention and performance* (Vol. 9, pp. 173–186). Hillsdale, NJ: Erlbaum.

Lee, W. A. (1984). Neuromotor synergies as a basis for coordinated intentional action. *Journal of Motor Behavior, 16*(2), 135–170.

Linsker, R. (1988). Self-organization in a perceptual network. *IEEE Computer, 21*(3), 105–117.

Luria, A. R. (1973). *The working brain*. New York: Penguin Psychology Series.

Lynch, G. (1985). *Synapses, circuits, and the beginnings of memory*. Cambridge, MA: MIT Press.

Lynch, G., Granger, R., Larson, J., & Baudry, M. (1989). Cortical encoding of memory: Hypotheses derived from analysis and simulation of physiological learning rules in anatomical strictures. In L. Nadel (Ed.), *Neural connections, mental computations*. Cambridge, MA: MIT Press.

Lynch, K. (1960). *The image of the city*. Cambridge, MA: MIT Press.

Maxwell, T., Giles, C. L., Lee, Y. C., & Chen, H. H. (1986). *Non-linear dynamics of artificial neural systems*. Paper presented at the Snowbird Conference, Utah.

Mountcastle, V. B. (1979). An organizing principle for cerebral function: The unit module and the distributed system. In F. O. Schmitt & F. G. Worden (Eds.), *The neurosciences: Fourth study program* (pp. 21–42). Cambridge, MA: The MIT Press.

Neves, D. M., & Anderson, J. R. (1981). Knowledge compilation: mechanisms for the automatization of cognitive skills. In J. R. Anderson (Ed.), *Cognitive skills and their acquisition* (pp. 47–84). Hillsdale, NJ: Erlbaum.

Newell, A., & Rosenbloom, P. S. (1981). Mechanisms of skill acquisition and the law of practice. In J. R. Anderson (Ed.), *Cognitive skills and their acquisition* (pp. 1–56). Hillsdale, NJ: Erlbaum.

Nestor, (1987). *Learning systems based on multiple neural networks*. Providence, RI: Nestor, Inc.

O'Keefe, J., & Nadel, L. (1978). *The hippocampus as a cognitive map*. Oxford, England: Clarendon Press.

Pribram, K. H., Nuwer, M., & Baron, R. J. (1974). The holographic hypothesis of memory structure. In D. H. Krantz (Ed.), *Contemporary developments in mathematical psychology: Measurement, psychophysics, and neural information processing* (Vol. 2, pp. 420–459). San Francisco, CA: W. H. Freeman.

Rosenblatt, F. (1961). *Principles of neurodynamics: Perceptrons and the theory of brain mechanisms*. Washington, DC: Spartan Books.

Rumelhart, D. E., Hinton, G. E., & Williams, R. J. (1986). Learning internal representations by error propagation. In D. E. Rumelhart & J. L. McClelland (Eds.), *Parallel distributed processing* (Vol. 1). Cambridge, MA: MIT Press.

Rumelhart, D. E. Smolensky, P., McClelland, J. L., & Hinton, G. E. (1986). Schemata and sequential thought processes in PDP models. In J. L. McClelland & D. E. Rumelhart (Eds.), *Parallel distributed processing* (Vol. 2). Cambridge, MA: MIT Press.

Schneider, W., & Shiffern, R. M. (1977). Controlled and automatic information processing: Detection, search, and attention. *Psychological Review, 84*(1), 1–66.

Schwartz, E. L. (1980). Computational anatomy and functional architecture of the striate cortex: a spatial-mapping approach to perceptual coding. *Vision Research, 20*, 645–670.

Selverston, A. I. (1985). *Model neural networks and behavior*. New York: Plenum.

Shepherd, G. (1984). *Neurobiology*. New York: Academic Press.

Shiffern, R. M. & Dumais, S. T. (1981). The development of automatism. In J. R. Anderson (Ed.), *Cognitive skills and their acquisition* (pp. 111–140). Hillsdale, NJ: Erlbaum.

Smith, E. E., & Medin, D. L. (1981). *Categories and concepts*. Cambridge, MA: Harvard University Press.
Sperling, G. (1963). A model for visual memory tasks. *Human Factors, 5*, 19–31.
Spinelli, D. N., & Jensen, F. E. (1979). The mirror of experience. *Science, 203*, 75–78.
Szentagothai, J. (1978). The neural network of the cerebral cortex: A functional interpretation. *Proceedings of the Royal Society of London, B, 201*, 219–248.
Tinbergen, N. (1958). *Curious naturalists*. Garden City, NY: The Natural History Library, Anchor Books.
Tolman, E. C. (1948). Cognitive maps in rats and men. *Psychological Review, 55*, 189–208.
Vidyasagar, M. (1980). Decomposition techniques for large-scale systems with non-additive interactions: Stability and stabilizability. *IEEE Transactions on Automatic Control, 25*(4), 773–779.
Widrow, B., & Stearns, S. D. (1985). *Adaptive signal processing*. Englewood Cliffs, NJ: Prentice Hall.
Winograd, T., & Flores, F. (1986). *Understanding computers and cognition*. Norwood, NJ: Ablex Publishing Corp.
Zeki, S. (1974). The mosaic organization of the visual cortex in the monkey. In R. Belloirs & E. G. Gray (Eds.), *Essays on the nervous system*. Oxford, England: Clarendon Press.

APPENDIX 1

$$\epsilon^i \frac{dx^i}{dt} = -A^i x^i + T^i g^i(x^i) + W^i h^i(\mathbf{Y}) + I^i \tag{1}$$

where

M is the number of Columns in the whole system.
N^i is the number of ShR nodes in the ith Column.
M^i is the number of LRC nodes in the ith Column.
x^i_j is the state of the jth ShR node in the ith Column.

$x^i = (x^i_1, x^i_2, \ldots, x^i_{N^i})^T$

$\mathbf{X} = (x^{1T}, x^{2T}, \ldots, x^{MT})^T$, and has dimension $\sum_{k=1}^{M} N^i$

y^i_j is the state of the jth LRC node in the ith Column.

$\mathbf{Y} = (y^{1T}, y^{2T}, \ldots, y^{MT})^T$, and has dimension $\sum_{k=1}^{M} M^i$

A^i_j is the decay rate of the jth ShR node

A^i a $N^i \times N^i$ diagonal matrix, with diagonal elements A^i_j

T^i_{jk} is the synaptic weight of the connection from ShR node k to j, both in Column i. The form of this matrix is retricted by lateral inhibition and by the symmetric distribution of interneuron axon terminations.

T^i is an $N^i \times N^i$ matrix, with elements T^i_{jk}

$g^i_j\,(x^i_k)$ is the transformation of postsynaptic potential (PSP) in the kth ShR node into a firing rate.

$$g^i(x^i) = (g^i_1(x^i_1),\ g^i_2(x^i_2),\ \ldots,\ g^i_{N^i}(x^i_{N^i}))^T$$

W^{ij}_{kl} is the synaptic weight of the connection from LRC node l in Column j to ShR node k in Column i. Only one LRC node in a column sends input to nodes in any other column, and the weight is the same for all ShR nodes in Column i; i.e., the weight is independent of k.

W^i is an Mi $\times$ M matrix with all rows identical.

${}^j h^i(y^j)$ is the transformation of the post-synaptic potential (PSP) of the LRC node in Column j into a firing rate that goes to all nodes in Column i.

$$h^i(Y) = [{}^1h^i(y^1),\ {}^2h^i(y^2),\ \ldots,\ {}^Mh^i(y^M)]^T$$

I^i_j is the input vector from the environment to the jth node. In most computations, it is assumed that external input varies slowly over the average time it takes the system to reach a steady state.

$$I^i = (I^i_1,\ I^i_2,\ \ldots,\ I^i_{N^i})^T$$

e^i is a scaling factor which gives the ShR level fast dynamics compared to the other hierarchical levels.

The equation governing the behavior of the LRC nodes is

$$\frac{dy^i}{dt} = -B^i y^i + V^i g^i(x^i) + W^i h^i(Y) \tag{2}$$

where the notation is the same as in Equation 1, and

B^i is an $M^i \times M^i$ diagonal matrix of decay rates.

V^i_{jk} the synaptic weight of the connection from ShR node k to the LRC node j, both in Column i. The form of this matrix is retricted by lateral inhibition and by the symmetric distribution of interneuron axon terminations.

V^i a $M^i \times M^i$ matrix, with elements V^i_{jk}

Note that the e^i at the front of Equation 1, but not Equation 2, means that activity on the ShR nodes changes much faster than the activity of LRC nodes. Also note that the output of a single column is identical for every node in a target column, although it varies for different columns.

4

Competitive Activation Mechanisms in Connectionist Models*

James A. Reggia
Granger Sutton
Sungzoon Cho
Department of Computer Science
University of Maryland
College Park, MD

1. INTRODUCTION

Recently, a new approach to producing "competitive" or inhibitory effects in connectionist models has been proposed (Reggia, 1987). Rather than implementing competitive/inhibitory interactions directly through explicit structural features (inhibitory connections) of a network, they are produced indirectly by the functional mechanism or rule used by nodes to control the spread of activation. With this approach the nodes in a network "compete" for any externally applied activation, and for this reason are said to use a *competitive activation mechanism*. Models using competitive activation mechanisms have a number of advantages over those using traditional methods; e.g., they require substantially fewer connections in some applications.

Initial computer simulations (Reggia, 1987) and mathematical analysis (Wang, Seidman, & Reggia, 1988) with small, simple networks using competitive activation mechanisms were encouraging and demonstrated the basic validity of this idea. However, this initial work did not provide any indication of whether such an approach could function meaningfully in the large, complex networks that might be encountered in real-world applications. In particular, two significant barriers to effective use of competitive activation mechanisms seemed evident initially. First, different versions of competitive activation mechanisms can exhibit quantitative and even qualitative differences in behavior. It is not obvious in general how one should go about devising a specific competitive activation mechanism for individual applications. Second, in contrast to more conventional activation mechanisms, no learning methods exist that have been studied in connectionist models which use a competitive activation mechanism.

---

* J. Reggia is also with the Institute for Advanced Computer Studies and the Dept. of Neurology at the University of Maryland. This work was supported by NSF Award IST-8451430, NASA Award NAG1-885, and by NIH Award NS-29414.

This chapter focuses on efforts to address these two issues. During the last 2 years we have studied a number of methods for deriving competitive activation mechanisms for use with associative networks relevant to cognitive science, artificial intelligence, and control applications. In this chapter some of the methodological concepts that have emerged in the context of these applications are presented. The material is divided into three sections. First, the basic idea of a competitive activation mechanism is described. Second, representative examples of deriving specific competitive activation mechanisms are presented. Two of these are described in some detail: a print-to-sound model in which a trial-and-error approach was used successfully, and a diagnostic hypothesis generator in which nonlinear optimization techniques were applied. The effectiveness of these two approaches to devising activation rules is confirmed by computer simulations which demonstrate that the activation mechanisms so derived perform well with complex networks of appreciable size. The third section describes initial work on formulating learning methods that work with competitive activation mechanisms. The chapter ends by describing some implications of this work and directions for further research.

2. COMPETITIVE INTERACTIONS IN CONNECTIONIST MODELS

In the following, each node n_i in the network of a connectionist model is viewed as having an activation level $a_i(t)$ at time t, and the pattern of activation over the entire network is represented as a time-varying vector $\mathbf{a} = (a_1, a_2, \ldots, a_n)$. Each node receives activation from other nodes over weighted connections, where weight w_{ij} designates the weight on the connection directed from node n_j to node n_i. Incoming activation over n_i's input connections as well as any externally applied input to node n_i forms a resultant input $in_i(t)$. Each node can be viewed as following an *activation rule/mechanism,* a local function/procedure which the node uses to update its activation level as a function of its input and current activation level.

Two nodes in a connectionist model are said to be *competitors* if the gain of one occurs at the expense of the other, i.e., if their functional relationships are inhibitory in nature. For example, models using continuous time and activation levels where the ith node follows an activation rule

$$\frac{da_i}{dt} = f_i(\mathbf{a}), \qquad (1)$$

can be said to involve *competitive interactions* between nodes i and j if $\partial f_i / \partial a_j < 0$ when $i \neq j$ (Grossberg, 1982; Hirsch, 1987). Note that this definition of competition indicates inhibitory interactions but says nothing about the underlying mechanisms involved in producing those inhibitory interactions.

It is critical to the following to appreciate that the *mechanism* by which competition (inhibitory interactions) occurs can vary from situation to situation. *Direct* or *antagonistic competition* occurs when entity i directly interacts with rival entity j in a fashion that suppresses j's activity (wrestling match, predator–prey relations). *Indirect allocational competition* occurs when two rivals require and/or consume the same limited resource, the consumption by one rival resulting in less for the other to consume (animal populations sharing a common food source, businesses selling in the same market). These two mechanisms for producing competition are not mutually exclusive.

Given the distinction between the antagonistic and allocational mechanisms that can underly competitive (inhibitory) interactions, one can inquire how previous connectionist modeling efforts have used these two mechanisms. To the authors' knowledge, all previous activation mechanisms developed in connectionist modeling have been based on the assumption that competitive/inhibitory effects during spread of activation are brought about solely by antagonistic mechanisms (Amari & Arbib, 1982; Feldman & Ballard, 1982; Grossberg, 1982; Reggia & Sutton, 1988). In other words, two "competing nodes" have direct inhibitory connections to one another. The inhibitory connections used in these models are often intended to produce a *winner-takes-all situation* in which an equilibrium is achieved with one node maximally activated and the other nodes having zero activation (e.g., Feldman & Ballard, 1982, p. 218).

As will be seen in subsequent sections of this chapter, many formulations of competitive activation mechanisms are possible. For illustrative convenience, we will assume that $a_k(t)$ and w_{ji} are restricted to the interval (0, 1) unless specifically noted otherwise (this restriction is *not* an essential property of a competitive activation mechanism). Typically, competitive activation mechanisms are implemented by letting the flow of activation from n_i to n_j be a time-varying function of a_j, the destination node activation level. As a specific example, the amount of activation $out_{ji}(t)$ flowing from node n_i to node n_j can be given by

$$out_{ji}(t) = \frac{a_j(t)\, w_{ji}}{\sum_k a_k(t) w_{ki}} \cdot a_i(t) \tag{2}$$

where the summation is over all nodes k to which node n_i sends connections. Here the output from node n_i going to node n_j depends, not only on a_i and w_{ji}, but also on receiving node n_j's activation level a_j (as well as the sum in the denominator). This approach to implementing competitive interactions can be contrasted with that used in more traditional connectionist models. For example, with a noncompetitive activation mechanism the value

$$out_{ji}(t) = w_{ji}\, a_i(t) \tag{3}$$

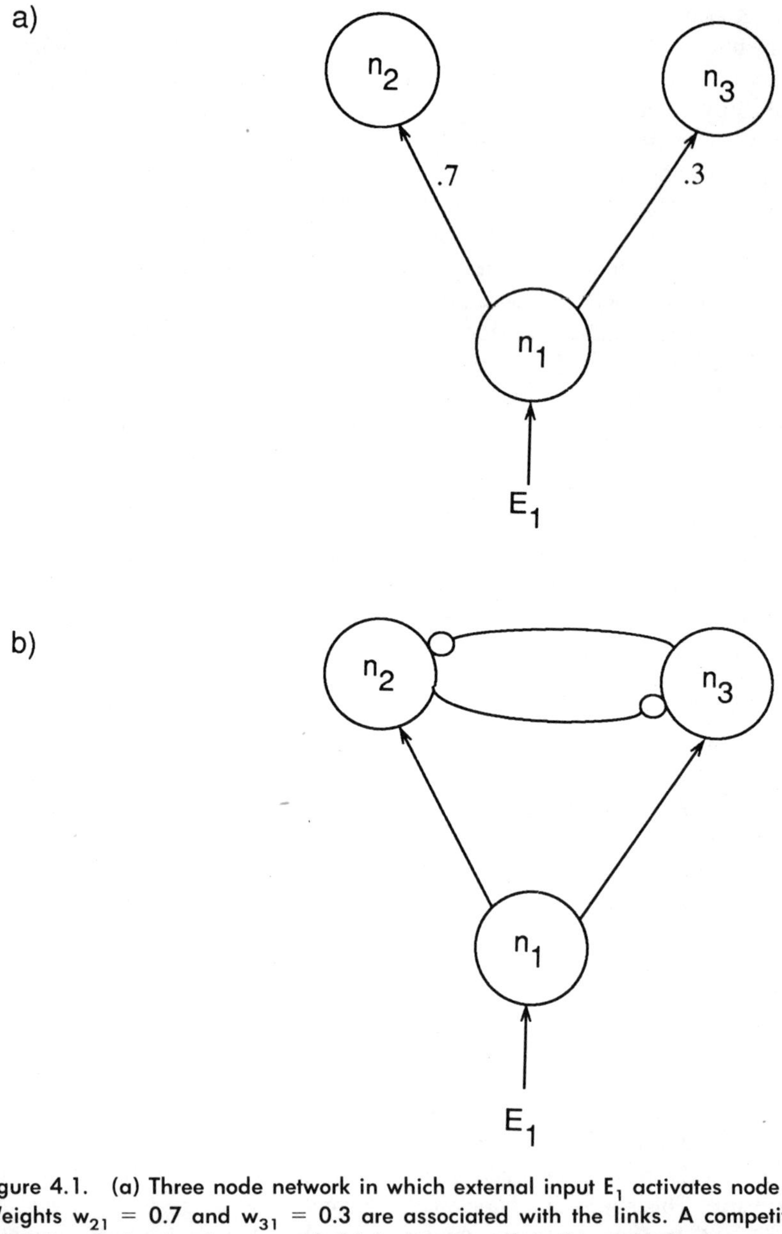

Figure 4.1. (a) Three node network in which external input E_1 activates node n_1. Weights $w_{21} = 0.7$ and $w_{31} = 0.3$ are associated with the links. A competitive activation mechanism is assumed. (b) Architecture of similar network when a more traditional noncompetitive activation mechanism is used. Note the inhibitory links (end with small circles) between n_2 and n_3.

Table 4.1. Node Activations Over Time

Time	a_1	a_2	a_3
0	0	0	0
0.25	0.39	0.045	0.017
2	0.72	0.449	0.027
5	0.85	0.700	0.007
10	0.92	0.831	0.000
20	0.96	0.910	0.000

might be used so that $out_{ji}(t)$ is not influenced by the activation $a_j(t)$ of the node n_j receiving node n_i's output.[1]

The dynamics of connectionist models using competitive activation mechanisms can be most easily appreciated from example simulations. Consider the simple network in Figure 1a; there are no inhibitory connections in this network. A single external input E_1 activates node n_1, which in turn connects to and activates nodes n_2 and n_3. Note the larger weight 0.7 on the connection from n_1 to n_2. Suppose that each node here follows the activation rule

$$\frac{da_i}{dt} = (in_i - a_i)(1 - a_i) \qquad (4)$$

where

$$in_1(t) = E_1(t),$$
$$in_2(t) = out_{21}(t),$$
$$in_3(t) = out_{31}(t),$$

and $out_{ji}(t)$ is given by Equation 2. Assume all $a_i(0) = 0.0$, and $E_1(t) = 1$, for $t > 0$. At $t = 0$ in this simulation, both the numerator and denominator in Equation 2 are 0. We define $out_{ji}(t) = w_{ji} \cdot a_i(t)$ to hold whenever this is the case. Numerical simulation of this system exhibits the behavior given in Table 4.1. Node n_1 quickly becomes activated. Initially, activation levels a_2 and a_3 both grow, but eventually a_2 approximates 1 and $a_3 \rightarrow 0$. This is an example of *winner-takes-all* or *choice* behavior in that an activation pattern over a set of nodes (n_2 and n_3) reaches equilibrium with one node fully activate and other nodes fully inactive.

Figure 4.1b shows a similar network that exhibits the same behavior when a traditional noncompetitive activation mechanism is used. The difference is that the two competing nodes n_2 and n_3 now have inhibitory connections to each other (indicated by connections with circular terminators). With this second network, as n_2 becomes more active than n_3, it directly suppresses activation of n_3 via its inhibitory connection ($w_{32} < 0$).

[1] All weights w_{ji} are taken to be dimensionless in this chapter as a matter of convenience. Units could be introduced via appropriate constants if desired.

Using competitive activation mechanisms rather than inhibitory links between competing nodes is desirable from the perspective of developing connectionist models directly from existing associative networks in artificial intelligence and cognitive science. Such networks do not incorporate inhibitory links, and in many cases it would be neither desirable nor feasible to introduce them. There are several reasons that this is the case. First, most connections/links in semantic networks correspond to empirical associations with at least theoretically measurable frequencies of occurrence. In contrast to this well-defined correspondence between model components (excitatory connections) and the entities being modeled (measurable associations), there is no generally recognized analogous real-world correspondence to inhibitory connections in AI/cognitive psychology theory. This is very different than the situation one encounters with connectionist models of neural circuitry in the brain (inhibitory connections between neurons are common).

Another reason for desiring to minimize inhibitory connections in networks is combinatorial. For example, if there are n nodes in a set of competing nodes and they must directly inhibit one another to produce a winner-takes-all phenomenon, then close to n^2 inhibitory connections would be required. For example, 1,000 nodes would require almost 1,000,000 inhibitory connections. (There are ways to minimize such connections without using competitive activation mechanisms requiring on the order of 3n connections, but their generality remains to be established.) Thus, scaling up to large networks while using explicit inhibitory links in this fashion would clearly require a large number of connections and large fanouts. Preliminary experiments on parallel computers suggest that a critical element in achieving speed-up in such a framework is the fanout of nodes (Tagamets & Reggia, 1989). This implies that a competition-based activation mechanism may have significant advantages over implementing competition directly via explicit inhibitory links, even on parallel architectures.

Furthermore, implementing direct competition via inhibitory links is at best problematic in situations where multiple simultaneous "winners" are desired (see diagnosis model below). If a set of competing nodes with direct, mutually inhibitory links tries to sustain multiple winners simultaneously, these winners will tend to extinguish each others' activations. Further, in some situations, two nodes may be considered to be in competition, while in other situations the same two nodes may not be competitors and may actually "cooperate" to formulate a solution to a problem (Peng & Reggia, 1989). Allocational competition appears to provide a clean solution for determining such relationships dynamically.

Finally, there is a fundamental difference that arises when a competitive rather than a noncompetitive activation mechanism is used. Consider a feedforward network composed of several layers of nodes and using a *non*competitive activation mechanism. In this case, output node activations cannot influence one another (they are not directly connected to each other in a feedforward-only network; e.g., n_2 and n_3 in Figure 1a). In contrast, with a competitive activation mechanism, even though a feedforward network is involved, activation levels of nodes in one layer are used in a retrograde fashion to guide the forward flow of activation from the preceding layer. This occurs because $out_{ji}(t)$ is a function of the destination node n_j's activation level. Thus, as the output nodes' activation levels stabilize, they have exerted a powerful indirect influence on each others values.

Initial simulations (Reggia, 1987) and theoretical analysis (Wang et al., 1988) with small, very simple networks demonstrated that the basic concept of a competitive activation mechanism is sound. Models using a suitable formulation of this approach generally reach equilibrium states where the network activation forms a circumscribed pattern. Clear cut, context-sensitive winner-takes-all behavior can be produced. For example, had there been an additional, very small input to n_3 in the earlier example (Figure 4.1a and Table 4.1), then node n_3 would have emerged as the "winner" in its competition with node n_2. It is in this sense that determination of a "winning node" is context sensitive. All of these features make competitive activation methods an attractive new connectionist modeling method.

3. DEVELOPING COMPETITIVE ACTIVATION METHODS FOR APPLICATIONS

For a specific application, it is not obvious a priori how to derive a high-performance competitive activation mechanism. Thus, to clarify further the properties of connectionist models using competitive activation mechanisms, and to extend the ideas involved, recent work has focused effort on developing the methods needed to apply this approach in larger, more complex networks. Two exploratory studies, representative of this effort, are now described. These two examples deal with print-to-sound conversion and diagnostic problem solving. The implementation described in each case was achieved using a general-purpose software environment called MIRRORS (D'Autrechy, Reggia, Sutton, & Goodall, 1988). This environment supports a very high-level, nonprocedural language for specifying nodes, their connections, and the details of specific experimental simulations. Some additional examples are mentioned briefly at the end of this section.

3.1. Print-to-Sound Transformation

Print-to-sound transformation (reading aloud a single printed word) was selected as the first large-scale test of competitive activation mechanisms, because it provides a challenging but relatively circumscribed problem. The print-to-sound transformation is challenging in that the existence of two hypothesized "routes" by which information flows through the underlying associative network implies that nodes serving as outputs for the model might receive conflicting information about what their activation levels should be. Such conflicts must be resolved by these nodes based on locally available information as node activations approach equilibrium. On the other hand, compared to many other cognitive tasks involving associative memory (e.g., natural language processing at the semantic level), the underlying network is relatively circumscribed; hence a fairly significant subset of it can be captured in a model. There is also a relatively large amount of empirically derived information upon which to base network structure, assignment of weights to connections, and analysis of simulation results.

In reading a word aloud, a sequence of printed graphemes is transformed into a sequence of spoken phonemes. A *grapheme* is defined to be one or a few printed characters serving as the written representation of a phoneme. For typographic convenience, phonemes will be represented by lower-case letters between slanted lines, graphemes by upper-case letters, and word/morphemes by double-quote marks. For example, the word "onion" consists of five graphemes, O N I O N, which correspond to five phonemes, /uh$^+$ n y uh$-$ n/.

The cognitive task of word naming or reading aloud is often thought of as information flow and transformation through two routes (Ellis, 1984). Figure 4.2 illustrates the two routes by which information flows as it is transformed from written to spoken form in our connectionist model. Circles are *sets* of nodes (G_i = graphemes, P_i = phonemes, W = words) and arrows are *sets* of connections in this figure. One route is the *grapheme–phoneme correspondence or GPC route* (bottom of Figure 4.2). Reading aloud via this route involves mapping graphemes onto their corresponding phonemes. The second route is the *lexical route* (top of Figure 4.2). Reading aloud via this route involves the mapping of graphemes onto morphemes/words via the visual word recognition system, and then onto their phonemic representation. The *dual-route model* of reading is strongly supported by evidence from empirical studies of both normal skilled readers and individuals with acquired dyslexia.

The network in the connectionist model of print-to-sound transformation uses a local representation of information. Nodes represent graphemes, phonemes, and words, while connections represent positively weighted associations between these entities. Running a simulation involves selective application of an externally supplied source of input to the appropriate grapheme nodes, thereby driving up their activation levels. Activation then spreads from grapheme nodes to phoneme nodes (via the GPC route), and from grapheme nodes to "hidden" word nodes to phoneme nodes (via the lexical route). The activation levels of phoneme nodes represent the network's output.

Since each word node in the network connects to multiple grapheme/phoneme nodes occurring in specific positions there are actually multiple copies or *instances* of grapheme and phoneme node sets in any situation. The exact number of instances of grapheme and phoneme node sets is determined by the number of graphemes that are designated as input. If a specific simulation involves the presentation of a sequence of n graphemes as input, this is implemented in the model by dynamically constructing n copies of the grapheme nodes prior to initiating the simulation. Each set of grapheme nodes corresponds to one input

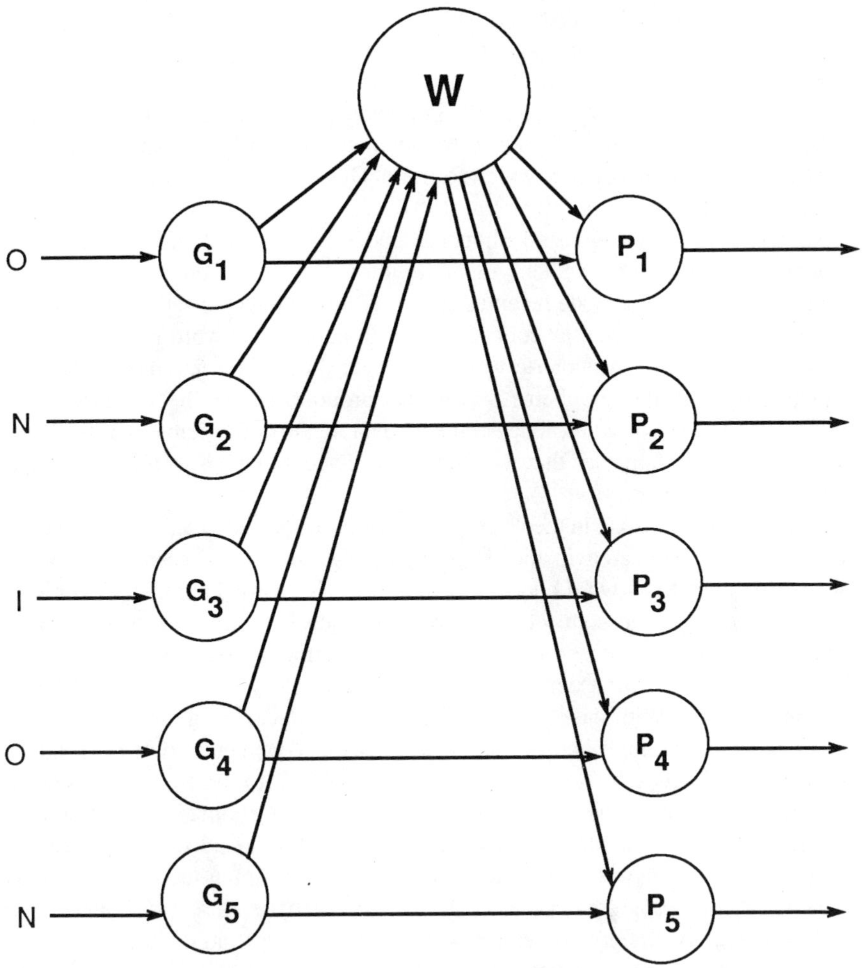

Figure 4.2. Structure of the network in the print-to-sound model. Each circle is a set of nodes (G_i = graphemes, P_i = phonemes, W = words). When the five graphemes of the word "onion" serve as input, there are five position-specific copies of each set of grapheme and phoneme nodes.

position, where positions are numbered from 1 (initial position) to n (final position). For each set of grapheme nodes so constructed, a corresponding set of phoneme nodes is generated (recall that a grapheme is defined as the orthographic representation of a single phoneme), along with all relevant connections from graphemes to phonemes in one position. Thus, for an input sequence of n graphemes, counting the set of word nodes there are 2n + 1 interconnected sets of nodes present. Figure 4.2 illustrates the specific example where the connectionist model is presented with five graphemes (O, N, I, O, and N) as input. The network contains five sets of grapheme nodes and five sets of phoneme nodes.

There are 48 phonemes and 168 graphemes represented as nodes in *each* position-specific set in the print-to-sound model's associative network. These nodes and their connections, which form the GPC route, are based on published data (Berndt, Reggia, & Mitchum, 1987). An example of a single grapheme node I and its connections to phoneme nodes in a path of the GPC route is illustrated in Figure 4.3. Each grapheme node also sends connections to word nodes. Each phoneme node receives additional incoming connections from other grapheme nodes, as well as connections from appropriate word nodes, that are not shown here. Each numeric weight in Figure 4.3 represents the conditional probability that the grapheme I will be pronounced as the corresponding phoneme. The set of word nodes contains over 1,000 two-syllable words with a wide range of frequencies that were not preselected on the basis of orthographic or phonetic structure.

Each grapheme node in the ith grapheme set is connected to all words in which that grapheme appeared in the ith position. The weight on each link from a grapheme node to its word nodes is 1/n, where n is the total number of words to which that grapheme connected. Each word node has forward connections to phoneme nodes in the appropriate position-specific phoneme sets. The word node for "onion," for example, has a connection to /y/ in the third set P_3 of phoneme nodes. With the exception of 17 words with common multiple pronunciations, a word node has one connection with a weight of 1.0 to a single phoneme node in each phoneme set (or no connections to some phoneme sets, if the number of phoneme sets exceeded the number of phonemes in the word).

In summary, the associative network in the print-to-sound model consists of numerous positively weighted, forward connections forming multiple, position-specific paths through two routes (Figure 4.2). There are no reverse connections (phonemes to words or graphemes, words to graphemes), no inhibitory connections, and no connections between any two phonemes, any two graphemes, or any two words. The complete network involved in a simulation is relatively large. For example, for the input graphemes O N I O N, there are a total of 2,110 nodes (5 times 168 grapheme nodes, plus 5 times 48 phoneme nodes, plus 1,030 word nodes) and roughly 12,000 forward connections. The use of a competitive activation mechanism, however, avoids the need for more than a million lateral inhibitory connections that would normally be required to produce winner-take-all behavior among word nodes and among each position-specific set of phoneme nodes.

The method used to derive the competitive activation mechanism for the print-to-sound model was a computer-assisted, heuristic search process that can be characterized as follows. Starting with a small prototype network and versions of equations 1 and 2 described by Reggia (1987), a number of trial simulations were

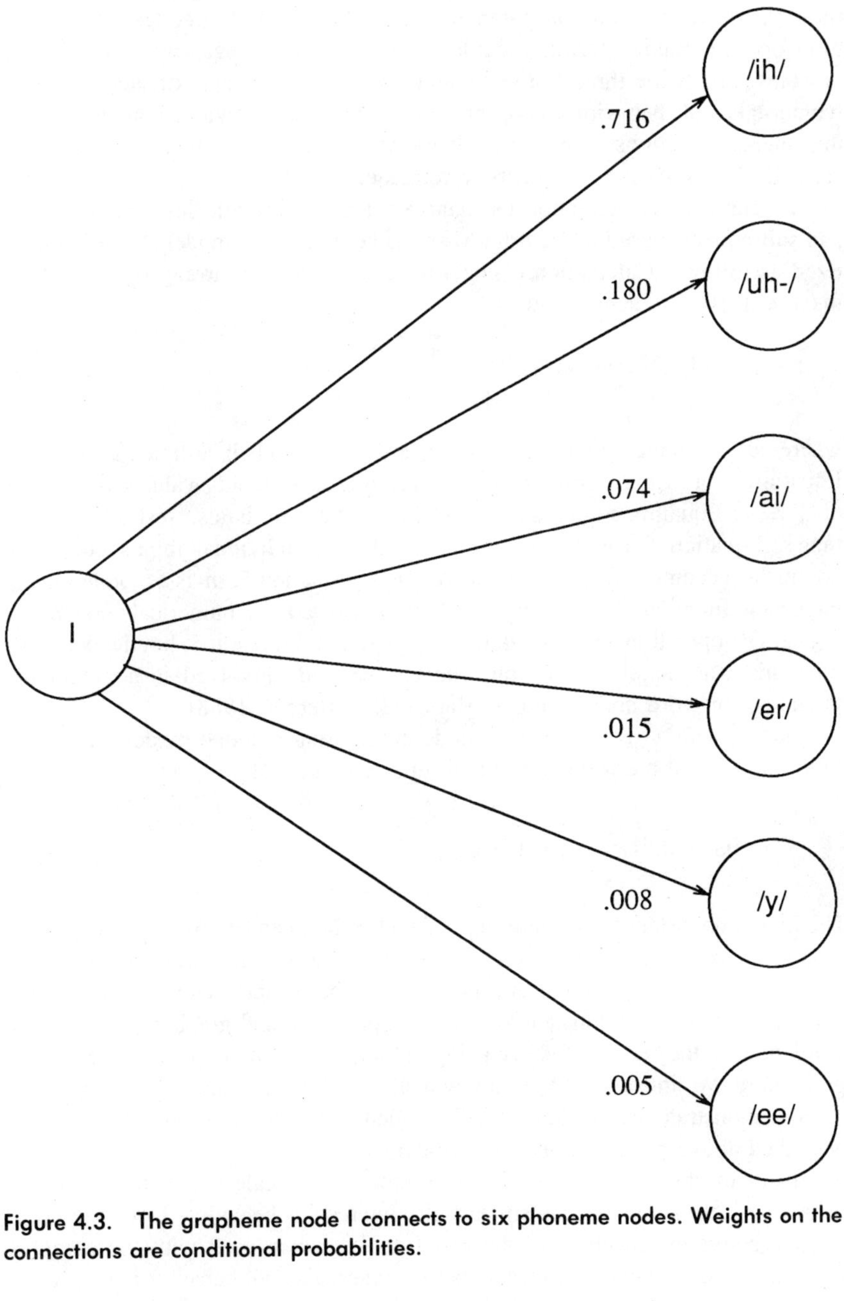

Figure 4.3. The grapheme node I connects to six phoneme nodes. Weights on the connections are conditional probabilities.

run. With each trial, variations to the activation mechanism equations were made (new factor added, constant parameter altered, etc.), and three test cases were run (input graphemes forming regularly spelled word, irregularly spelled word, or nonword). If the three test simulations more closely approximated a correct winner-takes-all behavior among phoneme nodes than previous equations, then the altered equations were kept; otherwise, the changed equations were discarded. No timing measurements were made.

The competitive activation mechanisms derived through this search process and subsequently used in the print-to-sound connectionist model can be summarized as follows. Calculation of $in_i(t)$ for each node n_i is arranged so that $0 \leq in_i(t) \leq 1$. This is achieved using

$$in_i(t) = 1 - \prod_k (1 - out_{ik}(t)) \tag{5}$$

where $out_{ik}(t)$ is the output from node n_k arriving at node n_i at time t as given by Equation 2, or is an external input to n_i. As long as each out_{ik} value satisfies $0 \leq out_{ik} \leq 1$, Equation 5 guarantees that the resultant in_i is also restricted to this range. Equation 5 can be viewed as combining individual inputs out_{ik} in a nonlinear, accumulative fashion. According to Equation 5, in_i is a monotonically increasing function of every out_{ik}, and can be viewed as a numerical version of a logical OR operation. Input to all nodes is based on Equation 5, but the details of how this was done depends on whether the node involved is a grapheme, phoneme, or word node [Reggia, Marsland, & Berndt, 1988].

Starting with $a_i(0) = 0.0$, each node in the print-to-sound model uses Equation 2 and 5 and the following rule to update its activation level:

$$\frac{da_i}{dt} = k_i \cdot [in_i - 2a_i (1 - in_i)] (1 - a_i). \tag{6}$$

The first nonconstant factor here, $in_i - 2a_i (1 - in_i)$, can be positive or negative. This factor causes a_i to increase whenever $in_i > 2a_i(1 - in_i)$, to decrease whenever $in_i < 2a_i(1 - in_i)$, and insures that $a_i \geq 0$. The second factor insures 1.0 as a maximum value. The constant k_i is 1.0 for phoneme and grapheme nodes. For word nodes, the value of k_i is a logarithmic function of p_i, a node's prior probability. We introduced k_i to allow analysis of word frequency effects.

To demonstrate that the heuristically guided, computer-assisted search process described above produced an effective competitive activation mechanism, it is necessary to show that the resultant complete, full-scale connectionist model using this activation mechanism exhibits interesting behavior. Does the competitive activation mechanism described above, when used with the complex print-to-sound network, produce suitable winner-takes-all behavior among word nodes and phoneme nodes in the absence of lateral inhibitory connections? In particular, it was not obvious a priori that competitive activation mechanisms could work well in the context of conflicting input signals to phoneme nodes arriving over two separate routes.

A single brief example of a representative simulation with the print-to-sound model is given here to illustrate its ability to activate correctly word and phoneme nodes with a sharply defined winner-takes-all performance. The sequence of five graphemes, O N I O N, representing an irregular word, serves as input to the model. Table 4.2 gives activation levels as a function of time for selected nodes in the network. The symbol "– " means "inactive" ($a_i < .001$) and the symbol "****" means saturated" ($a_i > .99$). Each 10 iterations (first column) represents one unit of simulated time.

Grapheme nodes quickly become saturated (second column). While a fair number of word nodes are activated early in the simulation, activation levels are given for only the target word "onion" and one of its orthographic neighbors, "union," which has four of five graphemes in common with the target word. These are the most highly activated word nodes during this simulation. Early in the simulation, the node representing the orthographic neighbor "union" is *more* activated than the node for "onion." However, eventually "onion" dominates and becomes fully activated, while activation of all other word nodes (both those shown here and all others) dies out. The clear-cut winner-takes-all behavior arises completely through allocational competition, with "onion" eventually dominating because of its perfect match with the input graphemes in this case. The larger early activation of the node representing the orthographic neighbor "union" arises primarily as a word frequency effect.

The rightmost columns in Table 4.2 illustrate activation levels of selected phoneme nodes. Allocational competition results in clear-cut, winner-takes-all activation of exactly those phoneme nodes representing the correct pronunciation

Table 4.2. Example Simulation with Print-to-Sound Model

		Words		Phonemes		
Iterations	Grapheme	"onion"	"union"	$/ih/_3$	$/y/_3$	$/n/_5$
0	—	—	—	—	—	—
10	.651	.063	.134	.001	—	.029
20	.878	.211	.164	.001	—	.166
30	.958	.383	.097	—	—	.360
40	****	.657	.023	—	.253	.613
50	****	.884	.002	—	.658	.803
60	****	.967	—	—	.875	.942
70	****	****	—	—	.956	.979
80	****	****	—	—	.985	****
90	****	****	—	—	****	****

of the word "onion." Activation of phoneme nodes is slower than that of word nodes because, especially early on, their activation depends on receiving significant input from *both* the lexical and GPC routes. The rightmost column illustrates the mapping of grapheme N_5 to phoneme $/n/_5$ in the fifth position. In this case, the GPC route connection $N_5 \rightarrow /n/_5$ in the final position has the large weight .975. Further, the most highly active word nodes ("onion" and "union") both have a $/n/_5$ in their phonemic realization. Thus, $/n/_5$ receives reinforcing input simultaneously from the lexical and GPC routes, and rapidly activates with little significant competition. In contrast, in the third position grapheme I_3 connects to six phonemes (Figure 4.3). Activation levels for two of these phonemes, $/ih/_3$ and $/y/_3$, are given in Table 4.2. Weights on the GPC route connections are .716 for $I_3 \rightarrow /ih/_3$ and .008 for $I_3 \rightarrow /y/_3$, the latter being the correct phonemic realization of I_3 in "onion." The very low weight on the GPC connection to $/y/_3$ and support for $/ih/_3$ from the word route (e.g., from "prison," "exist," etc., in this case) result in the slow activation of $/y/_3$ relative to $/n/_5$; see Table 2. However, a clean winner-takes-all activation of $/y/_3$ still eventually occurs.

To examine word frequency and regularity effects on the model's performance, data consisting of four sets of words with 16 words per set were used to test the model (Reggia et al., 1988). Words for each of these sets were selected from those in the associative network's lexicon based on word frequency (high vs. low) and regularity (very regular vs. very irregular). In all 64 runs where a word contained in the model's lexicon was introduced as input, the correct set of phonemes eventually attained a 1.0 activation level, and all remaining phoneme nodes in each of the phoneme sets had a 0.0 activation level. Thus, clear-cut winner-takes-all behavior for the correct phoneme node always occurred with these simulations in a fashion similar to that demonstrated with "onion" above (Table 4.2). Measurements were recorded with the print-to-sound model of the time $t_{.5}$ required for the correct set of phoneme nodes in each of the 64 words to attain a 0.50 activation level. These data were averaged for the 16 words in each data set and are given in columns 3–4 of Table 4.3 for each of the four sets of test words where k_i is based on word frequency. Phonemes for low-frequency irregular words had a delayed activation rate compared to phonemes in the other three sets of words.

The performance of the print-to-sound model was also tested using nonwords

Table 4.3. Simulation Results (Print-to-Sound Model) $t_{.5} \pm$ sd

Word Group	n	phonemes	word
1. High Freq. Reg.	16	27.9 ± 0.73	18.8 ± 1.29
2. High Freq. Irreg.	16	30.6 ± 2.39	18.9 ± .89
3. Low Freq. Reg.	16	33.3 ± 2.50	26.1 ± 4.06
4. Low Freq. Irreg.	16	46.7 ± 9.45	35.3 ± 14.27
5. Non-Words	10	66.6 ± 12.55	NA

as input. The set of nonwords consisted of arbitrarily selected, 2-syllable words which were not contained in the model's lexicon. For 10 nonwords for which winner-takes-all behavior was attained for all phonemes, the mean $t_{.5}$ value for phonemes was 66.6 (see bottom row, Table 3). This was a significantly greater $t_{.5}$ value than for the four sets of test words.

These results are qualitatively similar to empirical results with normal readers described in the literature. In research measuring the time taken for normal subjects to read words aloud (pronunciation latency), it has been found, in general, that words with regular pronunciations can be read faster than irregular words. Further, this effect of regularity on pronunciation latency is detectable only for words of low frequency. High-frequency words, whether regular or irregular, are pronounced uniformly quickly relative to low-frequency words. Thus, not only does this activation rule produce clear cut "winner-takes-all" behavior, but it also produces pronunciation latencies similar to those seen with adult readers (Reggia et al., 1988).

3.2. Diagnostic Hypothesis Generation

Several probabilistically oriented causal models have been developed during the past few years for diagnostic problem solving in situations where multiple disorders may occur simultaneously (Peng & Reggia, 1987, 1989). In these models disorders and manifestations are connected by causal links associated with probabilities representing the strengths of the causal associations. A hypothesis, consisting of one or more disorders with the highest posterior probability for the given set of manifestations (findings), is typically taken as the optimal problem solution. Conventional sequential search approaches in AI that solve diagnostic problems formulated in this fashion suffer from combinatorial explosion. We recently postulated that a globally optimal diagnostic explanation (set of disorders) could be approximated by a connectionist model using a causal network, if a suitable competitive activation mechanism could be identified (Peng & Reggia, 1989).

The diagnostic inference process whose computation is carried out by the connectionist model is based on a formalization of the causal and probabilistic associative knowledge underlying diagnostic problem solving. The particular formulation we use is called *parsimonious covering theory* (Reggia, Nau, Wang, & Peng, 1985). In parsimonious covering theory there is a set of disorders D, a set of manifestations M, and a relation C representing the causal associations between disorders and manifestations (see Figure 4.4). Saying that disorder d_i may cause manifestation m_j corresponds to a link in Figure 4.4. A subset of M, denoted M^+, represents the subset of all manifestations that are present, while $M^- = M - M^+$ represents the subset of all manifestations assumed to be absent. Based on the relation C, two sets, effects(d_i) and causes(m_j), are defined

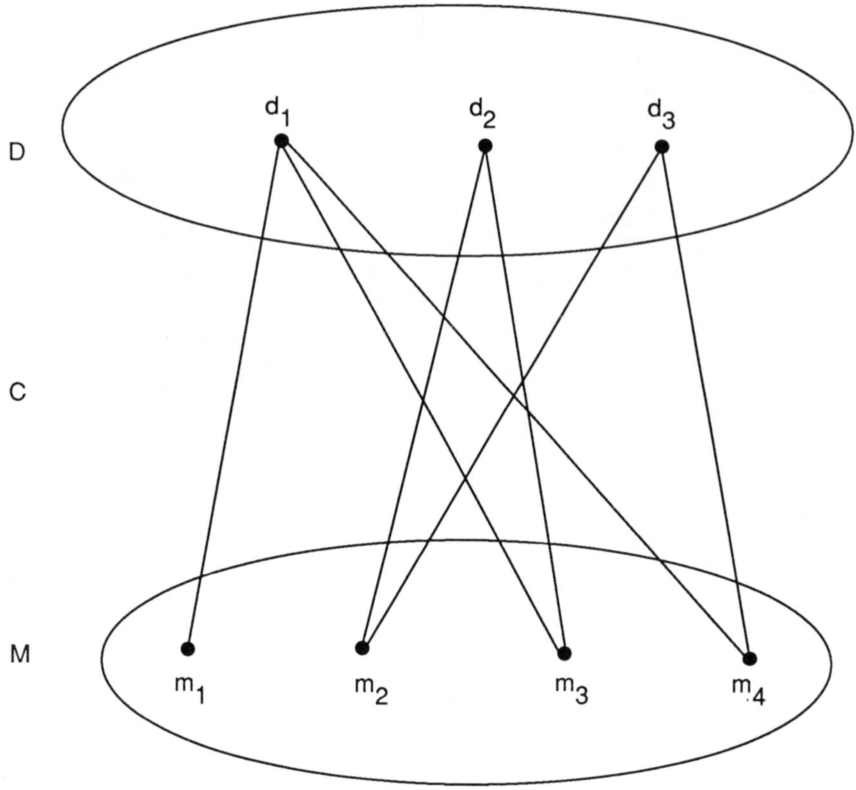

Figure 4.4. Two-layer diagnostic problem. The set D represents disorders, M represents manifestations, and C represents the causal associations between them.

for each $d_i \epsilon$ D and each $m_j \epsilon$ M, respectively: effects(d_i) = {m_j| d_i causes m_j} and causes(m_j) = {d_i| d_i causes m_j}. Intuitively, effects(d_i) are all manifestations that d_i can cause, and causes(m_j) are all disorders that can cause m_j. A set of disorders D_I is called a *cover* of the given M^+ if it is a set of disorders which, when present, could cause or account for all of the manifestations in M^+. A set of disorders D_I is said to be a *hypothesis* (or *explanation*) if (a) D_I is a cover of M^+, and (b) D_I is parsimonious. A number of criteria exist for what makes a set D_I parsimonious (Peng & Reggia, 1987; Reggia et al., 1985); we will not consider those criteria here.

The causal network in parsimonious covering theory can be augmented with relevant probabilities (Peng & Reggia, 1987). Each $d_i \epsilon$ D is associated with a number $p_i \epsilon$ (0, 1), representing its prior probability. Each causal link, such as that between disorder d_i and manifestation m_j is associated with a number $c_{ij} \epsilon$ (0, 1), the *causal strength* from d_i to m_j, representing how frequently d_i causes m_j. In other words, $c_{ij} = P(d_i \text{ causes } m_j \mid d_i)$. If there is no causal link between d_i and m_j, then c_{ij} is assumed to be zero. It is assumed that the disorders d_i are independent of each other, that whenever d_i occurs, it always causes m_j with the same probability c_{ij}, and that no manifestation can be present without being caused by some disorder. Based on these assumptions, a "relative likelihood measure" for a hypothesis D_I given M^+ can be derived according to Bayes' Theorem (Peng & Reggia, 1987). This measure is

$$L(D_I, M^+) = \prod_{m_j \in M^+} [1 - \prod_{d_i \in D_I} (1 - c_{ij})] \cdot \prod_{m_l \in M^-} \prod_{d_i \in D_I} (1 - c_{il}) \cdot \prod_{d_i \in D_I} \frac{p_i}{1 - p_i} \quad (7)$$

The first product here, over all present manifestations M^+, can be thought of as a weight reflecting how likely D_I is to cause the manifestations given in M^+; the second product can be thought of as a weight based on expected but absent manifestations (M^-); and the third product represents a weight based on prior probabilities of disorders in D_I. The relative likelihood $L(D_I, M^+)$ calculated in Equation 7 differs from the posterior probability $P(D_I \mid M^+)$ calculated with Bayes's Theorem only by a constant.

To solve a diagnostic problem means to identify one or more most probable diagnostic hypotheses with the highest relative likelihood (L value) among all possible hypotheses. Since disorders are assumed to occur independently of one another, any combination of disorders is possible. Provably correct problem-solving methods have been developed for this task using search programs cast within the traditional symbol-processing framework of AI. However, the potential search space for a solution is generally extremely large (i.e., $2^{|D|}$) and thus, as noted earlier, diagnostic problem solving in this formulation is combinatorially difficult.

A probabilistic causal network in parsimonious covering theory (e.g., Figure 4.4) can be used directly as a connectionist model network: disorders D and manifestations M are represented by two sets of nodes, and causal relation C is represented by the set of weighted links connecting these nodes. There are no inhibitory or intraset links. In formulating a diagnostic problem as a connectionist model, each disorder node d_i has an activation level at time t during the computation, denoted as $d_i(t) \in (0, 1)$, which serves as a measure of confirmation. Each manifestation node m_j has an activation level $m_j(t) \in (0, 1)$. Initially, $d_i(0) = p_i$. When a simulation equilibrates with $d_i(t) \approx 1.0$ at time t, the disorder d_i is confirmed to be occurring (or is said to be a "winner") and thus becomes an element of the solution; when $d_i(t) \approx 0.0$ then d_i is disconfirmed or rejected. Each manifestation node m_j is marked as to whether it is present ($m_j \in M^+$) or absent ($m_j \in M^-$). This marking represents the external input to the connectionist network.

Each causal link (connection) is associated with a constant weight equal to the appropriate causal strength c_{ij} which, during a computation, can be accessed solely by the two nodes d_i and m_j. Note that all weights c_{ij} are positive or excitatory. For each $m_j \in M^+$, its neighboring nodes (nodes in causes(m_j)) can be viewed as competing with each other for activation. Processing continues until equilibrium is reached at time t_e. If the model converges on a set of winners, i.e., for each d_i, $d_i(t_e)$ approximates either 1 or 0, then the set of disorders $D_S = \{d_i | d_i(t_e) \approx 1\}$ is taken to be the connectionist model's problem solution. In other words, the connectionist model derives D_S as its candidate for the most probable cover D^+ of the given features M^+.

The crucial point here is that a set of disorders D_S is to be derived through the concurrent *local* interactions occurring in the connectionist model, where D_S represents a hypothesis about the identity of the *globally* optimal set of disorders D^+ as determined by the likelihood measure (Equation 7). Since each node's processing is driven solely by local information, it is not guaranteed a priori that the resultant locally optimal solution will correspond to a globally optimal solution or even to a set of multiple winners.

The competitive activation mechanism used, outlined below, was derived by decomposing the formula for identifying a globally Bayesian-optimal set of disorders (Equation 7) into local rules used by each node to update its activation level (Peng & Reggia, 1989). This was done in three steps. First, Equation 7 was converted into a continuous function of all disorder node activation levels. Second, this objective function was partially localized and made a function $q_i(d_i(t))$ of a single disorder's activation level, $d_i(t)$. Third, the input $in_i(t)$ to disorder node d_i was derived based on the ratio $q_i(1)/q_i(0)$. This ratio is a completely local computation and thus suitable for use in a connectionist model. Using this ratio to determine input is based on the rationale that we wish to derive whichever of $d_i(t) = 1$ or $d_i(t) = 0$ will maximize q_i under the assumption that all other $d_k(t)$ are fixed. Further details can be found in Peng and Reggia (1989); the resultant activation mechanism is described below.

At the beginning of a simulation, the manifestation nodes are separated into two subsets referred to as M^+ and M^-, manifestations which are present and those which are absent, respectively. The influence of M^- nodes and prior probabilities on disorder activations is a constant K_i, which is therefore computed once for each disorder node d_i at the beginning of a simulation. The nodes which continuously participate in a simulation's computations consist of the manifestation nodes in M^+ and all of the disorder nodes. Assuming a discrete representation of time, let $d_i(t)$ be the activation level of node d_i at time t, and $m_j(t)$ be the activation level of node m_j at time t. Both of these quantities lie between 0.0 and 1.0, inclusive. The manifestation nodes in M^+ are updated using the activation rule

$$m_j(t) = 1 - \prod_{d_i \in \text{causes}(m_j)} (1 - c_{ij} d_i(t-1)) \tag{8}$$

(Compare with Equation 5.) At the start of a simulation, disorder node activations are initialized to the values of their respective estimated prior probabilities ($d_i(0) = p_i$ for all disorders). Activation values for manifestation nodes are computed at each iteration using Equation 8, and for disorder nodes using the sigmoid function

$$d_i(t) = \frac{1}{1 + e^{-in_i(t)/T(t)}}. \tag{9}$$

Here T(t) is a control parameter analogous to an annealing temperature in simulated annealing systems. Parameter T is started at an initial value T_0 and progressively decreased. The variation of the control parameter T(t) for the connectionist model is of the form $T(0) = T_0$, and $T(t) = \delta * T(t - 1)$, where $0 < \delta < 1$. The value $in_i(t)$ is determined by the rule

$$in_i(t) = K_i \cdot \prod_{m_j \in M_i^+} \left(1 + c_{ij} \frac{1 - m_j(t)}{m_j(t) - c_{ij} d_i(t-1)}\right) - 1 \tag{10}$$

where $M_i^+ = M^+ \cap \text{effects}(d_i)$. Note that Equations 8–10 are all based on information locally available to the node doing the computation.

To see how competition plays a role in this computation, note that by Equation 8 we can rewrite Equation 10 as

$$in_i(t) = \prod_{m_j \in M_i^+} \left[1 + \frac{c_{ij}}{\dfrac{1}{\prod\limits_{\substack{d_k \in \text{causes}(m_j) \\ d_k \neq d_i}} (1 - c_{kj} d_k)} - 1}\right] \cdot K_i - 1.$$

where variable t has been omitted for brevity. This equation shows that the ith disorder's input, in_i, will tend to decrease if activation d_k ($k \neq i$) of some other disorder in causes(M_i^+) increases, and in_i will tend to increase if d_k decreases. In this sense, the ith disorder competes with all other disorders in causes(M_i^+), and whether d_i should increase or decrease depends on this competition as well as the constant K_i. (For further analysis and discussion of this issue, see Wald, Farach, Tagamets, and Reggia, 1989.)

To show that the activation mechanism derived in the above fashion is effective, it was first studied using three small, abstract networks having randomly generated nodes and connections (Peng & Reggia, 1989). Each network had 10 manifestations, 10 disorders, and a maximum of 40 connections (causal associations) between individual disorders and their manifestations. Each of the 2^{10}

possible subsets of manifestations was used as M^+ in testing the resultant connectionist model. These simulations showed that 87% of the time the connectionist model successfully activated as D_s the globally most probable *set* of disorders D^+ when a set of manifestations M^+ was activated. As with the print-to-sound model, clear-cut winners ($d_i = 1$) and losers ($d_i = 0$) occurred. If partial resettling was done (a few repeat simulations during which each initially activated disorder is clamped off in turn and the altered set of activated disorders examined), accuracy rose to 99%. While encouraging, these initial simulations were limited by the small size and the artificial nature of the networks used (i.e., randomly generated associations and weights).

To examine whether this specific formulation of a competitive activation mechanism for diagnostic problem solving scales up to larger and more realistic networks, a substantially larger network having 56 manifestations, 26 disorders, and 384 causal links in a medical domain was implemented (Wald et al., 1989). On first thought, this network may not seem impressive, but it should be understood that the potential hypothesis space involved with such a network is enormous compared to that of the previous simulations. A network with 10 disorders represents $2^{10} = 1{,}024$ possible diagnostic hypothesis; in contrast a network with 26 disorders represents $2^{26} = 67{,}108{,}864$ possible hypotheses. In addition, this network is based on a real diagnostic application. The network structure (causal associations) and connection weights were provided by physicians and were not randomly generated. As a result, the connectionist model used in this experimental study was not only larger, bu also more realistically structured than the previous ones.

In attempting to scale up the diagnostic model, it was observed that frequently the system failed to converge on a problem solution and instead began to oscillate. While some oscillations had occurred in the earlier study, this problem had been overcome by increasing the initial value of the control parameter T (Peng & Reggia, 1989). Attempts to correct the undesirable oscillatory behavior in the larger network with a similar approach failed. An analysis was therefore undertaken to establish why oscillations occurred and, in particular, how the annealing schedule might be altered to improve performance. This analysis suggested two conclusions (Wald et al., 1989). First, as long as T_0, the initial T value, is large enough so that simulations begin outside a critical period when decisions are made, the value of T_0 should not matter, except in a random way. Second, by increasing δ, there should be a greater chance of disorders winning and suppressing other disorders during the critical period. Further, it is possible to estimate an expected T value for the critical period. Once one has an estimate for this critical value T_c, a value for T_0 can be calculated prior to starting a simulation by deciding how many ticks to start before the critical point.

Table 4 illustrates the kinds of results one obtains using the medical causal network and the above methodology. Each of 50 test cases was run with $T_0 = 1.0$, well above T_c, and with different δ values. Many simulations oscillated at δ

Table 4.4. Simulations with Varying δ (T_0 = 1.0; 50 test cases)

δ	Number (%) Reaching Equilibrium	Number (%) Deriving Most Probable Hypothesis	Number (%) Deriving One of Top Three Hypotheses
.5	7 (14%)	7 (14%)	7 (14%)
.7	22 (44%)	17 (34%)	20 (40%)
.8	28 (56%)	24 (48%)	28 (56%)
.9	41 (82%)	33 (66%)	37 (74%)
.95	50 (100%)	37 (74%)	45 (90%)
.99	50 (100%)	38 (76%)	46 (92%)

= 0.5 and none at δ = 0.99 (Table 4.4). Once δ was increased to 0.95, every simulation reached a stable equilibrium. For all simulations that stabilized at any δ value, a clear cut set of winners was identified (i.e., all d_i values were 0.0 or 1.0 and not in between), and the set of disorders with $d_i \approx 1.0$ was always a cover for M^+. Without using resetting, roughly 90% of simulations produced one of the three globally optimal (most probable) diagnostic hypotheses (Table 4.4).

3.3. Other Applications

A number of other applications of competitive activation mechanisms have been developed, and we mention some of these here. One problem that has been studied is tracking and photographing designated targets with cameras on a spacecraft (Whitfield, Goodall, & Reggia, 1989). The scenario, simplified from real life, involves three mobile cameras that are available to photograph designated locations as the spacecraft passes over them. The problem to be solved is for the cameras to move so as to track incoming target locations; the cameras are to automatically position themselves to take a photograph just before the targets pass under the spacecraft. The cameras "compete" for targets in determining which camera is assigned to each oncoming photographic target, and a competition-based activation mechanism is used to implement this competition. An initial set of experimental tests has been done (Whitfield et al., 1989). Photographic targets were randomly generated at varying target densities. In simulations with target densities from 1% to 50% of possible locations, the percentage of targets photographed varied from 100% to 88%. When the model was "damaged" by deleting a significant number of nodes, performance was mildly degraded, but in general it showed remarkable fault tolerance. Subsequent, more challenging experimental tests also gave good results (Goodall & Reggia, 1990).

This research demonstrated for the first time that competitive activation mechanisms have potential applications to real-time control systems.

Another problem that has been studied is the vertex covering problem. Given an arbitrary graph, the goal is to identify a minimum size set of vertices that will cover all of its edges. A competitive activation mechanism was developed for solving such problems and tested experimentally using 80 randomly generated graphs of differing sizes (Peng, 1989). The connectionist model identified a minimum vertex set in about two-thirds of these problems. This was significantly better than a standard sequential algorithm ("greedy algorithm") performed against the same test data.

A third application that is being studied is optimal scheduling of communications between satellites and ground antennae (Bourret, Goodall, & Samuelides, 1989). As low-level satellites pass over a ground antenna, there is a short time interval during which they can transmit information. When several satellites and several antennae are involved, optimally determining a communication schedule involving several constraints (amount of information that must be sent, satellites cannot share antennae, etc.) is a difficult problem. A connectionist model using competitive activation methods was tested on limited examples and provided "proof of concept," but much work is needed to further analyze and test this approach.

4. LEARNING

As noted in the *Introduction* to this chapter, a second barrier to more widespread use of competitive activation mechanisms is that no learning methods have been developed for them. This is an important issue since adaptability is one of the major strengths of connectionist modeling technology. For this reason, we have recently been developing and studying learning methods for use with competitive activation mechanisms. Here, one aspect of this work involving *competitive learning* is described (Sutton, Reggia, & Maisog, 1989).

Competitive learning is an unsupervised learning rule which groups input patterns into classes based on the patterns' structure (Rumelhart & Zipser, 1986; Grossberg, 1987). The basic competitive learning network is a two-layer, feedforward network. Every input node connects to every output node. The set of weights on the incoming connections to an output node is its weight vector, and a network classifies an input vector (or pattern, i.e., the ordered set of activation levels of nodes in the input layer) by its similarity to the weight vector associated with each output node. The output node with the weight vector most similar to a given input vector (judged by the inner product) is said to "win" the competition for that input vector. The winning output node's weight vector is then adjusted to be even more similar to the input vector, so that the winning node is more likely to win that input vector the next time it appears. Competitive learning, by adjusting an output node's weight vector to be similar to all of the input vectors for which the output node wins, creates weight vectors which serve as prototypes for classes of input vectors.

Competitive learning has been implemented and studied with competitive activation mechanisms using the specific activation rule for output node j of

$$a_j(t + 1) = in_j(t) = \sum_i out_{ji}(t), \tag{11}$$

where index i ranges over the input nodes and out_{ji} was determined using Equation 2. The specific competitive learning rule used was

$$\Delta w_{ji}(t + 1) = \epsilon[a_i(t) - w_{ji}(t)]a_j(t + 1) \tag{12}$$

where ϵ is a small positive constant ("learning rate"). This competitive activation rule tends to produce winner-takes-all behavior among the output nodes following initiation of a pattern of activation over the input nodes. The learning rule used here assumes that the incoming weights to an output node sum to 1.0, and that the activations of input nodes also sum to 1.0.

In experimental simulations with this unsupervised learning rule and a competitive activation mechanism, competitive learning was basically found to duplicate the performance of competitive learning and a noncompetitive activation mechanism described elsewhere (Rumelhart & Zipser, 1986). However, analysis shows that a competitive activation mechanism has the advantage of automatically correcting for pattern classification distortions that arise when one assumes weight vector components sum to 1.0 (Sutton et al., 1989). This unexpected observation suggests that competitive activation mechanisms may have some useful advantages over noncompetitive ones, but this issue will require further study.

Competitive learning is traditionally an unsupervised learning scheme. It differs from reinforcement learning where positive and negative performance cues are available and from supervised learning where node-specific teaching signals are provided. Reinforcement and supervised versions of competitive learning have also been developed and studied recently in conjunction with competitive activation mechanisms (Sutton et al., 1989). Equation 12 is still used in these learning methods but is applied selectively, as described in Table 4.5. These learning methods have been demonstrated to work effectively when applied to dipole classification problems, with the supervised version learning more quickly than the reinforcement version.

Finally, it should be mentioned that work is underway to develop general error back propagation learning methods for use with competitive activation mechanisms. This work is expected to result in powerful training procedures for information processing applications.

Table 4.5. Definition of the Reinforcement and Supervised Learning Rules

Reinforcement Learning			Supervised Learning		
Reinforcement Signal to all Output Nodes	Output Node a_i's Activation	Result	Teaching Signal to Output Node j	Output Node Activation a_i	Result
+	loses	does not learn	win	loses	learns
+	wins	learns	win	wins	learns
−	loses	learns	lose	loses	does not learn
−	wins	does not learn	lose	wins	does not learn

5. DISCUSSION

For competitive activation mechanisms to be more useful, it is important to identify effective methods for developing task specific activation rules. This chapter has described two such methods. In the first, a heuristic, computer-assisted trial-and-error search process was used to create an activation mechanism for the large, complex print-to-sound network. The competitive activation mechanism created in this fashion was able to produce clear cut and correct "winner-takes-all" performance, even for nodes that received conflicting input information (phoneme nodes). Interestingly, measures of the time for activation of winning output nodes paralleled human reaction time measures of the reading aloud process being modeled.

The second method described here for creating a competitive activation mechanism involved decomposing a global optimization equation into local optimization criteria that were used as activation mechanisms by individual nodes. Of course, such an approach is only possible when a measure of global optimality exists, as it does for the class of diagnostic problems considered in this chapter. Again, simulations showed that the competitive activation mechanism created in this fashion resulted in equilibria with a set of winning nodes fully activated, and that these nodes were or closely approximated globally optimal problem solutions.

In addition, this chapter has summarized the recent development of learning rules that can function effectively with competitive activation mechanisms. The specific unsupervised, reinforcement, and supervised learning methods studied show promise, both experimentally and analytically. Further work on additional learning methods is underway.

While previous work with competitive activation mechanisms has suggested that the basic idea of using allocational competition is valid, the work described in this chapter is the first demonstration that this approach scales up to sizable problems of interest in cognitive science and artificial intelligence, and that this approach can work in adaptive systems. Further, the methods used to create the competitive activation mechanisms described here should be widely applicable to other areas where connectionist models might be developed. These results are very encouraging, and further study will no doubt uncover additional ways to derive competitive activation mechanisms and learning rules for other specific applications.

REFERENCES

Amari, S., & Arbib, M. (Eds.). (1982). *Competition and cooperation in neural nets.* New York: Springer-Verlag.

Berndt, R., Reggia, J., & Mitchum, C. (1987). Empirically-derived probabilities for grapheme-to-phoneme correspondences in English. *Behavioral Research Methods, Instruments and Computers, 19,* 1–9.

Bourret, P., Goodall, S., & Samuelides, M. (1989). Optimal scheduling by competitive activation: Application to the satellite antennae scheduling problem. *Proceedings of IEEE International Joint Conference on Neural Networks, I,* 565–572.

D'Autrechy, C. L., Reggia, J., Sutton, G., & Goodall, S. (1988). A General Purpose Simulation Environment for Developing Connectionist Models. *Simulation, 51,* 5–19.

Ellis, A. (1984). *Reading, writing, and dyslexia.* Hillsdale, NJ: Erlbaum.

Feldman, J., & Ballard, D. (1982). Connectionist models and their properties. *Cognitive Science, 6,* 205–254.

Goodall, S., & Reggia, J. (1990). Competitive activation mechanisms for dynamic control problems. *Proceedings International Joint Conference on Neural Networks,* in press. Washington, DC.

Grossberg, S. (1982). *Studies of mind and brain.* Dordecht: Reidel.

Grossberg, S. (1987). Competitive learning: From interactive activation to adaptive resonance. *Cognitive Science, 11,* 23–63.

Hirsch, M. (1987). Convergence in neural networks. *Proceedings IEEE International Conference on Neural Networks, II,* 115–125.

Peng, Y. (1989). A connectionist solution for vertex cover problems. *Proceedings International Joint Conference on Neural Networks.*

Peng, Y., & Reggia, J. (1987). A probabilistic causal model for diagnostic problem-solving. *IEEE Transactions Systems, Man and Cybernetics, 17,* 146–162, 395–406.

Peng, Y., & Reggia, J. (1989). A connectionist model for diagnostic problem solving. *IEEE Transactions on Systems, Man & Cybernetics, 19,* 285–298.

Reggia, J., Nau, D., Wang, P., & Peng, Y. (1985). A formal model of diagnostic inference. *Information Sciences, 37,* 227–285.

Reggia, J. (1987). Properties of a competition-based activation mechanism in neuromimetic network models. *Proceedings of the First International Conference on Neural Networks, II,* 131–138.

Reggia, J., & Sutton, G. (1988). Self-processing networks and their biomedical implications. *IEEE Proceedings, 76,* 680–692.

Reggia, J., Marsland, P., & Berndt, R. (1988). Competitive dynamics in a dual-route connectionist model of print-to-sound transformation. *Complex Systems, 2,* 509–547.

Rumelhart, D., & Zipser, D. (1986). Feature Discovery by Competitive Learning. In D. Rumelhart, J. McClelland, & the PDP Research Group (Eds.), *Parallel distributed processing* (Vol. I, pp. 151–193). Cambridge, MA: MIT Press.

Sutton, G., Reggia, J., & Maisog, J. (1989, April). *Implementing competitive learning in connectionist models using competitive activation rules* (CS-TR-2224). College Park: Dept. of Computer Science, University of Maryland.

Tagamets, M., & Reggia, J. (1989). A data flow implementation of a competition-based connectionist model. *Journal of Parallel and Distributed Computing, 6,* 704–714.

Wald, J., Farach, M., Tagamets, M., & Reggia, J. (1989). Generating plausiblc diagnostic hypotheses with self-processing causal networks. *Journal of Experimental & Theoretical Artificial Intelligence, 1,* 91–112.

Wang, P., Seldman, S., & Reggia, J. (1988). Analysis of competition-based spreading activation in connectionist models. *International Journal of Man-Machine Studies, 28,* 77–97.

Whitfield, K., Goodall, S., & Reggia, J. (1989). A connectionist model for dynamic control. *Telematics & Informatics, 6,* 375–390.

5

Decentralized Control of Access to Resources in a Network: Interdependence of Strategies in a Challenge Ring Model

Ross A. Gagliano
Department of Mathematics and Computer Science
Georgia State University

Mark E. Schaefer
Department of Economics
Georgia State University

1. INTRODUCTION

In this chapter, we present a decentralized alternative to a centralized host as a way to control the allocation of scarce resources in a ring network. Using simulation, we compare our *challenge ring* (CR) model of hostless allocation to more traditional *server ring* (SR) and *mover ring* (MR) models of hosted allocation. In all versions of the models, agents with specific mission requirements sequentially poll separate resource nodes identified by class (e.g., processor, database, communication port or printer) and by availability (idle or busy).

In the SR, agents wait for service at each appropriate busy node, using the standard disciplines of either first-in-first-out (FIFO) in the queue version or last-in-first-out (LIFO) in the stack version. In the MR, agents always move to the next node in the ring if the current one is busy. In the CR, when an agent finds a node with the next needed resource, the agent uses it, if it is idle, or challenges the current user for the node, if it is busy, according to individual strategies and specific rules of encounter.

For given network configurations and agent arrival rates, we examine the relationship between the mix of agent strategies and the system performance as measured by: (a) the ratio R of actual time required to complete service in a congested ring to the minimum time that would be required if the ring were empty, and (b) the proportion P of agents that completed processing. Cases are presented in which the hostless environment, exemplified by the challenge ring model, performs better than the hosted environment, represented by the server ring and mover ring models.

1.1. Background

Recently, considerable interest has been shown in the concept of a *market*, as defined in Section 2 below, to replace a host in controlling environments that support multiprocessing or multitasking (Fraser, Gagliano, & Schaefer, 1989; Gagliano, Fraser, & Schaefer, 1987, 1988; Huberman, 1988, 1989; Malone, Fikes, & Howard, 1983). Using simulation, we have previously investigated the possibility of hostless control in generic computing environments, for the cases of sealed-bid auctions and barter exchanges (Fraser et al., 1989; Gagliano et al., 1987, 1988). Our interest in self-organizing systems continues earlier work on synchronization, cybernetic, and organizational models (Gagliano, 1976, 1983; Gagliano & Lebkowski, 1979; Gagliano & Schwartz, 1981). Independently, the market concept has been applied to hostless operating systems for actual workstation networks in the current Spawn Project at the Xerox Palo Alto Research Center (PARC) (Huberman, 1988, 1989) and in the previous Enterprise project (Malone et al., 1983).

In addition to the market approach, other hostless resource allocation schemes can include the voting approach (Vitanyi, 1984; Railey, 1986; Windeknecht & Gagliano, this volume) and the threshold approach (Baran, 1988; Reggia, 1985). Voting models have been used to resolve deadlocks caused by many jobs contending for access to a single database. Threshold models are employed for lifelike processes, often incorporating connectionist structures to study pattern recognition, adaptation, and learning, e.g., neural networks.

Some of the advantages of the market approach are that it: (a) is self-organizing; (b) facilitates mutually beneficial exchanges which maximize system performance; (c) encourages cooperation as a globally efficient, long-run strategy; (d) economizes on the information needed to allocate resources; (e) is inherently versatile through a wide variety of network structures in which resources are linked but reconfigurable; (f) is generalizable in different ways, although here it is specialized to pair-wise competitive challenges; (g) can be simplified to yield a ring of servers that either allows priority service (the stack) or prevents it (the queue); and (h) can be interpreted, if funds are used in the exchanges, as a pool discipline, rather than the wait-in-line discipline of a queue, in which priority for getting earlier service is determined by the willingness of agents to pay.

Using markets to control multiprocessor computing environments is natural, given the rapid rate of innovation in operating systems, transputers, intelligent networks, non-von Neumann architectures, systolic arrays, distributed systems, and parallel processing (Dongarra, 1987). Moreover, market approaches are amenable to operating systems for state-of-the-art network architectures, such as the ethernet or the token ring (Tanenbaum, 1984).

1.2. Hostless Environments

The decade of the 1980s has witnessed an explosion of interest in networks of computing resources. Prior to networks, mainframes were used as batch processors, which economized on machine time at the expense of user convenience. The desire by users to have more immediate response led to the development of time-sharing, which was a stopgap measure that allowed many users nearly simultaneous access, but with the high overhead cost of repeatedly swapping jobs into and out of main memory.

The development of free-standing personal computers (PCs) encouraged small, independent tasks to migrate from mainframes to PCs not connected to larger machines. The convenience of PCs led users to attempt ever larger tasks, eventually pressing against the capacity limits of PCs. PC users found that they needed to communicate with each other, for example, when using the same dynamically changing database. Attempts were then made to link PCs together in networks in order to distribute the processing of larger tasks over other temporarily idle nodes and to allow shared access to common databases. Such networks offer the potential benefits of economizing on hardware and of tailoring to each job both its processing and its access to databases.

Although hosted environments may be more suitable for mainframes, batch processing, and time-sharing, the most appropriate approach to the control of resources in networks has not yet been determined. We suggest that networks require alternatives to hosted operating systems, and we offer the CR model as one such alternative. This chapter represents an early step in a research program whose long range objective is the determination of the conditions under which hostless architectures may be superior to hosted architectures.

2. MARKETS AND MODELS

We designed the CR model to emphasize only a few essential features of markets, as discussed in the next section, and we chose the Prisoner's Dilemma algorithm as the paradigm for the interaction of agents when contending for access to resources in a hostless system, as discussed in the subsequent section. These basic features of markets have manifested themselves repeatedly throughout human history and across different cultures, even as the specific functions of markets have evolved over time.

For purposes of this chapter, we define *the market process* to include a spectrum of behaviors ranging from conflict (resources seized by threats or force) to negotiated exchange (with or without money). We use this broad notion to devise an exhaustive taxonomy of market systems in Figure 5.1, from which the CR model is one case. To implement the CR, we use a discrete element approach

(Gagliano, in preparation) which facilitates the incorporation of a challenge algorithm for resolving contention based on the Prisoner's Dilemma.

2.1. Markets

A market is usually described as a process in which exchanges occur through the interaction of sellers and buyers (Samuelson, 1985). Specialized markets arise, such as *monopolies* (a market in which there is a single seller), *duopolies* (only two sellers), and *oligopolies* (a market within which a small number of buyers and sellers interact). In the CR model, we focus on the interaction of only two agents at a time, as this captures the most fundamental issues of cooperation and competition over access to resources.

A general market system in Figure 5.1 is conceptualized as consisting of *resources, rules of encounter,* and *agents.* Resources can have a variety of attributes, including class, status, and connectivity. Likewise, they can be either separable, such as display and CPU, or inseparable, such as a chip set for a video display card. In the separable case, each discrete resource can be connected to

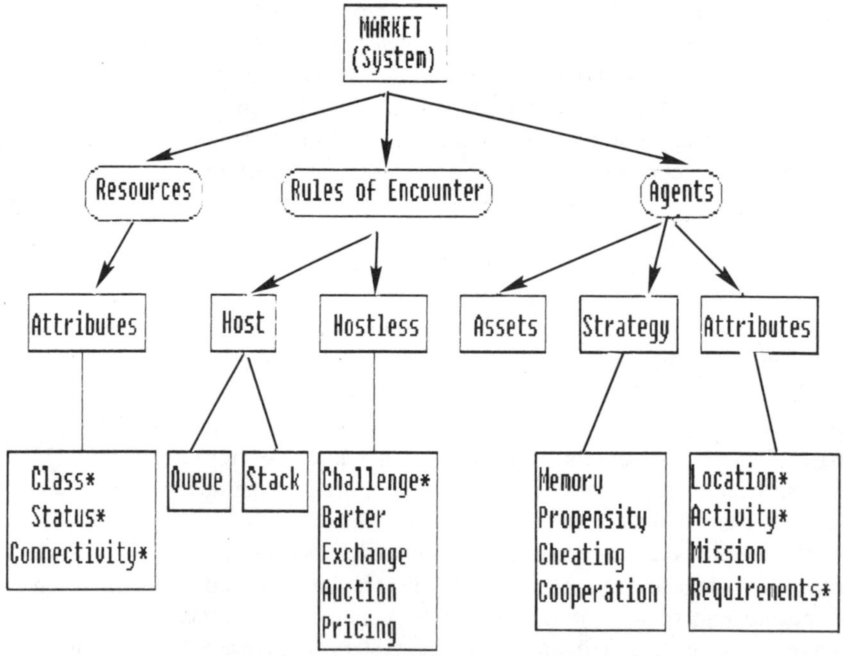

Figure 5.1. Taxonomy of Market Systems.

others or disconnected. Connected resources can be configured as networks such as a ring, star, mesh, cube, hypercube, and so on (Franklin, 1982).

Rules of encounter are the procedures that the agents follow when interacting to gain access to resources in either hosted or hostless environments. Under a host, these rules implement either a no-priority or queue (FIFO) versus a priority or stack (LIFO) system. The rules for hostless environments include the pure challenge case analyzed here and other cases such as barter (the exchange of goods for goods), purchase (the exchange of goods for money which can then be used to claim other goods), auctions (sealed-bid or silent and open-outcry, and English/rising-bid-price or Dutch/falling-ask-price), and simultaneous negotiations diffused over large-scale markets (regional, national, and international, for either immediate or future delivery).

Agents are described by assets, strategies, and attributes (location, activity, goal, and mission requirements). Assets can be initially endowed or dynamically acquired through exchanges. Strategies are decision-choosing algorithms that individual agents invoke prior to taking such actions as cooperating or cheating, and can be based on memory of past treatment by others and on inherent tendencies.

The starred items in Figure 5.1 were selected for emphasis in the CR model; then, from the CR model, the SR and MR models were created as benchmarks for comparison.

2.2. Models of Markets

Mathematical models of markets can be broadly classified as either aggregated or disaggregated. *Aggregated* market models typically emphasize summarizing concepts such as market-wide supply and demand. Quantity is expressed as a macroscopic function of price and other factors, with the behavior of individuals hidden implicitly in the summarizing function. Cournot's (1897) duopoly model and Chamberlin's (1933) monopolistic competition model are early examples of the aggregate analysis of the structure and dynamics of exchange.

Disaggregated models of markets explicitly describe the behavior and interactions of individual agents. Their complexity, however, often precludes the closed-form analysis usually available with aggregated models, so that numerical simulation must be used instead. The first major treatise on the disaggregated approach provided a theory of games and economic behavior (von Neumann & Morgenstern, 1953) that has been applied to the analysis of markets (Shubik, 1980). Two important disaggregated models that have been extensively studied are the zero-sum game and the Prisoner's Dilemma (Hofstadter, 1985). For our purposes here, disaggregated models provide more insight into the relationship between *agents* and the broader context of *markets*. Accordingly, disaggregated models provide more insight in the analysis of macrobehavior of system variables based on the microspecifications of discrete parameters (Schelling, 1978).

2.3. Prisoner's Dilemma

The Prisoner's Dilemma (PD) models the pair-wise interaction of agents in which overall cooperation pays, although each agent is tempted to cheat on the other. The PD mimics economic activity through its focus on individual choices either to cooperate, by adhering to a prior agreement, or to defect, by not behaving as previously promised. Since both competitive and cooperative behaviors of individual agents are possible, the PD is appropriate to the CR.

The term *Prisoner's Dilemma* was derived from a situation in which two suspects are held as prisoners in separate cells so that they cannot communicate. The interrogators offer leniency to the first prisoner who cheats on their prior agreement to remain silent. The dilemma arises because each prisoner must make a choice either to cooperate with the other prisoner by remaining silent (they both get a lighter sentence by keeping silent) or to defect by giving evidence against the other (thus getting off free).

Their decisions are obviously based on imperfect information about their situations (since they cannot be sure whether the other will talk) and on their individual strategies (Axelrod, 1984). The PD can be represented as a game with two players, A and B, each of whom chooses either to COOPERATE with or DEFECT from the other, with the associated matrix of payoffs to each player as shown in Figure 5.2.

The PD requires four relationships among the payoffs. First, simultaneous cooperation must be better overall than simultaneous cheating ($R + R > L + L$, or $R > L$). Second, to have a dilemma at all, each player must be tempted to cheat, so cheating by one player, while the other cooperates, must improve the cheater's payoff ($T > R$), while worsening the other's payoff ($R > S$). Third, a cooperating player, who has encountered a defection, must be able to improve his or her payoff by also switching from cooperation to defection ($L > S$). Together, the first three conditions imply that $T > R > L > S$. Fourth, the total payoff for cooperation must exceed the total payoff when only one party defects ($R + R > T + S$). In other words, a player is tempted to cheat to improve his or her individual payoff at the expense of the other if he or she is not sure that the other will cooperate, knowing that, if both cheat, then they will both be worse off.

Surprisingly, in the face of strong temptation for individual cheating, computer tournaments (Axelrod, 1984; Hofstadter, 1985), in which players randomly "encounter" other players and "exchange" payoff values, have demonstrated that cooperation can emerge as a more successful alternative under a simple strategy known as *tit-for-tat*. Our results likewise show that superior system performance can arise from cooperative individual strategies in the CR.

		Player B	
		Cooperates	Defects
Player A	Cooperates	(R,R)	(S,T)
	Defects	(T,S)	(L,L)

Figure 5.2. The Prisoner's Dilemma Payoff Matrix.

2.4. Discrete Element Methodology

To develop the CR model, a method was needed that would facilitate the construction of a hostless environment based on the pair-wise interactions of the PD. We selected the *discrete element methodology* (DEM) (Gagliano, in preparation), which has been used to analyze models such as Conway's Game-of-Life, Tug-of-War, Heart-beat, Synchronously-flashing-fireflies, and Neural-nets.

The DEM has similarities to the physics of the many-body problem, but overcomes some modeling shortcomings with features from discrete event simulation and numerical methods. From statistical mechanics, the DEM assumes the notion that the interaction of particles at the microscopic level can produce qualitatively different observable effects at the macroscopic level. From *discrete event simulation* (Banks & Carson, 1984), the DEM borrows the concepts of arrival processes, discrete time, statistical distributions, and queues. From the *finite element method,* which uses piece-wise linear local numerical approximation to solve partial differential equations, the DEM provides iterative computation implemented primarily through boolean functions.

The DEM has benefited from the significant amount of computer simulation activity of the late 1960s and early 1970s (Dutton & Starbuck, 1971). The DEM facilitates the representation of small groups of decision makers in a manner similar to the "stereotype approach," which was used to model such diverse situations as prairie-dog towns, voting processes, human neighborhoods, and elementary schools (Windeknecht & D'Angelo, 1975). Expanded from the first ideas of that approach (Gagliano, 1976), the DEM has been employed in simulations of synchronization, stabilization, and pattern completion (Fraser et al., 1989; Gagliano et al., 1987; Gagliano, in preparation).

3. CHALLENGE RING MODEL

In this section, we describe the *challenge ring* (CR) model and compare it to the *stack* and the *queue* versions of the *server ring* (SR-S and SR-Q) and to the *mover ring* (MR). In the next section, the implementation of the models in several simulation programs is explained. Only the key algorithms and data structures of the models are provided here, but the complete simulation programs, written in TURBO Pascal, are available upon request.

The CR model is a special case of a general market system (from Figure 5.1) in which challenges, among contenders for computing resources arranged as nodes in a ring network, are used to control access to those resources. The system performance under the CR as the mix of individual strategies changes is then compared to the performance under the SR and MR.

3.1. Resources in the CR Model

Arranging the resources in the CR model in a ring allows agents to inspect the nodes in sequence and then to recycle through the ring until all the computing mission requirements are completed. The simple, continuous ring structure is the basis of a variety of games (Levy, 1988) in each of which the effect of player strategy on system performance can be analyzed, e.g., the time path of net worth in the board game of Monopoly.

The ring structure consists of n nodes (<= 20), each of which can be assigned (randomly or manually) to a resource class. The nodes are connected in a clockwise direction, causing a one-dimensional "flow" of agents. Agents must all enter the ring at the same point on the ring, but may exit from any point whenever their mission requirements are completed.

In the CR model, nodes must be in one of the following states: I (for Idle, when no agents are currently using it); S (for Single, one user); D (for Double, two agents contending for its use); H (for sHare, two agents sharing) and K (for Killer, two agents both attempting use it after each has defected on the other). Any node that is not idle is busy, indicating that an agent located there intends to use it.

3.2. Rules of Encounter in the CR Model

Again, resources are allocated in the CR model through challenges. In the spirit of the PD, the challenge rule of encounter allows pairs of contending agents to

		N2 (Occupant)	
		C	D
N1 (Challenger)	C	(P,W) H	(M,P) S
	D	(P,M) S	(A,P) K

Figure 5.3. Challenge Ring Payoff Matrix.

reach one of four outcomes when competing for a given resource (see Figure 5.3). We emphasize the basics of contention by allowing only two agents to interact at any given time. When extending the analysis to more than two agents, processes such as barter or auction can replace the PD.

The CR rule of encounter dictates that a new arrival at busy node can challenge the current user if no other agent is waiting. If the node already has a user and a waiter (i.e., the node is in states D, H, or K), then the arriving agent must move to the next node.

By contrast, under the queue (SR-Q) or FIFO rule of encounter, each new arrival at a busy node must take the last place in line and use the free resource in turn. But under the stack (SR-S) or LIFO rule, the new arrival goes in front of every one else. In the mover ring (MR), each arriving agent seeks an idle needed node, and moves from any busy needed node to the next node rather than wait for the busy one to become free.

In all cases, only one agent is allowed to use any node at a time. If a second agent arrives at a busy node, then, as shown in Figure 5.3, four CR outcomes are possible: (a) both N1 and N2 cooperate, and the node is shared (state H, in which current processor P shares with new waiter W); (b) the challenger N1 defects by seizing the node and becoming P, while the incumbent N2 cooperates by moving on M, so the node is monopolized (state S); (c) the reverse of case 2; or (d) both defect, so the node is retained by the current processor (state K, in which the unsuccessful attacker A remains to rechallenge the current processor P after one time period). In cases (a) and (d), other arriving agents who may be interested in processing at this node cannot challenge. Since no more than two agents are allowed to contend for a single node at any given time, other interested agents must pass through, as do arriving agents who do not need the node.

3.3. Agents in the CR Model

Agents arrive at a single entry point in the ring (location 0) with mission requirements (<= 9 items) of resource class (<= 3 classes) and durations (<= 5 time units each). Agents traverse the ring (nodes 0 through n-1), searching for available resources that match their current requirements.

Agents have an identification number (ID), a location (0 through n-1), a mission (represented as an array of required resources and durations of processing at each resource), and activities (M for move, P for process, W for wait when sharing, E or F for the challenge states when entering an encounter, A for attacker that is the loser of the last encounter remaining to challenge again, and D for done, when all mission requirements have been completed and the agent leaves the system).

The strategy of an agent is expressed in terms of p (the probability of unprovoked defection) and q (the influence of the treatment received during the previous encounter on the present choice to cooperate or to defect). The pure strategies are: C for always Cooperate (p = 0, q = 0); D for always Defect (p = 1, q = 0); T for Tit-for-tat (p = 0, q = 1); and R for Random (p is Uniform Random Variate, q = 0). Variations on these strategies are: W (p = URV, q = URV); X (p = URV, q = PRV); Y (p = NRV, q = URV): and Z (p = NRV, q = PRV), where URV is the uniform random variable, PRV is positively ramped random variable and NRV is negatively ramped random variable.

3.4. Algorithms to Update Agents and Nodes

The two major algorithms in the CR model are: Check_nodes, which discovers the current state of each node, and Mark_agents, which determines the activity of the agents in the next time period (I, S, D, H, or K), based on what happened this period, and tags the agents accordingly. Figures 5.4 and 5.5 show the possible transitions of the node states, which depend on the activities of the agents in the previous time period.

A node is designated as in the I (or Idle) state from the busy state only when the current processing agent P moves on and is marked as M, or is done D. A node enters the S (or Singleton) state from I when an arriving M agent becomes a P, or from D when an encounter is resolved. A node enters the D (or Doubleton) state from S when a challenger arrives to contend. A node enters the H (or

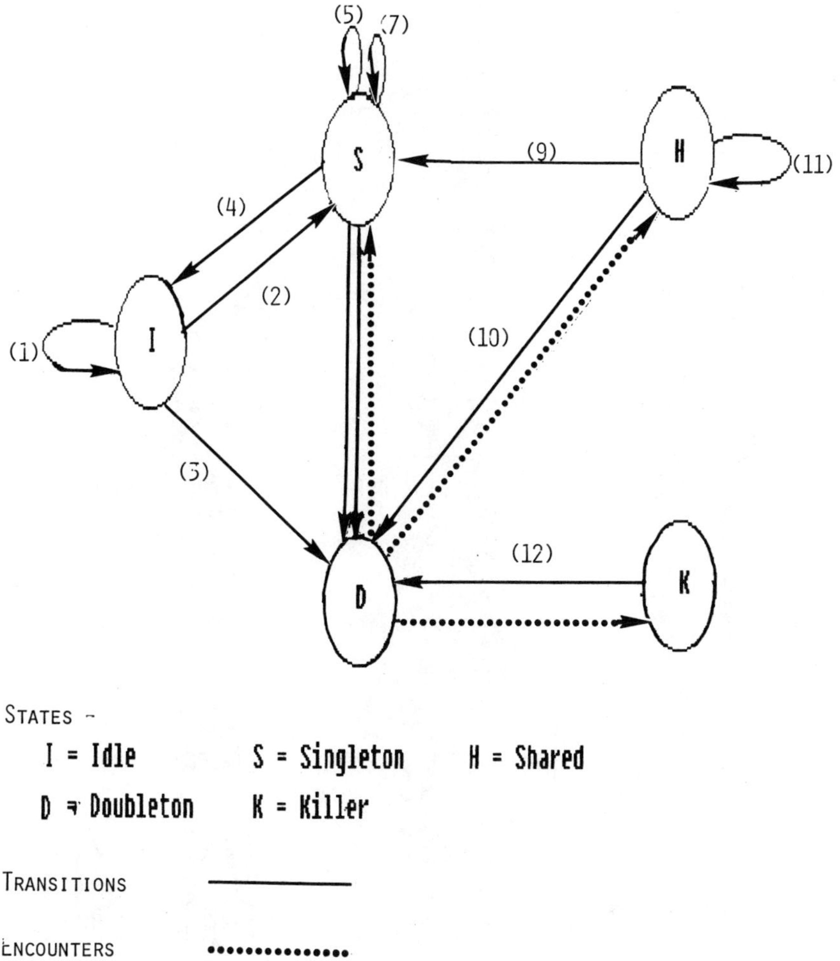

Figure 5.4. CR Node State Transition Diagram.

sHared) state from D when both contenders cooperate, but enters K when both defect. The new state of the node is then used to mark the agents for their next activity. For example, H swaps the agents that are sharing a node, as well as moving any agents that are passing through.

3.4. Example of the CR Model

The following example illustrates the operation of a CR model using a total of 10 nodes. The first agent arrives at time 0. Table 5.1 shows the status of the nodes

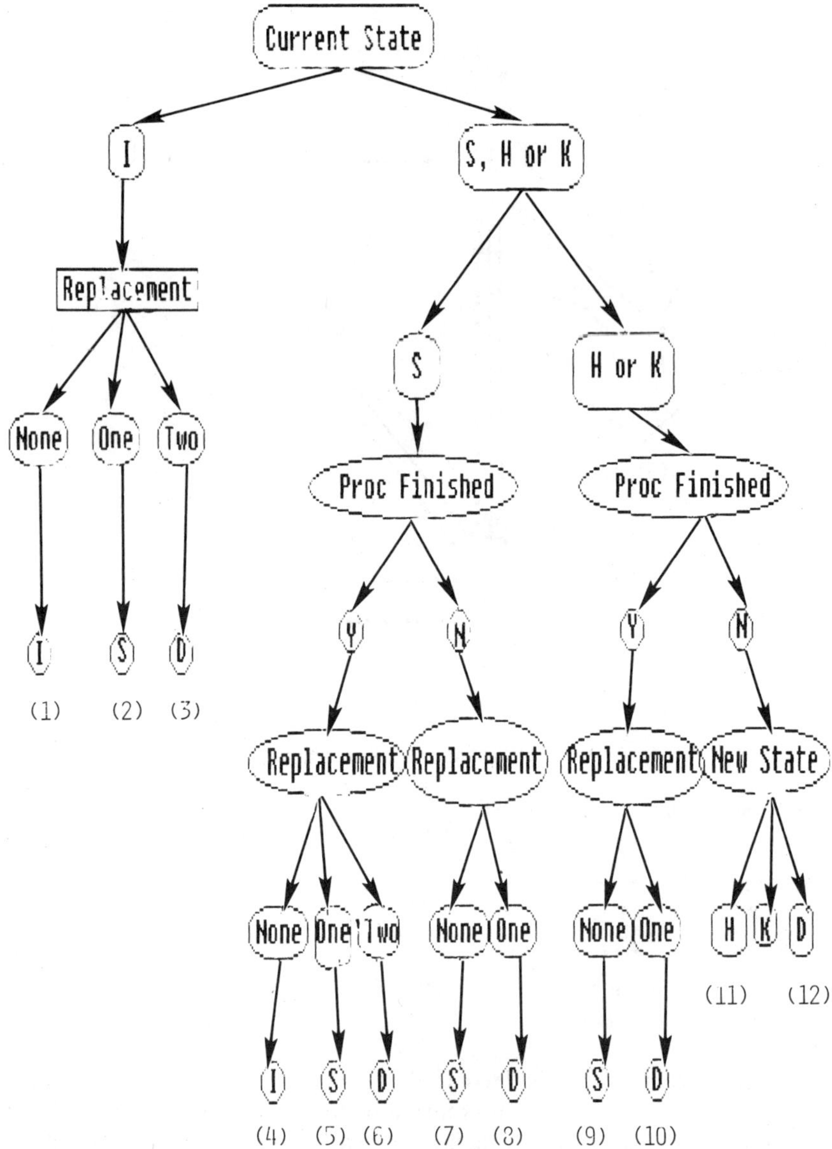

Figure 5.5. Diagram of CR Node Transitions.

for the initial (or zero) time period with the following identifiers: Loc is the location of the node on the ring, Cls is the class of the resource at the node, Ste is the state of the node, Prt is the number of time periods that the node has been busy, Usr is the current user's number, Wtr is the current waiter's number, Num

Table 5.1. Initial (Time = 0) Node Configuration.

Loc	Cls	Ste	PrT	Usr	Wtr	Num	Occupants...
0	3	I	0	0	0	1	1
1	1	I	0	0	0	0	V
2	2	I	0	0	0	0	V
3	1	I	0	0	0	0	V
4	1	I	0	0	0	0	V
5	3	I	0	0	0	0	V
6	2	I	0	0	0	0	V
7	2	I	0	0	0	0	V
8	1	I	0	0	0	0	V
9	1	I	0	0	0	0	V

is the number of agents at that node, and Occupants shows either the ID number(s) of the agents currently at that node or a V for a vacant node.

Table 5.1 also shows the initial state of the 10 nodes in this ring. It is important to note that there are three classes of resources, all nodes are initially in state I (Idle), and the other resource attributes are initialized to zero (or V for Vacant). This first agent has arrived at node 0.

Table 5.2 shows the format for the listing of the agents. Since at time 0, only the first (whose arrival started the simulation) is shown with: ID = identification number; Loc = location; St = Strategy; p = probability of defecting, q = influence of the last encounter; Lst = what happened (Cooperate or Defect) to that agent in the last encounter; Act = current activity; Nxt = next activity; ArT = arrival time; RqT = time required to complete the mission; AcT = actual time to complete the mission (NA means not applicable if agent has not completed); Cur = number of the requirement currently being processed (e.g., 3rd); Num = total number of requirements in the agent's entire computing mission, and Class/Duration provides the sequence of requirements by class and duration.

Agent 1 has a strategy D (always Defect) and a mission of 5 requirements. Since Agent 1's first requirement is of class 1, Agent 1 cannot use the resource (of class 3) at node 0, so the agent will move to node 1. At time 2, Agent 2

Table 5.2. Listing of the 1st Agent.

ID	Loc	St	p	q	Lst	Act	Nxt
1	0	D	1.00	0.00	C	M	M

ArT	RqT	AcT	Cur	Num	Class/Duration
0	16	NA	1	5	1/3 2/1 3/1 1/4 3/1

Table 5.3. Node Configuration at First (Time = 14) Encounter.

Loc	Cls	Ste	PrT	Usr	Wtr	Num	Occupants...	
0	3	I	1	0	0	0	V	
1	1	I	11	0	0	0	V	
2	2	D	6	4	5	2	4	5
3	1	I	0	0	0	0	V	
4	1	I	0	0	0	0	V	
5	3	I	3	0	0	1	3	
6	2	I	0	0	0	0	V	
7	2	I	0	0	0	0	V	
8	1	S	1	1	0	1	1	
9	1	I	0	0	0	0	V	

arrives, and so on until time 14, when the first encounter occurs as Agents 4 and 5 both contend for node 2 (see Table 5.3).

In Table 5.3, all of the nodes except 2 and 8 are shown to be idle. Node 8 has one processor (Agent 1) that is working on its fourth requirement. At node 2, Agent 4 is the current processor but has been challenged by Agent 5, causing the node to be in the doubleton state D. Agent 3 is at node 5 but cannot utilize that resource at this time.

The results of the first encounter are shown in Table 5.5, where the state of node 2 is H (a sHared state), since Agents 4 and 5 are sharing that resource.

In time 19 (see Table 5.6), agents 1 and 7 compete for node 0, but this time, they both defect, and the node goes from State D (Doubleton) to the state K (Killer).

Thus, Agent 1 gains the resource and completes, while Agent 7 assumes the resource after waiting to compete (see Table 5.7).

The entire sequence of activities over the time horizon for nodes and agents is summarized in Table 5.8.

Table 5.4. Listing of Agents at Time = 14.

ID	Loc	St	p	q	Act	Nxt	ArT	RqT	AcT	Cur	Class/Duration				
1	8	D	1.00	0.00	P	P	0	16	NA	4	1/0	2/0	3/0	1/3	3/1
2	99	W	0.70	0.66	D	D	2	12	12	3	3/0	1/0	2/0		
3	5	X	0.45	0.75	P	M	5	12	NA	3	2/0	3/0	1/4		
4	2	C	0.00	0.00	P	E	8	11	NA	2	1/0	2/2	3/1		
5	2	C	0.00	0.00	M	F	12	14	NA	1	2/2	1/4	2/1	3/2	

Table 5.5. Listing of Nodes at Time = 15.

Loc	Cls	Ste	PrT	Usr	Wtr	Num	Occupants...
0	3	I	1	0	0	1	6
1	1	I	11	0	0	0	V
2	2	H	6	4	5	2	4 5
3	1	I	0	0	0	0	V
4	1	I	0	0	0	0	V
5	3	I	3	0	0	0	V
6	2	I	0	0	0	1	3
7	2	I	0	0	0	0	V
8	1	S	2	1	0	1	1
9	1	I	0	0	0	0	V

Table 5.6. Nodes at Time = 19.

Loc	Cls	Ste	PrT	Usr	Wtr	Num	Occupants...
0	3	D	1	1	7	2	1 7
1	1	I	11	0	0	0	V
2	2	I	10	0	0	1	5
3	1	I	0	0	0	1	4
4	1	I	0	0	0	1	6
5	3	I	3	0	0	0	V
6	2	I	0	0	0	0	V
7	2	I	0	0	0	0	V
8	1	S	6	3	0	1	3
9	1	I	0	0	0	0	V

Table 5.7. Nodes at Time = 20.

Loc	Cls	Ste	PrT	Usr	Wtr	Num	Occupants...
0	3	K	1	1	7	2	1 7
1	1	I	11	0	0	0	V
2	2	I	10	0	0	0	V
3	1	S	0	5	0	1	5
4	1	I	0	0	0	1	4
5	3	I	3	0	0	1	6
6	2	I	0	0	0	0	V
7	2	I	0	0	0	0	V
8	1	S	7	3	0	1	3
9	1	I	0	0	0	0	V

Table 5.8. Example (through Time = 21).

Time	Agent	Mission	Activity	0	1	2	3	4	5	6	7	8	9
			Location	0	1	2	3	4	5	6	7	8	9
			Resource Type	3	1	2	1	1	3	2	2	1	1
			Activity	Occupants									
0	1	1/3 2/1 3/1 1/4 3/1	M	1	V	V	V	V	V	V	V	V	V
1			M	V	1	V	V	V	V	V	V	V	V
2	2	3/1 1/5 2/2	PM	2	1	V	V	V	V	V	V	V	V
3			PP	2	1	V	V	V	V	V	V	V	V
4			PM	V	1,2	V	V	V	V	V	V	V	V
5	3	2/2 3/2 1/4	MPM	3	2	1	V	V	V	V	V	V	V
6			PPM	V	2,3	1	V	V	V	V	V	V	V
7			MPM	V	2	3	1	V	V	V	V	V	V
8	4	1/3 2/3 3/1	MPPM	4	2	3	V	1	V	V	V	V	V
9			MPPM	V	2,4	3	V	V	1	V	V	V	V
10			PMMP	V	4	2	3	V	1	V	V	V	V
11			MPMP	V	4	2	V	3	V	1	V	V	V
12	5	2/2 1/4 2/1 3/2	MPMPM	5	4	2	V	V	3	V	1	V	V
13			MDPMM	V	5	4	V	V	3	V	V	1	V
14			P PPM	V	V	4,5	V	V	3	V	V	1	V
15	6	2/2 3/1 1/3	P MWPM	6	V	5,4	V	V	V	3	V	1	V
16			P MPWM	V	6	4,5	V	V	V	V	3	1	V
17			P MWPM	V	V	*	V	V	V	V	V	1,3	V
18			M PPMW	V	V	4,6	5	V	V	V	V	3	1
19	7	3/3 2/2 1/3 2/3	M PMPPM	1,7	V	6	5,4	V	V	V	V	3	V
20			P PMPPA	1,7	V	6	5	4	V	V	V	3	V
21			D PMPMP	7	V	V	5,6	V	4	V	V	3	V

* 5,4,6

4. SIMULATION EXPERIMENTS

A series of simulation experiments were run using the CR model, the MR model, and the SR model (with both SR-Q or SR-S). The program for the CR model is the largest of the three programs, with approximately 1100 lines of code, while the other two each contain about 800 lines of code. The SR and the MR provide baselines against which the performance of the CR may be compared. In these prototyping runs, the programs allowed maximum constants of: 100 nodes, 1,000 agents, 10 requirements per agent, 3 classes of each requirement, 10 time units duration for each requirement, and 1,000 total time units for the system (time_horizon).

After initializing the system, the main simulation loop followed this sequence:

1. Generate a new agent (if an arrival is scheduled for this time);
2. Check the nodes to indicate their next state;
3. Mark the agents to indicate their next activity;
4. Advance the system clock;

5. Update the agents as they perform their next activity; i.e., Move, Process, Encounter, Wait, and Done;
6. Collect pertinent statistics; and
7. Repeat steps 1 through 6 as necessary.

4.1. System Performance

The simulation experiments were constructed to show the effect of various mixes of strategies, arrival rates and sizes of the ring, on steady-state system performance as measured by: (a) the proportion (P) of all agents that complete, and (b) the ratio (R) of the actual time (A) to complete processing to the minimum time (M) required when no other agents are present to contend for resources. Actual time A varies with congestion and the mix of strategies, while both A and M depend on mission requirements and computing resources.

Congestion may be measured in several different ways. First, the average number of agents in the system per node (APN) yields the most visible interpretation of crowding. Second, the actual time to complete (A) focuses on the delay which an individual agent experiences, which would be the most obvious concern of an agent in a hurry to complete. Third, the system-wide proportion of all agents completing (P) captures the productivity of the whole system, which is the appropriate concern of a group of agents that choose one system over another.

We chose a fourth way: the ratio (R) of A to M, because R shows system congestion in a way consistent to both arriving agents and to a description of system-wide performance. If R is unity, then agents are finishing in the minimum possible time which is good for agents, but probably wasteful for the system, because, without contention, resources must be frequently idle. As resources become more intensively used, idle time drops and contention occurs, so R must

Table 5.9. Strategies (T, C, D, R, W, X, Y, Z).

Strategy	T	C	D	R	W	X	Y	Z
p	0.0	0.0	1.0	0.5	URV	URV	NRV	NRV
q	1.0	0.0	0.0	0.0	URV	PRV	URV	PRV

Strategy Mix	T	C	D	R
A	10%	20%	30%	40%
B	10%	40%	40%	10%
C	40%	10%	10%	40%
D	40%	30%	20%	10%

rise. Optimizing R requires an explicit valuation (pricing) of the time of agents relative to the time of nodes, which was not a focus of this chapter. Instead, we found the minimum R as a function of the mix of strategies, the number of nodes, the number of requirements, and the arrival rate. Our simulations indicate that R is a stable function of the mix of strategies, so system performance can be manipulated through the choice of a suitable mix of strategies across agents. The various strategies are shown in Table 5.9.

4.2. Data Structures

The two principal data structures represent the agents and the resource nodes whose variables are contained in Pascal arrays of records and whose data declarations have the Pascal constants shown below.

```
const
   max_num_of_agents_in_sys = 1000;
   max_num_of_nodes = 100;

type
   Long_type = 0 . . max_num_of_agents_in_sys;
   Short_type = 0 . . 10;
   Loc_type = 0 . . max_num_of_nodes;

req_record = record
      class: Short_type;
      duration: Short_type;
   end;

   Req_array = array [Short_type] of req_record;
   agents_data = record
      ID: Integer;
      location: Loc_type;
      num_of_res_req: Short_type;
      res_required: Req_array;
      req_transit_time: Long_type;
      arrival_time: Integer;
      strategy: Char;
      p: Real;
      q: Real;
      first_encounter: Boolean;
      last_encounter: Char;
      activity: Char;
      next_activity: Char;
      current_req: Short_type;
      completed: Boolean;
      actual_transit_time: Integer;
```

```
    rartt: Real;        {Rates of actual to}
end;                    {required transit time}

resource_data = record
    address: Loc_type;
    class: Short_type;      {Class of resource}
    state: Char;            {Idle, etc.}
    num_at_node: Long_type;
    current_processor: Long_type;
    current_waiter: Long_type;
    proc_time: Integer;
    usage_factor: Real;
end;
```

These Pascal record structures have the advantage of allowing a separate record to be maintained for each agent and for each node.

4.3. Numerical Results

Simulation runs were made over a horizon of 1000 time periods for the CR, SR, and MR models, using an arrival rate of 0.5 per time unit and a ring with 20 nodes, each could be one of three possible resource classes (adjacent nodes had different resource classes).

The arrival rate, the number of nodes, and the time horizon were chosen after exploration established a suitable baseline. The low intensity (computing requirements) runs allowed no more than six uniformly distributed mission requirements per agent. In the high intensity runs, the number of mission requirements was increased by 50%, that is, to nine requirements (also uniformly distributed) for each agent. Figure 5.6 provides a compact view of the results of the two sets of runs.

A major conclusion derived from these numbers is that the hostless environment can outperform the hosted environment in some cases. Specifically, in busy systems, cooperation between contending agents gives the fastest average completion time for all agents.

For the system as a whole, R is understated, since A is understated for nonfinishers until they complete processing, which explains why R for all agents can sometimes be less than R for agents that finish.

Figure 5.6 further shows that, for the mover ring (MR), the proportion (P) of agents who completed by the end of the horizon fell from 97.0% (max of six requirements) to 62.5% (max of nine requirements). For agents that finished, the ratio Rf (actual time required to complete relative to minimum possible time) rose from an average of 1.79 (the low intensity ratio for all agents Ra was 1.73) to 4.90 (Ra was 5.14).

For the server ring with the queue rule (SR-Q), P decreased from 90.8%

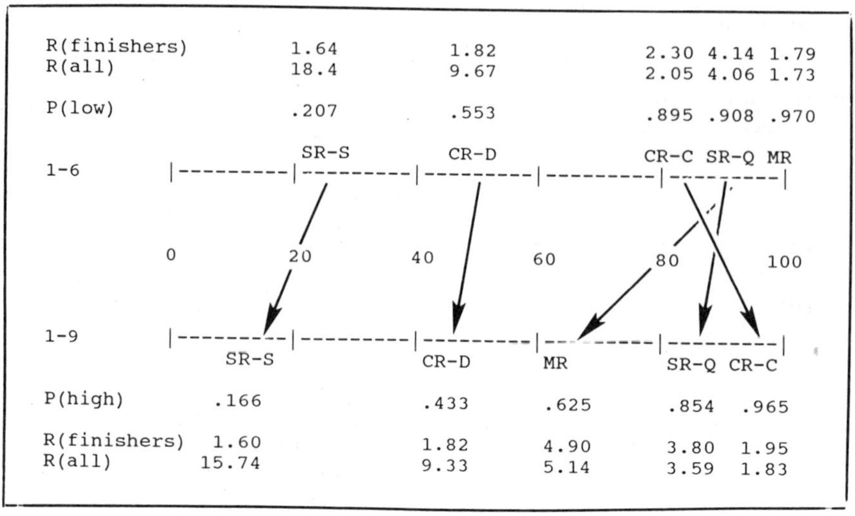

Figure 5.6. Comparison of Proportions of Agents Completing (by strategy and small/large requirements).

(maximum of six requirements) to 85.4% (maximum of nine requirements), while Rf decreased from 4.14 (Ra was 4.06) to 3.80 (Ra was 3.59). For the server ring with the stack rule (SR-S), P decreased from 20.2% (maximum of six requirements) to 16.6% (maximum of nine requirements), while Rf decreased from 1.64 (Ra was 18.4) to 1.60 (Ra was 15.74).

Tables 5.10 and 5.11 present summary results for CR runs with strategies fixed for all agents as always Defect and Tit-for-tat, respectively. The number of agents in the system (k), and the number of agents that have finished (Cmp), are provided, along with the instantaneous, average, and standard deviation of the ratios for both the agents finished (Ratio, Avg_R and SSD_R) and all agents (TRatio, TAvg_R and TSSD_R).

For agents utilizing the strategy of Tit-for-tat ($p = 0$, $q = 1$), identified as CR-C, P actually increased from 89.5% to 96.5%, while Rf decreased from 2.30 (Ra 2.05) to 1.95 (Ra 1.83). For agents who always defect ($p = 1$) and forget the past ($q = 0$), identified as CR-D, P decreased from 55.3% to 43.3%, while Rf remains constant at 1.82 (Ra decreased slightly, from 9.67 to 9.33).

By varying p and q, a spectrum of R and P values are generated (see Tables 5.12, 5.13, and 5.14). Table 5.12 shows Rf, the average ratios for agents that have finished. Note that the smallest values in this table occur for the largest values of p, indicating either that defection pays or that selfishness is good for the lucky agents who find the resource type that they need.

In Table 5.13, the average ratios for all agents are shown. Note that this time, however, the largest values in this table occur for the largest values of p, indicating here that refusing to share nodes does not yield faster completions.

Table 5.10. Results of run for CR-C (p = 0, q = 1).

Time	Idx	k	Cmp	Ratio	Avg_R	SSD_R	TRatio	TAvg_R	TSSD_R
50	1	27	11	1.5389	1.5389	0.0000	1.1128	1.1128	0.0000
100	2	58	35	1.7714	1.6552	0.1163	1.4692	1.2910	0.1782
150	3	81	57	1.8397	1.7167	0.1288	1.5862	1.3894	0.2013
200	4	112	85	1.8753	1.7563	0.1310	1.6562	1.4561	0.2092
250	5	134	115	1.9387	1.7928	0.1380	1.8528	1.5355	0.2453
300	6	165	146	1.9678	1.8220	0.1419	1.8549	1.5887	0.2536
350	7	188	174	1.9463	1.8397	0.1384	1.8689	1.6287	0.2544
400	8	216	191	1.9482	1.8533	0.1343	1.8190	1.6525	0.2462
450	9	240	217	1.9585	1.8650	0.1309	1.8687	1.6765	0.2418
500	10	264	245	1.9562	1.8741	0.1271	1.8811	1.6970	0.2375
550	11	289	266	1.9631	1.8822	0.1239	1.9010	1.7155	0.2339
600	12	317	290	1.9807	1.8904	0.1217	1.9082	1.7316	0.2302
650	13	340	313	1.9959	1.8985	0.1202	1.9400	1.7476	0.2280
700	14	370	341	2.0087	1.9064	0.1193	1.9410	1.7614	0.2253
750	15	403	376	2.0281	1.9145	0.1192	1.9566	1.7744	0.2231
800	16	433	406	2.0303	1.9217	0.1188	1.9691	1.7866	0.2211
850	17	465	436	2.0413	1.9288	0.1186	2.0001	1.7992	0.2203
900	18	495	475	2.0444	1.9352	0.1183	1.9979	1.8102	0.2188
950	19	518	498	2.0457	1.9410	0.1177	2.0176	1.8211	0.2180
1000	20	547	528	2.0612	1.9470	0.1177	2.0268	1.8314	0.2171

In Table 5.14, the proportions P of agents completing are shown. In this table, it should be noted that the smaller values are located in the upper left (high p and low q) and the larger values occur in the lower right (low p and high q), indicating that the strategy of Tit-for-tat gets more agents through the system than strategies of forgetful defection do.

Table 5.11. Results of run for CR-D (p = 1, q = 0).

Time	Idx	k	Cmp	Ratio	Avg_R	SSD_R	TRatio	TAvg_R	TSSD_R
50	1	23	5	1.5379	1.5379	0.0000	1.0380	1.0380	0.0000
100	2	51	18	1.8749	1.7064	0.1685	2.0677	1.5528	0.5148
150	3	86	32	1.8620	1.7583	0.1559	2.6577	1.9211	0.6693
200	4	109	46	1.0118	1.7717	0.1370	3.5925	2.3390	0.9272
250	5	138	57	1.8246	1.7823	0.1243	4.4416	2.7601	1.1820
300	6	158	69	1.8202	1.7886	0.1144	5.4421	3.2071	1.4708
350	7	188	79	1.8171	1.7927	0.1064	6.1437	3.6266	1.7060
400	8	212	95	1.8151	1.7955	0.0998	7.0601	4.0558	1.9585
450	9	238	105	1.8170	1.7979	0.0943	7.9264	4.4859	2.2112
500	10	260	118	1.8150	1.7996	0.0896	8.8470	4.9220	2.4723
550	11	286	130	1.8419	1.8034	0.0863	9.6333	5.3503	2.7186
600	12	310	141	1.8333	1.8059	0.0831	10.5590	5.7843	2.9745
650	13	344	151	1.8423	1.8087	0.0804	11.2285	6.2031	3.2049
700	14	370	165	1.8334	1.8105	0.0777	12.2320	6.6338	3.4567
750	15	399	176	1.8256	1.8115	0.0752	13.1251	7.0665	3.7113
800	16	423	184	1.8327	1.8128	0.0730	14.2145	7.5133	3.9883
850	17	457	197	1.8299	1.8138	0.0709	14.9813	7.9526	4.2496
900	18	483	207	1.8362	1.8151	0.0691	16.0138	8.4004	4.5239
950	19	506	218	1.8234	1.8155	0.0673	17.1204	8.8594	4.8145
1000	20	529	229	1.8206	1.8158	0.0656	18.1897	9.3259	5.1143

Table 5.12. Ratios for Finishers under CR (p vs q).

p \ q	0.0	0.2	0.4	0.6	0.8	1.0
1.0	1.8158	1.7170	1.8790	2.0859	2.0081	2.6841
0.8	1.9579	1.9776	1.9839	1.9882	2.5216	1.9909
0.6	2.3073	2.8668	2.7810	2.2583	2.4361	2.1007
0.4	2.3356	2.1750	2.3664	2.0435	2.7612	2.0052
0.2	2.5990	4.5471	2.0417	2.3548	3.1727	2.9303
0.0	2.1669	2.7018	2.1341	3.6677	2.0143	1.9470

4.4. Interpretation of Results

The numerical results consider only the pure cases of MR, SR-S, SR-Q, and CR. It is possible that intermediate cases could give better results if changing the rule of encounter were allowed at crucial times, e.g., switching from FIFO to LIFO when a high priority agent arrives, or switching from MR to SR-Q when rising agent traffic occupies all previously idle nodes.

The results indicate that cooperation (lower p and higher q) is beneficial for the system overall, but perhaps less so for particular agents. Thus, there can be conflicting interests between what is good for the group versus the individual. Also, the more robust strategies are Cooperation in CR and Queuing in SR, since P does not change substantially with the increase in the number of requirements (from <= 6 to <= 9).

Further, the stack rule (SR-S) is obviously best for later arrivals, since these agents complete quickly. In fact, the later they arrive, the smaller are their ratios, R. For systems with many free nodes, moving on is better for individual agents than waiting, but for systems that are full, just the reverse is true: individual agents should wait rather than continue moving and looking for idle nodes.

For the Stack, R is small while P is large, since newcomers appear to zip

Table 5.13. Ratios for all Agents under CR (p vs q).

p \ q	0.0	0.2	0.4	0.6	0.8	1.0
1.0	9.3259	7.0557	7.6650	5.9775	3.6562	2.5303
0.8	7.8185	7.7297	5.8114	3.9178	4.6574	1.8686
0.6	4.8542	8.5390	6.2830	3.5511	2.7190	1.9433
0.4	3.4869	3.0144	3.0318	1.9780	2.7398	1.8812
0.2	2.4938	4.8014	1.8983	2.1866	3.0656	2.7010
0.0	2.0086	2.5183	1.9832	3.5501	1.8963	1.8314

Table 5.14. Proportions Completing under CR (p vs q).

p \ q	0.0	0.2	0.4	0.6	0.8	1.0
1.0	0.433	0.555	0.525	0.608	0.826	0.942
0.8	0.553	0.518	0.598	0.759	0.737	0.963
0.6	0.719	0.469	0.620	0.804	0.910	0.950
0.4	0.823	0.881	0.856	0.938	0.918	0.949
0.2	0.940	0.725	0.949	0.957	0.821	0.947
0.0	0.961	0.953	0.956	0.856	0.974	0.965

through while oldtimers must wait. Agents that finish do so quickly, while early arrivals are "pushed down in the stack," possibly remaining indefinitely. In summary, it seems that, when nodes are scarce, queues are efficient, because moving agents cannot find idle resources, so a strategy of waiting is better. However, when resources are plentiful, moving on pays, because an idle node will be found.

Our underlying hypothesis throughout has been that a decentralized, self-organizing hostless system can, under certain conditions, be more efficient than a hosted system. A host is more efficient whenever there is perfect information available to it, e.g., whenever the host (a) knows everything that is happening (b) everywhere and has this information (c) instantly and (d) costlessly. Whenever one or more of these four conditions is not met, then a hostless system may be more efficient. In reality, information is incomplete, scattered, tardy, and expensive, particularly for physically dispersed locations with imperfect communication.

In real hostless settings, a self-organizing collection of agents is superior to a hosted environment whenever the environment is so complex that the host is unable to manage (to know about and implement swiftly enough) all possible beneficial exchanges. For example, when packaged rations are dispensed en masse to soldiers, they often swap among themselves to get something closer to their personal preferences. In another common circumstance, whenever official rules of exchange become unworkable, unofficial or "black" markets arise. Thus, hostless control of resources seems to emerge naturally whenever swapping is either advantageous to the entrepreneurial agents or necessary to accomplish local or global tasks.

4.5. Future Research

The simulation results presented here, while provocative, barely scratch the surface of our topic: finding optimal decentralized processes for controlling the allocation of network resources. Future plans in our research will include steps to:

(a) conduct more simulation experiments to explore the properties of the CR model; (b) optimize the CR model from the viewpoint of both individual agents and the system as a whole, with incentives to harmonize conflicts; (c) allow agents to return to the system on subsequent missions (so that "track records" count in the estimation of likely future behavior of other agents) while living within budget constraints; (d) vary the intensity of participation; (e) allow individuals to switch strategies in response to recent experience (learning as you go), with the result that the behavior of the current group influences the newly arriving agent's choice of strategy (a Darwinian approach); and (f) investigate other network structures.

5. SUMMARY

In this chapter, we have examined some properties of an approach to resource allocation in networks which is decentralized, or hostless, and thus self-organizing. Such an approach may be applicable to operating systems for networks of intelligent nodes. We focused on one special case, the challenge ring (CR), where agents either utilize an appropriate resource at a node, if idle, or challenge the current user based on strategies leading to cooperation or defection in the context of past experience.

We tested a range of strategies by varying the probability of defection (p) and the sensitivity to past experience (q). System performance, measured by the proportion (P) of completions and the ratio (R) of actual to minimum times to complete, was manipulated by varying the mix of strategies. Our major findings are (a) that cooperation in hostless environments may be better for individuals, and (b) that a hostless system can perform more effectively than traditional hosted FIFO or LIFO systems.

REFERENCES

Axelrod, R. (1984). *The evolution of cooperation.* New York: Basic Books.

Banks, J., & Carson, J. S. (1984). *Discrete-event simulation.* Englewood Cliffs, NJ: Prentice-Hall.

Baran, R. H. (1988, May). Monte Carlo evaluation of a receiver structure based on the Hopfield. *Proceedings of the 19th Annual Pittsburgh Conference on Modeling and Simulation,* pp. 2005–2011.

Chamberlin, E. H. (1933). *The theory of monopolistic competition.* Cambridge, MA: Harvard University Press.

Cournot, A. (1897). *Research into the mathematical principles of the theory of wealth.* New York: Macmillan.

Dongarra, J. J. (Ed.). (1987). *Experimental parallel computing architectures.* Amsterdam, Netherlands: North-Holland.

Dresher, M. (1961). *Games of strategy, theory and applications.* Englewood Cliffs, NJ: Prentice-Hall.

Dutton, J., & Starbuck, W. (1971). *Computer simulation of human behavior.* New York: Wiley & Sons.

Franklin, W. R. (1982, May). On an improved algorithm for decentralized extrema finding in circular configurations of processors. *Communications of the ACM, 25*(5), 336–337.

Fraser, M. D., Gagliano, R. A., & Schaefer, M. E. (1989, March). The simulation of a distributed control model for resource allocation and the implied pricing. *Proceedings of the 22nd Annual Simulation Symposium* (pp. 81–92). New York: IEEE Computer Society Press.

Gagliano, R. A. (1976, March). Some reflections on societal modeling. *Proceedings of the 7th Annual Pittsburgh Conference on Modeling and Simulation,* Instrument Society of America (ISA), pp. 766–770.

Gagliano, R. A., & Lebkowski, K. S. (1979). Cybernetics and a general theory of organization. In *Progress in Cybernetics and Systems Research* (Vol. VII, pp. 143–148). Washington, DC: Hemisphere Publishing Co.

Gagliano, R. A., & Schwartz, A. P. (1981). Systems, models and the jazz orchestra. In G. E. Lasker (Ed.), *Applied systems and cybernetics* (pp. 687–691). New York: Pergamon Press.

Gagliano, R. A. (1983, May). Systems and solutions of people problems. *Proceedings of the 1983 Conference of the Society for General Systems Research* (pp. 767–774). New York: Interscience Publications.

Gagliano, R. A., Fraser, M. D., & Schaefer, M. E. (1987, August). *A market model for distributed control: The role of algorithms for the initial endowment of wealth.* Paper presented at the International Symposium on Systems Research, Informatics and Cybernetics, Baden-Baden, West Germany. (To appear in the forthcoming *Proceedings of 4th International Symposium on Systems Research, Informatics and Cybernetics.*)

Gagliano, R. A., Fraser, M. D., & Schaefer, M. E. (1988, March). Simulation of a market model for distributed control. *Proceedings of the 21st Annual Simulation Symposium* (pp. 171–187). New York: IEEE Computer Society Press.

Gagliano, R. A. (in preparation). *Discrete element models and simulation.*

Hofstadter, D. R. (1985). The Prisoner's Dilemma computer tournaments and the evolution of cooperation. In *Metamagical themas.* New York: Basic Books.

Huberman, B. (1988). The behavior of computational ecologies. In *The ecology of computation.* New York: Elsevier.

Huberman, B. (1989). PARC brings Adam Smith to computing. *Science, 244,* 145–146.

Levy, D. N. (1988). *Computer games II.* New York: Springer-Verlag.

Malone, T. W., Fikes, R. E., & Howard, M. T. (1983). *Enterprise: A market-like scheduler for distributed computing environments* (Working Paper). Palo Alto, CA: Xerox (PARC), Palo Alto Research Center.

Railey, M. R. (1986, January). *Dynamic control structures for cooperating processes.* Unpublished doctoral dissertation, University of Illinois.

Reggia, J. (1985). Virtual lateral inhibition in parallel activation models of associative memory. *Proceedings of the 9th International Joint Conference On Artificial Intelligence* (pp. 244–248).

Samuelson, P. A. (1985). *Foundations of economic analysis*. Cambridge, MA: Harvard University Press.

Schelling, T. C. (1978). *Micromotives and macrobehavior*. New York: W. W. Norton & Co.

Shubik, M. (1980). *Market structure and behavior*. Cambridge, MA: Harvard University Press.

Tanenbaum, A. S. (1984). *Structured computer organization* (2nd ed.). Englewood Cliffs, NJ: Prentice-Hall.

Vitanyi, P. M. B. (1984). Distributed elections in an Archimedean ring of processors. *Proceedings of the 16th ACM Symposium on the Theory of Computing* (pp. 542–547).

von Neumann, J., & Morgenstern, O. (1953). *Theory of games and economic behavior*. Princeton, NJ: Princeton University Press.

Windeknecht, T. G., & D'Angelo, H. (1975, March). The stereotype approach to the modeling and simulation of an elementary school. *IEEE Transactions on Systems, Man and Cybernetics*, pp. 216–225.

6

Network Models of Motor Systems With Many Degrees of Freedom*

F. A. Mussa-Ivaldi
E. Bizzi
Massachusetts Institute of Technology
Dept. of Brain and Cognitive Sciences
Cambridge, MA

P. Morasso
University of Genova
Department of Computer, System and Communication Sciences (DIST)
Genova, Italy

N. Hogan
Massachusetts Institute of Technology
Dept. of Mechanical Engineering
Cambridge, MA

1. INTRODUCTION

In this chapter, we will examine some motor control issues from the perspective of distributed processing models. In particular, we will focus on kinematics and control problems arising in redundant manipulator systems, both biological and artificial. These systems are characterized by an excess of degrees of freedom with respect to the number of parameters required for specifying a task. For example, only six kinematic parameters are required to express the location of a rigid tool in the workspace. In contrast, the human arm has at least seven degrees of freedom, not including those associated with the fingers and with the shoulder-girdle complex. Other examples of motor redundancy can be found in a wide variety of tasks ranging from the generation of a desired net torque at a mechanical joint operated by a multitude of tendon-like actuators to the implementation of dexterous manipulation by robot hands or multiple coordinated arms.

In general, it is widely acknowledged that adding degrees of freedom to a manipulator can significantly improve its dexterity—its ability to perform differ-

* This work was supported by the National Science Foundation, Grant EET-8613104, by the Office of Naval Research, Grant N00014/88/k/0372, and by the National Institute of Neurological Disease and Stroke Research, Grant NS09343.

ent tasks in a wide range of environmental conditions. Redundancy appears to be the key to versatility in human movements, and, for this reason, it has attracted an increasing interest in robotics research.

We can distinguish between two types of redundancy: structural and task-dependent. Structural redundancy arises from fixed constraints such as the presence of multiple muscles acting about a single joint. In contrast, task-dependent redundancy results from specific requirements that may change from one task to another. For example, one may carry an object without being concerned about its orientation or, on the contrary, one may control an orientation, as when transporting a glass, without spilling its contents. In general, the degree of redundancy, that is, the difference between the number of parameters specified by a task and the number of independently controlled actuators, may change from one task to another. For this reason, any general-purpose manipulator is bound to be used with some degrees of redundancy whenever the task requirements become less stringent than those which guided the design process.

Both structural and task-dependent redundancy result in so-called ill-posed problems: problems for which solutions either are not unique or do not exist.[1] We may identify many ill-posed problems in the study of the motor system. One is the problem of determining the coordinated rotations of the arm joints for a planned trajectory of the hand. At the same time, other aspects of sensory-motor information processing involve direct problems that are perfectly well posed, i.e., that admit unique solutions. This is the case when the task is to derive the position of the hand with respect to the body from the knowledge of joint angles measured by locally available sensors. Thus, intelligent control of motor behavior requires the solution of both ill-posed and well-posed problems.

The problem of kinematic redundancy has been addressed by a number of neural network models. Kawato (Kawato, Maeda, Uno, & Suzuki, 1988) has developed a network that generates coordinated trajectories by implementing a minimum torque-rate constraint. A general network architecture for generating sequences of actions has been formulated by Jordan (1986). Using this architecture, Jordan (1988) addressed the problem of redundancy by defining an error functional which incorporates both linear and nonlinear constraints in task coordinates. Jordan used the transpose of the Jacobian matrix to transform this error from task to articulatory space.

Here, we present a different approach based upon the idea of exploiting the mechanical and geometrical properties of motor systems for deriving distributed representations of the control and planning processes. This approach exploits the notion of motor impedance: a function that characterizes the force output generated by a system in response to an external perturbation.

---

[1] Given a system of N equations in M unknowns, a multiplicity of solutions occurs when N is less than M. In contrast, when N is larger than M, it is generally impossible to satisfy simultaneously all the equations with any setting of the unknowns.

Mechanical impedance can be either related to intrinsic mechanical properties such as inertia, viscosity, and stiffness, or it can be a convenient way to represent the action of a controller at the interface with the environment (Hogan, 1987; Slotine & Li, 1987; Colgate & Hogan, 1988). For example, a one-dimensional PD (proportional-derivative) controller generates a force, F, proportional to the error between actual and nominal position, $x - x_n$, and to the current velocity x':

$$F = K_P (x - x_n) + K_D x'. \tag{1}$$

The same expression also represents the behavior of a passive mechanical system composed of a spring (with stiffness K_P and rest-length x_n) and of a dashpot (with viscosity K_D). An external observer whose only source of information was the mechanical interaction between the environment and a system characterized by the above equation would not be able to establish whether he is dealing with a passive viscoelastic object or with a PD-controlled device.

This *physical equivalence* is the conceptual foundation of impedance control (Hogan, 1987). Controlling the impedance of a manipulator has been proven effective in a variety of interactive tasks (Hogan, 1980, 1985b; Mason, 1981). In particular, it has been recently demonstrated (Colgate & Hogan, 1988) that a necessary and sufficient condition for stability during contacts with the environment is that the manipulator can be described, at the interface with the environment, as a passive mechanical impedance. Impedance-control schemes have also been proposed in robotics for planning of movements within cluttered environments (Hogan 1985b; Kathib, 1986; Koditschek, 1987). Obstacle avoidance can be achieved by associating to each object a repulsive potential energy field and to the target position an attractive potential energy field. Since energy functions can be combined, the resulting net potential energy field is a "landscape" with hills and valleys. Therefore, the navigation of the manipulator becomes equivalent to gradient descent.

Here, we show how mechanical impedance (in particular its "elastic" component[2]) leads to a natural representation and regularization of kinematic redundancy. In fact, an important physical property of a system characterized by elastic properties is that it tends to assume configurations of minimum potential energy. This minimum-energy principle is satisfied by any passive physical system which "derives" the configurational change produced by an external perturbation when the number of degrees of freedom exceeds the number of kinematic constraints.

Consider, for example, the network of springs shown in Figure 6.1. If a displacement, dX, is imposed at the point P, each spring will move by an amount depending upon its own stiffness. At the same time, the global configuration of

---

2 The elastic component of the mechanical impedance, also known as *stiffness*, establishes the relation at steady state between input displacements and output forces.

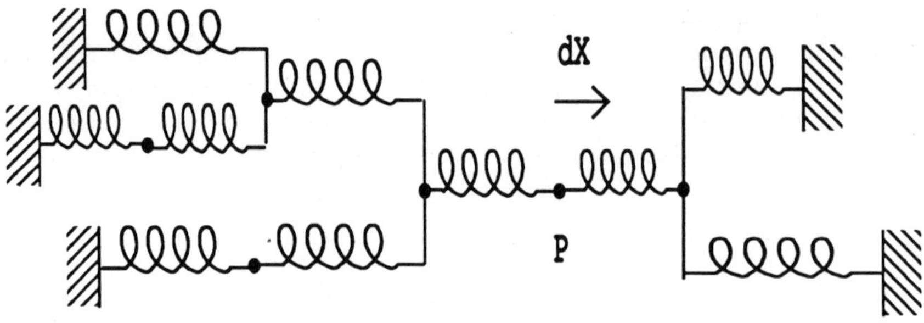

Figure 6.1. A network of springs.

the network will correspond to a minimum potential energy compatible with the location of P. The mathematical description of this physical process leads directly to a distributed representation, since the interactions among mechanical components are intrinsically local. *The minimization of potential energy is a "global" property arising from local interactions.* Similar principles have been widely used in control theory to study the dynamic stability of complex systems by means of Lyapunov functions. For example, Hopfield (1982) has succeeded in characterizing the dynamical behavior of large networks of linear threshold units by means of global potential functions. In a Hopfield network each unit, on the basis of its own inputs, determines its own state update. Any such local decision contributes to the minimization of a global potential function. The same happens in a perturbed mechanical system. However, in the latter case, the global potential function is not an abstract computational concept but a direct expression of the system's elastic properties.

One can extend the solution corresponding to a passive motion to actively controlled systems by choosing to update the control input of each element so as to cancel the stress induced by a simulated external perturbation. This approach has been named the *passive-motion paradigm* (Mussa-Ivaldi, Morasso, & Zaccaria, 1988). The simulated perturbation, for example, can force the hand along a desired trajectory. When the input signals obtained by this process are generated in the absence of a perturbation, the system will tend to reproduce the same trajectory.

In this chapter, we will present the notion of impedance control both in the biological and in the robotics domain. In particular, we will focus on the consequences of the actuator's mechanical properties, with respect to the problem of generating trajectories and interactive behavior. Then, we will consider the general formulation of the passive-motion paradigm, and we will show that this approach leads to a distributed representation of kinematic constraints. This is a tree-structured scheme in which each node represents either a common-position or a common-force constraint. For each type of node, specific algorithms are defined which simulate both passive and active changes of position and effort variables. Finally, we will discuss two different implementations of the passive-motion paradigm. One is based upon the explicit algebraic representation of kinematic transformations. The other is a model that approximates the explicit kinematic representation but implements the constraints in an implicit way through a relaxation algorithm.

2. ACTUATOR MECHANICS AND COMPUTATION

2.1. Some Facts about Muscles

Several investigators of biological systems (Feldman, 1966; Rack & Westbury, 1969; Bizzi, Polit, & Morasso, 1976; Nichols & Houk, 1976) have focused on the role of the muscle's mechanical properties in motor control. Gordon, Huxley, and Julian (1966) studied the force/length relationship at steady-state in individual muscle fibers. These authors related the development of tension at different muscle lengths to the degree of overlap between actin and myosin filaments[3] (see Figure 6.2). The process of generating force within the muscle is caused by the interaction between actin and myosin filaments (Huxley, 1963, 1969). Briefly, when the motoneuronal drive to a muscle increases, new chemical bonds or *cross-bridges* are formed between the actin and myosin filaments. Consequently, an increase of muscle tension is generated concomitantly with an increase of muscle stiffness.

Despite the complexity of the molecular processes underlying the generation of muscle force, at the macroscopic level, a muscle can be characterized as a tunable elastic element. This property is illustrated in Figure 6.3, where tensions measured in the cat's soleus muscle are plotted against muscle lengths at various level of neural activations. The data were obtained by Rack and Westbury (1969), who devised a method for applying a set of stimuli to different portions of the same nerve. All the stimuli had the same frequency but different phases in order to avoid synchronous stimulation of all muscle fibers. Then for each tested frequency, Rack and Westbury measured the steady-state tension corresponding to different muscle lengths.

Conceptually, a muscle's spring-like behavior can be summarized as follows:

1. For a fixed value of the motoneuronal input, the force generated at steady state is a function of muscle length.
2. This force/length function can be integrated to derive a potential function

[3] In the structural organization of vertebrate striated muscles, sarcomeres are the constituent units which are repeated longitudinally along the muscle fibers. These units consist primarily of comb-like arrays of overlapping actin and miosin filaments.

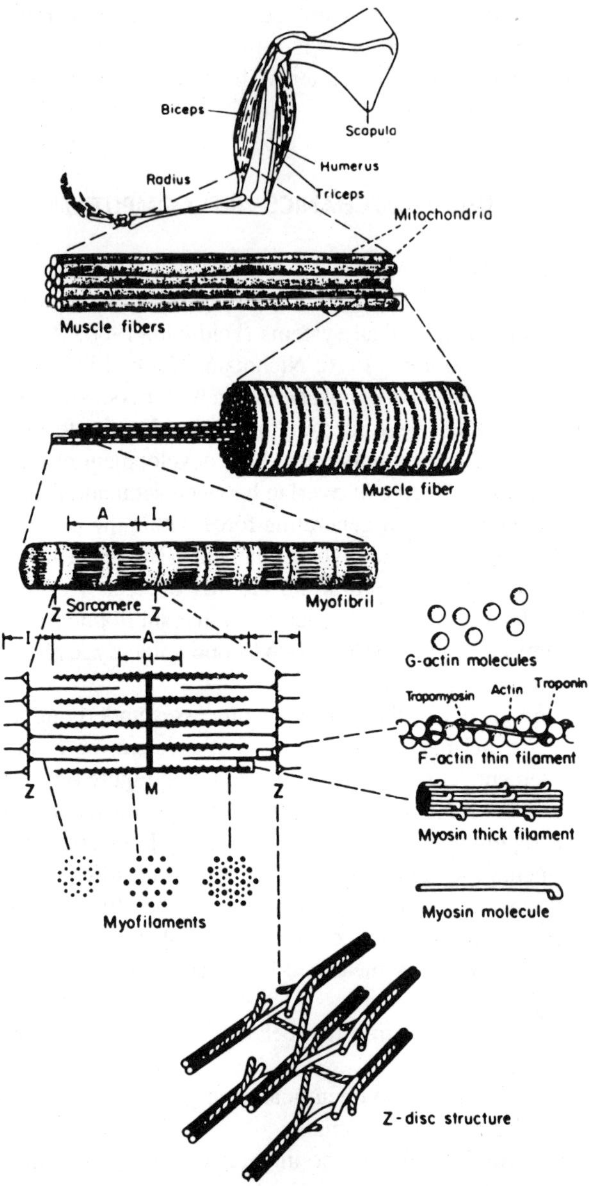

Figure 6.2. Organization of striated muscle structure. (From T. A. McMahon, *Muscles, reflexes and locomotion*. Princeton, NJ: Princeton University Press, 1984.)

equivalent to the energy stored (or released) during an externally imposed displacement.

3. Changes of neural input to the muscle smoothly affect the force/length relationship without drastically changing its shape.

Indicating by f, l, and u the tension, the length, and the neural input to a muscle, and by E the stored elastic energy, we may summarize the above statements by the expressions:

f = f(l, u) and

$$E = \int_{l_1}^{l_2} f(l,u)dl \tag{2}$$

We want to stress that, in the above definition of spring-like behavior, the force/length relation is not required to be linear. As a matter of fact, the force/length curves in Figure 6.3 display considerable nonlinearity. However, for any value of length, there is a locally linear relation between displacements, dl, and effort changes, df:

df = k(l) dl.

In the above expression, $k = \frac{\partial f}{\partial l}$ is the local muscle *stiffness* which, in general, depends upon muscle length. Whenever the stiffness is not zero, it is also possible to define a local *compliance*, $c = k^{-1}$, which maps a change in input force into an output displacement. Figure 6.3 shows that, for most activation levels, the physiological force/length curves display a maximum, that is a point of zero stiffness, followed by a decline of tension at increasing length. At such points, the muscle compliance is not defined.

Muscles are arranged about the joints in agonist–antagonist configurations. A limb's posture is maintained when the forces exerted by the agonist and antagonist muscle groups are equal and opposite. When an external force is applied, the limb is displaced by an amount depending both upon the external force and upon the stiffness of the muscles.[4] When the external force is removed, the limb should return to the original position. Experimental studies of motor behavior in

---

[4] For the present discussion it is immaterial that part of the muscle's "restoring force" may be due to reflexes. In fact, the static reflex response can be modelled by expressing the input, u, as the combination of a centrally originated signal, u_c, and a feedback signal, $u_R(l)$, which is a function of l. Then, we have $f = f(l, u_R(l), u_c) = f'(l, u_c)$, and the reflex behavior is equivalent to a stiffness component, $k_R = \frac{\partial f'}{\partial l} = \frac{\partial f}{\partial u_R}\frac{\partial u_R}{\partial l}$

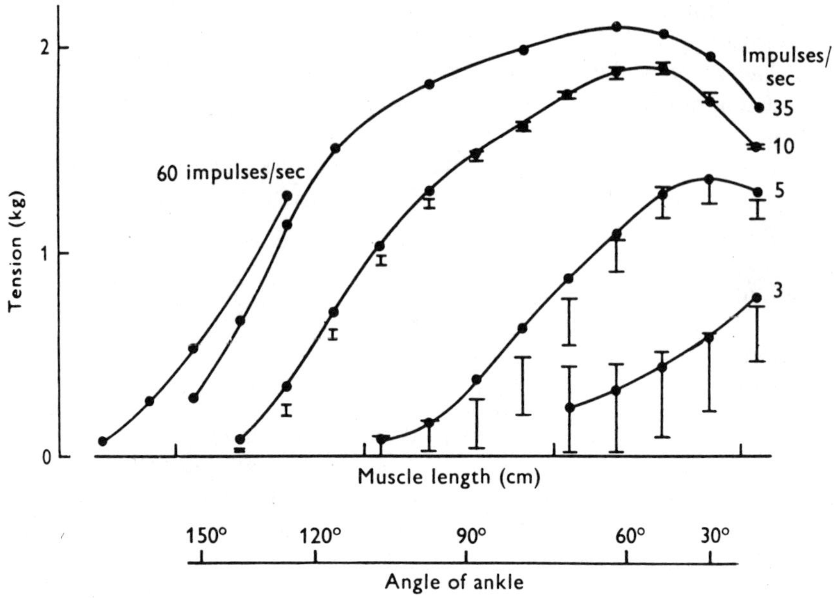

Figure 6.3. Length-tension curves measured in the cat's soleus muscle. Different curves correspond to different stimulus rates. The vertical lines show the limits of tension fluctuations during synchronous stimulation. (From P. M. H. Rack & D. R. Westbury, *The effects of length and stimulus rate on tension in the isometric cat soleus muscle. J. physiol., 204,* 443–460, 1969.)

humans and monkeys have confirmed that arm posture is indeed characterized by spring-like properties (Bizzi, Accornero, Chapple, & Hogan, 1984; Mussa-Ivaldi, Hogan, & Bizzi, 1985).

2.2. Virtual Trajectories

This view of posture has been extended to the analysis of movement and trajectory formation (Bizzi et al., 1984; Hogan, 1984; McKeon, Hogan, & Bizzi, 1984; Flash, 1987). The observation that posture is maintained by the equilibrium between the length–tension properties of opposing muscles led to the idea that movements result from a shift of the equilibrium point caused by a change in neural input. This hypothesis was first proposed by Feldman (1966). The studies by Kelso (1977), Kelso and Holt (1980), and Bizzi et al. (1984) provided the related experimental evidence.

Here we discuss the implications of the moving equilibrium hypothesis in a computational perspective. To this end, we start with a formal definition of the concept of virtual trajectory. A detailed discussion of related control issues can be found in Hogan (1985a).

Let us first consider the case of a simple, one-dimensional system characterized by the tunable-elastic behavior of Equation (2). Let the stiffness be defined, locally about a given length and at constant input, as $k = \frac{df}{dl}$. The equilibrium position of the system, in the absence of external forces, is given by the condition f(l,u) = 0. A stable equilibrium position is characterized by negative stiffness (i.e., the forces about the equilibrium are attractive): whereas a positive stiffness implies an unstable equilibrium, similar to the equilibrium of a ball on the top of a hill.

If the input is a continuous function of time, u(t), the static equilibrium condition becomes:

$$f_e(l,u(t)) = 0 \tag{3}$$

where the subscript, e, indicates that f_e is the "elastic" or "steady-state" component of the total force acting on the system. If the environment does not prevent the system from moving as the input changes in time, the total force may also contain significant inertial and viscous components.

The above equation defines implicitly a (unique) map from u(t) to l:

$$l_e(t) = l(u(t)) \tag{4}$$

with $l_e(t)$ and u(t) satisfying Equation (3), provided that the stiffness, k, at each equilibrium position, $l_e(t)$, is not zero. This result is a direct consequence of a fundamental theorem on implicit functions. For two variables, x and y, this theorem can be stated as follows. Let F(x,y) be a function continuous with its first partial derivatives in a region R of the plane x,y and let the following conditions be satisfied: (a) $F(x^0,y^0) = 0$ at a point $P^0 = (x^0,y^0)$ in R, and (b) the partial derivative $\frac{\partial F}{\partial y}$ is different from zero at the point P^0. Then, the expression F(x,y) = 0 can be solved; i.e., a single-valued function can be defined in the vicinity of P^0.

The function $l_e(t)$ is the system's *virtual trajectory,* which corresponds to the input function u(t). A few important features of the virtual-trajectory concept are highlighted by the above unidimensional example. In particular:

- the virtual trajectory is not a "hypothesis" but a direct consequence of muscle spring-like properties.
- it can be regarded as a map from the control input (u) to an entity (l_e) which

has the same physical dimension as a state component (l, the actual position of the system at any time).

- this map is given by an algebraic, rather than by a differential, equation.[5]

The fact that a muscle is characterized by significant stiffness properties (i.e., that k is generally different from zero) implies that it cannot be considered a "good" force generator. An ideal force generator, like an ideal voltage source in an electric circuit, should have negligible output impedance. In other words, the output force should not depend upon the operating position but only upon the control input. This criterion has been followed in the design of many robotic actuators, such as conventional torque motors. In contrast, biological evolution seems to have chosen a different route by developing muscles whose stiffness not only is significant but also depends on the level of neural activation. The notion of virtual trajectory transforms this feature into a strength rather than a weakness of the biological design. Actually, according to the implicit-function theorem, the actuators *must* have nonzero stiffness for mapping a sequence of control inputs into a sequence of well-defined equilibrium lengths. However, we will show that points of zero muscle stiffness do not necessarily constitute a problem in a multidimensional situation.

The extension of the virtual-trajectory concept to a multidimensional system is straightforward. Let us consider, for example, a serial arrangement of n limb segments interconnected by rotational joints. The configuration of this system is the array $q = [q_1, \ldots, q_n]^T$ of joint angles, and the net torque is the array $T = [T_1, \ldots, T_n]^T$ of joint torques. Furthermore, the limbs are driven by a set of m muscles with $m > n$; i.e., there are more muscles than joints. Collectively, the muscles are represented by a length array, $l = [l_1, \ldots, l_m]^T$, by a force array, $f = [f_1, \ldots, f_m]^T$, and by an array of input activations, $u = [u_1, \ldots, u_m]^T$. In the hypothesis that each muscle is characterized by tunable spring-like properties, the overall muscle behavior is described by the vector equivalent of Equation (2), namely:

$$f = f(l, u) \tag{5}$$

The n-dimensional joint-torque vector is obtained from the m-dimensional muscle-tension vector by multiplying the latter by the matrix of moment arms, μ.

---

[5] In general, for a dynamic system, a map of the form $x' = g(x, u)$ is defined. This map allows one to derive the future time course of the system state, x, given the input function u(t) and the initial value of the state, x_0. Since the state equation is a differential equation, its solution depends on the arbitrary selection of the initial conditions. In contrast, the virtual trajectory, being the result of an algebraic equation, does not contain arbitrary terms. Actually, the virtual trajectory defines the initial conditions for the state equations since the system is at static equilibrium before the onset of a movement.

The elements of μ, $\mu_{i,j}$ are the partial derivatives $\frac{\partial l_i}{\partial q_j}$. The relation $l = l(q)$, which uniquely defines the muscle-length array as a function of the joint configuration is, in general, nonlinear. Therefore, the matrix of the moment arms is also a function of joint configuration. Using Equation (5), the net joint torque vector becomes:

$$T = \mu(q)^T f = \mu(q)^T f(l(q), u) = T(q, u) \tag{6}$$

When the input array is a function of time, $u(t)$, the static equilibrium condition, $T = 0$, defines implicitly the joint virtual trajectory as a function of $u(t)$:

$$q_e(t) = q(u(t)) \text{ such that } \quad T(q_e(t), u(t)) = 0 \tag{7}$$

which is analogous to Equation (4.) From the fundamental theorem on implicit functions, the necessary and sufficient condition for the existence and uniqueness of the virtual trajectory, $q_e(t) = q(u(t))$, is that the determinant of the joint stiffness matrix R, whose elements are $R_{ij} = \frac{\partial T_i}{\partial q_j}$ (i, j = 1, . . . , n), doesn't vanish[6] at any equilibrium point.

This condition is equivalent to requiring nonzero stiffness in a one-dimensional systems. Here, a negative joint-stiffness determinant corresponds to stable equilibrium whereas a positive determinant implies unstable equilibrium. Note, however, that asking for a nonzero joint-stiffness determinant is less stringent than requiring nonzero stiffness for each muscle. As we have already pointed out, individual muscles may actually be operating at points of zero stiffness. However, the stiffness about a joint is obtained from a weighted sum of the stiffness supplied by all the muscles operating about that joint. Hence, in order to have nonzero joint stiffness, it is not necessary to require nonzero muscle stiffness. Actually, there is experimental evidence (Mussa-Ivaldi et al., 1985) that the multijoint elastic forces during posture are attractive. In that case, the condition for defining virtual trajectories in hand or joint coordinates is satisfied.

The muscle's spring-like properties allow mapping the input, u, into a lower dimensional entity, the equilibrium arm-configuration, which has the physical

---

[6] The theorem of implicit functions is readily generalized to a system of n equations:

$$F_i(x_1, \ldots, x_m, y_1, \ldots, y_n) = 0 \quad ; \quad i = 1, \ldots n$$

by requiring that at a solution point, $P^0 = (x_1^0, \ldots, x_m^0, y_1^0, \ldots, y_n^0)$, the functional (or Jacobian) determinant, $\frac{\partial F}{\partial y}$ is different from zero. Then, the above n equations can be solved for y_i, i.e., n functions, $y_i = f_i(x_1, \ldots, x_n)$, can be defined, in the vicinity of P^0.

dimension of a position variable. Hence, the virtual trajectory, together with the joint stiffness, can be regarded as a summary of all the inputs involved in the execution of a movement.

An important consequence of virtual trajectories is that they can be used to avoid the computation of inverse dynamics. The inertial and viscous components of the dynamics equations can be treated as "perturbing torques" that make the arm deviate from the desired path, which is specified as a sequence of static equilibrium configurations. At moderate speeds and accelerations, the difference between actual and virtual motion is small and can be neglected. Clearly, as speed and acceleration increase, limb inertia and viscosity would be expected to cause larger deviations from the virtual trajectory. However, these deviations can be corrected by increasing the stiffness and/or by modifying the virtual trajectory itself.

The elastic properties of the actuators also provide stability to the planned movements (Hogan, 1985a). In a computational approach based on the explicit solution of inverse dynamics, problems arise when external perturbations (as in a collision with an obstacle) cause a deviation from the preprogrammed path. In such a case, the dynamics must be recomputed or some special servocontrol mechanisms must be provided. In contrast, if one obtains movement by shifting the equilibrium position defined by elastic actuators, a deviation from the intended path simply results in larger restoring forces, without the need of computation or of particular control schemes (McKeon et al., 1984).

2.3. Position and Force Control

The idea of generating movements via virtual trajectories is also the key to representing and solving more complex problems arising in functional manipulation. Indeed, very few motor tasks merely involve controlling the trajectory of a manipulator. Functional behavior also requires a manipulator to interact with objects in its environment. This dynamic interaction would be expected to have a profound effect on the performance of the system.

There are many possible ways in which a control system might deal with dynamic interaction, and indeed finding the best way is a focus of intensive research in robotics. Here, we consider one way which is a direct generalization of the virtual trajectory concept. The central hypothesis is that movements are planned as temporal sequences of static equilibrium positions. Then, if the manipulating system encounters an object, the same strategy is also an effective way to control contact.

Consider the following one-dimensional example. A robot hand (Figure 6.4a) must move downwards to contact a surface and push on it. The hand is assumed to be controlled such that a simple relation between force and position is maintained. For simplicity, let the force, F, be proportional to the separation between

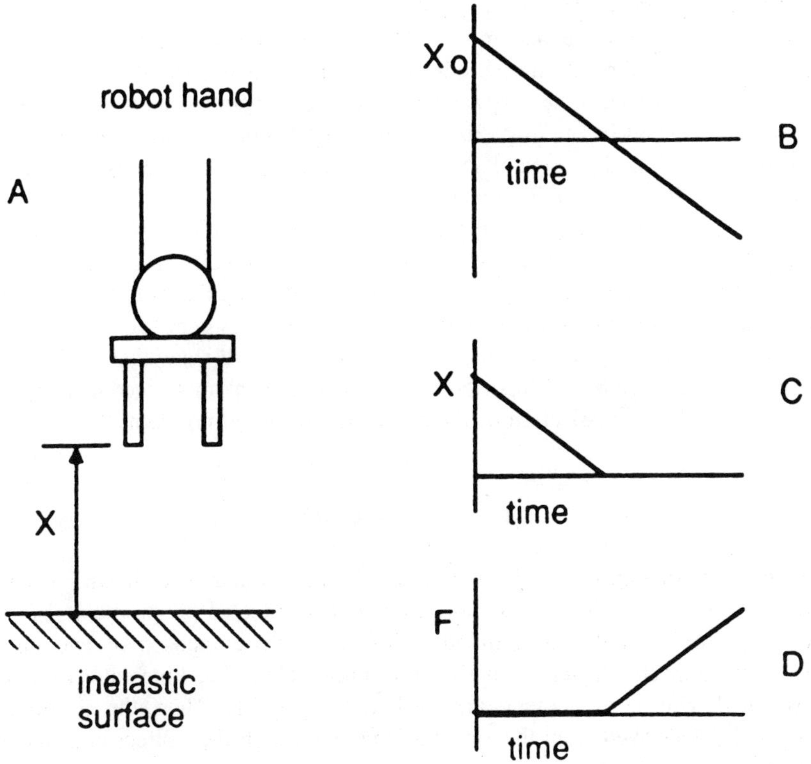

Figure 6.4. (a) One-dimensional contact task; (b) Virtual position; (c) Actual position; (d) Contact force.

the virtual position, X_0, and the actual position, X, of the robot hand: $F = K(X - X_0)$ where K is a proportionality constant.

Next, assume that the virtual position is moved slowly and steadily downwards as shown in Figure 6.4b. As long as the robot's hand is clear of the surface, the force is zero and the actual position of the hand tracks the virtual position as shown in Figure 4c. As soon as the hand contacts the surface, the actual position can no longer follow the virtual position, because of the physical constraint imposed by the surface. But once the hand is in contact with the surface, the task is to control the force exerted. This is easily accomplished by specifying the depth the virtual position "penetrates" into the surface. As the virtual position moves deeper into the surface, the force rises proportionally as stated by the relation between force and position (see Figure 6.4d).

This simple example illustrates that the virtual trajectory is an effective way to represent the control of free motion and the control of interaction forces. With separate representations for motions and contacts, the planner should carefully establish at which point in time one type of controller takes over the other one. In this case, it is intuitive that even moderate uncertainty in the model of the environment could result in severe instability at the contact surface. In contrast, with a unified virtual-trajectory representation, uncertainties about the environment simply result in an effort error which depends continuously upon the error in surface location. This type of approach has been shown to insure stable contact (Wlassich, 1986; Colgate & Hogan, 1988).

In summary, we have shown that tasks as diverse as maintaining posture, generating movements, and controlling interaction forces may be considered within a unique framework by adopting the view that the inputs to the actuators select the equilibrium configuration of the controlled system together with its impedance properties. In the following sections, we will show that this control hypothesis also leads to a distributed representation of motor redundancy together with the regularization of the associated ill-posed problems.

3. PASSIVE MOTION

The task of generating coordinated motion in a redundant mechanism has been conventionally described as an ill-posed inverse kinematics problem. Let us consider, for example, an extremely simple system composed of two linear elements connected in series, as shown in Figure 6.5a. The kinematic variables associated with these elements are the lengths l_1 and l_2. Then, the net system length, L, is derived from the element lengths through the "direct kinematics" equation:

$$L = l_1 + l_2 \tag{8}$$

Given the above expression, the inverse kinematics problem consists in finding the values of l_1 and l_2 that correspond to a desired total length, L. A geometrical interpretation of this problem is shown in Figure 6.5b, where the kinematic space of the system is represented as a two-dimensional coordinate frame. Each axis of this frame represents the length of one element. The oblique line is at a distance L from the origin and corresponds to the constraint Equation (8). Then, all (and only) the pairs of values (l_1, l_2) corresponding to the points on this line are solutions of the inverse-kinematic problems for a desired displacement, L. Optimization methods result in the selection of a specific point by adding some further constraint. For example, the point $D = \left(\frac{L}{2}, \frac{L}{2}\right)$, located at the intersection of the solution line with the perpendicular drawn from the origin, corresponds to a minimum-norm criterion.

The most common engineering approach to an underdetermined problem consists in defining cost functions according to specific goals, which include

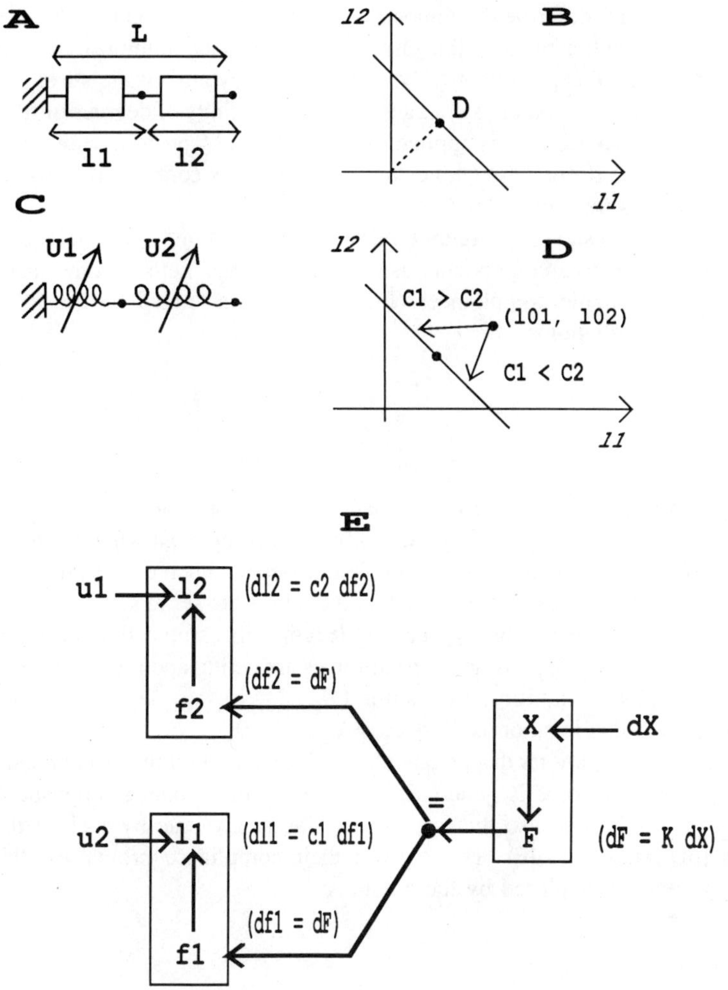

Figure 6.5. Passive Motion in a simple system (see text).

avoiding singular configurations (Bailleul, Hollerbach, & Brockett, 1984), minimizing joint torques (Hollerbach & Suh, 1985), joint motion (Brooks, 1982), or kinetic energy (Kathib, 1983). Here we present a different point of view, based on simulating passive motions within a field of elastic forces. This approach was introduced by Mussa-Ivaldi et al. (1988) and has been named the *passive-motion paradigm*. Essentially, the passive-motion paradigm exploits the fact that a passive displacement of a physical system characterized by impedance properties always leads to a well-posed problem. This is the case regardless of the imbalance between the system's degrees of freedom and the number of dimensions necessary to fully describe the imposed displacement. The regularization principle implicitly implemented by this physical solution is the minimization of potential energy. This fact is dramatically demonstrated by any elastic sheet, such as the surface of a drum which is characterized by an infinity of degrees of freedom. When a local displacement is applied at a point (e.g., by pushing with a pencil at the center of the drum), the whole surface changes its configuration so that the strain-energy is minimized.

In the example shown in Figure 6.5, the passive-motion paradigm requires the definition of the two components as elastic elements. Let's assume that these elements are tunable compliances (Figure 5c) characterized by the following length/tension relations:

$$l_1 = c_1(u_1)\, f_1 + l0_1(u_1)$$

$$l_2 = c_2(u_2)\, f_2 + l0_2(u_2). \tag{9}$$

The parameters c_1 and c_2 are the element compliances. The parameters $l0_1$ and $l0_2$ are rest-lengths (the lengths assumed by each component when the tension is zero). Both the compliance and the rest-length depend upon each element's input in a known way. Let us also assume that the inputs are set to some initial value, $u_{1,\ INIT}$, $u_{2,\ INIT}$. Accordingly, the rest-length will assume the corresponding values $l0_{1,\ INIT}$, $l0_{2,\ INIT}$. If no external forces are acting upon the system, it will settle to a "global" equilibrium position $L0_{INIT} = l0_{1,\ INIT} + l0_{2,\ INIT}$. The net compliance at this location is $C = c_1 + c_2$ ($C \neq 0$).

If at this point, a total displacement, dL, is imposed on the system endpoint, then a net elastic force is generated, $dF = C^{-1}\, dL$, which is opposite to the displacement. This is also the force "seen" at steady state by each of the elements ($df_1 = df_2 = dF$). Then, given their compliance properties, the two elements will be displaced by the amounts:

$$dl_1 = c_1\, dF = \frac{c_1}{c_1 + c_2}\, dL \tag{10}$$

$$dl_2 = c_2\, dF = \frac{c_2}{c_1 + c_2}\, dL.$$

Thus, we have effectively an inverse kinematic map from dL to the pair dl_1, dl_2.

It is readily seen that this solution corresponds to the point of minimum potential energy compatible with the kinematic constraint:

$$dl_1 + dl_2 = dL. \tag{11}$$

In fact, the potential energy, E, in the vicinity of the equilibrium configuration, $l0_{1,INIT}$, $l0_{2,INIT}$, is

$$E = \frac{dl_1^2}{2c_1} + \frac{dl_2^2}{2c_2} \tag{12}$$

Then, the first (second) Equation (10) is directly obtained by substituting Equation (11) for dl_2 (dl_1) in Equation (12) and finding the solution for $\frac{\partial E}{\partial l_1} = 0$ $\left(\frac{\partial E}{\partial l_2} = 0.\right)$

From this simple example, it is possible to make some important observations. First, the minimum norm solution, $dl_1 = dl_2 = \frac{dL}{2}$, is the "natural" response to a passive displacement when $c_1 = c_2$. By choosing different patterns of compliance, one obtains different points on the solution set (Figure 6.5d) in a way that is strictly consistent with the notion of impedance: the more one element is compliant (relative to the others), the more it will tend to contribute to the global motion. In general, different settings of the elastic properties associated with the degrees of freedom will yield different configurations of minimum potential energy, given the same externally imposed displacements. Since we are assuming that the control signals can tune the local elastic properties of the actuators, we have at our disposal a mechanism to generate different patterns of movements, given a single kinematic task.

The second observation concerns information processing. The computational scheme that we used for deriving the expressions (10) is inherently modular and distributed. In Figure 6.5e, each physical element is represented by a processing unit which computes its position and effort on the basis of the environmental constraints and of the unit's elastic behavior. Furthermore, a computational unit is introduced representing the elastic behavior of the whole system: the unit's effort and position variables are F and L, respectively, and its compliance is C ($= c_1 + c_2$.)

Each element derives its own effort and position changes on the basis of locally available information. When a displacement, dL, is imposed by the environment on the element representing the net system, the latter derives the effort change, dF, multiplying dL by its own stiffness. Then, this element sends this information to the elements representing smaller components. These compute their displacements independently of each other on the basis of their compliance. All the coupling information, in this case the net compliance, $C = c_1 + c_2$, is concentrated in the elastic elements which represent the whole system.

It is possible to go one step further in the passive-motion paradigm by letting each element change its input so that the new position is at equilibrium. Denoting by σ_i the sensitivity of element i's length to a change in input, $\sigma_i = \frac{\partial l_i}{\partial u_l}$ and assuming that σ_i^{-1} exixts, an input update $du_i = \sigma_i^{-1}\, dl_i$ applied independently to each controlled element is sufficient to bring the whole system to equilibrium in the new position $L' = LO_{INIT} + dL$.

As happens with other types of network (Hopfield, 1982), the overall behavior of the system is characterized by a global energy function. In our case, this function is the actual potential energy associated with the system's spring-like properties. Following the local input-update rule outlined above is equivalent to requiring that the potential energy is minimized on a global scale. At the same time, the input-update carries out the task of displacing the system by the required amount dL.

In the next sections, we will focus on the application of the passive-motion paradigm to more complex motor geometries involving both common-position and common-effort constraints as well as significant non-linearities. We will show that the passive-motion paradigm leads to a distributed representation which is consistent with the physical properties of the controlled system.

4. KINEMATICS AND CONNECTIONS

In the following discussion, an *element* is formally defined as a pair of position and effort variables plus a function relating these variables at steady state. This function can have either *stiffness causality* or *compliance causality*. In the former case, the effort is derived from the position whereas in the latter, the position is derived from the effort. An element is said to be *reversible* if both relations are defined.

An N-dimensional geometrical space is associated with each element. In this space, efforts and positions are defined as arrays with a specific physical interpretation.[7] For example, a muscle is represented by a one-dimensional element in which effort and position are tension and length variables. The end-effector of a manipulator is a six-dimensional element whose position is an array of translational and rotational components and whose effort is the corresponding force/torque array.

The term *connection* will be used here in a generalized sense to indicate a set of transformations between effort and position variables belonging to different elements. These transformations arise from kinematic constraints which can occur in two forms: as generalized common-position constraints, establishing

[7] In a more rigorous definition, an element's generalized position (or configuration) is a point within an N-dimensional manifold. Given a point on the configuration manifold, infinitesimal displacements (and velocities) are vectors lying in the plane tangent to the manifold at that point. Generalized forces are N-dimensional vectors in the cotangent space of the configuration manifold. Here, however, we only want to stress that positions, displacements, and efforts are N-dimensional objects.

parallel connections, and as generalized common-effort constraints, establishing *serial* connections.

A connection is established between a set of *component* elements and a single *compound* element. Occasionally, the notions of compound and component elements is directly related to actual physical connections within an assembly. For example, two muscles (component elements) may operate about a given joint (compound element). In other cases, however, the distinction between compound and component elements corresponds to a hierarchical relation between controlled and task-related variables. For example, when a single element representing the joint-space description of a manipulator is connected to a single element representing the end-effector space, the former element is considered a component and the latter a compound. A connection is said to be *redundant* when the sum of the number of dimensions of the component elements exceeds the number of dimensions of the compound element.

In the following discussion of connection topologies we will use lower-case letters to represent variables belonging to component elements and upper-case letters for the compound-element variables. Thus, for a connection involving N components, the following entities are defined:

- x_i = the position vector of the ith component element ($x_{i,j}$ is the jth coordinate of this vector)
- X = the position vector of the compound element (X_l is the eth coordinate of this vector)
- f_i = the effort vector of the i-th component element.
- F = the effort vector of the compound element
- c_i = the compliance matrix of the i-th component element; $c_{i,l,m} = \dfrac{\partial x_{i,l}}{\partial f_m}$
- C = the compliance matrix of the compound element; $C_{l,m} = \dfrac{\partial X_l}{\partial F_m}$.
- k_i = the stiffness matrix of the i-th component element; $k_{i,l,m} = \dfrac{\partial f_{i,l}}{\partial x_m}$
- K = the stiffness matrix of the compound element; $K_{l,m} - \dfrac{\partial F_l}{\partial X_m}$.

4.1. Parallel Connections

The transformations defining a parallel connection are:

$$x_i = x_i(X) \quad ; i = 1, \ldots, N \tag{13}$$

$$F = \sum_{i=1}^{N} J_i(X)^T f_i \tag{14}$$

The matrices J_i are the Jacobians of (13): $J_i = \frac{\partial x_i}{\partial X}$.

The first expressions, (13), represent a generalized common-position constraint: the positions of the component elements are uniquely determined as functions of the compound element position. In a redundant connection, these functions cannot be inverted to derive X from an arbitrary set of x_i since there are more constraint equations than unknowns. The second expression, (14), which is also noninvertible in a redundant connection, is a direct consequence of Equation (13) and of the principle of virtual work. This principle states that the mechanical work (the inner product of force and displacement) is invariant by coordinate transformations, that is:

$$\sum_{i=1}^{N} f_i^T \, dx_i = \sum_{i=1}^{N} f_i^T \, J_i(X) \, dX = F^T \, dX.$$

A biological example of parallel connection is provided by the relation between the muscles and the skeleton. Given a set of muscles operating about a number of joints, the joint torques are uniquely derived from the muscle tensions and moment arms. The moment arms are the partial derivatives of the functions mapping joint angles into muscle lengths. In this case, we have two different ill-posed problems:

1. Finding the joint angle corresponding to an arbitrary set of muscle lengths. There are more constraint equations than unknowns. Thus, the problem may have no solutions: muscle lengths cannot be selected arbitrarily.
2. Finding the muscle forces corresponding to a given joint-torque. There are more unknowns than equations. Therefore, the problem has an infinity of solutions.

In a parallel connection, the local elastic properties of the components are transformed into the corresponding local properties of the compound element. In particular, the net stiffness K about a point (X_0, F_0) is given by:

$$K = \sum_{i=1}^{N} (\Gamma_i + J^T{}_i \, k_i \, J_i) \qquad (15)$$

This expression is obtained by differentiating Equation (14) with respect to X and by taking into account that for each component element the force depends upon the position, i.e., $f_i = \mathrm{f}_i(x_i)$. The matrices Γ_i are required to account for non-linearities in the transformations (13). These matrices vanish when (a) Equations

(13) are linear or, (b) the operating forces f_i are zero, i.e., when the component elements are at equilibrium. The element $\Gamma_{i,j,l}$ of Γ_i is given by:

$$\Gamma_{i,j,l} = \sum_{k=1}^{Ni} \frac{\partial^2 x_{i,k}}{\partial X_j \partial X_l} f_{i,k} \tag{16}$$

(N_i is the number of dimensions of the ith component element.)

If the compound element is invertible, i.e., if $\det(K) \neq 0$, its compliance is:

$$C = K^{-1}. \tag{17}$$

4.2. Serial Connections

The description of a serial connection is dual to that of a parallel connection:

$$X = X(x_1, x_2, \ldots, x_N) \tag{18}$$

$$f_i = J^T{}_i F \tag{19}$$

where $J_i = \dfrac{\partial X}{\partial x_i}$. The forces of the component elements are uniquely determined, given the compound-element force, by the generalized common-force constraint (19). On the other hand, the position of the compound element is expressed as a function of the positions of the component elements. As was the case for the common-position constraint, in this case the force transformations (19) are a direct consequence of the principle of virtual work applied in conjunction with the position transformation (18).

To derive the compound compliance from the compliances of the component elements, we must again take into account the nonlinearity of Equation (18). Thus, we obtain a correction matrix γ_i for each component element i, with:

$$\gamma_{i,j,l} = \sum_{k=1}^{M} \frac{\partial^2 X_k}{\partial x_{i,j} \partial x_{i,l}} F_k. \tag{20}$$

Here, M is the dimension of the compound element and j,l = 1..Ni (dimension of the ith component).[8] Let us assume that a change in effort, dF, is imposed

[8] For simplicity, we assume here that, given two distinct elements, e1 and e2, $\dfrac{\partial^2 X_k}{\partial x_{e1,j} \partial x_{e2,l}} = 0$. When this is not the case (as in the transformation from relative joint angles to hand coordinates), we add an intermediate compound element, E, such that $X_E = [x_{e1}, x_{e2}]^T$.

upon the compound element. Then at steady state, the corresponding effort change on the component i is given by:

$$df_i = J^T{}_i \, dF + \gamma_i \, dx_i.$$

The second term on the right-hand side accounts for the fact that, at steady-state, the element position is changed by an amount dx_i and that, in a nonlinear system, the Jacobian, J_i, is position-dependent. The displacement dx_i is related to df_i by the compliance matrix c_i. Hence, using the above expression for df_i, we obtain for dx_i:

$$dx_i = (I - c_i \, \gamma_i)^{-1} \, c_i \, J^T{}_i \, \mathrm{dF} = (c_i^{-1} - \gamma_i)^{-1} \, J^T{}_i \, dF.$$

Finally, the net displacement dX of the compound element is obtained from the component displacements, dx_i by differentiating the expression (18):

$$dX = \sum_{i=1}^{N} J_i \, dx_i = \sum_{i=1}^{N} J_i (c_i^{-1} - \gamma_i)^{-1} \, J^T{}_i \, dF.$$

Then, the compound compliance is:

$$C = \sum_{i=1}^{N} J_i \, (c^{-1}{}_i - \gamma_i)^{-1} \, J^T{}_i. \tag{21}$$

The compound stiffness is:

$$K = C^{-1} \tag{22}$$

whenever the compound element is invertible. Note that the compliance transformation for a serial connection and the stiffness transformation for a serial connection are not reciprocally "dual." That is, one transformation cannot be derived from the other by transposing the Jacobians and exchanging the role of effort and position variables. This lack of symmetry is due to the nonlinearity of the transformations (18) and (13). In a parallel connection the Γ-matrices appear as correction terms applied to the compound stiffness (Equation (15)). In contrast, in a serial connection the corrections γ_i are applied to the component stiffnesses before transforming them in the compound compliance.

An example of serial connectivity is provided by the transformation between joint and hand coordinates in a redundant arm. In this case the ill-posed problems are:

1. Finding the hand-force corresponding to an arbitrary set of joint torques. Since there are more constraint equations than unknowns, this problem may have no solutions. Joint torques cannot be selected arbitrarily.
2. Finding the joint configuration corresponding to a given hand position. There are more unknowns than equations, and the problem has infinite solutions.

4.3. Significance of the Gamma Matrices.

The geometrical transformations for position variables in both serial and parallel cases (Equations (18), (13)) are not required to be linear but only to be sufficiently differentiable (i.e., up to the second partial derivatives). With linear transformations, the Jacobian matrix is a matrix of constants; otherwise, it is a function of position. Hence, when a differential change of force is considered (df_i in Equation 14 or dF in Equation 19), one must take into account that, at steady state, the Jacobian will also be changed, because the element upon which it depends will move to a new equilibrium position. The Gamma-matrices, Γ_i and γ_i, have been introduced to account for such changes in the Jacobians. They have the physical meaning of additional stiffness terms generated by the nonlinearity of the position map.

In a parallel connection, the matrix Γ corresponds to an additional stiffness "seen" by the environment. To illustrate this, let us consider the case of two ideal force-generators pulling on a rope in two opposite directions. By definition, these force-generators are characterized by zero stiffness, and they are supposed to be at equilibrium (i.e., $f_1 = f_2$). Hence the rope can be displaced in the direction of the forces without encountering any resistance, since the net stiffness along that direction is also zero. However, a displacement orthogonal to the line connecting the two force-generators is resisted by a restoring force. Clearly, this force cannot be a consequence of the intrinsic actuator-properties, because the actuators have no stiffness. This elastic force is instead a consequence of the nonlinear geometry of the system. (Given a point outside the straight line connecting the two force generators, the relation between the cartesian coordinates of this point and its distance from any of the two force generators is not linear.) A similar interpretation can be given to the matrix γ in the serial case.

From the above example, it is also evident that the matrix Γ can play a simplifying role in our computational approach. In fact, without such a correction term, the stiffness orthogonal to the line connecting two elastic actuators would be zero, and, accordingly, the transverse compliance would be singular. In contrast, the Gamma-matrix, which reflects the physical behavior of the system, provides an additional stiffness term and eliminates this singularity, thus adding static stability to the system.

However, the sign of the stiffness contributed by nonlinear geometries can be either negative (i.e., corresponding to an attractive force field) or positive (i.e., corresponding to a repulsive force field). A simple pendulum in a gravitational field illustrates this point. When the pendulum is oriented downwards and parallel to the direction of gravity, we have a stable equilibrium, and the matrix γ (which represents in this case the "apparent joint stiffness" induced by the field) is negative. If, instead, the pendulum is pointing upwards, we have an unstable equilibrium, and γ is positive. Thus, γ may also impair the static stability of a system.

4.4. Mixed Topologies

More complex topologies, expressing both common force and common position constraints, are represented by combining parallel and serial connections in a tree structure where each nonterminal node represents an elastic element connected to its descendants according to one of the basic topologies. An example of such a situation is illustrated in Figure 6.6.

Here, the modelled kinematics is that of a person controlling a steering wheel with two hands (Figure 6.6a). The corresponding tree structure is shown in Figure 6.6b. On one extreme, there is the root node representing the task space, which contains the wheel angle and torque with respect to the environment. On the opposite extreme, the terminal nodes are elastic elements representing each independently controlled muscle. Between these two extremes, there are elements corresponding to intermediate representations. The right and left hand are connected to the wheel via a common-position constraint: the location of each hand is uniquely determined by the wheel angle, and the wheel torque is obtained from the forces applied by the two hands. Then, each hand representation is related via a common force constraint to a description of the corresponding arm in joint coordinates. At this stage, position and efforts are seven-dimensional arrays whose elements correspond to the degrees of freedom of each joint. There are three rotational components at the shoulder, two at the elbow and two at the wrist.

This lumped joint-arm representation is further decomposed into lower-dimensional elements corresponding to individual joints and to pairs of joints. This operation is carried out by simple projection operators applied to the joint-angle vector. The projection operators are equivalent to a common-position constraint: given a total joint angle vector, a set of shoulder-position parameters is uniquely derived as:

$$[q_1, q_2, q_3]^T = [1, 1, 1, 0, \ldots, 0]\,[q_1, q_2 \ldots, q_7]^T$$

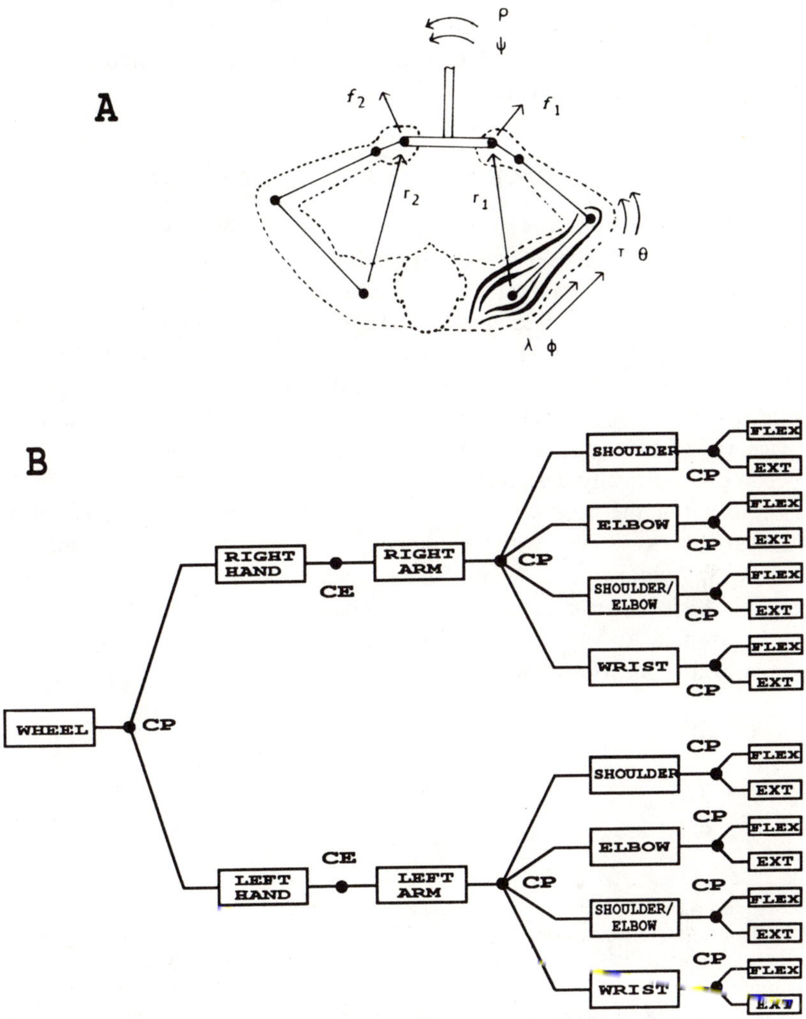

Figure 6.6. Representing mixed connection topologies. (a) Wheel-steering task. Task space (position: ϱ, effort: ψ); Hand space (position: r, effort: f); Joint space (position: θ, effort: τ); Muscle space (position: λ, effort: ϕ.) (b) Tree-structured representation. CP: Common position (parallel) connection; CF: common force (serial) connection. In this scheme we assume that the muscles are organized in pairs of flexors (FLEX) and extensors (EXT). (Modified from F. A. Mussa-Ivaldi, P. Morasso, & R. Zaccaria, *Kinematic networks. A distributed model for representing and regularizing motor redundancy. Biological Cybernetics, 60,* 1–16, 1988.)

Conversely, the seven-dimensional joint-torque vector is obtained by injecting[9] and adding the torque components associated to the joint subsets. Finally, the muscles are connected in parallel to the joints or a group of joints upon which the muscles exert a direct mechanical action.

5. BACKDRIVING ALGORITHMS

In the previous section, we have introduced a distributed representation of kinematic structures as trees of serial and parallel connections. Here, we define the operations which one can carry out on this representation. In particular, we consider the problem of finding which changes must be applied to the control inputs (acting on the "leaves") in order to obtain a desired change of the effort and position variables at the root-node of the tree. For example, we may wish to change position without changing the effort at the interface with the environment or vice versa. This goal is achieved by the concurrent application of a set of procedures specifically designed for parallel and serial connections.

Let us define the *state,* S, of a connection as the ordered set of position and effort variables associated with the compound and the component elements: $S = \{X, F, x_i, f_i\}$, with $i = 1, \ldots, N$. For each type of connection, we will consider a number of ideal recursive procedures which produce an infinitesimal[10] state change, from S to S+dS. These procedures, or *maps,* will be explicitly expressed as a set of *transitions:*

$$X \rightarrow X + dX$$
$$F \rightarrow F + dF$$
$$x_i \rightarrow x_i + dx_i$$
$$f_i \rightarrow f_i + df_i.$$

---

[9] Given a vector $x = [x_1, x_2, \ldots, x_n]^T$ and a set of k indices $\{i_1, \ldots, i_k\}$, the projection $\pi_{i_1,\ldots,i_k}$ is the linear operator which maps an n-dimensional vector, x, into a k-dimensional vector, $x' = [x_{i_1}, \ldots, x_{i_k}]^T$ $(k \leq n)$. Conversely, an injection $i_{i_1,\ldots,i_k}$ is a linear operator which maps a k-dimensional vector $y = [y_1, \ldots, y_k]$ into an n-dimensional vector x $(n \geq k)$ with $x_l = y_k$ if $l = i_k$ for some k, or $x_l = 0$ otherwise. It is readily seen that $i_{i_1,\ldots,i_k} = \pi_{i_1,\ldots,i_k}{}^T$. Now, consider an n-dimensional elastic element characterized by a pair (X, F) of position and effort vectors. If m projectors $\{\pi_1, \ldots, \pi_m\}$ are applied to the position vector, then we have a set of transformations, $x_i = \pi_i X$. Each transformed position vector, x_i, is associated to an effort vector f_i. The principle of work invariance states that:

$$\sum_{i=1}^{m} f_i^T dX_i \sum_{i=1}^{m} f_i^T \pi_i dX = F^T dX.$$

Thus, the effort F can be expressed as $F = \sum_{i=1}^{m} i_i f_i$. In other words, the projection operators applied to the position vector define a common position constraint whose transposed Jacobians are the injectors $i_i = \pi_i{}^T$.

[10] Clearly, a real procedure can only generate *finite* state changes δS.

Procedures will be also indicated as functions with two arguments, $\phi(S, d)$. The first argument is the initial state of a connection, and the second is an increment of some state variable (dX or dF or dx_i or df_i). The value of this function is a transformed state, $S' = S + dS$.

Since we are dealing with a tree-structured representation of kinematics, these maps are intrinsically recursive. In fact, a component element at any level can also be a compound element at a lower level. For instance, in the wheel-steering task shown in Figure 6.6, the "left-hand" element is a component element with respect to the wheel, and at the same time, it is a compound element with respect to the joint representation of the left arm. Thus, the application of a map generating a rotation of the wheel will result in a change of position and eventually of effort at the two hands. The latter changes will activate other maps generating variations of angles and torques at the joints, and so on.

The passive motion paradigm will be formally described by three sets of procedures:

1. *Active changes,* simulating changes in position or effort generated by the component elements. In particular, when the component elements are directly operated by a control input, the active changes correspond to changes in state produced by changes in input.
2. *Passive changes,* simulating changes in position or effort which are imposed by the environment on the compound element.
3. *Driving procedures,* which are combinations of passive and active changes. As a net result, these procedures achieve a desired change in position and effort according to the passive motion paradigm.

5.1. Parallel Connections

In a parallel connection, the position of the component elements is determined by the position of the compound element. The effort of the compound element is obtained from the efforts generated by the components. Thus, from the point of view of information flow, the component elements should be treated as impedances (position in, effort out).

For a parallel connection, an *active change* is a transition in which each component-element effort is modified by an amount df_i while the environment is maintaining a constant position (i.e., while $dX = dx_i = 0$). If the component element is directly operated by a control input, $f_i = f_i(x_i, u_i)$, then such a change is produced by a variation, $du_i = \sigma^{-1}\, df_i$, with $\sigma = \dfrac{\partial f_i}{\partial u_i}$. Otherwise, if the component is an intermediate node, the effort change, df, is the result of an active change generated at a lower node. Thus, active changes propagate along the tree from the leaves (controlled elements) to the root (task space).

The map, $\phi_A(S, df_i)$, corresponding to an active change is given by the following transitions:

$$\begin{aligned} X &\rightarrow X \\ F &\rightarrow F + dF = F + \sum J_i^T df_i \\ x_i &\rightarrow x_i \\ f_i &\rightarrow f_i + df_i \end{aligned} \tag{23}$$

5.1.1. Passive Changes

When a passive change, dX, is imposed on the compound element, the following transitions occur:

$$\begin{aligned} X &\rightarrow X + dX \\ F &\rightarrow F + dF = F + \sum J_i^T f_i + \Gamma\, dX. \\ x_i &\rightarrow x_i + dx_i = x_i + J_i\, dX \\ f_i &\rightarrow f_i + df_i = f_i + c_i\, dx_i \end{aligned} \tag{24}$$

(For simplicity we have set $\Gamma = \Sigma\, \Gamma_i$.) In functional notation, we indicate this set of transitions as the map $\phi_D(S, dX)$.

Similarly, when a passive change of effort dF is imposed (this operation is defined as a *passive push*), we have the following transitions:

$$\begin{aligned} X &\rightarrow X + dX = X + C\, dF \\ F &\rightarrow F + dF \\ x_i &\rightarrow x_i + dx_i = x_l + J_i\, C\, dF \\ f_i &\rightarrow f_i + df_i = f_i + k_i\, J_i\, C\, dF. \end{aligned} \tag{25}$$

The passive push is indicated by the function $\phi_P(S, dF)$. Both types of passive changes tend to propagate from the root node to the leaves.

Note that the last and the first transitions in ϕ_P are mutually consistent, since:

$$dF = \Sigma\, J_i^T\, df_i + \Gamma dX.$$

Then, eliminating dX (= CdF) and df_i (= $k_i dx_i$ = $k_i J_i CdF$), one obtains the following expression:

$$(I - \Gamma\, C)\, dF = \Sigma\, J_i^T\, k_i\, J_i\, C\, dF.$$

which is an identity, since:

$$(I - \Gamma C) = (K - \Gamma)C = K_{LIN}\, C \tag{26}$$

with $K_{LIN} = \Sigma\, J_i^T\, k_i\, J_i$. In the last expression, the term K_{LIN} is the *linearized compound stiffness,* that is, the stiffness that the compound element would have if the connection geometry were linear (i.e., if J were not position-dependent).

5.1.2. Backdriving

The *backdriving map,* $\phi_B(S, dX)$ is defined as the combination, $\phi_B(S, dX) = \phi_A(\phi_D(S_1, dX), -df_i)$. It corresponds to the application of a passive displacement, dX, followed by an active change, $-df_j$, applied independently to each element, i. The active change locally cancels the efforts induced by the passive displacement. The corresponding transitions are:

$$
\begin{aligned}
&X \rightarrow X + dX \rightarrow X + dX \\
&F \rightarrow F + \sum J_i^T df_i + \Gamma\, dX \rightarrow F + \Gamma\, dX \\
&x_i \rightarrow x_i + J_i\, dX \rightarrow x_i + J_i\, dX \\
&f_i \rightarrow f_i + df_i \rightarrow f_i
\end{aligned}
$$

Note that ϕ_B causes a change in the compound position *as well as* in the compound effort, $dF = \Gamma dX$. The latter is a consequence of the non-linear connection geometry and vanishes with linear connections or at equilibrium (if $F = 0$, then $\Gamma = 0$). Thus, the map ϕ_B is generally not sufficient to generate a position change at constant effort. This task is effectively carried out by the position-driving map ϕ_X described below.

5.1.3. Force Driving

The goal of *force driving* is to generate a change in force dF at constant X. Let us consider the application of a passive push, $\phi_P(S, dF)$, followed by a backdriving, $\phi_B(S, -CdF)$, towards the original position. We have the following transitions:

$$
\begin{aligned}
&X \rightarrow X + C\, dF \rightarrow X \\
&F \rightarrow F + dF \rightarrow F + dF - \Gamma\, dX = F + K_{LIN}\, C\, dF. \\
&x_i \rightarrow x_i + J_i\, C\, dF \rightarrow x_i \\
&f_i \rightarrow f_i + k_i\, J_i\, C\, dF \rightarrow f_i + k_i\, J_i\, C\, dF
\end{aligned}
$$

The effort change differs from dF by the factor $K_{LIN}C$ (which reduces to the identity matrix in a linear connection). Thus, in order to generate a desired force, dF, the passive push must be $dF' = KC_{LIN}dF$ with $C_{LIN} = K_{LIN}{}^{-1}$. With this correction, the force-driving procedure is a map $\phi_F(S, dF) = \phi_B(\phi_P(S, dF'), -CdF')$ corresponding to the transitions:

$$
\begin{aligned}
&X \rightarrow X \\
&F \rightarrow F + K_{LIN}\, C\, dF' = F + dF. \\
&x_i \rightarrow x_i \\
&f_i \rightarrow f_i + k_i\, J_i\, C_{LIN}\, dF
\end{aligned}
\tag{27}
$$

5.1.4. Position Driving

The goal is to achieve a displacement, dX, of the compound element at constant effort, F. We achieve this goal in two steps: first, a backdriving $\phi_B(S, dX)$ is executed towards the desired position; then a force driving $\phi_F(S, -\Gamma dX)$ is used to cancel the effort change induced by the previous step. Thus, *position driving* is a map, $\phi_X(S, dX) = \phi_F(\phi_B(S, dX), -\Gamma dX)$, corresponding to the transitions:

$$\begin{aligned} &X \rightarrow X + dX \rightarrow X + dX \\ &F \rightarrow F + \Gamma\, dX \rightarrow F. \\ &x_i \rightarrow x_i + J_i\, dX \rightarrow x_i + J_i\, dX \\ &f_i \rightarrow f_i \rightarrow f_i - k_i\, J_i\, C_{LIN}\, \Gamma\, dX \end{aligned} \tag{28}$$

Note that, with linear connection geometry or at equilibrium, we have $\phi_X = \phi_B$.

5.2. Serial Connections

In a serial connection, the component elements must be treated as compliances (force in, position out). Thus, the active update consists in changing the element position by an amount dx_i while the environment is exerting a constant effort, F, on the compound element (i.e., with dF = 0). If the component elements are directly controlled, then their behavior is given as $x_i = x_i(f_i, u_i)$. Differentiating this expression, we obtain:

$$dx_i = \sigma_i\, du_i + c_i\, df_i$$

where $\sigma_i = \dfrac{\partial x_i}{\partial u_i}$. Each element's effort-change, df_i, is related to the net effort change, dF, as:

$$df_i = J^T{}_i\, dF + \gamma_i\, dx_i.$$

Thus, by requiring that dF = 0, we obtain:

$$dx_i = \sigma_i\, du_i + c_i\, \gamma_i\, dx_i$$

and the corresponding input update rule is:

$$du_i = \sigma_i^{-1} c_i k_{LIN,i} dx_i$$

with $k_{LIN,i} = c_{LIN,i}{}^{-1} = (k_i - \gamma_i)$.

In summary, the *active change* for a serial connection is a map $\pi_A(S, dx_i)$ which corresponds to the following transitions:

$$
\begin{aligned}
&X \rightarrow X + \sum J_i dx_i \\
&F \rightarrow F \\
&x_i \rightarrow x_i + dx_i \\
&f_i \rightarrow f_i + \gamma_i dx_i
\end{aligned} \tag{29}
$$

5.2.1. Passive Changes

When a change in effort, dF, is imposed by the environment on the compound element, the following transitions occur:

$$
\begin{aligned}
&X \rightarrow X + C\,dF \\
&F \rightarrow F + dF \\
&x_i \rightarrow x_i + dx_i \\
&f_i \rightarrow f_i + J^T{}_i\,dF + \gamma_i dx_i.
\end{aligned} \tag{30}
$$

The increments dx_i in the above expressions are:

$$dx_i = c_{LIN,i} J^T{}_i dF$$

We indicate this passive push as a map $\pi_P(S, dF)$.

When instead of an effort change, the environment imposes a displacement dX, we have the map $\pi_D(S, dX)$ corresponding to the following transitions:

$$
\begin{aligned}
&X \rightarrow X + dX \\
&F \rightarrow F + K\,dX \\
&x_i \rightarrow x_i + dx_i \\
&f_i \rightarrow f_i + J^T{}_i K\,dX + \gamma_i\,dx_i
\end{aligned} \tag{31}
$$

with $dx_i = c_{LIN,i}\, J^T{}_i\, K\, dX$.

5.2.2. Force Driving

The goal of the *force-driving* map $\pi_F(S, dF)$ is to set an effort change dF at constant position. This result is achieved by simulating a passive push $\pi_P(S, dF)$ followed by an active change π_A, which cancels the displacements dx_i; thus we have, $\pi_F = \pi_A(\pi_P(S, dF), -dx_i)$. Accordingly, we have the following transitions:

$$
\begin{aligned}
&X \rightarrow X + C\,dF \rightarrow X \\
&F \rightarrow F + dF \rightarrow F + dF \\
&x_i \rightarrow x_i + dx_i \rightarrow x_i \\
&f_i \rightarrow f_i + J^T{}_i\,dF + \gamma_i dx_i \rightarrow f_i + J^T{}_i\,dF.
\end{aligned}
$$

5.2.3. Position Driving

The goal of the *position-driving* map $\pi_X(S, dX)$ is to set a displacement dX at constant force (dF = 0). This result is obtained by a passive displacement $\pi_D(S, dX)$, followed by a force driving π_F which cancels the effort change KdX: $\pi_X(S, dX) = \pi_F(\pi_D(S, dX), -KdX)$. Thus, we have the following transitions for π_X:

$$
\begin{aligned}
&X \rightarrow X + dX \rightarrow X + dX \\
&F \rightarrow F + K\, dX \rightarrow F \\
&x_i \rightarrow x_i + dx_i \rightarrow x_i + dx_i \\
&f_i \rightarrow f_i + J^T{}_i K\, dX + \gamma_i\, dx_i \rightarrow f_i + \gamma_i\, dx_i
\end{aligned}
\tag{32}
$$

with $dx_i = c_{LIN,i}\, J^T{}_i\, K\, dX$.

5.3. Combined Driving Maps

An important property of the force- and position-driving maps is that their combination is commutative, that is:

$$\phi_F \cdot \phi_X = \phi_X \cdot \phi_F$$

and

$$\pi_F \cdot \pi_X = \pi_X \cdot \pi_F$$

Thus, it is possible to define unambiguously two *combined* maps, $\phi_{F,X}$ and $\pi_{F,X}$, as:

$$
\begin{aligned}
\phi_{F,X}(S, dF, dX) &= \phi_F(\phi_X(S, dX), dF) = \phi_X(\phi_F(S, dF), dX) \\
\pi_{F,X}(S, dF, dX) &= \pi_F(\pi_X(S, dX), dF) = \pi_X(\pi_F(S, dF), dX).
\end{aligned}
\tag{33}
$$

In other words, for each type of connection, it is possible to activate a driving procedure which provides any desired change in effort and position of the compound element. If the component elements are terminal nodes of the kinematic tree, the driving procedure results in the specification of appropriate changes of the control inputs. Otherwise, if the component elements are intermediate nodes, the driving procedure specifies a change in component effort and position; this change is enforced by a recursive call to another driving procedure.

To illustrate the process of combining local procedures, let us consider the kinematic tree in Figure 6. Let us assume that the desired change at the root node is a rotation, $d\psi$, at constant torque ($d\rho = 0$). Then, a position-driving map $\pi(S, d\psi)$ is applied to the parallel connection describing the relation between the wheel and the two hands. The map requires each hand to update the positions and efforts by the amounts dF_i, dX_i (i = "right" or "left"). This is done by invoking a combined driving $\phi_{F,X}(S, dF_i, dX_i)$ at each of the common-force connections expressing the joint-to-hand transformations for each arm. Consequently, each arm will be required to generate a change in configuration, dq_i, and torque, dT_i. This request activates a pair of combined-driving maps, $\pi_{F,X}(S, dT_i, dq_i)$, at the two projection nodes, which disassemble the arm configurations into single and double-joint components. Finally, each joint component will then activate a procedure $\pi_{F,X}(S, dT, dq)$ at the common position node to which the muscle element are directly connected. Thus, the procedure requires each muscle to generate an effort change df by an input reset du. When this input reset is applied to all of the muscle elements, the entire kinematic tree will be in a new consistent state with the root node being in the desired position and at the desired effort.

6. PASSIVE MOTION IS INTEGRABLE

In the previous section, we described a set of ideal procedures or maps whose effect is to induce some infinitesimal change in state, dS. For example, let us consider the passive-displacement map $\pi_D(S, dX)$, which derives the change of configuration, dx, of a redundant serial linkage, given an externally imposed displacement of the end-point, dX. This map is effectively a local solution to the inverse-kinematics problem for this mechanism. Algebraically, this solution corresponds to the application of a *weighted generalized inverse* of the Jacobian matrix, $J = \dfrac{\partial X}{\partial x}$. In fact, using $\pi_D(S, dX)$, we obtain:

$$dx = c_{LIN}\, J^T\, (J\, c_{LIN}\, J^T)^{-1} \tag{34}$$

where

$$c_{LIN} = (k - \gamma)^{-1}.$$

The general expression for the weighted generalized inverse of J is:

$$P_w = w\, J^T\, (J\, w\, J^T)^{-1} \tag{35}$$

where w is some weight matrix. With this generalized inverse, the configuration change $dx = P_w\, dX$ is guaranteed to satisfy the kinematic constraint:

$$dX = J\, dx$$

while, at the same time, minimizing the quadratic form:

$$E_w = dx^T\, w^{-1}\, dx.$$

In particular, when w is the unit matrix, I, the quadratic form E_I is the norm of the configuration change, $dx^T dx$. Thus, the generalized inverse $P_I = J^T(J\,J^T)^{-1}$, which is known as the Moore-Penrose pseudoinverse of J, corresponds to a minimum norm criterion (Ben-Israel & Greville, 1980). The map corresponding to an externally imposed displacement is equivalent to the application of a generalized pseudoinverse $P_{c_{LIN}}$. Using this pseudoinverse is consistent with the physical requirement that the passive change of configuration is constrained by a minimum potential-energy criterion.

So far, we have described differential transformations which find a configuration displacement corresponding to a given end-point displacement, dX. There is no a priori guarantee that such procedures are *integrable,* or in other words that they are, within some domain of the workspace, the Jacobians of some inverse kinematic functions mapping any given position X into a corresponding configuration x. Whenever such a map exists, then iterating the related incremental procedure from a starting position X_0 to a final position X_1 results into a final configuration x_1, depending upon the initial configuration x_0 *but not upon the particular workspace path chosen to join* X_0 *to* X_1. Equivalently, if a local generalized-inverse map is integrable, then iteration along any closed path brings the system back to the same starting configuration.

A number of investigations (Liegeois, 1977; Klein & Huang, 1983; Hollerbach & Suh, 1985; Wampler, 1987) have demonstrated that the most common generalized-inverse operators *do not* provide integrable maps. Most notably, Klein and Huang (1983) showed that iterating the Moore-Penrose pseudoinverse along closed paths can produce a variety of non-cyclic behaviors (Figure 6.7). In some cases, as the hand passes repeatedly through the same point, the joint configuration changes until a limit configuration is reached (Figure 6.7a). However, this limit configuration may depend upon the direction of travel around the path (Figure 6.7b). In other cases, the configuration keeps changing without reaching any limit (Figure 6.7c). The most common solutions to the integrability problem Liegeois, 1977; Bailleul, 1985) involve the combination of the Moore-Penrose pseudoinverse with some null-space motion (a configuration change that doesn't change the end-point position). These null-space motions are chosen so as to optimize some predefined criterion such as the manipulability index or the distance from singular configurations.

Using a different approach, Mussa-Ivaldi and Hogan (1989) have recently demonstrated that the weighted generalized inverse, $P_{c_{LIN}}$, corresponding to an externally imposed displacement, is integrable within any simply connected domain in which the manipulator end-point doesn't loose mobility (i.e., in which $\det(J\, c_{LIN} J^T) \neq 0$). This result is consistent with the physical notion that the minimum potential-energy constraint is sufficient to uniquely define a configuration corresponding to a given location of the end-point. Consider, for example, a redundant serial kinematic chain. Let each joint be characterized by a fixed

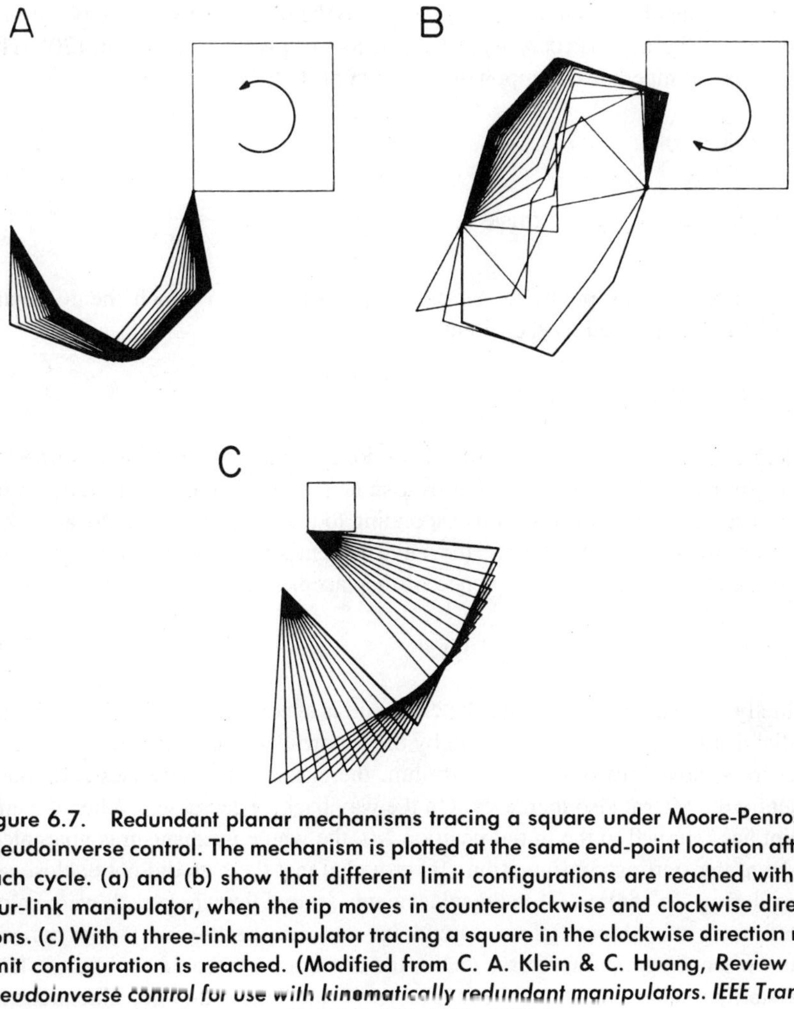

Figure 6.7. Redundant planar mechanisms tracing a square under Moore-Penrose pseudoinverse control. The mechanism is plotted at the same end-point location after each cycle. (a) and (b) show that different limit configurations are reached with a four-link manipulator, when the tip moves in counterclockwise and clockwise directions. (c) With a three-link manipulator tracing a square in the clockwise direction no limit configuration is reached. (Modified from C. A. Klein & C. Huang, *Review of pseudoinverse control for use with kinematically redundant manipulators. IEEE Trans. System Man and Cybernetics, SMC-13,* 245–250, 1983.)

torque/angle relation so that the linkage is at equilibrium at a configuration x_0 corresponding to a tip-location X_0. This relation can be simply obtained by placing a "winding spring" on each joint. It is intuitively evident that, if we force the tip along a closed path terminating back at X_0, the whole mechanism will return to the starting configuration. It is also intuitive that the only way to achieve a different configuration is by "winding" the joint springs. This can be achieved by moving the tip along a path that encloses some singular points of the workspace, thus carrying out the iteration in a domain that is not simply connected.

From an algebraic point of view, the key to the integrability of passive motion is provided by the matrix γ whose elements are given by Equation (20). This matrix is an impedance component which contributes to the expression of c_{LIN}:

$$c_{LIN} = (k - \gamma)^{-1}$$

where $k = c^{-1}$ is the "intrinsic" joint-stiffness matrix, $k = \frac{\partial f}{\partial x}$.

To illustrate this point, let us consider a situation in which the following control law is applied to each joint.

$$f_i = k\,(x_i - x0_i)$$

where k is the same constant for all the joints. Then, the net joint stiffness is proportional to the unit matrix. Let us assume that the mechanism is at the initial equilibrium configuration x0, corresponding to the initial end-point location X0. As the end point is forced by the environment to follow a closed path, the configuration undergoes a sequence of displacements:

$$dx = (I - \gamma(x))\, J^T (J\,(I - \gamma(x))^{-1}\, J^T)^{-1}. \tag{36}$$

Initially, γ is equal to zero since the end point is at equilibrium (F = 0). Thus, the initial displacement is simply given by the Moore-Penrose pseudoinverse, P_1. As the tip is moved away from equilibrium, the elastic force increases and consequently the γ term also increases. On the way back, γ decreases. When the end-point has returned to the initial position X0, the whole mechanism is guaranteed to be at the starting configuration x0 (provided that the path did not enclose any singularity). In contrast, if the displacements around the whole path were calculated using the Moore-Penrose pseudoinverse (i.e., with $\gamma = 0$ everywhere), then, when the endpoint returns to X0, the configuration would be different from the starting value, x0. Thus, the matrix $\gamma(x)$ is a configuration-dependent correction which is equivalent to a memory of the initial conditions.

7. IMPLEMENTATIONS

So far, we have described a general algebraic framework for representing the geometrical and the mechanical constraints of a redundant, articulated mechanism. We have also introduced a set of differential maps corresponding to passive and active changes of effort and position. In this section, we present two computational models which effectively implement these maps: kinematic networks (Mussa-Ivaldi et al., 1988) and motor-relaxation networks (Morasso, Mussa-

Ivaldi, Vercelli, & Zaccaria, 1989). The former model is based upon the explicit representation of kinematic constraints as Jacobian matrices. In contrast, in motor-relaxation networks, these constraints are simulated as elastic links, or *ligaments,* between adjacent body segments. Both models have been implemented as simulation tools in a previously developed animation environment, NEM, which allows the definition of body models and action patterns in 3D (Marino, Morasso, & Zaccaria, 1986).

7.1. Kinematic Networks

A *kinematic network* is a directed graph whose nodes are either generalized forces or generalized displacements and whose links represent two types of causal relations:

- geometric causality, expressed by Jacobian matrices
- elastic causality, expressed either by compliance or by stiffness matrices.

Pairs of generalized force and displacement vectors associated with a given element are grouped into a single computational unit called a *work unit* (WU). Work units are distinguished in two groups according to the type of elastic causality that they implement: *stiffness WUs* store a stiffness matrix, K, and *compliance WUs* store a compliance matrix, C (Figure 6.8).

In complex kinematic structures, we have a ramification of limbs connected serially or in parallel. In a serial connection of limbs, the same force is *assigned* to all the composing limbs, and the global displacement is the *sum* of the composing limbs. Dually, in a parallel arrangement the same displacement is assigned to all the limbs, and the global force is obtained by summing the forces generated by the limbs. Therefore, parallel and serial connections of multiple limbs are implemented by sum and assignment nodes (Figure 6.8). Using these elements, the kinematic network of a wheel-steering operation is obtained, as shown in Figure 6.9.

The network is built in three stages.

1. First, a work unit with unspecified elastic causality is assigned to each coordinate system or limb involved in the task. Thus, there is one WU representing the wheel, one representing each hand in spatial coordinates, one representing each arm in joint coordinates, and one for each arm in muscle coordinates.
2. Then, the geometric causality is established and is indicated by a set of oriented arrows joining positions and effort variables across different WUs. Each arrow corresponds to the application of a Jacobian operator. Redundancy implies that the direction of each arrow is fixed and cannot be inverted.

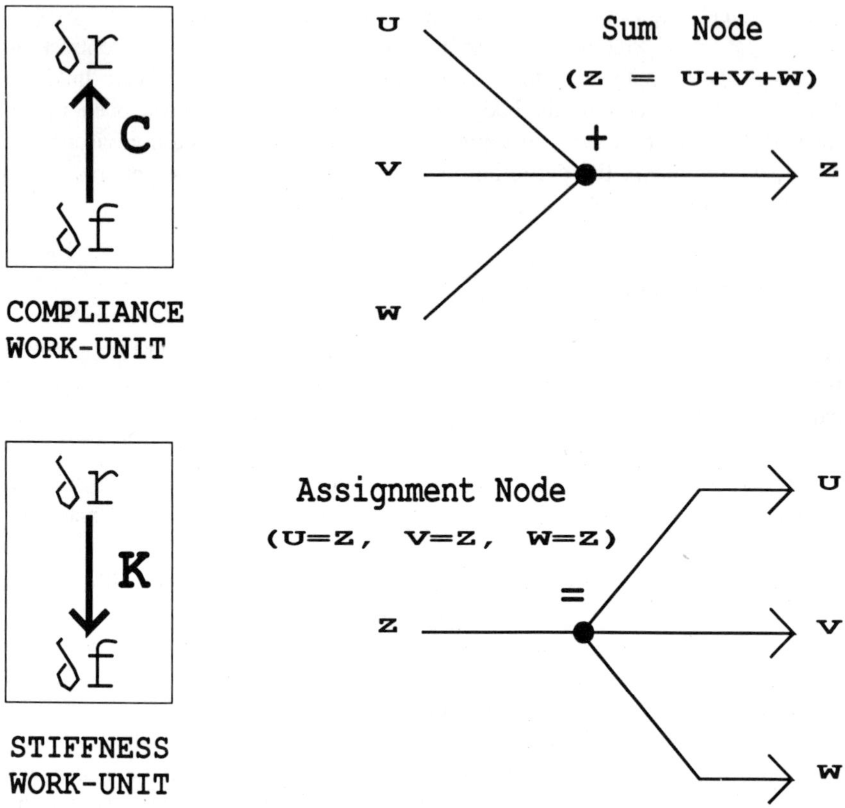

Figure 6.8. Kinematic network elements. (From Mussa-Ivaldi et al., 1988).

3. Finally, the directions of the elastic transformations are chosen so as to satisfy a requirement of *circularity:* All the loops in the kinematic network must be closed. This requirement has the effect of making any node in the network accessible through a path starting from any other node.

As a consequence of the last step, each WU is characterized either as a stiffness or as a compliance. Therefore, in the wheel-steering example, the joints must be controlled as compliance elements (force input and position output).

Once the kinematic network has been fully specified, the driving algorithms described in Section 5 are applied to generate the actuator commands corresponding to a given task. Here, movements are temporal sequences of "virtual positions" (Section 2). Accordingly, the controls are sequences of joint equilibrium configurations. In Figure 6.9, we present three photograms of a simulation run during which the wheel was steered first to the left and then to the right. Figure 10 shows the joint-rotation patterns generated by the kinematic network

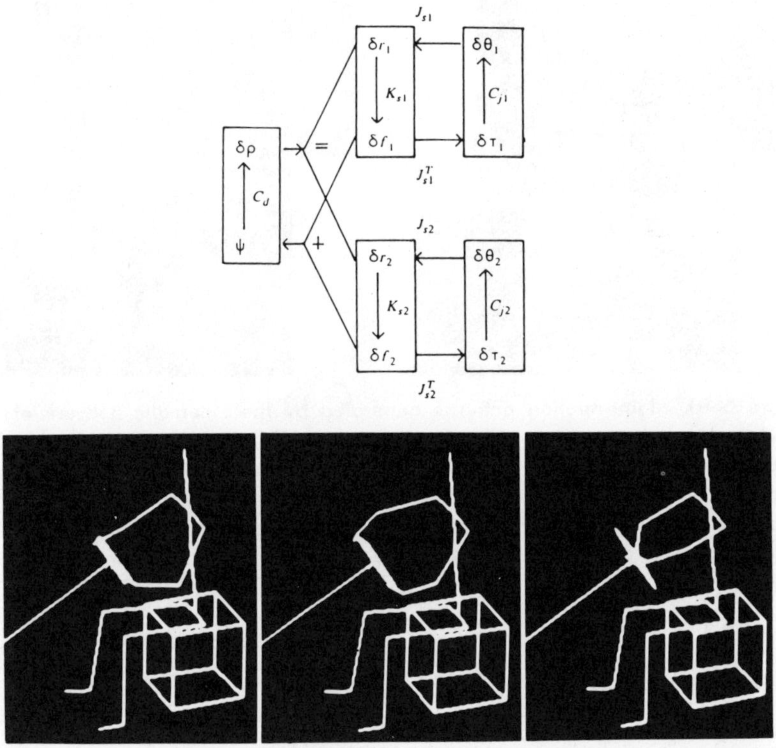

Figure 6.9. Top: Kinematic network for the wheel-steering task supposing that the trunk is fixed. (See Figure 6 for the notation.) Here, muscle spaces are not represented. Bottom: three photograms of a simulation run that involves steering the wheel first to the left and then to the right. (Modified from Mussa-Ivaldi et al., 1988.)

for such a planned motion of the steering wheel. A remarkable feature of the patterns generated by the kinematic networks is that almost all the degrees of freedom are put into action despite the few parameters specified by the task.

7.2. Kinematic Networks and Body Models

A kinematic network is tree-structured, and different tasks require different structures. The mechanism for generating these structures is based on *body models* properly connected to the environment.

A body model (Figure 6.11), like those developed for ergonomic modeling and biomechanics (Badler & Smoliar, 1979; Kingsley, Schofield, & Case, 1981; Korein, 1985; Marino et al., 1985), typically consists of a tree of rigid *segments* connected by *joints*. The nodes of these trees correspond to the body segments (the root node is the pelvis), and the links correspond to the joints. Of the two

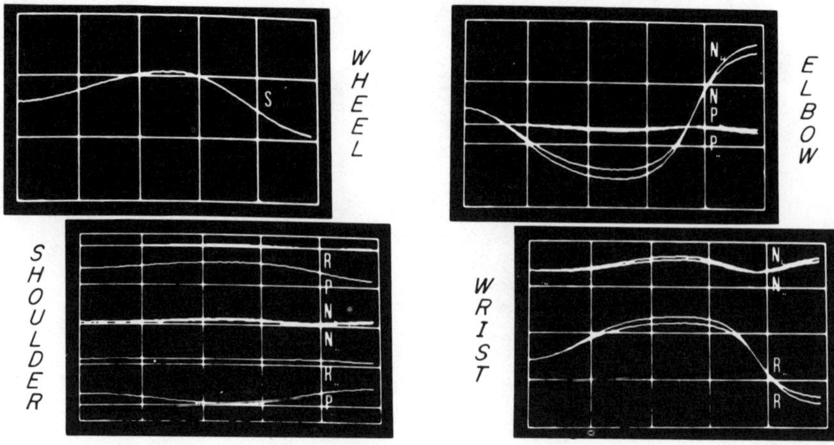

Figure 6.10. Joint-rotation patterns generated by the kinematic network of the previous figure for a planned steering movement that involves a rotation to the left followed by a rotation to the right. Both rotations are performed with a bell-shaped velocity profile. S is the planned profile of the steering movement. N, P and R are the Euler angles of each joint for the right and left arm, respectively. Vertical calibration: 1 rad; horizontal calibration: arbitrary time-units. (From Mussa-Ivaldi et al., 1988.)

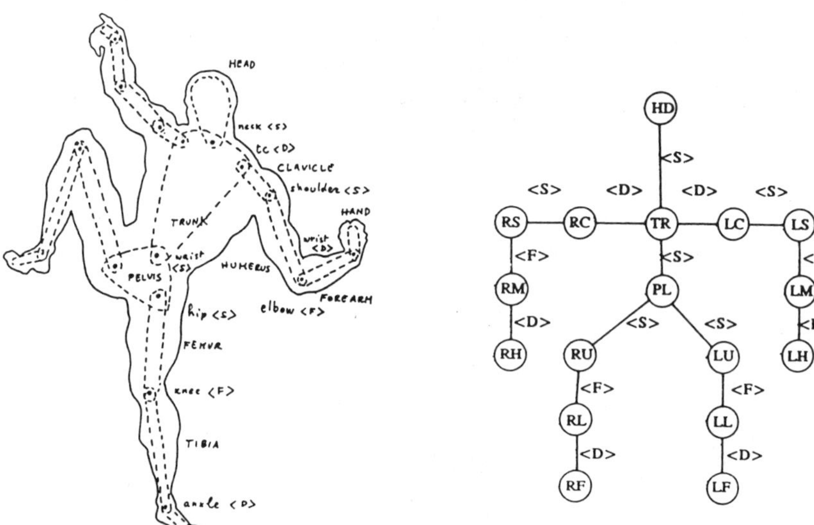

Figure 6.11. A body model. Left: body segments. Right: body tree. Nodes represent links. Arcs represent joints which are classified in three types: S, F, D. The S-type (e.g., shoulder) has three dof's; the three axes are the x,y,z axes of the proximal segment. The F-type (e.g, elbow) has two dof's; one axis is the y-axis of the proximal segment, and the other is the z-axis of the distal segment. The D-type (e.g., wrist) has also two dof's arranged in a different way: one axis is the y-axis of the proximal segment, and the other is the x-axis of the distal segment.

segments that meet at a joint, the one closer to the pelvis is labeled *proximal* and the other one is labeled *distal*. This distinction is necessary because, in general, rotation operators are not reversible.

A chain of segments identifies a *limb*. Some segments, such as the pelvis or the trunk, join two or more limbs. The directionality of joints (from proximal to distal) expresses the need to define a default direction for the kinematic transformations and the corresponding Jacobian matrices. Clearly, this default direction does not depend upon any task. Therefore, the specification of a body model is not sufficient to establish a kinematic network. Each task has its own geometric structure that needs to be considered in order to obtain the necessary Jacobians at the interface between the body and the *task device*.

The task device (a wheel or a tool, for example) is the starting point for building a kinematic network. From this point we may enter the body model, branching the kinematic network into serial and/or parallel configurations, down to the directly controlled elements that are relevant for the particular task. We also need to specify the model's connection to "ground." This is necessary for determining which parts of the body model are kinematically involved in a given task and which parts are not. For example, in the steering-wheel context, if we can assume that the chest is grounded, then the kinematic network will grow from the steering wheel to the arms and will stop there. This assumption was used in building the network in Figure 6.9. In other cases, this assumption is inappropriate, as when the steering-wheel operator is standing. Then the kinematic network must be developed on more levels.

A body model supplemented with ground connections and task devices is topologically a graph. Thus, a *task graph* is defined as a body model augmented with both ground nodes and task nodes. The automatic generation of kinematic networks can then be reduced to the extraction of tree structures embedded in a task graph. During a complex action the body model obviously does not change its structure, whereas the task and the ground connections will generally change. The kinematic network must change accordingly.

In this context, a motor plan is specified as a virtual trajectory of the task node. A kinematic network is built first by creating a work unit for this node, then by identifying which nodes are actually required by the task. The answer can be easily found by considering that nodes that cannot be reached by a target-ground path are kinematically irrelevant.[11] Therefore, exploring all the possible paths from the target to ground, we can go on building the kinematic network. Consecutive path elements involve serial connectivity, and multiple paths meet-

[11] A node is said to be *kinematically irrelevant* with respect to a task if its motion does not directly affect the task. For example, the left arm is kinematically irrelevant with respect to the task of reaching an object with the right hand. However, in this same context the motion of the left arm may be relevant with respect to the concurrent task of maintaining the body balance.

ing at a node involve parallel connectivity. This procedure requires only standard graph-manipulation techniques.

7.3. Motor-Relaxation Networks

In Sections 4 and 5 we detailed a distributed representation of kinematic constraints that makes explicit all the possible transformations of force and displacement vectors. These transformations are exact and depend on two kinds of operators: Jacobian and gamma matrices. Using these operators in actual robotics applications may prove time-consuming and computationally expensive.

To address these problems, a class of analogic models, called *motor-relaxation networks,* has been developed by Morasso et al. (1989). Motor-relaxation networks are essentially mechanical circuits, composed of spring elements which connect the skeletal segments. The spring elements correspond to three entities: (a) muscles (active springs), (b) ligaments (passive springs), and (c) targets (virtual springs). In the framework of this model, trajectory formation is the simulation of the network's behavior for a given initial configuration and a given set of inputs (the targets).

Motor-relaxation networks are multiple-constraint satisfaction networks that are similar to Hopfield nets (Hopfield, 1982), since it is possible to define a global function, E, which, under many circumstances, has the property of a Lyapunov function. In Hopfield nets, E is an abstract computational concept, although a significant analogy has been established with the physical behavior of a particular material, the spin glass. In contrast, in a motor-relaxation network, E is the elastic energy stored by the muscles, and is the direct consequence of a physical phenomenon of biological significance. Therefore, this is an analogical model in a double sense: the computational process is a dynamic system, and there is a direct correspondence between the structure of the model and the underlying physicals system.

Three types of units are present in motor-relaxation networks:

- skeletal segment units (s-units),
- muscle units (m-units), and
- ligament units (l-units).

Let us now consider in detail their structure and function.

S-units model the different skeletal body-segments, represented as rigid bodies to which three sets of forces (muscle forces, ligament forces, external forces) are applied. These units are more complex than those usually considered in a neural-network model, because they deal with vector quantities (force, velocity, and rotation vectors) and perform operations such as vector products. The input is a set of force vectors $\{f_1, f_2, \ldots, f_n\}$ applied to a set of insertion points $\{p_1, p_2, \ldots, p_n\}$ distributed over the skeletal segment. The outputs are the positions of the same insertion points. The transformation operated by an s-unit is characterized by the following steps:

1. Computing the resultant force and torque vectors (F and T), i.e., the net vectorial input;
2. Computing incremental displacement and rotation vectors as sigmoidal functions of F and T, respectively;
3. Updating the insertion-point positions with a rigid translation/rotation.

M-units model the muscles as viscous-elastic elements characterized by a family of curves:

$$f = f(l, l', u)$$

indexed by the level of "neuromuscular" activity, u. (In this expression f is the muscle force, l is the muscle length, and l′ is the speed of contraction.) M-units are connected to two s-units in the case of single-joint muscles and to several s-units in the case of multijoint muscles (such as many muscles of the hand). The inputs are the insertion points of the muscle, from which the muscle length is computed. Two kinds of outputs are present: one is muscle force, which is transmitted to the connected s-units; the other is muscle activation, u. During the simulation of passive movements, muscle lengthening or shortening is accompanied by variations of u that keep the force output approximately constant.

L-units model the joints as elastic connections with high stiffness. Complex joints can be modeled with multiple l-units. This is true even for joints distributed over several skeletal segments, such as the wrist. Another function of l-units is to model joint limits in a soft way by generating increasingly stronger restoring forces as joints approach "forbidden" configurations. Note that joints and joint limits are not represented as hard constraints but as soft constraints. The power of this concept is that it brings geometry, kinematics, and actuator dynamics under a uniform representational scheme. From the operational point of view, l-units are simplified versions of m-units without a control input, u. Both l-units and m-units can store elastic energy.

M-units and l-units behave as impedances. They receive positional information and react by feeding back force information. S-units, on the contrary, behave as admittances, i.e., they receive force information and react by modifying position parameters. As we compare the motor-relaxation networks with usual connectionist models, m-units and l-units are analogous to connection weights. In our context, these weights have the meaning of stiffnesses, fixed in the case of ligaments and variable in the case of muscles.

A specialized s-unit is the "environment" (or "ground"). Gravity is represented by fictitious l-units that link all the regular s-units to the ground. Environ-

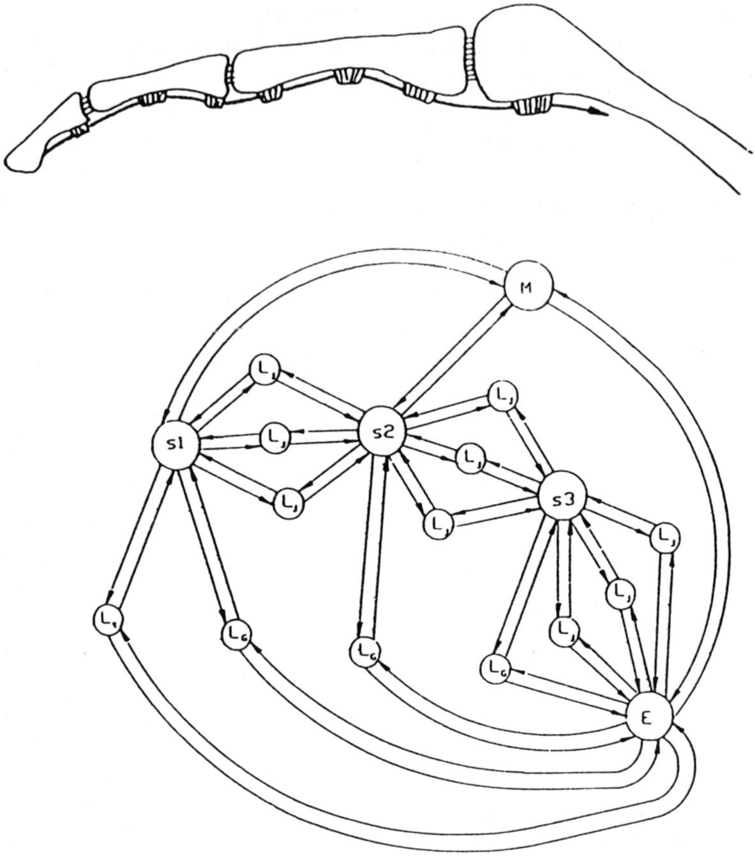

Figure 6.12. **Motor-relaxation network of a finger. (From P. Morasso, F. A. Mussa Ivaldi, G. Vercelli, & R. Zaccaria, *A connectionist formulation of motor planning*. In R. Pfeifer, Z., Schreter, F. Fogelman, & L. Steels (Eds.), *Connectionism in perspective*, Amsterdam: Elsevier, 1989.)**

mental constraints that do not allow the movement of some skeletal segments also can be represented by means of fictitious l-units as well as motor tasks. The latter can be represented as l-units linking goal-oriented s-units (e.g., a distal phalanx in a reaching task) to the environment. Concurrent tasks are represented in a natural way by the simultaneous activation of multiple l-units.

Figure 6.12 shows the motor relaxation network of a finger. The network contains the following units:

1. Three s-units (S1, S2, S3) correspond to the three phalanxes.
2. Another s-unit (E) identifies the environment.
3. Each of the three joints is represented by three l-units (denoted by lj). The

insertions of two of them are chosen in such a way to allow a one-degree-of-freedom rotation. The insertions of the third one are defined so as to avoid too much overextension of the joints.

4. Gravity is represented by means of l-units (lg) that connect the s-units to E.
5. For simplicity, only one m-unit is shown (it represent a multiple-joint muscle.)
6. An l-unit (lt), connected to E, represent the motor goal: a trajectory for the fingertip.

The input connections to s-units carry force vectors, and the output connections carry position vectors. In contrast, input connections to m- or l-units carry position vectors, and the outputs carry force vectors. Not shown in the picture is the set of outputs from the m-units. These outputs represent the motor commands generated by the network.

A motor-relaxation network works asynchronously. At equilibrium, the set of forces that enters each s-unit gives resultant force and torque vectors that must be null. As a consequence, the positions of the insertion points of all the muscles and ligaments remain stationary. However, even when the network is at equilibrium, muscles and ligaments may well be far from equilibrium and may in fact store considerable amounts of elastic energy.

A task node (lt in Figure 6.12) pulls the network out of equilibrium. This node corresponds to a spring which connects the fingertip to a point in space (the target point). The force generated by this node breaks the equilibrium of S1, and the disturbance propagates readily to the rest of the network. A whole trajectory can be generated if the end-point of such a fictitious spring is smoothly shifted towards the target.

8. CONCLUDING REMARKS

In this chapter, we have shown that the mechanics of a motor system lead to a natural solution of several ill-posed coordination problems. Our approach is based upon exploiting the solutions offered by the physics of passive motion.

We have shown that passive motion has indeed a set of valuable computational properties, namely:

1. Modeling passive motion leads to distributed representations based upon the exchange of force and position information between different physical elements as well as between different coordinate systems. This exchange is locally regulated by the principle of work invariance and leads to the minimization of the global potential energy. The same idea underlies the analysis of electrical circuits by Kirchhoff's current and voltage laws. In this respect, our approach is closely related to the modelling of physical systems by means of bond graphs (Paynter, 1961).

2. Passive motion offers a natural solution to the ill-posed nature of kinematic and static problems in redundant systems. This solution is based upon the principle that potential energy is minimized compatibly with the kinematic constraints.
3. The solutions offered by passive motion can be simply derived for complex kinematic structures containing any combination of open and closed chains. This is a significant advantage over the redundancy-resolution approaches currently developed in robotics (Liegeois, 1977; Klein & Huang, 1983; Baillieul, 1985). The latter can only be applied to serial kinematic chains for which a single Jacobian matrix can be defined.
4. The representation of passive motion as an incremental process can be integrated to provide global inverse kinematics solutions. These solutions do not depend upon the path that has been followed to reach an end-effector location from a given starting point. We have demonstrated that the integrability of passive motion is provided by a single operator, the gamma matrix, which compensates for kinematic nonlinearities.

Starting from these properties of passive motion, we have developed a method (the passive-motion paradigm) for generating the active coordination necessary to attain a planned goal. Coordination is achieved by combining a simulated passive motion with an update of the inputs controlling the actuators. The simulated passive motion implements the planned goal. The input update is chosen so as to cancel locally the stresses induced on the actuators by the passive motion. We have demonstrated that such a scheme is capable of attaining any combination of force and position goals.

It must be stressed that the central aim of this method is not to generate "unique solutions" to ill-posed motor problems. Instead, our goal was to implement a *repertoire* of solutions to any given goal. These multiple solutions are effectively parametrized, selecting different motor impedances by different motor commands. For example, if the goal is to produce a given trajectory of the hand, different coordinations are obtained by assigning a high stiffness to the wrist or to the elbow. In the former case, the wrist will tend to remain stationary, and the other joints will give a greater contribution to the overall arm movement. In the latter case, the elbow angle will remain nearly constant and the other joints, including the wrist, will experience larger displacements. This flexibility of the solutions offered by the passive-motion paradigm is, in our view, one of the major features that distinguish this method from others based upon fixed optimization criteria.

A final remark is related to the issue of neural networks. The models presented in this chapter cannot be considered as neural networks in a strict sense, i.e., according to the prevailing conventions in the field. In fact, it is true that the computational units representing elastic and kinematic elements implement transformations that are far more complex than the functions expressed by typical "model neurons." However, it can be reasonably assumed that such macroscopic units might correspond to assemblies of neurons behaving in some organized way, in a similar way to the cortical columns in the brain: in this context, the passive motion paradigm could be conceived as the collective behavior of interacting modular neural assemblies. Our models, moreover, fully share with neural modeling the key concepts of distributed representations, local interactions, asynchronicity, and analog problem solving via nonlinear dynamics.

As regards learning, which is a typical facet of neural modeling, we have not yet developed computational methods, but we think that the parameter-tuning methods used with more orthodox relaxation networks such as Hopfield networks or Boltzman machines could be extended to our distributed kinematic models. A source of complexity (but also an opportunity for structuring effectively a learning strategy) stems from the fact that our networks depend upon two types of parameters: kinematic parameters and muscular parameters. Learning is a distributed parameter identification problem with a lot of a priori knowledge which must be exploited.

As regards other types of neural network models used in conjunction with motor control, one of the most significant is that proposed by Jordan (1986), which extends the basic multilayer perceptron (MLP) in order to learn associations between input patterns (distributed over plan units) and a sequence of output patterns, related to motor variables (joint rotations or muscle contractions). There is obviously a deep conceptual difference between the two classes of models, which is typical of the neural modeling field at large:

1. For relaxation networks, the basic mode of operation is seeking stationary configurations of a nonlinear dynamical system.[12]
2. For Jordan's nets as well as for MLP's, the basic mode of operation is the feedforward association between an input pattern and an output pattern, and this entails an explicit supervised learning.
3. Motor-relaxation and kinematic networks are *somatotopic;* i.e., the connectivity pattern is directly derived from the topology of the controlled system.
4. On the contrary, MLP's and Jordan's nets are general purpose neural models whose structure is much more system independent.

Although kinematic and association networks have strongly different characteristics, in the motor control field they can play complementary roles. For example, it is possible to conceive a kinematic network that provides the teaching input for an association network specialized for a given task. This has been

[12] Motor relaxation networks find the solution of the system's dynamics via analogic simulation, whereas kinematic networks provide the exact solution of the same problem in the limit case of infinite ligament stiffness.

done recently for generating multijoint limb trajectories (Massone & Bizzi, 1989). In that application, the kinematic network simulated the geometrical and mechanical properties of the controlled arm. At the same time, the Jordan network implemented a map from a set of plan units to a set of output units generating the controls to the muscles. The kinematic network was used in two ways: (a) for deriving the direct transformation from the output unit activity to the motor behavior, and (b) for providing the teaching signals during the learning stage. The latter task was achieved by backdriving the kinematic network along a set of training trajectories. Thus, the training set was composed of minimum-potential-energy solutions to an ill-posed kinematics problem. As a result, the mature Jordan network demonstrated significant generalization capabilities together with noise rejection and attractor dynamics properties.

REFERENCES

Badler, N. I., & Smoliar, S. W. (1979). Digital representation of human movement. *Computing Surveys, 11,* 19–38.

Baillieul, J., Hollerbach, J. M., & Brockett, R. W. (1984, December). Programming and control of kinematically redundant manipulators. *Proceedings of the 23rd IEEE Conference on Decision and Control,* pp. 768–774. Las Vegas, Nevada.

Baillieul, J. (1985). Kinematic programming alternatives for redundant manipulators. *Proceedings IEEE Conference on Robotics and Automation,* pp. 722–728. St. Louis, MO.

Ben-Israel, A., & Greville, T. N. (1980). *Generalized inverses: Theory and applications.* New York: R. E. Krieger Publishing Co.

Bizzi, E., Polit, A., & Morasso, P. (1976). Mechanisms underlying achievement of final head position. *Journal of Neurophysiology, 39,* 435–444.

Bizzi, E., Accornero, N., Chapple, W., & Hogan, N. (1984). Posture control and trajectory formation during arm movement. *Journal of Neuroscience, 4,* 2738–2744.

Brooks, T. L. (1982). Optimal path generation for cooperating or redundant manipulators. *Proceedings of the 2nd International Computing and Engineering Conference,* pp. 119–122. San Diego, CA.

Colgate, J. E., & Hogan, N. (1988). Robust control of dynamically interacting systems. *International Journal of Control, 48,* 65–88.

Feldman, A. G. (1966). Functional tuning of nervous system with control of movement or maintenance of a steady posture. II. Controllable parameters of the muscles. III. Mechanographic analysis of the execution by man of the simplest motor task. *Biophysics, 11,* 565–578; 766–775.

Flash, T. (1987). The control of hand equilibrium trajectories in multi-joint arm movements. *Biological Cybernetics, 57,* 257–274.

Gordon, A. M., Huxley, A., & Julian, F. J. (1966). The variation in isometric tension with sarcomere length in vertebrate muscle fibers. *Journal of Physiology, 184,* 170–192.

Hogan, N. (1980). Mechanical impedance control of industrial manipulators. *Proceedings of the 1980 Joint Automatic Control Conference,* San Francisco, CA.

Hogan, N. (1984). An organising principle for a class of voluntary movements. *Journal of Neuroscience, 4,* 2745–2754.

Hogan, N. (1985a). The mechanics of multi-joint posture and movement control. *Biological Cybernetics, 53,* 1–17.

Hogan, N. (1985b). Impedance control: An approach to manipulation. Part I: Theory. Part II: Implementation. Part III: Application. *ASME Journal of Dynamic Systems Measurement and Control, 107,* 1–24.

Hogan, N. (1987). Modularity and causality in physical system modelling. *ASME Journal of Dynamic Systems Measurement and Control, 109,* 384–391.

Hollerbach, J. M., & Suh, K. C. (1985). Redundancy Resolution of Manipulators Through Torque Optimization. *Proceedings of the IEEE International Conference on Robotics and Automation,* pp. 1016–1021. St. Louis, MO.

Hopfield, J. J. (1982). Neural networks and physical systems with emergent collective computational abilities. *Proceedings of the National Academy of Sciences, USA, 79,* 2554–2558.

Huxley, H. E. (1963). Electron microscope studies on the structure of natural and synthetic protein filaments from striated muscle. *Journal of Molecular Biology, 7,* 281–308.

Huxley, H. E. (1969). The mechanism of muscular contraction. *Science, 164,* 1356–1366.

Jordan, M. I. (1986). Attractor dynamics and parallelism in a connectionist sequential machine. *Proceedings of the 8th Annual Conference of the Cognitive Science Society.* Hillsdale, NJ: Erlbaum.

Jordan, M. I. (1988). *Supervised learning and system with excess degrees of freedom* (COINS, Tech. Rep.). Amherst, MA: University of Massachusetts at Amherst.

Kathib, O. (1983, December). *Dynamic control of manipulators in operational space.* Paper presented at the 6th IFToMM Congress on Theory of Machines and Mechanisms, New Delhi.

Kathib, O. (1986). Real time obstacle avoidance for manipulators and mobile robots. *The International Journal of Robotics Research, 5,* 90–99.

Kawato, M., Maeda, Y., Uno, Y., & Suzuki, R. (1989). *Trajectory formation of arm movement by cascade neural network model based on minimum torque-change criterion* (Tech. Rep. No TR-A-0056). Kyoto, Japan: ATR.

Kelso, J. A. S. (1977) Motor control mechanisms underlying human movement reproduction. *Journal of Experimental Psychology, 3,* 529–543.

Kelso, J. A. S., & Holt, K. G. (1980). Exploring a vibratory system analysis of human movement production. *Journal of Neurophysiology, 43,* 1183–1196.

Kingsley, E. C., Schofield, N. A., & Case, K. (1981). SAMMIE: A computer aid for man-machine modelling. *Computer Graphics, 15,* 163–169.

Klein, C. A., & Huang, C. H. (1983). Review of pseudoinverse control for use with kinematically redundant manipulators. *IEEE, Transactions on System Man and Cybernetics, SMC-13,* 245–250.

Koditschek, D. E. (1987). *A strict global lyapunov function for mechanical systems* (Tech. Rep. 8707). New Haven, CT: Center for System Science, Yale University.

Korein, J. U. (1985). *A geoumetric investigation of reach.* Cambridge, MA: MIT Press.

Liegeois, A. (1977). Automatic supervisory control of the configuration and behavior of multibody mechanisms. *IEEE Transactions on System Man and Cybernetics, SMC-7,* 868–871.

Marino, G., Morasso, P., & Zaccaria, R. (1985). NEM: A language for the representation of motor knowledge. In P. Morasso & V. Tagliasco (Eds.), *Human movement understanding* (pp. 125–156). Amsterdam: North-Holland.

Mason, M. T. (1981). Compliance and force control for computer controlled manipulators. *IEEE Transactions on System, Man and Cybernetics, SMC-11*, 418–432.

Massone, L., & Bizzi, E. (1989). A neural network model for limb trajectory formation. *Biological Cybernetics, 61*, 417–425.

McKeon, B., Hogan, N., & Bizzi, E. (1984). Effect of temporary path constraint during planar arm movements. *Society for Neuroscience Abstracts, 10*, 337.

Morasso, P., Mussa-Ivaldi, F. A., Vercelli, G., & Zaccaria, R. (1989). A connectionist formulation of motor planning. In R. Pfeifer, Z. Schreter, F. Fogelman, & L. Steels (Eds.), *Connectionism in perspective*. Amsterdam: Elsevier.

Mussa-Ivaldi, F. A., Hogan, N., & Bizzi, E. (1985). Neural, mechanical and geometric factors subserving arm posture in humans. *Journal of Neuroscience, 10*, 2732–2743.

Mussa-Ivaldi, F. A., Morasso, P., & Zaccaria, R. (1988). Kinematic networks. A distributed model for representing and regularizing motor redundancy. *Biological Cybernetics, 60*, 1–16.

Mussa-Ivaldi, F. A., & Hogan, N. (1989). Solving kinematic redundancy with impedance control: A class of integrable pseudoinverses. *Proceedings of the IEEE International Conference on Robotics and Automation*, pp. 283–288. Scotsdale, AZ.

Nichols, T. R., & Houk, J. C. (1976). Improvement in linearity and regulation of stiffness that results from actions of stretch reflex. *Journal of Neurophysiology, 39*, 119–142.

Paynter, H. M. (1961). *Analysis and design of engineering systems*. Cambridge, MA: MIT Press.

Rack, P. M. H., & Westbury, D. R. (1969). The effects of length and stimulus rate on tension in the isometric cat soleus muscle. *Journal of Physiology, 204*, 443–460.

Slotine, J. J., & Li, E. (1987). On the adaptive control of robot manipulators. *International Journal of Robotics Research, 3*, 49–59.

Wampler, C. W. (1987). Inverse kinematic functions for redundant manipulators. *Proceedings of the IEEE International Conference on Robotics and Automation*, pp. 610–617. Raleigh, NC.

Wlassich, J. J. (1986, February). *Nonlinear force feedback impedance control*. Master's Thesis, M.I.T., Dept. of Mechanical Engineering, Cambridge, MA.

7

Stability, Convergence, and Computation of Stereotype Voting Groups

Thomas G. Windeknecht
Computer Science and Engineering Department
Oakland University

Ross A. Gagliano
Department of Mathematics & Computer Science
Georgia State University

1. INTRODUCTION

Voting is an important process, not only in the political connotation of resolving conflict and settling disputes, but also in the general systems notions of control and distribution of resources. Voting is a natural and common technique used in human communities, particularly democratic societies, to shape the collective value system, to establish the background of preferences, and to formulate consensus.

In both the political and general systems cases, group decision making through voting involves a global search process for dynamic equilibrium. A voting model is described in this article which provides a means to study dynamic stability and convergence. With this model, two related questions can be investigated: First, what kinds of human behaviors can be successfully represented in machines (artificial intelligence), and, second, what types of machine behaviors realistically mimic human behavior (parallel/distributed processing).

Human beings admit obvious stereotypes in various voting situations; e.g., John always votes as his friend does. Suppose that the individuals in a selected group of stereotype voters are polled regularly by an opinion survey and the results published for the group to consider. The stereotypes will then regularly change their votes in an analyzable manner. How do such groups behave? What is the relationship between group behavior and the stereotypes comprising it? In this chapter, a novel approach to the modeling of dynamic voting groups is presented, and a theory of stability and convergence is given, together with a computational approach to analysis.

2. BACKGROUND

The process of voting, or the formation of consensus or social choice, has been studied since the eighteenth century, when important work was done by Borda (assigning weights to alternative choices) and Condorcet (analyzing the effects of the sequence of alternatives). In recent years, particular attention has been paid to the game-theoretic aspects of voting, particularly in the context of committees (Black, 1958; Farquharson, 1969; Merrill, 1988; Moulin, 1983; Nurmi, 1987; Peleg, 1984).

The literature describing these processes is generally divided along the lines of game theory and political activity. Game theory presents a formal structure (definitions, lemmas, remarks, theorems, and corollaries) about idealized collections of voters and the activities associated with anonymity, monotonicity, neutrality, sincerity, and stability. Political activity seeks explanations for the outcomes in real elections and historical consequences of various voting processes.

Election or voting algorithms are also used for the control of processors and the resolution of deadlocks on databases (Garcia-Molina, 1982; Vitanyi, 1984). The ideas developed here go well beyond the problems of social choice and the discovery of rational human behavior. In fact, voting may be among the several possible alternative techniques that could be employed in future operating systems for networks of intelligent nodes (Gagliano & Schaefer, this volume).

This chapter extends earlier results (Windeknecht, 1972) which proposed a technique for the dynamic modeling and study of small groups of voters. The technique was based upon the so-called *stereotype modeling approach* (D'Angelo & Windeknecht, 1973a,b, 1975; Gagliano & Windeknecht, 1974). In the latter, each individual is represented in the model by a deterministic behavioral strategy (or stereotype), and the group response is then derived by analysis or simulation.

Such a modeling philosophy is particularly appropriate for voting groups, because human beings admit obvious stereotypes in various voting situations; e.g., John always votes as his friend does. Suppose the individuals in a selected group of stereotype voters take a sequence of public "show of hands" votes. Alternatively, suppose the group members are polled regularly by an opinion survey, and the results are published for the group to consider. The stereotypes will then regularly change their votes in an analyzable manner. How do such groups behave? What is the relationship between group behavior and the stereotypes comprising it?

In this chapter, the stereotype approach to the modeling and analysis of voting groups is presented, and a theory of stability, convergence, and computation of these groups is given. Stability will be described as the ability of the voting group to realize a single final state, whereas convergence is the property of realizing such a state. Computation is performed on the (discrete) time to achieve convergence.

3. THE STEREOTYPE MODELING APPROACH

For many years, there has been increasing interest in the application of mathematical analysis to socially relevant problems (Gagliano, 1983). In the realm of socioeconomic systems, a whole spectrum of important real systems is apparent in which the basic structure of the system is "an evolving society of individuals." In 1975, D'Angelo and Windeknecht discussed the need for basic innovations in the modeling of such systems for computer simulation. In particular, it was suggested that alternatives to a purely statistical approach to system description be investigated.

One such alternative is described in general terms by D'Angelo and Windeknecht (1975), together with a detailed example, the modeling of the learning and economic processes of a six-grade elementary school. The basic idea, in modeling a collection of interacting individuals, is to replace each real individual with one of a number of deterministic stereotype individuals whose behavior is similar to but much simpler than a real individual's. The basic conjecture underlying the approach is that such a collection of stereotypes will retain many of the properties of group behavior exhibited by collections of real individuals.

Since each real individual retains an identity in the model, it appears the model contains much more information than do the usual statistical models of the group. The model can account for the situation of the individual who is simply not average. The model is interesting from a theoretical point of view, because it retains the essential dynamic character of the real situation. Finally, the interactions of various individuals (which underlie and cause the system to evolve in a particular manner) are specifically accounted for and, in a simulation, are available for observations and analysis.

A particularly simple case of "an evolving society of individuals" is a voting group. In a voting group, the interactions of the members of the group are of a rather limited kind; thus, the simplicity. There are two good reasons for studying models of voting groups. First, the dynamic system encountered is representative of an important class of not well-understood systems and a relatively tractable one. Thus, some important insights can be gained and transferred to other systems. Second, the behavior of real groups of voters is an important aspect of the democratic process, one that should be understood as well as possible in order to preserve democratic processes.

In the next section, the stereotype voting group is defined, based on the stereotype voter. Examples of three-member and six-member voting groups are described in the next sections. Lastly, the issues of stability and convergence are discussed.

4. A DYNAMIC MODEL FOR VOTING GROUPS

A *voting group* is a collection of individuals who take a sequence of votes on some issue. A *stereotype voter* is a member of a voting group whose next vote is completely determined by the current votes of a subset (possibly empty or all) of the group members. A *stereotype voting group* is a voting group containing only stereotype voters.

Human beings admit a number of obvious stereotypes within voting groups. For example, consider the following:

1. Votes as his or her friend did last time
2. Votes as the majority did last time
3. Votes as the minority did last time
4. Always votes the same way
5. Always votes the same way unless no one else agrees, in which case he changes his or her vote
6. Cycles his or her vote through the alternatives
7. Votes as two other voters did last time provided they agree; otherwise, as he or she did last time
8. Votes as the majority of a certain subgroup did last time.

All of the above voting behaviors are examples of what we previously defined to be stereotype voters.

Granted that stereotype voters are at best an approximation to the behavior of real voters, how does a given mix of stereotype voters function as a group trying to make a decision?

Assume there are n voters in the group and they are presented with a set C of m alternatives on which to vote. They take a sequence of votes at $t = 0, 1, 2, \ldots$. Any collective vote of the group can be represented by an n-tuple

$$v(t) = (v_1(t), v_2(t), \ldots, v_n(t))$$

where $v_i(t)$ is the alternative selected by i^{th} voter at time t. If the ith voter is in fact a stereotype then $v_i(t + 1)$ is a function of v(t), i.e.,

$$v_i(t + 1) = f_i(v_1(t), v_2(t), \ldots, v_n(t))$$

Note: $f_i: C^n \to C$. If all of the voters are stereotype, then the group behavior is characterized by

$$\begin{aligned} v_1(t + 1) &= f_1(v_1(t), v_2(t), \ldots, v_n(t)) \\ v_2(t + 1) &= f_2(v_1(t), v_2(t), \ldots, v_n(t)) \\ &\cdots \\ v_n(t + 1) &= f_n(v_1(t), v_2(t), \ldots, v_n(t)) \end{aligned}$$

or, simply,

$$v(t + 1) = f(v(t)), \qquad t = 0, 1, 2, \ldots$$

where $f{:}C^n \rightarrow C^n$ is the unique function with projections $f_i{:}C^n \rightarrow C$ for $i = 1, 2, \ldots, n$. The function f is finite here and, hence, may be presented in tabular or graphical form.

5. A THREE-MEMBER VOTING GROUP

Let us take up an example. Suppose we have the following group of three stereotype voters who take a sequence of votes "aye" or "nay" on some issue:

1. Voter #1 always votes as he or she did last time unless alone, in which case he changes his or her vote
2. Voter #2 votes as #3 did last time
3. Voter #3 votes as the majority did last time.

For this group, the tabular representation of the function f is given in Table 7.1.

For example, if the vote of #1 is "aye" and those of #2 and #3 are "nay," then

$$v(t) = 100$$

Subsequently, #1 changes to 0 since he or she is alone in voting 1, #2 votes 0 following #3's current vote, and #3 votes 0 following the majority. Hence,

$$v(t + 1) = 000$$

Table 7.1. Transitions of Three-Member Voting Group.

v(t)	f(v(t))
000	000
001	010
010	000
011	111
100	000
101	111
110	101
111	111

Thus,

f(100) = 000

which is the fifth entry from the top in the table.

To make the dynamic voting behavior of the group more comprehensible, it is convenient to convert from the tabular representation of f, Table 7.1, to a transition graph. In the transition graph, each possible collective vote of the group is represented by a small circle, or *node,* and directed lines from node to node indicate the transitions under the function f. The transition diagram for the above group of three voters is contained in Figure 7.1.

By examination of the transition graph, one can readily understand the behavior of this voting group. We see the votes 000 (unanimous "nays") and 111 (unanimous "ayes") are so-called fixed points of f; i.e., no subsequent change in any member's vote occurs. We observe that the group starting with any initial vote converges to one of these fixed points after at most two votes. We note that a symmetry occurs upon interchanging "aye" and "nay" in the diagram, which results from the symmetry of the individual voting behaviors postulated. We conclude that the given group is a rather agreeable and stable voting group which can quickly reach unanimity on the given issue. That this is the case is *not* obvious from direct examination of the individual voting behaviors, despite the fact there are only three voters.

The example situation suggests the sort of questions we might ask about the behavior of stereotype voting groups in the general case. For example:

1. Is a fixed point always reached ultimately?
2. If so, do the fixed points represent unanimity?
3. If so, does every voter effect the ultimate outcome? Sometimes? In all cases?
4. Do a subgroup of the voters alone determine the outcome? Under what circumstances? Which voters? One voter?

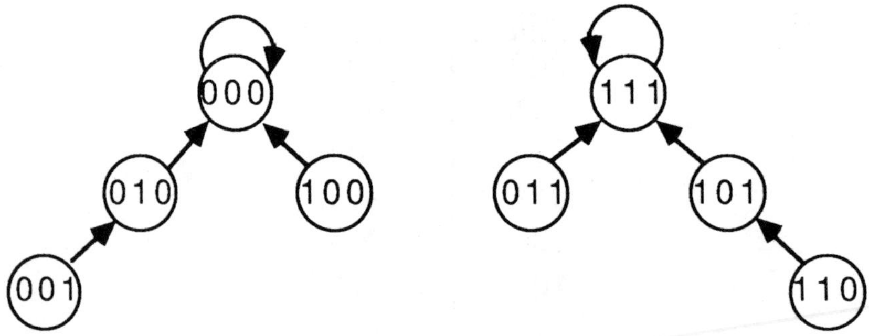

Figure 7.1. Transition Graph of Three-Member Voting Group.

5. Does an initial majority always win out in steady-state?
6. Can a voting group be manipulated by giving false information on the state of the voting group?

6. A SIX-MEMBER VOTING GROUP

As a more complex example, consider next the following group of six stereotype voters who vote "aye" or "nay" on some issue:

> voter #1 votes constant unless no one else votes the same way, in which case he or she changes his or her vote.

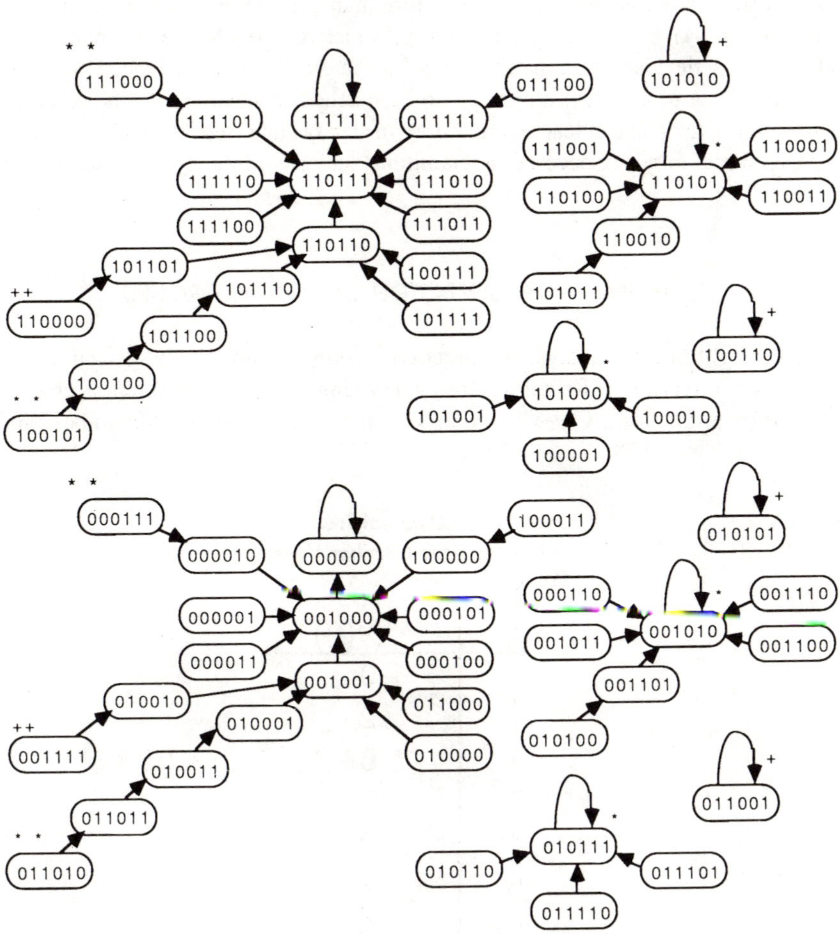

Figure 7.2. Transition Graph of Six-Member Voting Group.

voter #2 votes as the majority did last time provided a majority existed; otherwise constant.
voter #3 votes as the minority did last time if a minority existed unless he or she was alone in his or her vote or the vote was unanimous; otherwise constant.
voter #4 votes as #1 and #2 if they agreed; otherwise, constant.
voter #5 votes as #3 and #4 if they agreed; otherwise, constant.
voter #6 votes as #2 did last time.

The transition diagram for this voting group is given in Figure 7.2. The behavior of this group is considcrably more complex than that of the previous example. However, on the whole, the group is again a rather stable and decisive one. A fixed point is always reached. More than half of the possible initial states (38 out of 64) lead to a fixed point in which the final vote is unanimous. However, a tie vote (stalemate) is possible in steady-state (indicated by + in Figure 7.2), a four-to-two majority can be reached in steady-state (indicated by *), an initial tie vote can lead to unanimity in steady-state (see **), and, occasionally, an initial minority becomes a unanimous majority in steady-state (see ++ in Figure 7.2).

7. DECIMAL REPRESENTATION OF VOTING GROUPS

Some insight into the analysis of stereotype voting groups can be gained by the following observation. Recall a stereotype voting group with n voters is characterized by a function $f:C^n \rightarrow C^n$, where C is the set of m alternatives to be voted upon.

Table 7.2. Decimal Transition Table of Three-Member Voting Group.

v(t)	f(v(t))
0	0
1	2
2	0
3	7
4	0
5	7
6	5
7	7

If the alternatives to be voted upon in C are numbered 0, 1, . . . , m − 1, then a collective vote of the group

$$v(t) = (v_1(t), v_2(t), \ldots, v_n(t))$$

can simply be regarded as an integer in base-m representation. If we convert these base-m integers to decimal, then f becomes simply a transformation on the set {0, 1, . . . , $m^n - 1$} of integers.

In the above example of a three-member voting group, m = 2 and n = 3, so the collective votes of the group are binary integers; specifically, 000, 001, 010,

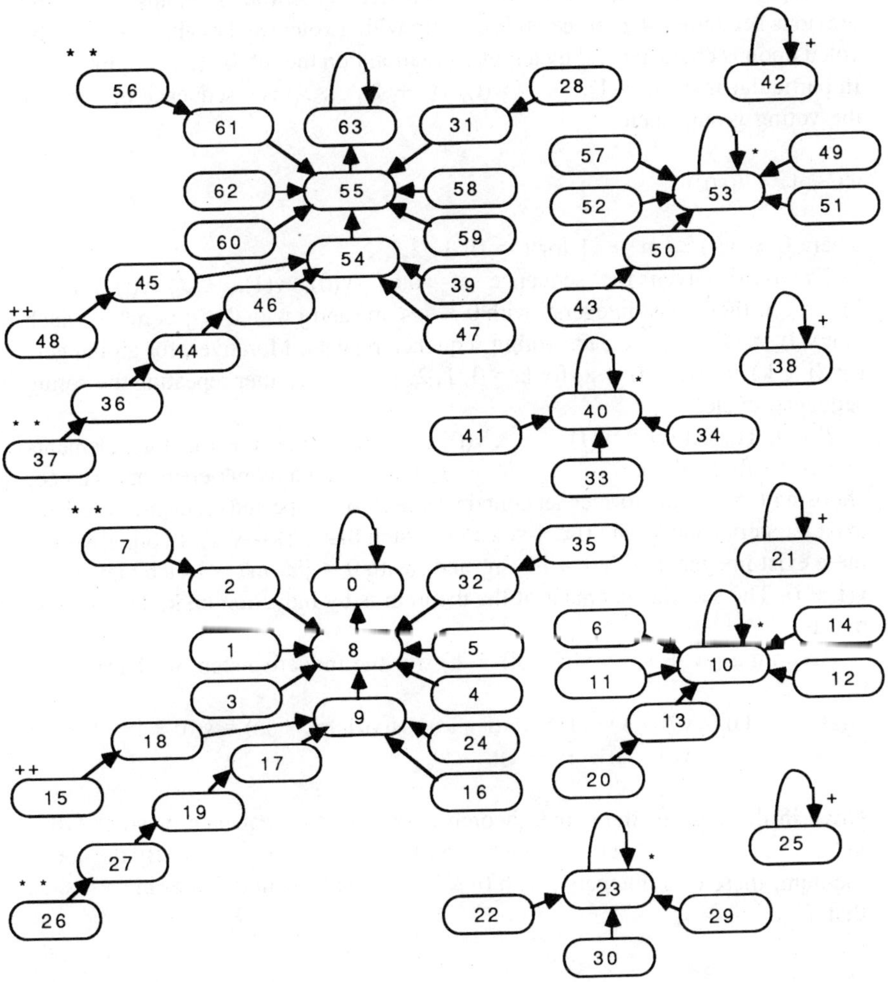

Figure 7.3. Decimal Transition Graph of Six-Member Voting Group.

011, 100, 101, 110, and 111. Converting to decimal integers, f becomes a transformation on {0, 1, 2, 3, 4, 5, 6, 7}; specifically, the transformation given in Table 7.2.

Similarly, for the above six-member example voting group, changing the binary integers representing collective votes to decimal integers yields the transition graph of Figure 7.3.

8. STABILITY AND CONVERGENCE OF VOTING GROUPS

For the remainder of the chapter, our goal is to address the problems of stability, convergence, and computation for general stereotype voting groups. As in the previous section, a stereotype voting group with n voters and m alternatives to be voted upon is characterized by a transformation f on the set $\{0, 1, \ldots, m^n - 1\}$. In particular if $\langle v(0), v(1), \ldots, v(t), v(t+1), \ldots \rangle$ is a sequence of votes of the voting group, then

$$v(t+1) = f(v(t))$$

where $0 \leq v(t) \leq m^n - 1$ for $t = 0, 1, 2, \ldots$.

Theorem: Given the sequence of votes $\langle v(0), v(1), \ldots, v(t), v(t+1), \ldots \rangle$, there exist integers i with $0 \leq i < m^n$ and j with $0 < j \leq m^n - i$ such that $v(i) = v(i + j)$; i.e., the voting sequence repeats. Moreover, for all integers k, $v(i + k) = v((i + j) + k)$ for $k = 0, 1, 2, \ldots$; i.e., after repeating the voting sequence cycles.

Proof: The set $\{v(0), v(1), \ldots, v(t)\}$ contains at most $t + 1$ distinct elements and is a subset of $\{0, 1, \ldots, m^n - 1\}$ which contains m^n elements. Hence, choosing $t = m^n$, the former set contains at least one repeated element; i.e., there exist integers i and k with $0 \leq i < k \leq m^n$ such that $v(i) = v(k)$. In other words, there exist integers i with $0 \leq i < m^n$ and j with $0 < j \leq m^n - i$ such that $v(i) = v(i + j)$. The second statement of the theorem is by induction on k. The basis is trivial.

Assuming $v(i + k) = v((i + j) + k)$, for the inductive step, we have

$$\begin{aligned} v(i + (k + 1)) &= v((i + k) + 1) = f(v(i + k)) = f(v((i + j) + k)) = v(((i + j) + k) + 1) \\ &= v((i + j) + (k + 1)) \qquad \square \end{aligned}$$

Now, in the light of the above theorem, consider the sequence of votes $\langle v(0), v(1), \ldots, v(t), v(t+1), \ldots \rangle$ where $v(0) = c$ is the initial vote. By the above theorem, there exist integers i with $0 \leq i < m^n$ and j with $0 < j \leq m^n - i$ such that

$$v(i) = v(i + j)$$

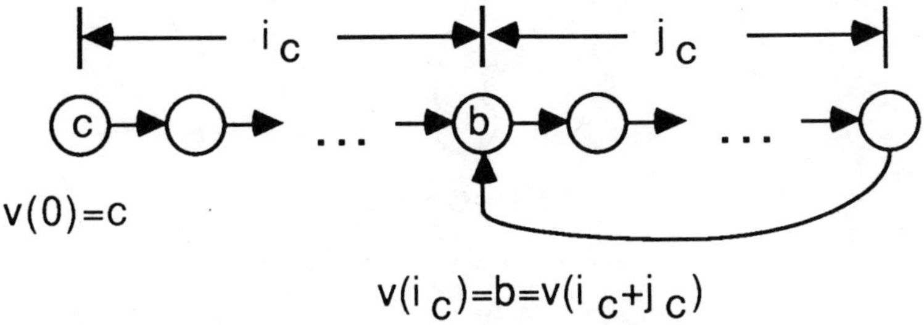

Figure 7.4. Graph of General Voting Behavior.

Given an initial vote, let i_c be the least integer such that

$$v(i_c) = v(i_c + j)$$

for some j and let j_c be the least integer such that

$$v(i_c) = v(i_c + j_c)$$

i_c is the *convergence time* of c and j_c is the *period* of c. Note: $0 \leq i_c < m^n$ and $0 < j_c \leq m^n - i_c$. The vote c is *transient* if $i_c > 0$ and *trapping* if $i_c = 0$. c is a *fixed point* if c is trapping ($i_c = 0$) and $j_c = 1$.

The above discussion shows the general behavior of a stereotype voting group. Starting with any initial vote c, a (possibly empty) sequence of i_c distinct votes occurs, followed by a sequence j_c distinct votes that is repeated endlessly, as shown in Figure 7.4.

When the initial state c is trapping ($i_c = 0$), then the graph of voting behavior simplifies to Figure 7.5.

Finally, when the initial state c is a fixed point, the graph of voting behavior simplifies to Figure 7.6.

With these definitions of convergence time, period, transient, trapping, and

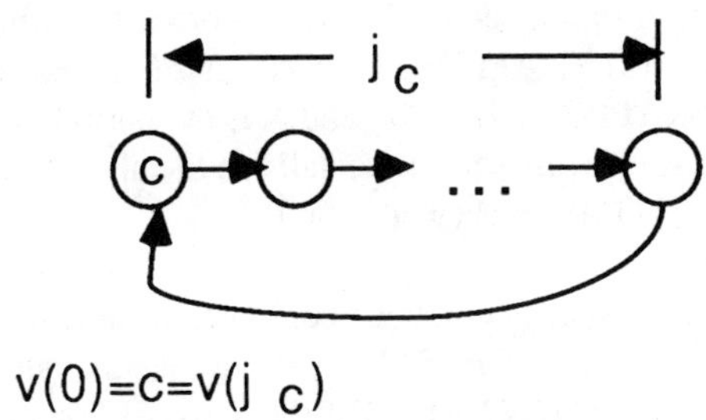

Figure 7.5. Graph of Trapping Behavior.

Figure 7.6. Graph of a Fixed Point.

fixed-point states, it is now possible to look at the computation of stereotype voting groups. We will primarily be concerned with the computation of convergence times and the determination of trapping states.

9. COMPUTATION OF CONVERGENCE TIMES AND PERIODS

One approach to the computational analysis of a stereotype voting group is (a) to classify each possible group vote as being transient or trapping, and (b) to determine the convergence time of each transient vote and the period of each trapping vote. This can be performed systematically, using four arrays for data storage:

1. NEXT with indices 0, 1, . . . , $m^n - 1$ is given containing values from the set {0, 1, . . . , $m^n - 1$} to describe the transition function f of the voting group in decimal representation. In other words, for each index I, NEXT[I] is f(I).
2. TRAPPING with indices 0, 1, . . . , $m^n - 1$ acquires values from the set {F, T} to classify the nodes as trapping (value = T) or transient (value = F). In other words, by computation, we make TRAPPING[I] = 'T' if node I is trapping and TRAPPING[I] = 'F' if node I is transient for each index I. The initial values of this array are arbitrary.
3. TIME with indices 0, 1, . . . , $m^n - 1$ acquires values from the set {0, 1, . . . , m^n}; namely, the convergence time for each transient node and the period for each trapping node. In other words, by computation, we make TIME[I] = N if (a) TRAPPING[I] = 'F' and N is the convergence time of node I or (b) TRAPPING[I] = 'T' and N is the period of node I. Note that N > 0 in either case. (This is used crucially in the algorithm to follow.) Let the initial values of TIME everywhere be 0.
4. REPETE with indices 0, 1, . . . , $m^n - 1$ acquires values from the set {F, T} to classify the nodes as having been computed or not. In other words, during computation, we make REPETE[I] = 'T' when values are assigned to TRAPPING[J] and TIME[J] and REPETE[I] = 'F' otherwise. Let the initial values of REPETE everywhere be F.

An efficient algorithm for computing the arrays TRAPPING, TIME, and REPETE given the array NEXT can be found using the insight of the previous section. With explanatory comment statements, the algorithm is:

```
{consider the nodes in order}
for I: = 0 to m^n − 1 do
   {if REPETE[I] = 'F', examine, mark, and count the successor nodes of I
   under f until a node J is reached such that REPETE[J] = 'T'}
   while REPETE[I] = 'F' do
      REPETE[I]: = 'T', COUNT: = 1, J: = NEXT[I]
      while REPETE[J] = 'F' do
         REPETE[J]: = 'T', COUNT:= COUNT + 1, J: = NEXT[J]
      endwhile
      {if TIME[J] = 0 then REPETE[J] was assigned 'T' inside the above loop
      and J is the first repeated successor node of I; thus, compute the
      period of J}
      if TIME[J] = 0 then
         PERIOD: = 1, K: = NEXT[J]
         while K ≠ J do
            PERIOD: = PERIOD + 1, K: = NEXT[K]
         endwhile
         {mark and store PERIOD in node J and the other nodes in the cycle}
         TIME[J]: = PERIOD, TRAPPING[J]: = 'T', K: = NEXT[J]
         while K ≠ J do
            TIME[K]: = PERIOD; TRAPPING[K]: = 'T', K: = NEXT[K]
         endwhile
         {if I ≠ J then mark and compute the convergence time of I and its
         successor nodes up to J}
         if I ≠ J then
            COUNT: = COUNT − PERIOD, TIME[I]: = COUNT, TRAPPING[I]: =
 'F',
            K: = NEXT[I]
            while K ≠ J do
               COUNT: = COUNT − 1, TIME[K]: = COUNT, TRAPPING [K]: =
 'F', K: = NEXT[K]
            endwhile
         endif
      else
      {if TIME[J] ≠ 0 then TIME[J] is the period of J if TRAPPING[J]= 'T' and
      TIME[J] is the convergence time of J if TRAPPING[J] = 'F'; in each case,
      mark and compute the convergence times of I and its successor nodes
      up to J}
         if TRAPPING[J] = 'F' then
            COUNT: = COUNT + TIME[J], TIME[I]: = COUNT, TRAPPING[I]: =
 'F',
            K: = NEXT[I]
```

NEXT

0	2	0	7	0	7	5	7
0	1	2	3	4	5	6	7

TRAPPING

T	F	F	F	F	F	F	T
0	1	2	3	4	5	6	7

TIME

1	2	1	1	1	1	2	1
0	1	2	3	4	5	6	7

Figure 7.7. Data Arrays for Three-Member Voting Group.

```
            else
                TIME[I]: = COUNT, TRAPPING[I]: = 'F', K: = NEXT[I]
            endif
            while K ≠ J do
                COUNT: = COUNT − 1, TIME[K]: = COUNT, TRAPPING[K]: = 'F', K:
    = NEXT[K]
            endwhile
        endif
    endwhile
endfor
```

For example, for the above three-member voting group, the array NEXT is given in Figure 7.7 together with the final arrays TRAPPING and TIME.

10. A PASCAL ANALYSIS PROGRAM

The above algorithm has been incorporated into a rudimentary TURBO PASCAL program using keyboard input and screen output for analysis of stereotype voting groups. The program reads:

```
program VOTETIME (input,output);
const
    max = 255;              {dimension for up to eight "aye"/"nay" voters}
    no_lines = 24;              {no. rows in screen display}
var
    i, j, k, no_voters, no_votes, count, period: integer;
```

```
   next: array[0..max] of Integer;
   trapping: array[0..max] of Boolean;
   time: array[0..max] of Integer;
   repete: array[0..max] of Boolean;
begin
   writeln('How many voters are there?');
   readln(no_voters);
   no_votes:=1;
   for i:=0 to no_voters-1 do
      no_votes:=no_votes*2;
   for i:=0 to no_votes-1 do
      begin
         time[i]:=0;
         repete[i]:=FALSE;
      end;
   writeln;
   writeln('Please define the next-states:');
   for i:=0 to no_votes-1 do
      begin
         write('What is the next state from state',i:3,': ');
         readln(next[i]);
      end;
   for i:=0 to no_votes-1 do              {main program}
         while not repete[i] do
         begin
            repete[i]:=TRUE
            count:=1;
            j:=next[i];
            while not repete[j] do
               begin
                  repete[j]:=TRUE
                  count:=count+1;
                  j:=next[j];
               end,
            if time[j]=0 then
               begin
                  period:=1;
                  k:=next[j];
                  while k<>j do
                     begin
                        period:=period+1;
                        k:=next[k];
                     end;
                  time[j]:=period;
                  trapping[j]:=TRUE;
                  k:=next[j];
                  while k<>j do
```

```
                begin
                    time[k]:=period;
                    trapping[k]:=TRUE;
                    k:=next[k];
                end;
            if i<>j then
                begin
                    count:=count-period;
                    time[i]:=count;
                    trapping[i]:=FALSE;
                    k:=next[i];
                    while k<>j do
                        begin
                            count:=count-1;
                            time[k]:=count;
                            trapping[k]:=FALSE;
                            k:=next[k];
                        end;
                end;
        end
    else
        begin
            if not trapping[j] then
                begin
                    count:=count+time[j];
                    time[i]:=count;
                    trapping[i]:=FALSE;
                    k:=next[i]
                end
            else
                begin
                    time[i]:=count;
                    trapping[i]:=FALSE;
                    k:=next[i];
                end;
            while k<>j do
                begin
                    count:=count-1;
                    time[k]:=count;
                    trapping[k]:=FALSE;
                    k:=next[k];
                end;
        end;
  end;                              {end of main program}
writeln('State Next-State Time Trap');
j:=0
for i:=0 to no_votes-1 do
```

```
        begin
            write(i:4);
            write(next[i]:8);
            write(time[i]:9);
            if trapping[i] then
                writeln('  T')
            else
                writeln('  F');
            j:=j+1;
            if j=no_lines then
                begin
                    readln(count);          {press RETURN key to continue}
                    j:=0;
                end;
        end;
end.
```

11. THREE EXAMPLES

In the following three examples, there are three voters and the outcome in the form of a graph of the behavior for each of the three voting groups is given in each case.

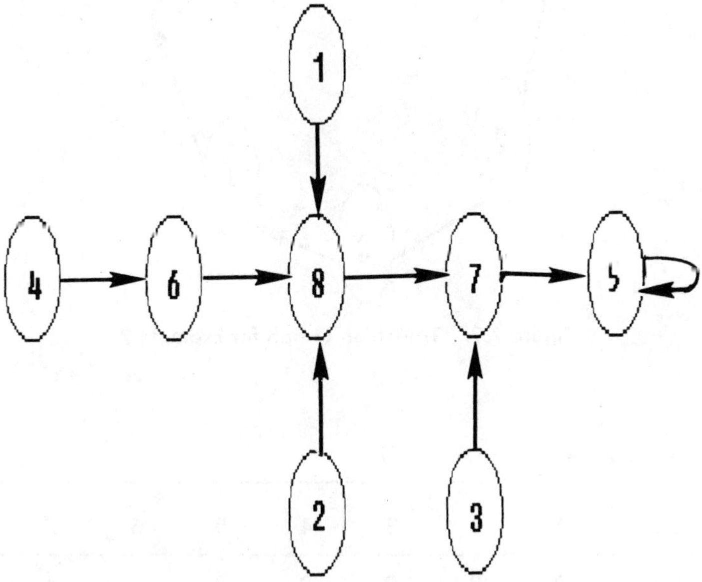

Figure 7.8. Transition Graph for Example 1.

Table 7.3. Data Array for Example 1.

State	1	2	3	4	5	6	7	8
Time	3	3	2	4	1	3	1	2

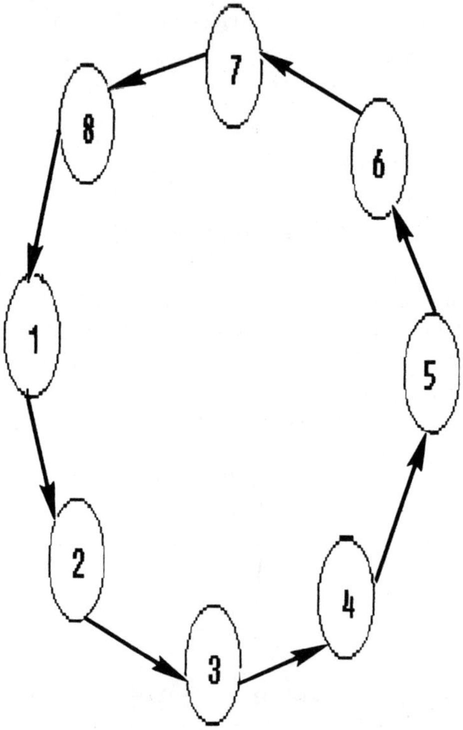

Figure 7.9. Transition Graph for Example 2.

Table 7.4. Data Array for Example 2.

State	1	2	3	4	5	6	7	8
Time	8	8	8	8	8	8	8	8

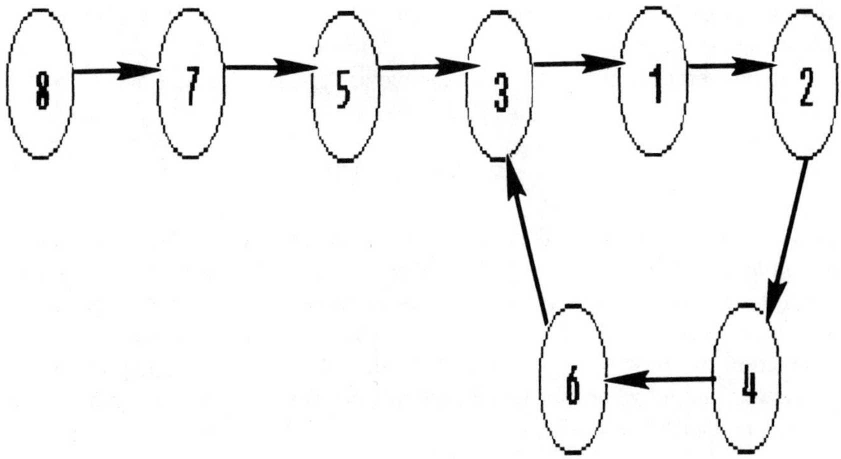

Figure 7.10. Transition Graph for Example 3.

11.1. Example 1

The transitions representing the states of this voting group appear in Figure 7.8. Again, there are three voters, thus there are eight states, of which state 5 is a fixed point.

The convergence times for this example are given in Table 7.3.

11.2. Example 2

For this second example, the transitions representing the states of this voting group appear in Figure 7.9. Again, with three voters, there are eight states, and none of the states is a trap state.

The convergence times for this example are given in Table 7.4.

11.3. Example 3

For this last example, the transitions representing the states of this voting group appear in Figure 7.10. Again, with three voters, there are eight states, of which,

Table 7.5. Data Array for Example 3.

State	1	2	3	4	5	6	7	8
Time	5	5	5	5	6	5	7	8

in this case, there are no trap states but convergence is determined by the nonrepeating sequence.

The convergence times for this example are given in Table 7.5.

12. CONCLUSION

This chapter has presented the stereotype approach to the modeling and analysis of voting groups and developed a theory of stability, convergence, and computation for stereotype voting groups. Several examples were developed in addition to a theorem on the cyclic nature of the voting states. An algorithm for the calculation of convergence times and the determination of trapping states was provided. Sample values for the algorithm were generated by a program implemented in TURBO Pascal.

IN MEMORIAM

The authors respectfully dedicate this article to the late Professor Henry D'Angelo of Boston University.

REFERENCES

Black, D. (1958). *The theory of committees and elections*. London: Cambridge University Press.

D'Angelo, H., & Windeknecht, T. G. (1973a). Modeling real decision-makers in an evolving society of individuals. *Proceedings of Sixth Asilomar Conference on Circuits and Systems* (pp. 365–369). North Hollywood, CA: Western Periodicals.

D'Angelo, H., & Windeknecht, T. G. (1973b). A system model of a prairiedog town. In W. G. Vogt & M. H. Mickle (Eds.), *Modeling and simulation* (Vol. 4, pp. 59–63). Pittsburgh, PA: University of Pittsburgh Press.

D'Angelo, H., & Windeknecht, T. G. (1975). The stereotype approach to the modeling and simulation of an elementary school. *IEEE Transactions on Systems, Man, and Cybernetics, 5*(2), 805–810.

Farquharson, R. (1969). *Theory of voting*. New Haven, CT: Yale University Press.

Gagliano, R. A. (1983). Systems and solutions of people problems. *Proceedings of the 1983 Conference of the Society for General Systems Research*. Lewiston, NY: Intersystems Publications.

Gagliano, R. A., & Windeknecht, T. G. (1974). A disaggregated model for neighborhood dynamics. In W. G. Vogt & M. H. Mickle (Eds.), *Modeling and simulation* (Vol. 5, pp. 41–46). Pittsburgh, PA: University of Pittsburgh Press.

Garcia-Molina, H. (1982). Elections in a distributed computing system. *IEEE Transactions on Computers, C-31*, 48–59.

Merrill, S. (1988). *Making multicandidate elections more democratic*. Princeton, NJ: Princeton University Press.

Moulin, H. (1983). *The strategy of social choice*. Amsterdam, Netherlands: North-Holland.

Nurmi, H. (1987). *Comparing voting systems*. Boston, MA: Dordrecht (Kluwer Academic Publishers).

Peleg, B. (1984). *Game-theoretic analysis of voting in committees*. New York: Cambridge University Press.

Vitanyi, P. M. (1984). Distributed elections in an archimedean ring of processors. *Proceedings 16th ACM Symposium on the Theory of Computation,* pp. 542–547.

Windeknecht, T. G. (1972). On the behavior of small groups of stereotype voters. *41st National ORSA Meeting,* New Orleans.

8

The CARELIA Simulator: A Development and Specification Environment for Neural Networks*

Pasi Koikkalainen
Erkki Oja
Lappeenranta University of Technology
Department of Information Technology
Lappeenranta, Finland

1. INTRODUCTION

The theory of computational neural networks has had significant advantages recently. As is the case with parallel processing and adaptive computing in general, they might provide the answers for many practical problems where traditional computer technology must give up. Up to now, neural networks have shown their strength in demonstrations and in special embedded problems. It remains to be seen what kind of contribution neural networks can give for the whole field of computer science.

In this work a neural networks development environment is introduced. It has been implemented in Occam parallel processing language and designed to run in a multi-Transputer processor network. The system is targeted for general purpose neural programming and design, which makes it ideal as a research tool. The requirement of generality forces us to search for a general formal model for neural networks and carefully study common features in neural network algorithms. We also want as the output from the system a specification for neural networks that could be compiled to other types of computer architectures, both parallel and sequential.

The motivation for neural development and simulation environments is quite clear: They are the first step for more general use of neural networks. The design of algorithms and network structures should be possible at a higher level than in traditional programming languages. Users should have tools for visualizing and monitoring network behavior during a development phase. Interactions between real world data and neural network development should be made easy. When developed, the neural network should be documented or specified so that it could easily be transferred to any type of computer architecture.

---

* This work was supported by Tekes Grant 4196/1988 under Finsoft project.

Before explaining in detail the organization of the CARELIA simulator in Section 6 below, some aspects of neural net software, hardware, and algorithms are briefly reviewed. Some typical recent software and hardware systems will be covered in Section 2, and neural network models and algorithms in Section 3. In Section 4, a general computational model is presented which underlies the design philosophy of the simulator. Section 5 points out similarities between neural network models and the formalism of communicating sequential processes that will be exploited in the design.

2. NEUROCOMPUTER SOFTWARE AND HARDWARE

As there are a number of definitions for neural networks and an even larger number of different algorithms, it seems difficult to create any general purpose development environment. Many simulators (for example, D'Autrechy, Reggia, Shutton, & Goodall, 1988; Feldman, Fanty, Goddard, & Lynne, 1988; Rumelhart, McClelland, & the PDP Research Group, 1986; Smith, 1987) are therefore based on special models. Some of those that can run many models are not programmable, which makes them useful only for demonstration purposes. In the more programmable environments, the development is usually done by traditional low-level programming style (Goddard, Lynne, & Mintz, 1988; Lester, 1978; Neural Networks, 1981; Smith, 1987). The first stage of so-called neurocomputing co-boards include a traditional programming language (usually C-like) and a subroutine library for the most common neural operations (Treleaven, 1989a,b). Some of the newest products have an object-oriented higher-level language for network design. The current trend is towards higher-level specifications of neural networks which are based on an abstract model of a neuron as a computing element.

Neural networks, by all the definitions, are massively parallel. However, many practitioners in the field program and specify their algorithms by sequential languages. This means that, when starting to build parallel hardware or doing simulations in parallel computers, there is a need to retranslate the sequential algorithms into parallel form. This may not be easy. Furthermore, different parallel machines have different ways of realizing parallelism (Ahuja, Carriero, Gelernter, & Kirshnaswamy, 1988; Hammerstrom, 1988; Wexler & Prior, 1989). For example, a sequential code that might be vectorized automatically might not be automatically compiled for a multiprocessor architecture such as a Transputer. In doing sequential specifications of networks, it is also easy to violate the laws of parallelism.

2.1. Software Models

The requirements for neural network study and research include parallel processing, i.e., running parallel algorithms in real parallel surroundings, efficiency, low cost, and adaptivity. The study of existing neural software did not show that these requirements could be met. When this work was started and the first look for available simulators was taken in the beginning of 1988, the number of choices was very low. Since then many new systems have been introduced (D'Autrechy et al., 1988; Treleaven, 1989a,b). Currently, there are several research projects aiming at neural programming environments. The following is a summary of some of the best known neural programming environments, with selected features (D'Autrechy et al., 1988; Goddard, Lynne, & Mintz, 1988; Hanson, Crutz, & Tam, 1987; Treleaven, 1989b; Paic, Gungner, & Skrzypek, 1987):

ANNE (Oregon graduate center)

- Neural simulator for Intel iPSC multiprocessor
- High-level network description language (NDL)
- Network operations are built-in C procedures

ROCHESTER CONNECTIONIST SIMULATOR (University of Rochester)

- Simulator for connectionist networks
- Available for SUN and Butterfly multiprocessor
- Network description language: C-programming language
- Network operations are built-in C procedures
- Simple graphics monitor

IBM CONE (IBM, Palo Alto)

- Neural programming environment for IBM PC/AT
- May use attached multiprocessor
- Network specification language GNL (made using YACC and LEX for C)
- Graphics display

UCLA SFINX (University of California at Los Angeles)

- High-level network specification language
- Network operations are built-in C procedures
- Command interpreter for user commands
- Some graphic operations

HNC ANZA (Hecht-Nielsen Neurocomputer)

- Neurocomputer co-board and development environment for SUN and PC
- Object-oriented specification language AXON
- C procedure library

SAIC DELTA (Scientific Applications International Corporation)

- Neurocomputer co-board and development environment for PC
- Object-oriented specification language ANSpec
- Graphics window support

A close look at these programming environments reveals similarities in their design. Many of them have some higher-level language for structural design of neural networks. Algorithmic programming is done using very traditional programming languages, many times in C, with the help of a procedure or function library.

2.2. Special Hardware

Typically, a neurocomputer implementation is not built on special "neural" hardware. Simulations are run in normal sequential machines, the most popular ones being PC's and workstations (Hanson et al., 1987; Goddard et al., 1988; Treleaven, 1989a,b). Neural co-processor boards (Treleaven, 1989a) have usually some popular processor like 68020 with FP unit for extra computing power, and therefore they are not really neural computers. This is understandable since a more neural-like hardware does not allow easy algorithm development. It seems more realistic that neural algorithms are developed in traditional computers and then transferred onto special hardware (Abu-Mostafa, & Psaltis, 1987; Bailey, Hammerstrom, Mates, & Rudnic, 1988; Hammerstrom, 1988; Ruckert & Goser, 1988; Salam, 1988).

There are some simulators that use parallel computers to boost simulation performance. In our work we have studied the use of a message-passing multiprocessor system for neural network simulations. The selected processor is the Transputer by Inmos Ltd. (*Transputer Databook,* 1988). This architecture has attracted a lot of interest (May, 1987; Wayman, 1987; Wexler & Prior, 1989), and many projects, especially in Europe, have selected it as their hardware platform for neural network implementations.

3. THE STATE OF THE ART IN NEURAL NETWORKS

This section investigates the current knowledge of neural networks in the general setting of computer science. To summarize the most important points of view, a study of abstract definitions, categories of models, and stages in typical algorithms is presented.

3.1. Abstract Definitions for Neural Networks

There are a multitude of definitions for neural networks. Many of these reflect the mechanisms observed in biological networks, which are a major source of innovations. A collection of definitions for neural networks can be found from references (for example, Anderson & Rosenfeld, 1988; Hecht-Nielsen, 1988b; Hinton & Anderson, 1981; Kohonen, 1988b; Rumelhart et al., 1986; Sejnowski, Koch, & Churchland, 1988). Some of the most common features in the definitions of neural networks can be given as follows:

1. Neurons can be described as individual processes that calculate an output signal from input signals, and from internal states, synaptic weights, or connection strengths, of the neuron (see Figure 8.1).
2. A neuron can change its internal state as a function of the inputs and the output.
3. All the neurons run in parallel, and there is no external synchronization for them.
4. All information between neurons is transferred via special one way channels, and no neuron can "know" the state of any other neuron without communication by such a channel.

By all the definitions, neural networks are processes that operate in parallel and communicate with each other via channels (Koikkalainen & Oja, 1988). This property will be discussed more in Section 5 in connection with the parallel specification of neural networks.

3.2. Categories in Neural Computing Models

There is a difference, made for practical reasons, between abstract definitions and computational models. This is because implementations of the neural networks will set extra constraints like synchronization, capacity, etc. It also seems useful to describe computational models via different levels of organization and abstraction. Kohonen (1988b) has found the following categories of neural models useful:

1. *Neuron-level:* studying the properties of a neuron.
2. *Network-level:* the interconnected network of neurons.
3. *Nervous-system-level:* competing or co-operating networks of type 2.
4. *Mental-operation-level:* high-level cognitive operations.

As Kohonen emphasizes, the current state of the art in neural networks theory cannot apply all the four levels simultaneously. The step in trying to model high-level cognitive operations based on functions in a single neuron is still too high.

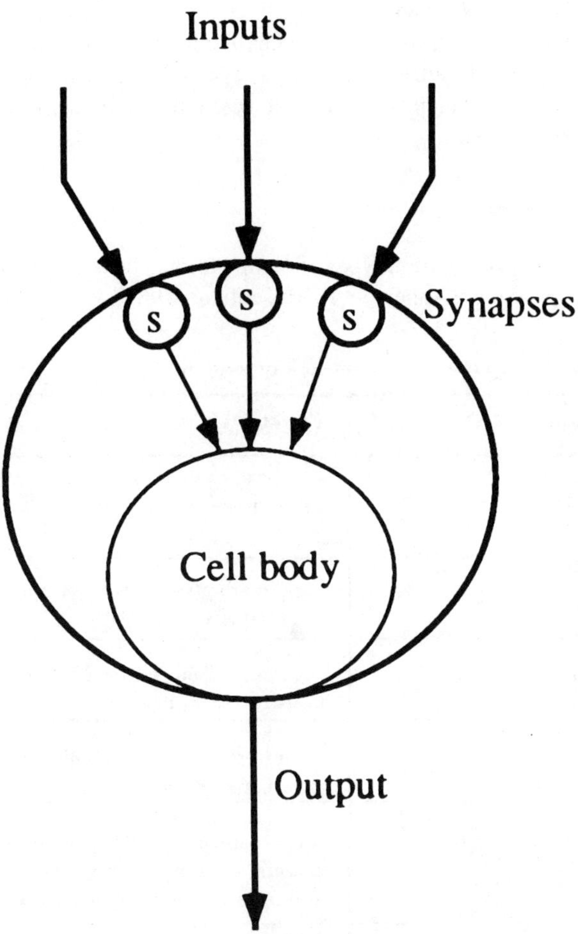

Figure 8.1. Idealization of a neuron.

The lower the level is, the more carefully models are usually designed to match what is known about the brain. Higher levels of models intend to imitate by manmade algorithms what has been observed in human information processing.

Most of the presently popular neural network algorithms are network-level type. The computational point of view is, then, that the neurons of the network are running under the control of the same algorithm. One notable exception to the above rule are connectionist models (Feldman et al., 1988), which should rather be categorized as mental-operation-level networks. The research on nervous-system-level models has not yet caught up with the popularity of the other models, although it can be expected with good reason that system-level networks will and should play an important role in neural networks research in the future. This suggestion is supported both by the biological organization of the brain

(Lindsay & Norman, 1977) and by the architecture of any general computational machine. They both have information processing localized for units or areas with specialized functions. In artificial neural networks this is also a natural way for reducing connectivity, which is a vital issue in simulating networks using parallel hardware (Ghosh & Hwang, 1989).

3.3. Neural Network Algorithms

The current number of different types of computational neural networks is around 100 and still growing (Anderson & Rosenfeld, 1988; Hecht-Nielsen, 1988;

Table 8.1. Some popular neural network algorithms.

Network model	Function
Associative memories (Anderson, 1972) (Kohonen, 1972)	Retrieval of memorized patterns by incomplete key
Perceptron (Rosenblatt, 1958)	Simple adaptive linear classifier of data patterns
Neocognitron (Fukushima,1983)	Invariant visual pattern recognition in hierarchical network
Back-propagation (Rumelhart et al., 1986)	Adaptive supervised nonlinear classifier of data patterns
Topological feature maps (Kohonen, 1982)	Self-organization and unsupervised classification of data patterns and ordering of reference vectors
ART (Grossberg, 1976)	Self-organization and classification of data patterns and detection of a new class
Boltzmann machine (Hinton et al., 1984)	Dynamic learning network for classification of data patterns
Learning subspaces (Oja, 1989)	Neural subspace classifier, orthogonalization of reference vectors
Hopfield net (Hopfield, 1982)	Finds given eigenstates of the network. Parallel optimization model
Counterpropagation networks (Hecht-Nielsen, 1988a)	Self-adapting look-up table. Combination of ART and topological feature maps

Kohonen, 1988b; Neural Networks, 1988). The simulator that will be described in this chapter is designed so that the best known algorithms could be realized using built-in subalgorithms, neural primitives (see Section 4).

To understand the role of neural primitives, we must first have a close look at some of the most significant neural network algorithms, and especially at the kinds of similarities that can be found between the algorithms. Some well-known algorithms are briefly summarized in Table 8.1.

3.4. Stages in a Typical Neural Network Algorithm

Despite the differences in the computational algorithms, some common stages can be detected. Typically in the first step, an input pattern is read, and, using some internal state of the neuron, an output pattern is computed. Secondly, output patterns are matched with "desired outputs" for error computing, or with each other, in order to find best matching units. In the last stage there is usually updating of the internal state of the neuron (weights). We term these stages of computation *forward computing, matching,* and *updating*. In the following, these stages are studied more carefully.

3.4.1. Forward Computing Stage

This stage in the algorithm is where the neural outputs are computed from the given input pattern and the internal weight vector. All these operations are parallel in nature for a set of neurons and therefore require no knowledge about the state of the other neurons. These are clearly neural-level operations. Examples for some of the models are given below:

Topological feature maps (Kohonen, 1988a):

$$Out = \sum_i |x_i - m_i|^n,$$

where n is 1 or 2, *Out* is the output of the neural unit, x is the input pattern and m is the weight (memory) vector.

Back propagation (Rumelhart et al., 1986):

$$Out = f\left(\sum_i x_i m_i\right),$$

where *Out, m,* and x are as above and $f(\alpha)$ is a nonlinear function, for example

$$f(\alpha) = \frac{1}{1 + e^{-(\alpha-\theta)}}.$$

Associative Memory (Anderson & Rosenfeld, 1988; Kohonen, 1988b):

$$Out = \sum_i x_i m_i,$$

where *Out*, *m*, and *x* are as above.

ART (Carpenter & Grossberg, 1988);

$$Out = \sum_i x_i m_i,$$

where *Out* is the neural output, *m* is the vector of bottom-up weights and *x* is the binary input vector.

3.4.2. Matching Stage

This is usually the most sequential part of a neural algorithm. In general this stage requires knowledge about the state of all the neurons in the network. This knowledge is used for cooperation or competition between neurons in the network. In unsupervised models this is usually the selection of the best matching unit, and in supervised models the back propagation of error or training values. These operations are network-level functions since they operate within a network of neurons. The knowledge of the state is passed to the updating equations through the variable t_i. For example:

Topological feature maps:

$$\begin{cases} t_i = \alpha & \text{if } i \text{ is the best matching neuron} \\ & \text{or one of its neighbours} \\ t_i = 0 & \text{otherwise} \end{cases}$$

Back propagation:

$$\begin{cases} t_i^k = o_i(1 - o_i)(t_i^{k+1} - o_i), & \text{for output neurons } i \text{ where } t_i^{k+1} \text{ and } o_i \\ & \text{are the desired and real outputs,} \\ t_i^k = o_i(1 - o_i) \sum_j t_j^{k+1} M_{ij} & \text{for hidden neurons } i \text{ at level } k \text{ where } t_j^{k+1} \\ & \text{are the } t \text{ values from the nex layer } k + 1, \\ & M_{ij} \text{ are the weights and } o_i \text{ are as above.} \end{cases}$$

3.4.3. Updating Stage

In this stage neural units adjust their internal weight values. Values are functions of the controls for the neurons that were defined in the matching stage. Since all the information is internal to a neuron, this stage can be computed in parallel for the neurons selected for updating. Like the operations in the forward stage, these are neural-level operations. For example, with M_{ij} denoting the jth weight on unit i:

Topological feature maps:

$$M_{ij} = M_{ij} + t_i * (x_j - M_{ij})$$

Back propagation:

$$M_{ij} = M_{ij} + \gamma t_i M_{ij}$$

4. THE GENERAL COMPUTATIONAL MODEL

A general purpose neural machinery must have a formalism that is flexible for many neural models and still simple enough for practical computing and high-level specification. The CARELIA neural networks simulator, presented in this chapter, is mostly based on the network-level of thinking. A very simple neuron-level approximation is also given to form a basis for general network-level algorithms. This is not intended to explain any biological behavior of a real neuron, but rather gives a basic design of an artificial neuron in a way that the network-level algorithms see it. The neuron-level computational unit is provided with operands and operations detected in most of the present computational models. These units are used in a network-level unit, a layer, which is a set of neurons provided with a superset of neuron-level operations (Figure 8.2). The realization of a layer in the simulator is usually a well-known algorithm or a part of it.

Multiple layers can be defined, and they can communicate with each other. The nervous-system-level can be built from such combination of layers. Since only few computational algorithms have been designed for this level in the present state of the art, we try to give the user as much freedom for system design as possible. The overall idea is that the system level is built as a network of communicating layers, where layers are networks of communicating neurons.

4.1. Neural Operands

A computational model of a neuron is a unit that operates with a set of neural operands S_N. In our model there are seven operands in the set S_N: $\{x, ex, m, o_i, t_i, c, a\}$ (Figure 8.3). Four of them, called *basic operands*, are required in every neural algorithm:

input vector	x
memory vector	m (= M_i for neuron i)
output scalar	o_i for neuron i
control scalar	t_i for neuron i

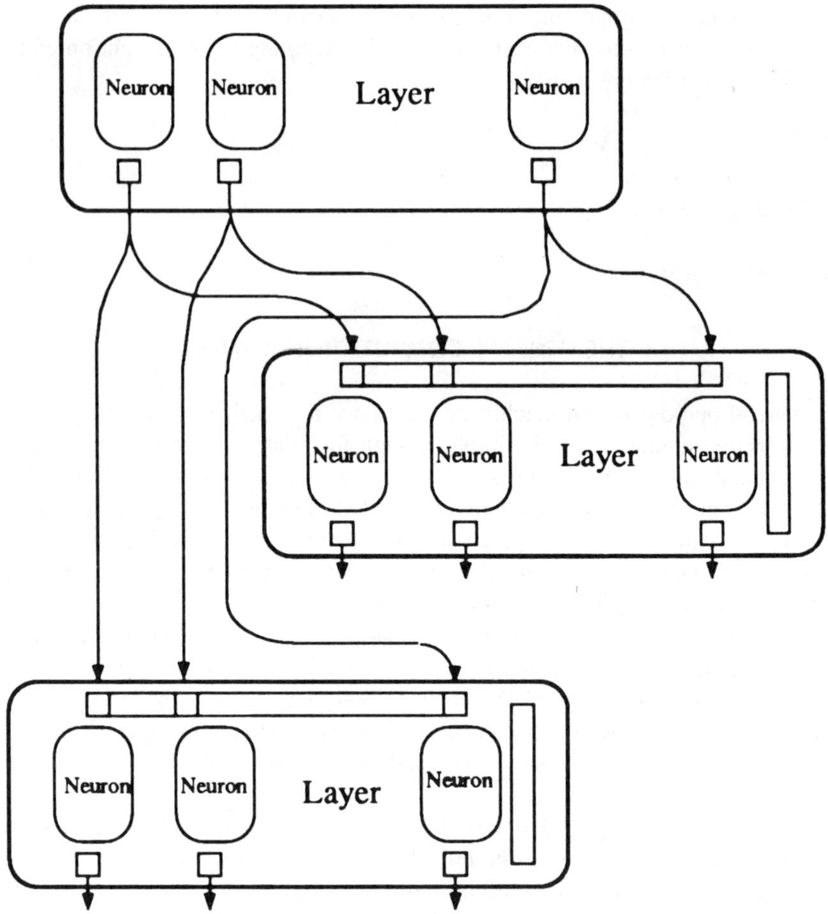

Figure 8.2. An illustration of layers and neurons.

Input vector x is a set of real (or binary) values, inputs to the neuron. Memory vector m is an internal operand of the neuron, usually used as a connection weight vector for the inputs. Output scalar o_i is a real or binary value typically computed from the input and memory vectors. Control scalar t_i is set by an external "layer" algorithm to control the updating of the memory vector. In many cases t_i is the "desired output" value, which is compared to the computed output of the neuron. The three operands left are for more special types of algorithms:

Extra input vector ex
Connection vector c
Attribute vector a

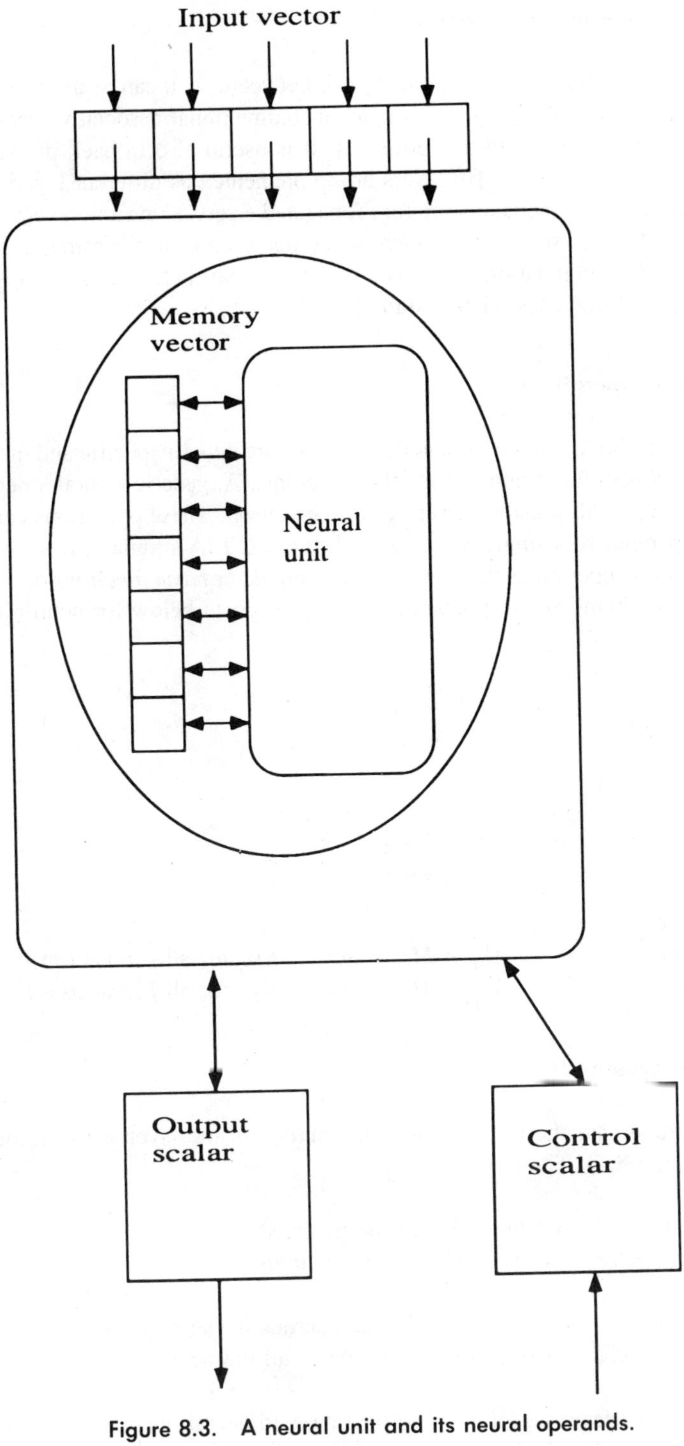

Figure 8.3. A neural unit and its neural operands.

Extra input *ex* has as many elements as input vector x. It can be used for cross-correlation computing, as, for example, in bidirectional associative memories (Kosko, 1988) or in subspace algorithms. It is useful also in back propagation algorithms, when different BP-layers are implemented as different layers in the simulator, as an intermediate store for propagated errors. Connection vector c is a vector of links and connection strengths to other neurons in the same layer. It is used for lateral computations in a layer of neurons. Attribute vector a can be used for any special purposes when required.

4.2. Neural Operations

As discussed above, the set of neural operations are neuron-specific and therefore do not access information from other neurons. A generic neural operation, $N(neuron, S_N)$, will update the set S_N for the *neuron*. These operations can only use the operands of a single neural unit. The CARELIA simulator has a built-in library of these operations that can be called *atomic* or *basic functions* of a neural network algorithm. Some typical operations are given below for neuron i:

$x \times m \rightarrow o_i$

eukl.dist	$o_i = \Sigma_j \lvert x_j - M_{ij} \rvert^2$
in.prod	$o_i = \Sigma_j x_j M_{ij}$

$o_i \rightarrow o_i$

sigmoi	$o_i = \dfrac{1}{1 + e^{-(o_i - \theta)}}$
thres.1	$o_i = sgn(o_i - \theta)$

$t_i \times o_i \times x \times m \rightarrow m$

upd.delta	$M_{ij} = M_{ij} + \alpha(o_i - t_i)x_j$ for all j in neuron i.
upd.topo	$M_{ij} = M_{ij} + t_i(x_j - M_{ij})$ for all j in neuron i.

4.3. Layer Operands

Layer operands are the ones connecting neurons in the layer with the outside world (Figure 8.4). The basic ones are:

input vector	x (shared by all the neurons)
extra input vector	*ex* (shared by all the neurons)
output vector	o (outputs of all the neurons in the network)
control vector	t (controls of all the neurons in the network)
memory matrix	M (memory vectors m of all the neurons)

Sometimes a layer algorithm may operate with neural operands like the connection vector c. In this case the operand is used for directing a neural operation

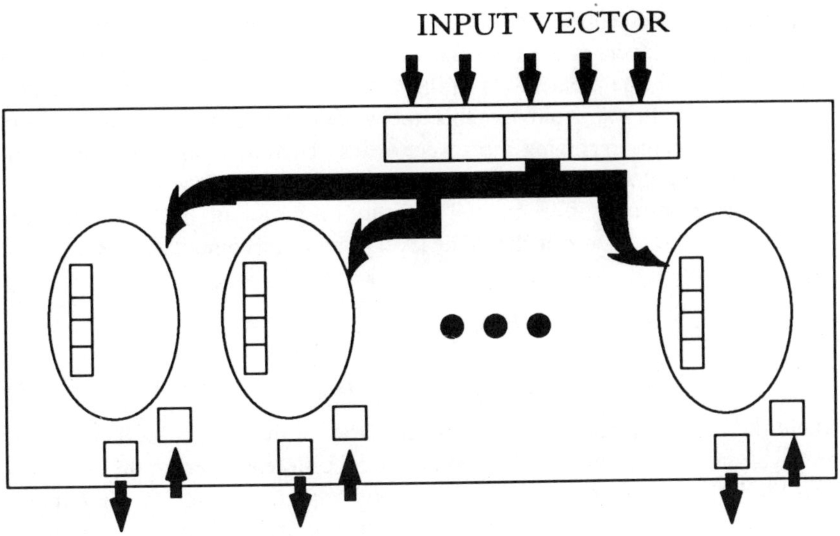

Figure 8.4. An illustration of a layer.

to the neurons that are connected to some selected neuron (see next section). The set of layer operands will be denoted S_L.

4.4. Layer Operations

Layer operations are a superset of neural operations. In the simplest case a layer operation, $L(layer, S_L)$, performs a neuron operation in parallel with all the neurons. All the neural operations are run by a layer operation. Layer operations are the primitives that a user can choose in neural network algorithm design. There are two groups of these operations, for computing and for communicating. The computing operations can furthermore be divided in five basic types: parallel, control, picking, targeting, and branching.

Parallel layer operations execute a neural operation in parallel with all the neurons in the network (for the Occam-like syntax, see Section 5):

Lpar$(layer, S_L)$: $(S_L \rightarrow S_L)$
  PAR *neuron* = first FOR number.of.neurons
    N$(neuron, S_N)$

Control operations belong typically into the matching stage of the algorithm. Operations can use information of the whole network to calculate control scalars for neural units. The form of the operation for control computing is:

Lctl$(layer, S_L)$: $(S_L \rightarrow S_L)$

In multilayer perceptron networks, the back propagation of the error is of this type. If different layers of the algorithm are implemented as different layers in the simulator as well, the input vector of the layer is received from the output vector of another layer. In a structure like this, the weights between the two layers are in the layer where the receiving input vector lies. Therefore, the backward computation of weighted errors for the sending layer must be done in the receiving one. Weighted errors are computed into the *ex* vector of the layer and sent backwards to the *t* vector of the other layer. The error computation is a typical control operation:

$t \times M \rightarrow ex$
BackErr $ex = M^T t$,

where the control vector *t* is used to store errors of the current layer. One back propagation layer can also be divided in several different layers in the simulator. This kind of grouping of neurons allows optimal partioning for the algorithm in terms of communication. If layers in the simulator are implemented in different processors as well, then the number of messages to be transferred between processors is of the degree $O(Ne)$, where Ne is the number of neurons in the layer (note that the degree of messages does not depend on the number of physical processors in the network).

Another example of a control operation where computation is very similar to the back propagation example is the bidirectional memory:

$o \times M \rightarrow ex$
BackBAM $ex = M^T o$

Picking operations are mostly used in unsupervised algorithms. They gather the information from all the neurons in the layer to select the "best matching" one. The picking operation is usually followed by a targeting or branching operation that targets its operations by the picked item. The form of the operation is:

$Lpick(layer, S_L)$: $(S_L \rightarrow neuron)$

For example, in the self-organizing topological feature maps the best matching unit is found by a picking operation. Before this operation, every neuron has computed in parallel the distance of its memory vector *m* from the layer input vector *x* and produced the output scalar o_i. Then a picking operation is used to find the minimal distance.

$o \rightarrow neuron$
PickMin $neuron$: $o_{neuron} < o_i$ for $\forall i \neq neuron$

The targeting operation requires a picking operation to be executed before it. It then uses the picked neuron index to target a neuron operation to that special neuron:

Lpoint(layer, S_L*)*: *(neuron* → S_N*)*
  N(neuron, S_N*)*

The branching operation is a special form of the targeting operation that uses the connection vector of the picked neuron to target a neural operation, not only to the picked neuron, but to all the neurons found in the connection vector as well. It can also use the connection strength to adjust control scalars in the targeted neurons. This operation is used in topological feature maps.

Lbranch(layer, neuron, S_L*)*: *(neuron* → S_L*)*
  PAR
    N(neuron, S_N*)*
    PAR *neib* = first FOR (for all the neighbours found in *c* vector of the best neuron)
      N(neib, S_N*)*

4.5. Communication Between Layers and External Devices

Layers are not only computational units; they also take care of communication. For this reason there is a set of noncomputational layer operations for information passing. Operations receive or send messages between layers or between a layer and the user. For the layer algorithms there are the following operations:

Get.inputs	to receive an input vector *x*
Get.training	to receive a control vector *t*
Get.ex	to receive an *ex* vector
Send.outputs	to send an output vector *o*
Send.ex	to send an *ex* vector

All communication is synchronized, so that a layer must wait for the receiving or sending partner to be ready before communication can happen. Layers usually communicate using these routines. The received data may come from another layer or from any device connected to the simulator. The user may also choose other similar routines for setting the initial values for the layers database, or for monitoring purposes.

4.6. Example Algorithms Using Basic Neural Operations

Here we illustrate by two simple examples how network algorithms can be built using primitive layer operations. The parameters that are set by the user and required by some of the operations are not shown here. They are set at the same time with the algorithm, and all are stored in the same stack, but the user may change them during the operation. During the operation the user may perform some controlling operations and ask for any data from the layer interactively and independently of the layer program.

Example 1. The Topological Feature Map Algorithm (Kohonen, 1988a)

```
1. Lcomm:      Get.inputs      % receive new input vector
2. Lpar:       Eukl.dist       % compute distances to neural outputs
3. Lpick:      PickMin         % pick minimum distance
4. Lbranch:    upd.topo        % use updating rule to neuron and it neighbours
5: Lcomm:      Send.weights    % send weights (for users monitor)
6: Lsys:       Restart         % goto 1
```

Example 2. A Simple Perceptron Using Delta Rule

```
1. Lcomm:   Get.inputs      % receive new input vector
2. Lcomm:   Get.training    % receive new desired output
3. Lpar:    In.prod         % compute neural response
4. Lpar:    Upd.delta       % update weights
5: Lcomm:   Send.outputs    % send outputs
6: Lsys:    Restart         % goto 1
```

5. SPECIFICATIONS OF NEURAL NETWORKS VIA A CSP-LIKE FORMALISM

From a point of view of parallel processing, neural network models belong to the more general class of *communicating sequential processes* (CSP). This makes it possible to specify neural networks using a CSP-like, fully parallel formalism. This specification can then be translated for many computer architectures, both sequential and parallel. It is also an ideal way for making automatic documents from the designed networks, using the neural networks development environment. Another obvious advantage is that the theory of communicating sequential processes has an efficient implementation in the Occam language and Transputer processors, in which case no translation is needed.

5.1. Communicating Sequential Processes, Occam and Transputer

The theory of communicating sequential processes (CSP) was introduced by C. A. R. Hoare (1978). The basic primitives of this specification language are sequential processes that can transfer messages between other parallel processes, using message channels. The channel is a point-to-point connection, and all other ways of communication between parallel processes are prohibited. The processes themselves include all normal programming structures, such as assignments, conditionals, replicators, and some special structures for communicating purposes. Communication occurs when both the sending and the receiving process are ready. If not so, the process that first tries to send or receive must wait until the second process is ready. A process can also be designed to communicate with one of several channels, depending on which one is ready first, by using an alternative statement.

The basic features of CSP are included in the programming language Occam (Wayman, 1987). Occam has been designed together with a special RISC architecture processor, the Transputer, by Inmos Ltd. (*Transputer Databook,* 1988). One processor is designed to run CS processes with great efficiency. It also has four serial links that behave like CSP channels, allowing communication with processes running in other similar processors. This offers an elegant way for increasing the computational power without major changes in software. The number of processors and serial links is a physical restriction only; on a logical level, any number of communicating parallel processes can be specified even in a one-Transputer physical processor.

For some readers it might prove to be useful to give a brief list of basic Occam primitives. The ones in the basic CSP theory may have different notation but are mostly functionally equivalent. The reason we use only Occam notation here is that it is fully implementable.

variable: = expression	assign expression to variable
channel ! expression	output expression to channel
channel ? variable	input variable from channel

Some of the constructional commands are:

Sequential execution of component processes $p_1, \ldots, p_n$

SEQ
  p_1
  . . .
  p_n

Parallel execution of component processes $p_1, \ldots, p_n$

PAR
  p_1
  . . .
  p_n

Alternative execution of processes, depending which input channel comes ready first

ALT
  channel$_1$? *variable*$_1$
    p_1
  channel$_2$? *variable*$_2$
    p_2
  . . .

Replicative execution of construct *b* (SEQ,PAR or ALT)
b i = *start* **FOR** *number.of.iterations*

A comparison between the definitions of neural networks (see Section 2) and the CSP-like formalism indicate that neural networks could be described in terms of the theory of communicating sequential processes.

5.2. An Example Specification

Here we show briefly how these specifications could be written for simple examples. We use the same algorithms as before. For the sake of clarity these examples are simplified from what they really would look like. However, it is easy to see how these specifications could be directly compiled from the algorithm and structure data of the layer database.

Example 1. Topological feature map

```
PROC F.map.layer([ ]CHAN OF ANY inputs,[ ][ ]CHAN weights)
  . . . definitions of variables and channels
  . . . definitions of processes
  WHILE active
    SEQ
      . . . get.inputs()
      PAR neuron=0 FOR number.of.neurons
        SEQ
          PAR input=0 FOR number.of.inputs
            dist[input][neuron]:=ABS(M[input][neuron] − x[input])
          o[neuron]:=Σ_input dist[input][neuron]
      picked:=MIN(o[neuron])
      PAR
        PAR input=0 FOR number.of.inputs
          M[input][picked]:=M[input][picked] +
                alpha*(x[input]-M[input][picked])
        PAR neuron=1.neib[picked] FOR numb.neib[picked]
          SEQ
            beta:=alpha*connection.strength[picked][neuron]
            PAR input=0 FOR number.of.inputs
              M[input][neuron]:=M[input][neuron]+
                        beta*(x[input]-M[input][neuron])
      . . . send.weights()
```

Example 2. Back propagation layer (hidden layer)

```
PROC F.hidden.layer([ ]CHAN OF ANY inputs,controls,e.inputs,outputs)
  . . . definitions of variables and channels
  . . . definitions of processes
```

```
WHILE active
  SEQ
    . . . get.inputs(x)
    PAR neuron=0 FOR number.of.neurons
      SEQ
        o[neuron]:=Σ_inputs x[input]*M[input][neuron]
        o[neuron]:=f_sigmoid(o[neuron])
    . . . send.outputs(o)
    . . . get.controls(t)
    BackErr(ex,M,t)      (ex = M^T t)
    . . . send.ex(ex)
    PAR neuron= 0 FOR number.of.neurons
      PAR input=0 FOR number.of.inputs
        M[input][neuron]:=M[input][neuron] + alpha*(t[neuron]*x[input])
```

6. THE SYSTEM ARCHITECTURE

The CARELIA simulator has been designed to be a general purpose development environment for neural networks. It provides many possibilities for algorithmic development and specification. The user communicates with the system via a command interpreter taking its input from the keyboard and a menu. Many graphical aids are supported to make network design and database monitoring easy. Graphics supports multiple windows for interactive operations. The user gives the system specifications for the layer algorithms and structures. By the *structure* we mean the number of neurons, inputs, connections, etc. These data are stored in the simulator database, which can then be used to simulate designed layers with the monitoring system and graphics. When required, a parallel specification of the network can be written out. These features of the simulator are illustrated in Figure 8.5.

The system is fully implemented using the Occam language in a Transputer network. The current version uses only one Transputer, but it will be distributed into a Transputer network of any size. We are now building tools that will do the distribution, loading, and routing automatically from the host to any Transputer-based multiprosessor, without any prior knowledge about the number of processors or their connection topology. For physical mapping problems, see Heath, Rosenberg, and Smith (1988).

There are two major processes in the system, the simulator process and the user interface process (Figure 8.6). The user interface process takes care of communication with output and input devices (screen, keyboard, files), and the simulator contains the runtime database and layer program interpreter. In the system, there can be one user interface process and several simulator processes (in different Transputers). The user interface process communicates with simulator processes via four message channels. A command channel pair is provided for

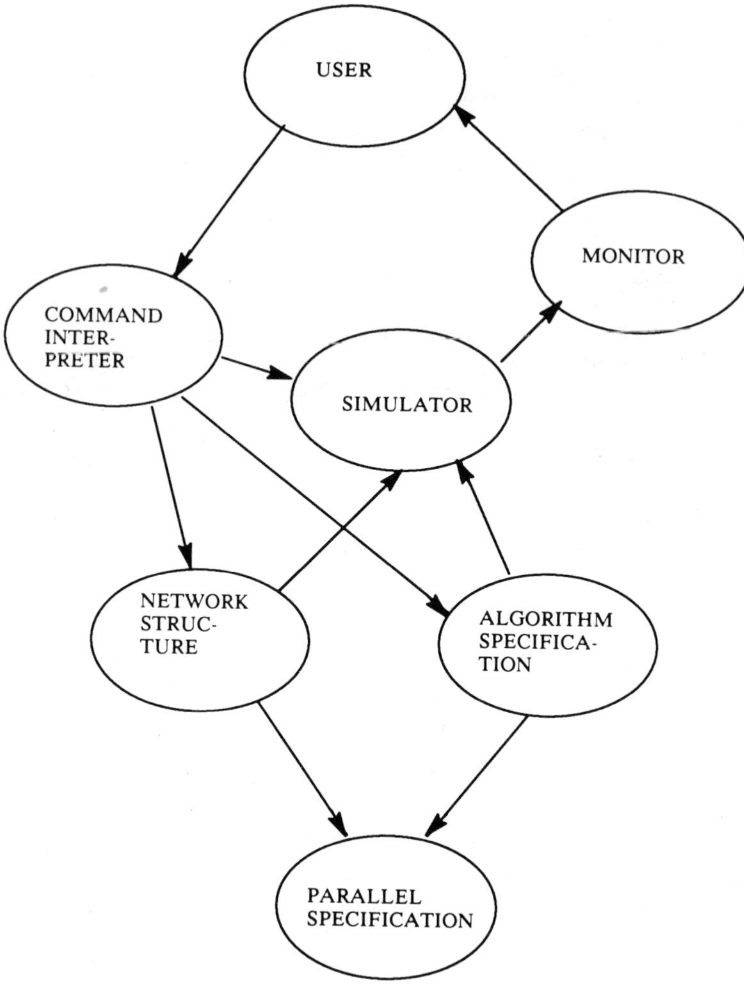

Figure 8.5. The system architecture of CARELIA neural networks development environment.

sending and receiving user messages and data to the simulator. The monitor channel is for time monitoring of the layer information during simulation. The error channel sends error messages to the user.

6.1. The User Interface Process

The user interface process is divided into two processes, the user command interpreter and the monitor. The command interpreter takes all inputs from the

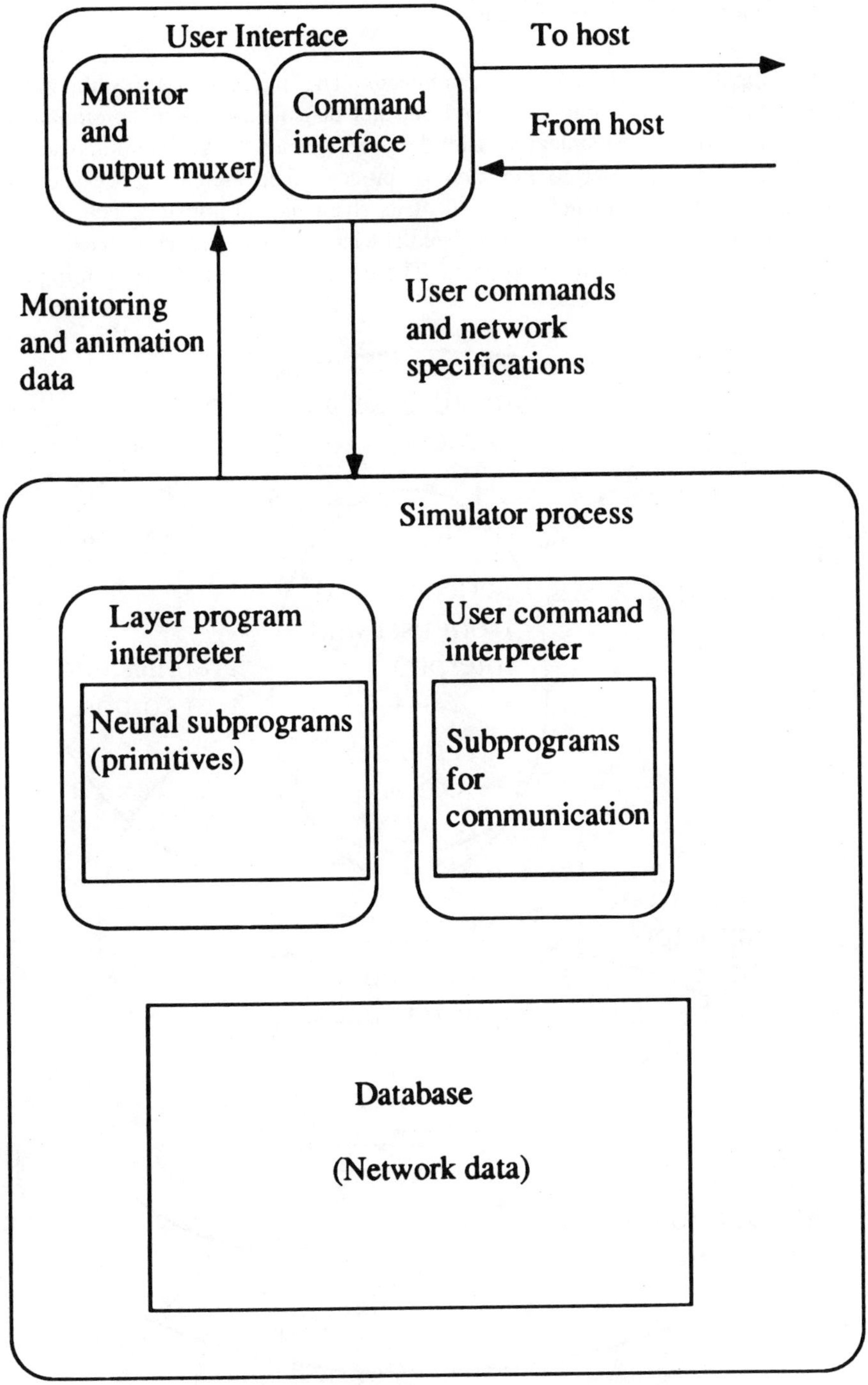

Figure 8.6. Simulator and user processes.

host computer and interprets user commands. The interpreter uses a library of communication subprograms to send and get data to and from the simulator processes. When communicating with the user, it reads the keyboard and sends messages from the user to the monitor process. The monitor process reads graphics and text commands from all of its channels and transfers them to the host computer display. It can also handle windows that will be created by a command from the interpreter process. These processes are illustrated in Figure 8.7.

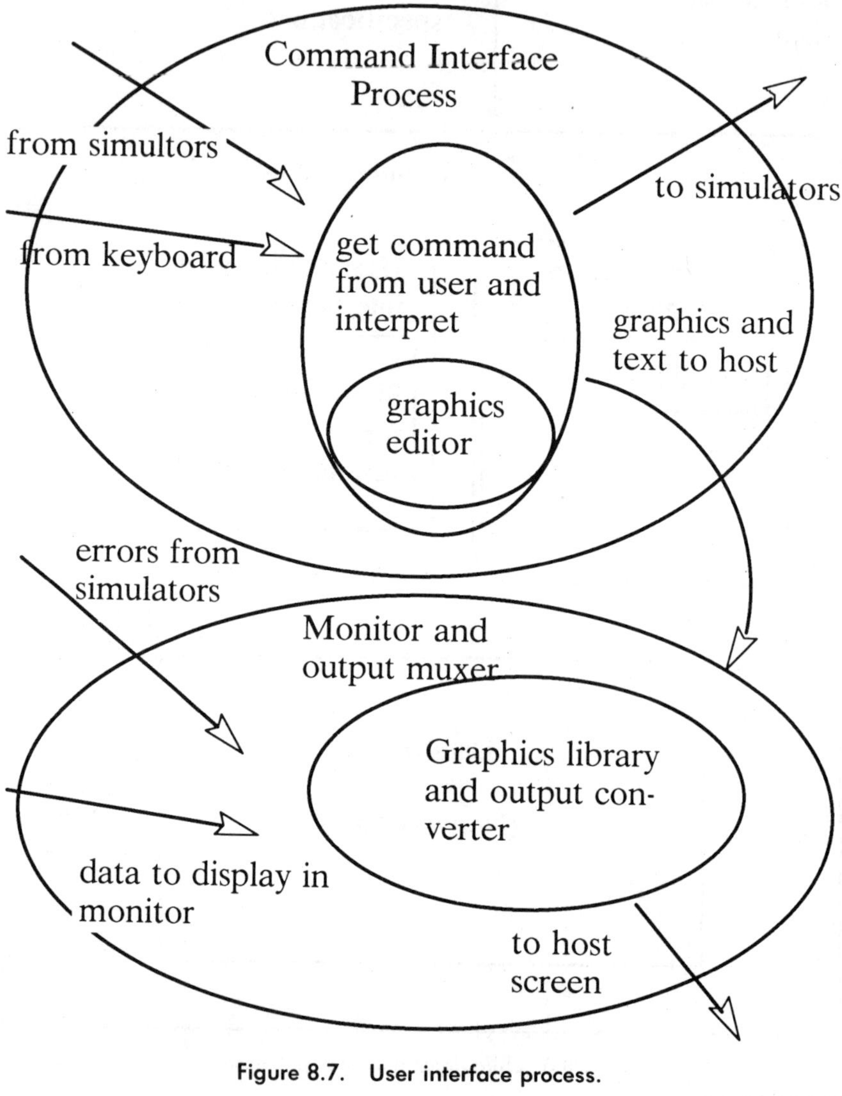

Figure 8.7. User interface process.

6.2. Simulator Process

The simulator process is the heart of the system. It contains the database for layers and primitive operations for computation and communication. All operations are performed by the interpreter for layer algorithms and user commands. It runs a cycle where it first checks if the user is sending any command, and, if so, executes it. If there is no communication from the user, and the database contains layers that are activated for simulation, the simulator undeterministically runs next step of the layer program for one of the activated layers. If there are no activate layers, then simulator waits for communication from the user to create and activate one.

6.3. The Database

The simulator database has been designed for efficient use of Transputer architecture for layer data and algorithms. Since there are no dynamic structures in Occam language, all data have been stored in arrays. This makes the system difficult to program but efficient to execute. The data structure of the layer is linked so that all the layers that are in an array have their pointers to the array of neurons, showing the starting indices for the block of neurons of that layer. Similar pointers refer to the array of all inputs and the array of layer programs. Neurons furthermore have pointers to weights, neighbour connections, and attribute arrays. The database structure is illustrated in Figures 8.8a and 8.8b.

The data are kept in arrays continuously from the beginning of the array. New data is always stored starting from the first free index of the array. This allows efficient use of the memory. The disadvantage is that when any data is deleted from the database, all arrays linked to the data must be reorganized. This is complicated but not inefficient. Since all the data are stored continuously in the arrays, the reordering can be made using the Transputer block move instruction, which is very fast.

6.4. Running Simulators in Multi-Transputer Systems

The current prototype of the system runs in one Transputer only. The plan is that it will be distributed in Transputer networks of arbitrary size and topology. When started, the system will automatically explore the Transputer network and load simulator processes to every available Transputer processor (Figure 8.9). The communication between simulators is done by the message transfer principle (see, for example, Knowles & Kantchew, 1989). Every processor in the network has at least three processes: the simulator (or the user interface), the message muxer, and the message router. In the system configuration stage, the message routers would analyze the topology of the physical processor network and com-

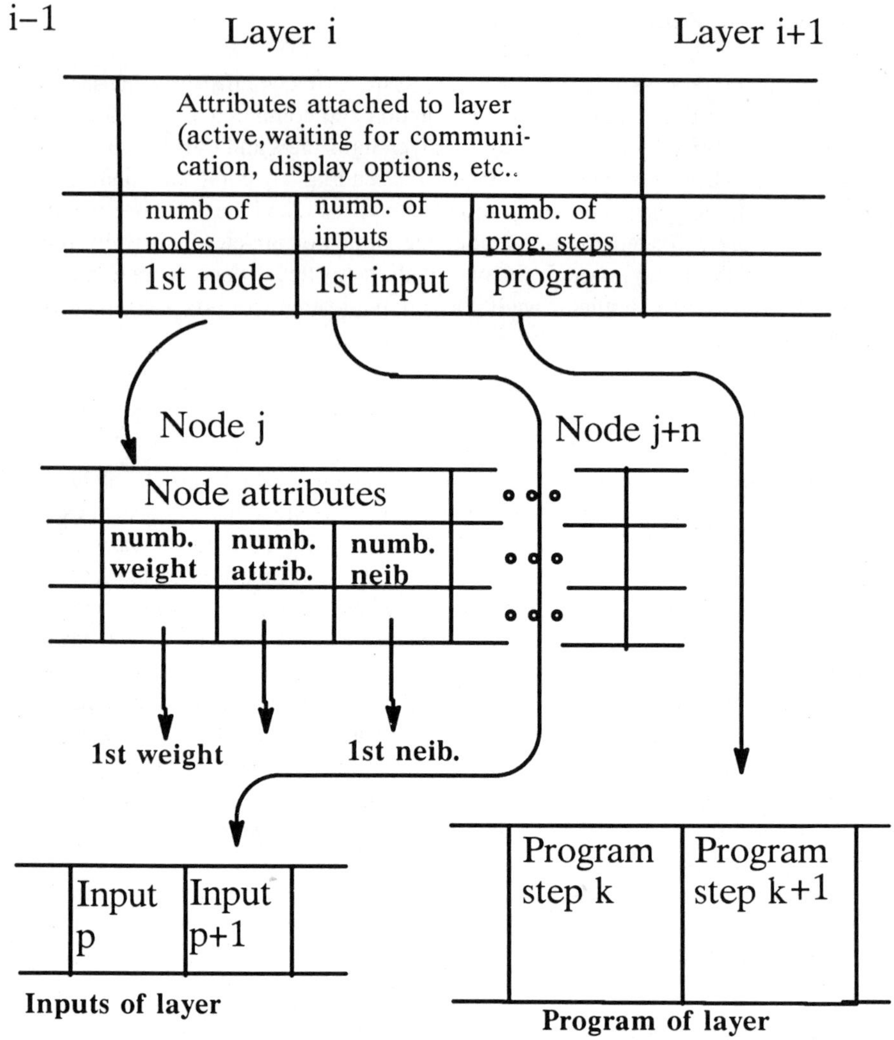

Figure 8.8a. Layer data in the simulator database.

pute optimal message pathways for interprocessor communications. The locations of the simulator processes in the processor network are included in every message in the muxer process after they are sent from the simulators. The router in every Transputer reads messages from a simulator (via muxer) and from every Transputer link. The router process is illustrated in Figure 8.10. It has 10 subprocesses running in parallel, one for each input and output link of the Transputer, and one for input and output to and from the message muxer process. The

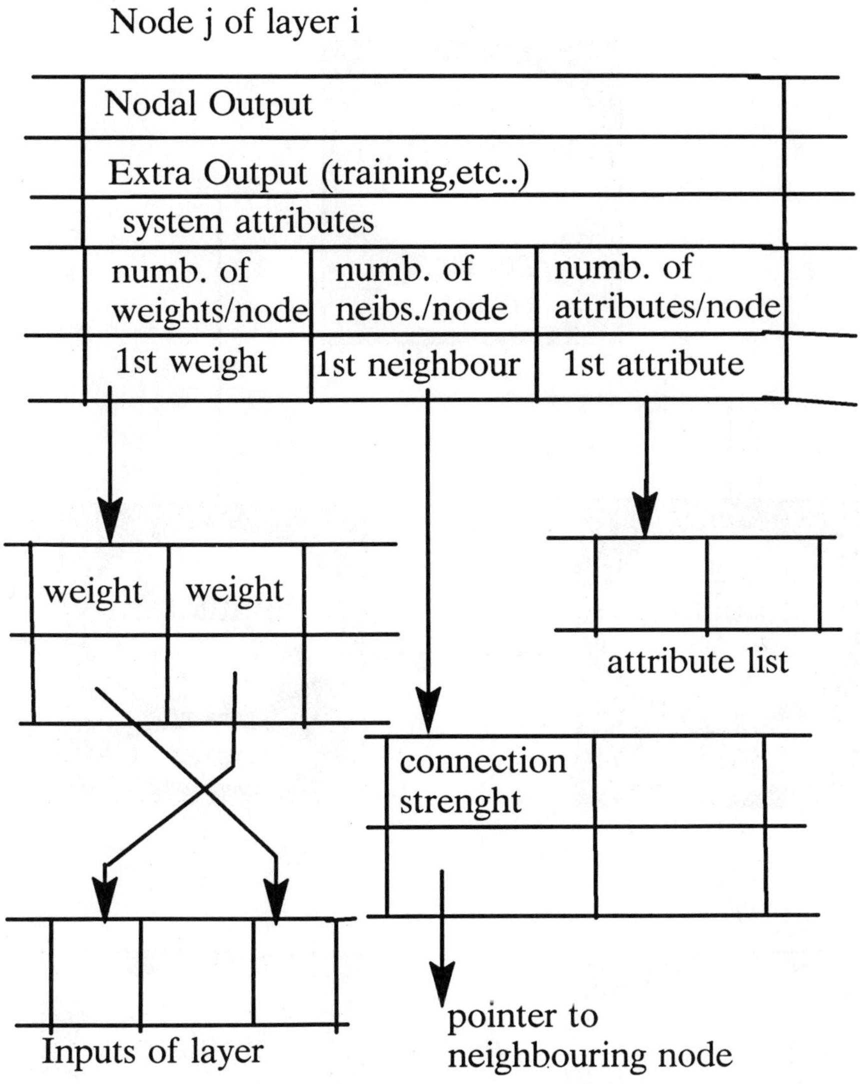

Figure 8.8b. Neural data in the simulator database.

message muxer is used for multiplexing channels in and out from the simulator. When a message is received, its destination is checked and it is directed to the optimal route towards its destination. This architecture may later be modified for dynamic load balancing and message routing.

Since every processor in a Transputer network has its own simulator, it is sometimes necessary to distribute neural network algorithms for multiple layers.

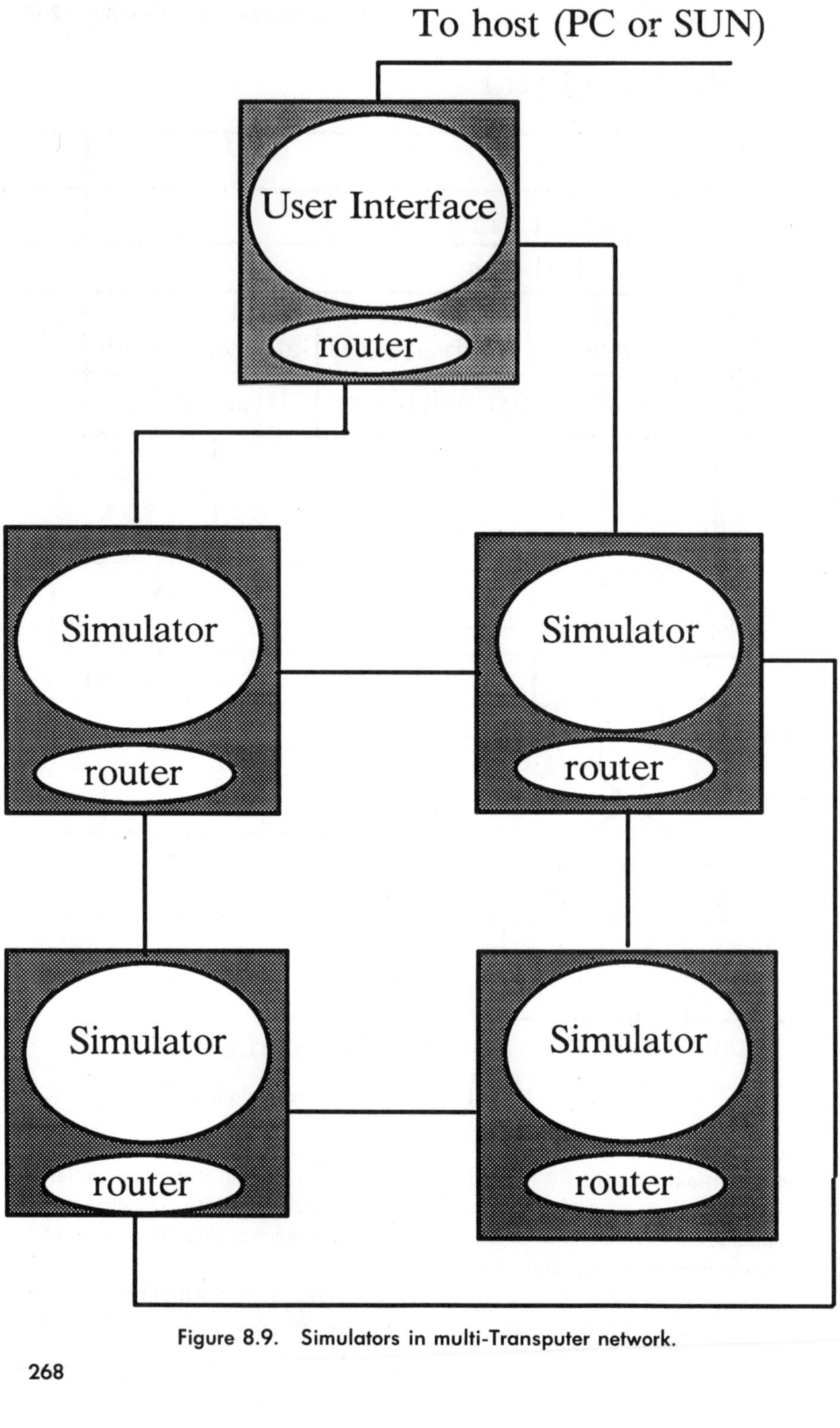

Figure 8.9. Simulators in multi-Transputer network.

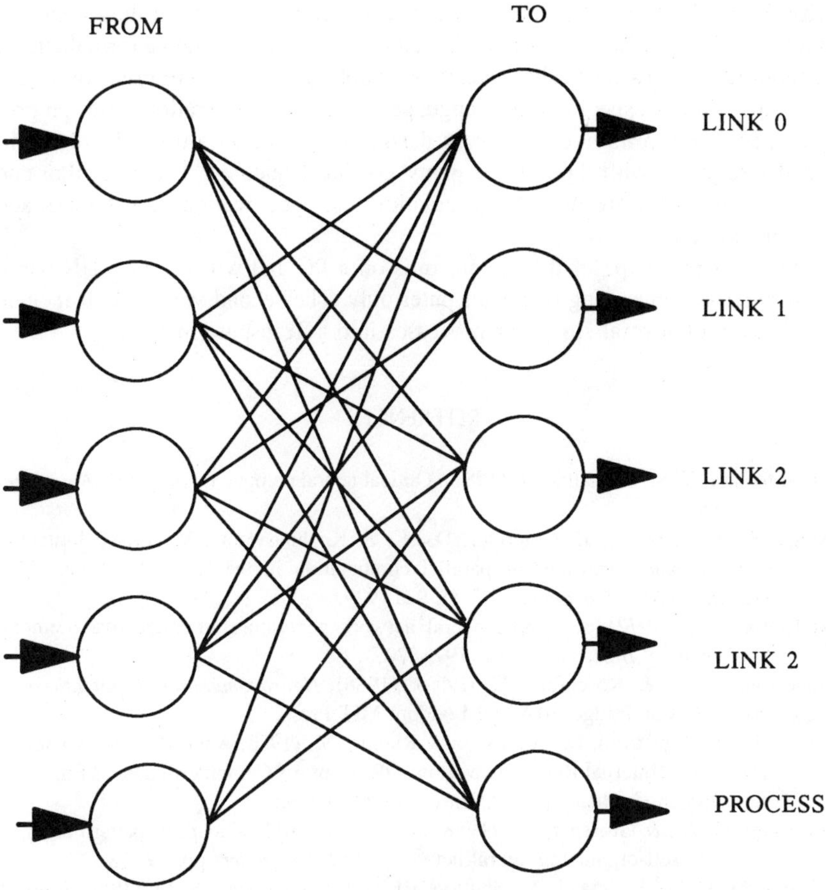

Figure 8.10. The router process.

For algorithms like back propagation this is not a problem, because all neurons in the network are laterally independent. This means that even one back propagation layer can be divided into multiple layers in the simulator (see Section 4.4). The problem for algorithms like topological feature maps is more severe, but in most cases distributed versions can be obtained without too much difficulty.

7. CONCLUSIONS

The aim of this work has been to develop a flexible neural networks development environment for research purposes. As algorithmic design is one of the main branches in our research, we require from the environment flexibility and adaptivity for many different neural network architectures. To obtain this, a careful study of existing neural network architectures was done to obtain a formalism for general neural network design. Features of this formalism were used for a high level algorithmic specification language, where the operations are preprogrammed neural primitives. Network design is done under a user-friendly command interpreter with the help of many graphical features. The algorithm and network structures are used for simulation and specification of networks and network systems.

The first prototype of the system runs on a PC and will run on SUN-based Transputer systems using one Transputer only. The second version will include distribution of several simulator processes into a Transputer network.

REFERENCES

Abu-Mostafa, Y. S., & Psaltis, D. (1987). Optical neural computers. *Scientific American, 256,* 88–95.

Ahuja, S., Carriero, N. J., Gelernter, D. H., & Kirshnaswamy, V. (1988). Matching language and hardware for parallel computation in the Linda Machine. *IEEE Transactions on Computers, 37*(8), 921–929.

Anderson J. A. (1972). A Simple neural network generating an interactive memory. *Mathematical Biosciences, 14*, 197–270.

Anderson, J. A., & Rosenfeld, E. (Eds.). (1988). *Neurocomputing: Foundations of research.* Cambridge, MA and London: MIT Press.

Bailey, J., Hammerstrom, D., Mates, J., & Rudnic, M. (1988, August). *Silicon association cortex* (Internal Rep.). Beaverton, OR: Dept. of Computer Science/ Engineering, Oregon Graduate Center, University of Oregon.

Carpenter, G. A., & Grossberg, S. (1988, March). The ART of adaptive pattern recognition by a self-organizing neural network. *IEEE Computer,* pp. 77–78.

D'Autrechy, C. D., Reggia, J. A., Shutton, III, G. G., & Goodall, S. M. (1988, July). A general purpose simulation environment for developing connectionist models. *Simulation,* pp. 5–19.

Feldman, J., Fanty, M., Goddard, N. H., & Lynne, K. J. (1988). Computing with structured connectionist networks. *Communications of the ACM, 31*(3), 170–187.

Fukushima, K., Miyake S., & Takayuki I. (1983). Neocognitron: A neural network model for a mechanism of visual pattern recognition. *IEEE Transactions on Systems, Man, and Cybernetics, SMC-13*, 826–834.

Ghosh, J., & Hwang, K. (1989). Mapping neural networks onto message-passing multicomputers. *Journal of Parallel and Distributed Computing, 6,* 291–330.

Goddard, N. H., Lynne, K. J., & Mintz, T. (1988, March). *Rochester connectionist simulator* (Tech. Rep. 233, revised). Rochester, NY: University of Rochester, Computer Science Dept.

Grossberg, S. (1976). Adaptive pattern classification and universal reading, I: Parallel development and coding of neural feature detectors. *Biological Cybernetics, 23*, 187–202.

Hammerstrom, D. (1988). *Hardware aspects of neural computation*. Tutorial at the Nordic Summer School on Neural Computation. Uppsala, Sweden: Uppsala University.

Hanson, W. A., Crutz, C. A., & Tam, J. Y. (1987, June). CONE—Computational network environment. *Proceedings of the IEEE 1st International Conference on Neural Networks*, pp. III-531–III-545.

Heath, L. S., Rosenberg, A. L., & Smith, B. T. (1988). The physical mapping problem for parallel architectures. *Journal of the ACM, 35*(3), 603–634.

Hecht-Nielsen, R. (1988a). Applications of counterpropagation networks. *Neural Networks, 1*(2), 131–139.

Hecht-Nielsen, R. (1988b). Neurocomputing: Picking the human brain. *IEEE Spectrum, 25*(3), 36–41.

Hinton, G. E., & Anderson, J. A. (Eds.). (1981). *Parallel models of associative memory*. Hillsdale, NJ: Erlbaum.

Hinton, G. H., Sejnowski, T., & Ackley, D. H. (1984, May). *Boltzmann machines: Constraint satisfaction networks that learn* (Tech. Rep. CMU-CS-84-119). Pittsburgh, PA: Dept. of Computer Science, Carnegie-Mellon University.

Hoare, C. A. R. (1978). Communicating sequential processes. *Communications of the ACM, 21*(8), 666–676.

Hopfield, J. J. (1982). Neural networks and physical systems with emergent collective computational abilities. *Proceedings of the National Academy of Sciences, 79*, 2554–2558.

Knowles, A., & Kantchew, T. (1989). Message passing in a transputer system. *Microprocessors and Microsystems, 13*(2), 113–123.

Kohonen, T. (1972). Correlation matrix memories. *IEEE Transactions on Computers, C–21*, 353–359.

Kohonen, T. (1982). Self-organized formation of topolography correct feature maps. *Biological Cybernetics, 43*, 59–69.

Kohonen, T. (1988a, March). The "neural" phonetic typewriter. *IEEE Computer*, pp. 11–22.

Kohonen, T. (1988b). *Self-organization and associative memory* (2nd ed.). Berlin, Heidelberg, New York, Tokyo: Springer-Verlag.

Koikkalainen, P., & Oja, E. (1988, July). Specification and implementation environment for neural networks using communicating sequential processes. *Proceedings of the IEEE International Conference on Neural Networks*, pp. I-533–I-540. San Diego, CA.

Kosko, B. (1988). Bidirectional associative memories. *IEEE Transactions on Systems, Man and Cybernetics, 18*(1), 1299–1306.

Lester, B. L. (1987, June). Neural network simulation language based on multi-Pascal. *Proceedings of the IEEE 1st International Conference on Neural Networks*, pp. III-347–III-354.

Lindsay, P. H., & Norman, D. A. (1977). *Human information processing* (2nd ed.). Orlando, FL: Academic Press.

May, D. (1987). *Communicating processes and Occam* (Tech. Note No. 20). Bristol, UK: Inmos Ltd.

Neural networks. (1988). *Abstracts of the 1st Annual INNS Meeting, 1*(1). New York: Pergamon Press.

Oja, E. (1989). Neural networks, principal components, and subspaces. *International Journal of Neural Systems, 1*(1), 61–68.

Paic, E., Gungner, D., & Skrzypek, J. (1987, June). UCLA SFINX—A neural network simulation environment. *Proceedings of the IEEE 1st International Conference on Neural Networks,* pp. III-367–III-375.

Rosenblatt, F. (1958). The Perceptron: A probabilistic model for information storage and organization in the brain. *Psychological Review, 65*, 386–408.

Ruckert, U., & Goser, K. (1988). VLSI architectures for associative networks. *Proceedings of the IEEE International Symposium on Circuits and Systems* (Vol. 2, pp. 755–770). Espoo, Finland: IEEE Press.

Rumelhart, D. E., Hinton, G. E., & Williams, R. J. (1986). Learning internal representations by error probagation. In D. E. Rumelhart & J. L McClelland (Eds.), *Parallel distributed processing: Explorations in the microstructures of cognition* (Vol. 1, pp. 318–362). Cambridge, MA: MIT Press.

Rumelhart D. E., & McClelland, J. L. (Eds.). (1986). Parallel distributed processing: Explorations in the microstructures of cognition (Vol. 1). Cambridge, MA: MIT Press.

Salam, F. M. A. (1988). On the analysis and design of neural nets with an implementation via CMOS VLSI. *Proceedings of the IEEE International Symposium on Circuits and Systems* (Vol. 2, pp. 1001–1004). Espoo, Finland: IEEE Press.

Sejnowski, T., Koch, C., & Churchland, P. (1988). Computational neuroscience. *Science, 241,* 1299–1306.

Smith, A. B. (1987, June). A parallel PDP network simulator. *Proceedings of the IEEE 1st International Conference on Neural Networks,* pp. III-377–III-384.

The Transputer Databook. (1988). Bath, UK: Inmos Ltd.

Treleaven, P. (1989a). *Neurocomputers* (Research Note No. 89/9). London: Department of Computer Science, University College.

Treleaven, P. (1989b). Hardware and software tools for neural networks. *Proceedings of the Nordic Symposium on Neural Computing.* Espoo, Finland: R. N. Institute.

Wayman, R. (1987). Occam 2: An overview from a software engineering perspective. *Microprocessors and Microsystems, 11*(8), 413–422.

Wexler, J., & Prior, D. (1989). Solving problems with transputers: Background and experience. *Microprocessors and Microsystems, 13*(2), 67–78.

9

The Maryland MIRRORS/II Simulation Environment for Developing Connectionist Models

C. Lynne D'Autrechy
James A. Reggia*
Department of Computer Science
University of Maryland

1. INTRODUCTION

During the last several years there has been a resurgence of interest in developing neurobiologically motivated parallel processing models of human memory and cognition (Feldman & Ballard, 1982; Hopfield, 1982; Rumelhart & McClelland, 1986). This interest has been driven by the desire to develop a better theoretical understanding of cognitive processes and their neural basis, by the recognition that existing artificial intelligence (AI) symbol processing models implemented on serial von Neumann machines face significant problems, and by the possibilities being opened up by parallel computing hardware architectures based on VLSI technology. These "massively" parallel systems are generally referred to as *connectionist models,* because they consist of a set of *nodes* which are connected together and communicate via *links.*

A great variety of approaches in developing connectionist models have been under study recently. Our research group has focused on developing a class of connectionist models using a new method to control the spread of network activation called *competition-based spreading activation* (Reggia, 1985, 1989; Millheim, 1986; Wald, Farach, Tagamets, & Reggia, 1989; Whitfield, Goodall, & Reggia, 1989). As a result of these and other experiences, a connectionist model simulation system called Maryland MIRRORS/II (pronounced "mirrors two") has been developed. Maryland MIRRORS/II will hereafter be referred to as MIRRORS/II. MIRRORS/II is *not* itself a connectionist model; it is a general-purpose software environment or "workbench" that helps a user develop and evaluate connectionist model simulations.

MIRRORS/II has three distinguishing features: a high-level nonprocedural

---

* Dr. Reggia is also with the University of Maryland Institute of Advanced Computer Studies, and the Department of Neurology. Supported in part by NS-29414 and in part by NSF Award IST-8451430.

language, a general-purpose event-handling mechanism, and an indexed library of system resources. These three features, all of which are user-modifiable, combine to make MIRRORS/II both general and powerful. By using the high-level language to describe the structure of a network, and by using the default system components from the MIRRORS/II library, a user can develop many kinds of connectionist models without doing any programming. However, MIRRORS/II also allows a user to experiment with connectionist models which require new language constructs and/or new system resources. For example, the MIRRORS/II language allows a user to define new attributes or properties for network elements, and also allows the substitution of user-written system resources for MIRRORS/II system resources during model construction. The general-purpose event handling mechanism gives the user complete control over the occurrence and timing of various events during a simulation. Finally, the MIRRORS/II library can also be extended to include new system resources.

The remainder of this chapter is organized as follows. Section 2 gives a brief overview of connectionist modeling terminology used in relation to MIRRORS/II. Section 3 briefly summarizes the overall organization of MIRRORS/II. Sections 4, 5, and 6 describe the three distinguishing features of MIRRORS/II discussed above: the language, the general-purpose event mechanism, and the library of system resources. Section 7 demonstrates these features of MIRRORS/II by example. Section 8 discusses implementation details of MIRRORS/II. Finally, Section 9 summarizes this work, compares it to related efforts, and offers ideas for further research.

2. CONNECTIONIST MODELS

To enable the reader less familiar with current work on connectionist models to follow the principal ideas embodied in MIRRORS/II, we introduce some basic concepts and terminology, simplifying somewhat for brevity. The term *connectionist model,* as used in this chapter, refers to models in which many, usually simple, processing elements operate in parallel and communicate via connections (links) between nodes. Such models are generally characterized by an analogy with a neurophysiological substrate or the distributed storage of items in memory, and by the absence of a central executive that coordinates processing (Rumelhart & Norman, 1981). For our purposes, it is convenient to view connectionist models as having three components: a network, a spreading activation method or rule, and a learning method or rule.

The *network* of a connectionist model consists of processing *nodes* connected together via *links*. Nodes directly connected to one another are said to be *neighbors* of each other. Typically, each node n_i in a connectionist network has an activation level $a_i(t)$ associated with it at time t, which may be a binary, integer, or real number. This activation level, or an output derived from it, is communicated from a node to its neighbors at each point in time, and the activation level that a node sees in its neighbors is used to update its own level of activation. *Weights,* numeric connection strengths, are often associated with the links in a network and are used during computations that update node activities.

The second component of a connectionist model, the *spreading activation method,* is a *local* rule or procedure that each node follows in updating its activation level in the context of neighboring node activation levels. For example, in the following representative local rule:

$$a_i(t + 1) = f(a_i(t), input_i(t)) \text{ where}$$
$$input_i(t) = E_i(t) + {}_j(w_{ij} \cdot a_j(t)),$$

the new activation value for node n_i at time step $t + 1$, $a_i(t + 1)$, is computed as a function of the current activation value, $a_i(t)$, and the current input, $input_i(t)$, to node n_i. The input to node n_i at any given time is calculated based on the sum of two values. One value is the external input E_i being applied to node n_i, representing input from outside of the network. The second value is the sum of the activation values a_j of neighboring nodes multiplied by the corresponding weight w_{ij} on the link between neighboring node n_j and node n_i. Typically, the goal in constructing and running a simulation with a connectionist model is to demonstrate that some *global* behavior (behavior of the network as a whole) can emerge from the concurrent *local* interactions between neighboring nodes during a simulation.

The third component of a connectionist model, the *learning method* or *rule,* describes how the weights on links should be altered as a function of experience over time. There are a great variety of approaches to learning; many of these can be viewed as a variant of *Hebb's Rule* or *Hebbian learning* (Hebb, 1949). With Hebb's rule the strength of the connection w_{ji} from node n_i to node n_j is adjusted in proportion to the product of the simultaneous node activation levels a_i and a_j. Like spreading activation, learning is based on a local rule which depends on the activation values of nodes connected by links. When learning is taking place in a network, the weights on the links of a network change more slowly than the activation values of the nodes.

A great number of connectionist models have been proposed and studied since the 1940s in cognitive science, artificial intelligence, and neurophysiological modeling (Reggia & Sutton, 1989). For our purposes, it is convenient to view these models as lying on a continuum based on their "level" with respect to cognition. At one end of the continuum are models characterized as *distributed connectionist models.* Each node in the typical case roughly corresponds to a neuron and links correspond to axons and dendrites. We refer to these models as *neural network models,* although the extent to which they mimic real biological neurons is usually very limited. A *concept* is represented as a pattern of activity over many processing nodes, and each node participates in representing multiple concepts.

At the other end of the continuum, connectionist models typically fit into the symbol processing, associative network framework of artificial intelligence and cognitive psychology. For example, each node in such a *local connectionist model* may represent a semantically oriented concept (e.g., *bird, yellow*), and links could represent associations between concepts (e.g., *has-color*). Processing in such *associative network models* is done by "spreading activation" using either numeric signals or by propagating symbolic labels. Although the idea of associative networks using spreading activation is intuitively plausible and is supported by empirical work, it is difficult to relate these latter models directly to the results of neural network modeling work.

It has often proven convenient to view connectionist networks as being partitioned into *sets* (*layers, levels, spaces, slabs,* or *pools*) of conceptually similar nodes, and to conceive of information as initially entering one "lowest" layer or level and propagating "upwards" to others. For example, Figure 9.1 shows a local network split into four levels intended to represent the various concepts involved in reading and disambiguating a single word (McClelland & Rumelhart, 1981; Rumelhart & McClelland, 1982; Cottrell & Small, 1983). Each of the layers contains many nodes. Connections between nodes occur within layers and between adjacent layers; there are no connections between nonadjacent layers. When nodes in a lower level (e.g., image features) directly connect to nodes at a higher level (e.g., letters), such connections may be called *forward* or *anterograde connections,* since they are in the direction of initial flow of activation. Conversely, connections in the opposite direction may be called *backward* or *retrograde connections*. Direct connections between nodes in the same layer can be referred to as *lateral connections* (indicated schematically by links on the right of each layer shown in Figure 9.1), because they are orthogonal to the direction of initial propagation of activation.

3. ORGANIZATION OF MIRRORS/II

MIRRORS/II consists of three principal components: a parser, a constructor, and a library of system resources (see middle of Figure 9.2). Although not part of MIRRORS/II proper, the MIRRORS/II environment also contains preprocessors and postprocessors.

Input to MIRRORS/II is a *specification file,* a simple ACSII file written in the MIRRORS/II specification language (see left part of Figure 9.2). This file is either generated by one of the MIRRORS/II preprocessors or is created by the user using a text editor. The MIRRORS/II specification language will be described in more detail in Section 4. Based on the information in the specification file, MIRRORS/II produces a connectionist model, a computer program which

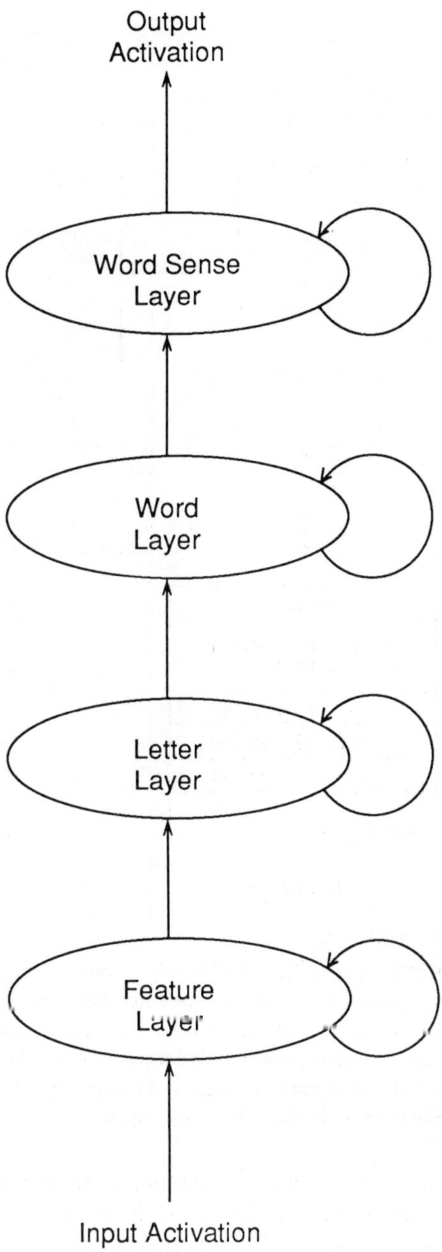

Figure 9.1. An idealized network with nodes partitioned into layers or sets. Each ellipse here represents a set containing numerous nodes. Each pictured link represents numerous connections between nodes in the sets.

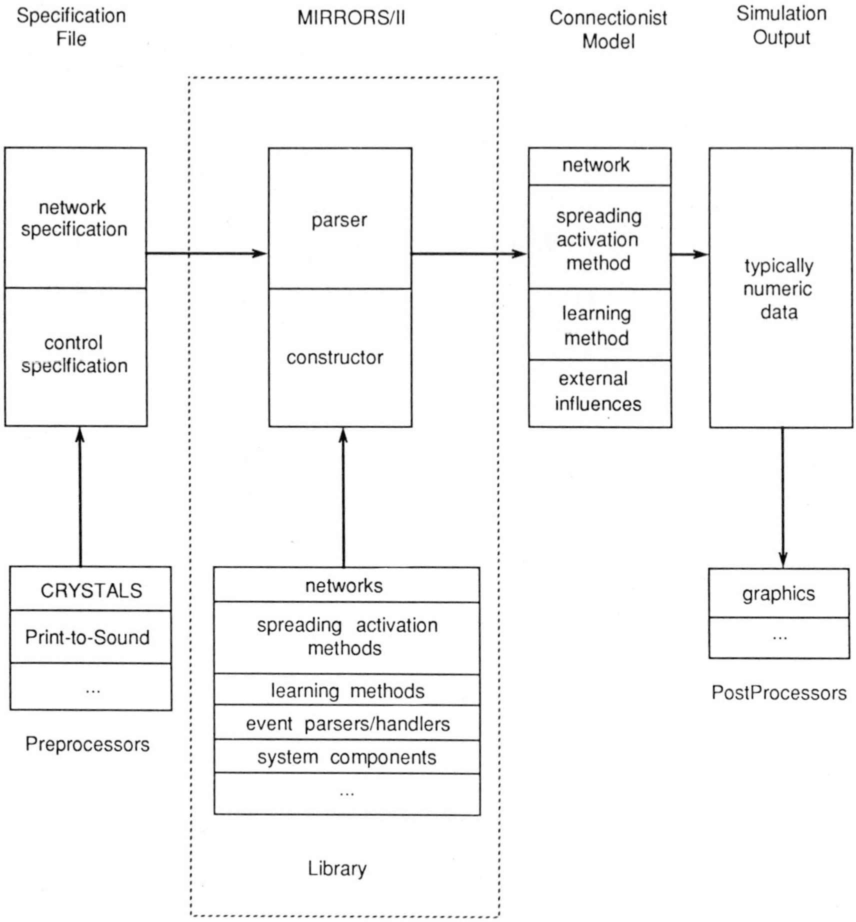

Figure 9.2. MIRRORS/II organization. MIRRORS/II consists of a parser, a constructor, and a library of system resources. A specification file, which may be either manually created or automatically generated by a preprocessor, serves as input to MIRRORS/II. The output is a connectionist model in the form of a computer program, which when run typically produces numeric data representing simulation results. This data may be analyzed with the aid of a postprocessor.

typically generates numeric output representing simulation results. A postprocessor, such as a graphics postprocessor, can be used to analyze the numeric simulation results produced by MIRRORS/II.

The MIRRORS/II processing that converts a specification file into a connectionist simulation typically consists of a three-phase PARSE-CONSTRUCT-RUN process. During the PARSE phase, the information in the user-supplied specification file is read line by line. The MIRRORS/II parser checks this information to make sure it consists of descriptive material that is correctly stated in the specification language. If the parser discovers an error, it notifies the user of this error and then tries to continue processing the rest of the specification file. As it reads in the description of the connectionist model during the PARSE phase, the MIRRORS/II parser is simultaneously constructing a *static network.* This static network is the internal representation of the sets, nodes, and connections as described in the network specification in the specification file.

Running a simulation with a connectionist model generally requires external influences. These represent external inputs, or *clamps,* that perturb or assign the current state of activation of individual nodes in the network. While the network, spreading activation method, and learning method together represent the connectionist model, the external influences represent the data on which a specific simulation is to be based.

When the parser first encounters an external influence "command" in the specification file, MIRRORS/II enters a second or CONSTRUCT phase of operation. During this phase, the constructor builds *external inputs* to the network and a *dynamic network* that is to be used during the desired simulation. The dynamic network is an augmented version of the static network that includes memory space with each node for storing current activation levels, incoming activation from external inputs, and other necessary information. In some instances more than one copy or *instance* of a node may be needed, and the creation of multiple node copies also occurs during the CONSTRUCT phase while building the dynamic network. Some default values and implicit connections not explicitly given in the specification file may also be filled in during the CONSTRUCT phase.

After completion of the CONSTRUCT phase, the third or RUN phase begins at the occurrence of a simulation initiation (run) command. The connectionist model the user has specified, and which was built during the first two phases, now "runs" or "executes." During each iteration of the simulation (i.e., during each "tick" of an internal clock), the method of spreading activation and learning specified by the user is typically applied to each node in the network, causing the state of the network (i.e, the activation levels of each node and the weights on each connection) to be updated. Periodically, according to user specification, activation levels of some or all of the nodes or other information of interest is displayed to the terminal screen or output to a file. At the end of the third phase MIRRORS/II either terminates or waits for additional instructions from the user.

4. SPECIFICATION LANGUAGE

MIRRORS/II has three important distinguishing features: a nonprocedural high-level language, a general-purpose event mechanism, and an indexed library of networks, spreading activation methods, learning methods, event parsers and handlers, and system components which make the system very flexible and easy to use. Often people interested in studying connectionist models, namely cognitive psychologists, neurophysiologists, linguists, and others, either do not have extensive computer programming expertise or simply prefer not to spend time doing software development. The MIRRORS/II language allows relatively inexperienced computer users in such application areas to express easily the structure of a network that they would like to study and the parameters which will control their particular connectionist model simulation. Users can also select an existing spreading activation method and learning method from the library to complete their connectionist model. No programming is required when using MIRRORS/II to simulate connectionist models in this manner if one is content to use the facilities available in the existing library. On the other hand, more advanced users with programming skills who are interested in research involving new methods for spreading activation or learning can also derive major benefits from using MIRRORS/II. In this situation, MIRRORS/II still provides a high-level, extendable language for network specification, automatic parsing of the specification file with error detection and construction of data structures, low-level access functions to data structures, and a user interface for the connectionist model. The user need only write functions for the desired procedural components; MIRRORS/II will automatically incorporate those components into the connectionist model for use at runtime.

As discussed previously, input to MIRRORS/II is in the form of a specification file written in the MIRRORS/II specification language. The specification file consists of two parts—the *network specification* and the *control specification*. The network specification describes the structure of a connectionist network and the methods of spreading activation and learning to be used, while the control specification describes the details of a specific simulation to be run using the given network. The following discussion is not intended to be a complete description of the language syntax; rather, it is intended to give the reader the flavor of the language and its capabilities. (See D'Autrechy, Reggia, Sutton, Goodall, Tagamets, & Marsland, 1988, for a more complete discussion of the MIRRORS/II language.)

The network specification consists of *descriptors* which describe sets and set connections, nodes and node connections, and set and node attributes. Each *set*- or *node*- descriptor provides the details for part of a network; the entire sequence of these descriptors specifies the network structure and functionality.

4.1. Set Descriptors

For our purposes, a connectionist network is viewed as being partitioned into *sets* (layers, etc.) of logically related nodes. In MIRRORS/II, sets have basically four components: the group of nodes which make up the set, connections to other sets, attributes, and a method of spreading activation and learning. Each of these is described in a *set*-descriptor, and we give simple examples of these in the following to illustrate the flavor of the language.

Set-descriptors are grouped together at the beginning of the network specification. The basic form of a *set*-descriptor is as follows:

[set *SetName SetStatement . . . SetStatement*].

A *SetName* can be virtually anything as long as it is unique among other set names in the network specification. *SetStatements* are used to describe the four set components listed above. In general, matching brackets ("[" and "]") and matching parentheses ("(" and ")") can be viewed as matching "begin" and "end" tokens in the MIRRORS/II language as illustrated here and subsequently. Also there are no reserved words, so even the names of descriptors, statements, or commands can be used anywhere in a specification file. For example, the word *set* can be used as a node name if the situation requires.

The nodes which are members of a set are described using a *SetStatement* that begins with the word *contains*. For example, the descriptor

[set treatment (contains pneumocillin neuromycin propranolol antacid)]

describes a set named *treatment* which *contains* four nodes named *pneumocillin, neuromycin, propranolol,* and *antacid*. A *contains*-statement is optional under certain conditions which will be discussed later.

Connections to other sets in the network specification are described using an optional *connects*-statement. A *connects*-statement in a *set*-descriptor means that it is legal for nodes in this set (designated as the "source set") to connect to nodes of other sets listed in the *connects*-statement (designated as "destination sets"). The general form of a *connects*-statement is

(connects (*DestSetName ConSpec . . . ConSpec*)
(*DestSetName ConSpec . . . ConSpec*)

where *DestSetName* is the name of any set for which a *set*-descriptor appears in the network specification and *ConSpec* is one of *optional, implicit, all, random,* one-to-one (*oto*), one-to-many (*otm*) or many-to-one (*mto*), and some others.

The *ConSpecs,* short for "connection specifications," in a *connects*-statement give more detail about the connections from the nodes in the source set to nodes in the destination set. A *ConSpec* of *optional* indicates that nodes in the source set may optionally specify connections to nodes in the destination set in the node specifications. The word *implicit* indicates that no explicit node connections can be specified between nodes in the source set *SetName* and nodes in the destination set *DestSetName*. These node connections will be generated by the constructor using other node connection information specified in the network specification. The symbol *all* is a special case of the *implicit ConSpec*. As with *implicit,* no explicit node connections can be specified. The symbol *all* differs from *implicit* in that the constructor will build connections from *each* node in the source set *SetName* to *every* node in the destination set *DestSetName* without requiring any additional node connection information in the network specification. The *random ConSpec* is very similar to the *all ConSpec;* the difference is that the *random ConSpec* causes the weights on the connections from the source set *SetName* to the destination set *DestSetName* to be randomly generated. These weight values lie between the maximum and minimum legal weights specified for the source set. Symbols *oto, otm,* and *mto* all designate the number of nodes in the source set *SetName* which may connect to the number of nodes in the destination set *DestSetName*. For example, in the following *set*-descriptors,

```
[set children  (contains Tom Mary Dick Sue)
               (connects (adults otm))]

[set adults  (contains Frank Deb Jim Barb)
             (connects (children otm implicit))]
```

nodes in the children set connect to nodes in the adults set with a *otm* relationship, indicating that each child may be related to at least one adult (e.g., mother, father) and vice versa. The connections from nodes in the adults set to nodes in the children set are *implicit,* because those connections can be inferred from the children-to-adults node connections. In other words, when connections from individual children to parent nodes are subsequently given explicitly in the specification file, reverse connections from adults to children nodes are automatically generated.

4.2. Node Descriptors

The *node*-descriptors follow the *set*-descriptors in the specification file and provide a detailed description of the network structure. The basic form of a *node*-descriptor is as follows:

[node *NodeName NodeStatement . . . NodeStatement*].

NodeName must be unique among the nodes in the same set; multiple nodes in different sets in a network can have the same name. *NodeStatements* are used for specifying set membership, connections to other nodes in the network (outgoing connections), and node attributes. Although nodes are often declared in their parent *set*-descriptor before their descriptor appears, if a separate *node*-descriptor exists for every node in a set, then a *contains*-statement in the *set*-descriptor is unnecessary.

A *member NodeStatement* is used to indicate the set of which the node is a member. For example, the *node*-descriptor

[node antacid (member treatment) . . .]

indicates that a node named *antacid* is a *member* of the set named *treatment*. We also refer to treatment as being the *parent* set of the node antacid in this case. A *member*-statement is mandatory because a network may contain more than one node with the same name in different sets.

Node connections are specified using a *Node-to-Node Connection (NNC) NodeStatement* of the form

(*DestSetName Bundle . . . Bundle*).

Here, *DestSetName* is the name of a set described earlier in the network specification and a *Bundle* is a group of connections which corresponds to a group of logically related links from the node whose descriptor contains this statement to nodes in the destination set *DestSetName*. A *NNC*-statement describes connections *from* the node in whose descriptor it appears (the source node) *to* nodes in *DestSetName* (the destination nodes). For example, the *NNC*-statement (in italics below) in the *node*-descriptor for node threshold

[node threshold *(treatment (/ (pneumocillin −0.01)(neuromycin −0.05) (propranolol −0.07)(antacid 0.09)))*]

indicates that node threshold connects to node pneumocillin, neuromycin, propranolol, and antacid in the treatment set. More than one *NNC*-statement may occur in the same *node*-descriptor, but each *NNC*-statement in the same *node*-descriptor must have a different *DestSetName*. There should be exactly one *NNC*-statement in a node's descriptor for each set to which the node may send connections to as specified in the *connects*-statement in the descriptor for the set of which the node is a member (unless an *implicit, optional,* or *all ConSpec* was used in the *connects*-statement).

One or more *Bundles* appear in every *NNC*-statement, and these specify connection logic and destination nodes which lie in *DestSetName*. A *Bundle* has one of the following formats:

1. (*/ Link . . . Link*)
2. (*& Link . . . Link*)
3. *Link*

In the first *Bundle* above, the connection logic "/" stands for "or," meaning that the following *Links* are considered to be *alternatives* to one another; the *Links* point at alternative nodes, one of which would typically be anticipated to be present (as in the example immediately above). A connection logic of "&"

stands for "and" meaning that *all* of the nodes listed as *Links* are typically anticipated to be present. Form three is used to indicate that a source node has a connection to only one destination node. As a simple example, the following *node*-descriptor:

```
[node Tom  (member children)
           (parents (& Frank Deb))
           (spouse Betty)]
```

contains a *NNC*-statement, (parents (& Frank Deb)), which indicates that node Tom in the children set has connections to nodes Frank *and* Deb in the parents set. The "&" logic indicates the "and" relationship of the connections. The statement (spouse Betty) indicates that the source node Tom has a connection to only one destination node, (Betty), in the destination set spouse.

A *Link* has two forms: *Node* or (*Node Weight*). In the simplest case, illustrated in the example *node*-descriptor immediately above, *Node* is the name of a node in the destination set to which a connection is being made. Since no connection weight is given, the weight is calculated by MIRRORS/II based on the connection logic used and the maximum weight allowed for connections from the source set to the destination set. In the second link form, *Node* is again the name of a node in the destination set. *Weight* is a connection strength between the minimum and maximum legal weights permitted on connections from the source set to other destination sets. For example, if node N37's descriptor is

```
[node N37 (member purkinje-neurons)
   (dentate-neurons (& (N35 −0.5)(N36 −0.75)(N37 −1.0)(N38 −0.75)(N39 −0.5)))]
```

then node N37 in the set of purkinje-neurons connects with a weight (synaptic strength) of −0.75 to node N36 in the set of dentate-neurons.

Note that more than one *Bundle* may appear in a *NNC*-statement. If more than one *Bundle* is present, then a *sequence* of destination nodes is being described. Each *Bundle* corresponds to one position in that sequence. For example, the NNC-statement

```
[node CONFLICT  (member words)
                (characters C O N F L I C T)]
```

indicates that node CONFLICT, a member of the words set, connects to the sequence of eight character nodes named C, O, N, F, L, I, C, and T in the characters set. Here each character node is a bundle.

4.3. Attributes

As noted earlier, sets and nodes each have *attributes* which can be explicitly specified by a user in the appropriate specification statement. If an attribute is not explicitly specified, it assumes a default value. The general form of an attribute statement is:

(*AttributeName Value*).

For example, the statement (minwt −1.0) in a *set*-descriptor indicates that the minimum weight permitted on a link from any node in this set is −1.0. The MIRRORS/II parser detects any violations of this constraint in subsequent *node*-descriptors.

The attributes defined by the MIRRORS/II system apply to both sets and nodes. Set attributes generally apply to all the nodes in a set, while node attributes override their parent set's attributes and only apply to the particular node whose specification contains the attribute statement. Examples of system-defined attributes are: the minimum activation value a node is allowed to achieve (*minact*), the maximum activation value a node is allowed to reach (*maxact*), the initial activation value of a node (*initact*), the resting activation value of a node (*restact*), a synonym for a set or node name (*synonyms*), the minimum weight of outgoing node connections (*minwt*), and the maximum weight of outgoing node connections (*maxwt*).

The MIRRORS/II language also provides a facility for users to define attributes in addition to those pre-defined in the MIRRORS/II system. There are two steps to defining a new attribute. First, the attribute must be declared in an *attribute*-statement in the *set*-descriptor whose member nodes can have that user-defined attribute. An *attribute*-statement defines a new attribute which will become a valid MIRRORS/II *NodeStatement*. The general form of an *attribute*-statement in a *set*-descriptor is:

(attribute *Attr-name Attr-detail . . . Attr-detail*)

The *attribute*-statement gives the name of the attribute, *Attr-name,* and other relevant *Attr-details* such as how to parse the user-defined *Attr-name* statements and the default value of the attribute. The second step in defining a new attribute is to include statements of the form (*Attr-name Value*) in *node*-specifications. The statement (*Attr-name Value*) assigns *Value* as the value of the attribute *Attr-name* for the node in whose descriptor the statement appears.

For example, suppose a user wants to use an activation method from the library which uses a threshold. The formulation of the method might be

$$a_i = \begin{cases} 0 \text{ if } \sum_j in_{ij} + E_i \leq \text{threshold} \\ 1 \text{ if } \sum_j in_{ij} + E_i > \text{threshold} \end{cases}$$

where threshold is a defined value for all nodes in a set. The user can define a user-defined attribute named *threshold* by doing the following:

```
[set Anyset  (contains x y z) (connects Otherset oto optional)
             (attribute threshold optional (default 0.25))]
```

Now, all nodes in set Anyset will have an attribute named *threshold* which has a value of 0.25 unless specified otherwise. Each node in set Anyset can have in its descriptor a statement of the form (threshold *Value*). To initialize the threshold value of node y to 0.3 one would do the following:

```
[node y (member Anyset) (threshold 0.3)].
```

One can also update the value of the "threshold" attribute at run time using an access function that is created by MIRRORS/II. This access function "hides" the details of the internal data structure from the user. A user-defined attribute differs from a system-defined attribute in that the user-defined *attribute*-statement in a set-descriptor *may* define a value for all the nodes in a set (if the user specifies a default value for the attribute) whereas system-defined attributes (except synonyms) *always* define a value for all the nodes in a set.

4.4. Implicit Information

As a convenience, the MIRRORS/II language has a third descriptor, the *implicit*-descriptor, which is used in the network specification part of a specification file. The *implicit*-descriptor is not involved with implicit set connections. Rather, it provides a mechanism for "factoring-out" statements which may appear in many consecutive *set*- or *node*-descriptors and telling MIRRORS/II that subsequent descriptors in the network specification *implicitly* contain these statements even though they are not *explicitly* present. The general format is

[implicit *Statement* . . . *Statement*]

where each of the zero or more *Statements* is a *member, method, attribute,* or a system- or user-defined attribute statement. This descriptor indicates that all subsequent *set*- and/or *node*-descriptors implicitly contain the indicated *Statements,* until such a time that those *Statements* are cancelled. If the *implicit*-descriptor precedes a *set*-descriptor then the *Statements* will be treated as *SetStatements,* whereas if the *implicit*-descriptor precedes a *node*-descriptor, then the statements will be treated as *NodeStatements.* For example, the following *implicit*-descriptor

```
. . .
[implicit (member children)]
[node Tom (parents (& Frank Deb))]
[node Sue (parents (& Jim Barb))]
. . .
```

indicates that the descriptors for nodes Tom and Sue are to be treated as if the statement (member children) appeared in them. Mechanisms for "turning off" such *implicit*-descriptor statements exist.

5. EVENT HANDLING MECHANISM AND SIMULATION CONTROL

The second distinguishing feature of MIRRORS/II is its general-purpose, user-modifiable, event handling mechanism that controls simulations at run time. The second part of the specification file used as input to MIRRORS/II, the control specification, is where the user specifies details about the running of a specific simulation. In general, the control specification is primarily composed of event commands. There are different kinds of events, such as *input, display,* and *learning*. An event command indicates which event is to occur, when it is to occur, and which part of the network it is to affect.

5.1. Events

The general purpose event-handling mechanism processes system-defined events (e.g., display, input) and user-defined events. This mechanism is based on a queue of queues. The main queue orders the different *types* of events (e.g., display, input, learn, etc.) as explained below. Each *type* of event has its own queue of event descriptions which is ordered based on a *time-of-occurrence* field (the starting time of the next event) in the description.

In any simulation generated by MIRRORS/II an internal clock is incremented by one after each iteration. At this time MIRRORS/II checks to see if any events are scheduled to occur during the next iteration, and, if so, it handles them appropriately. Typically, the activation levels of nodes in the network are updated during *each* iteration so there will generally always be at least one type of event for the generalized event mechanism to handle (i.e., node activation updating).

The main queue order is determined by an *events*-command in the control specification which has the general form:

[events (*EventType* (parser *File Function*) (handler *File Function*))
...
(*Event Type* (parser *File Function*) (handler *File Function*))].

The ordering of the statements within the *events*-command indicates the order in which different types of events will be handled when there is more than one event occurring at the same time. For example, the simple *events*-command in a control specification

[events (input)(learn)(display)]

indicates that, if both a learn and a display event occur "simultaneously" during a simulation (i.e., during the same iteration), then the event of type *learn* should be handled first.

An *EventType* may be a system-defined event (e.g., "display"; see below) or it may be a user-defined event (e.g., determining if the activation values of a network have reached equilibrium). MIRRORS/II provides default parsers and handlers for system-defined events, although a user may provide his or her own parser or handler for those events. If *EventType* is a user-defined event, the user must include the optional parser and handler statements in the *events*-command. The parser *Function* found in file *File* will parse an *EventType*-command when it appears in the control specification. The analogous handler function processes the event whenever it occurs at run time. If a user does not specify an *events*-command, then a default ordering of *input, output, clamp, learn, nextstate, distributeOutput, distributeUpdate, distributeLearn,* and *display* is used, and it is assumed that no user-defined events exist. If an *events*-command is used, it must appear before the first *EventType*-command.

While the *events*-command described above defines the precedence of different types of simultaneously-occurring events, individual *EventType*-commands are used repeatedly to indicate the specific events that are to occur during a desired simulation. An *EventType*-command describes an event in that it indicates which type of event is to occur, when it is to occur, and what part of the network is to be affected. A user can specify an *EventType*-command for any event type which appears in a previous *events*-command or for any system-defined event if no *events*-command was used. The general form of an *EventType*-command is

[*EventType When* ⟨*arguments specific to the type of event*⟩].

The appropriate MIRRORS/II event parser processes the first two arguments. *EventType* must be a valid system- or user-defined event. *When* typically indicates the starting and stopping time of an event as well as its frequency (e.g., every five iterations). Then, the parser specified in the *events*-command or the system default parser for *EventType* is used to parse the remaining arguments.

As an example of an *EventType*-command, consider the system-defined *EventType display,* i.e., the display command, which controls the information that is displayed during the running of a simulation. The syntax for a display command is:

[display *When Who What File Format*].

When indicates the starting and stopping time for this event as well as its frequency. *Who* indicates which nodes in which sets will be displayed. *What* indicates what data (e.g., current activation value, previous activation value, external input being received, connection weights, etc.) will be displayed. *File* indicates where the display output will be stored. *Format* provides output formatting information (e.g., the number of nodes to print per line, the number of decimal digits to print for floating point numbers, etc.). A specification application of this command might be

[display (? every 5) ? act myfile ((string (%s "tick: ") (%d *tick*)))]

which indicates that, throughout the entire simulation (the first "?" means "for all time"), at five iteration intervals, the activation values of all of the nodes (the second "?" means "for all nodes") in the network should be output to a file named myfile. The *Format* argument used indicates that numeric information output for an iteration should be preceded by a line beginning "tick: *n*" where *n* is the current iteration number.

Events such as *display* which occur at regular intervals (every *n* ticks) are handled as follows. After an event description is removed from the queue and the appropriate actions are taken, the time-of-occurrence field of the event description is incremented by *n* to obtain the next time-of-occurrence for the event. The event description is then reinserted into the queue based on its new time-of-occurrence.

Another type of system-defined event is external influences. External influences are inputs and outputs that affect the activation levels of nodes in a connectionist network or the clamping of a node to maintain its activation level at a fixed value. The syntax for a system-defined external influence *EventType*-command is:

[*ExtInfl When Who Amount CAmount*].

ExtInfl is one of *input, output,* or *clamp*. *When* indicates the starting and stopping time of the event. *Who* indicates which nodes in which set of the network will be influenced. *Amount* indicates the amount of influence that each node specified in *Who* will receive. *CAmount* is an optional argument and indicates the amount of influence that those nodes in the same set which were not specified in the *Who* argument will receive.

Each of these external influence *EventType*-commands generates an event description which is put on the appropriate event queue. The event description stores the starting time of the event, the stopping time of the event, and the next time-of-occurrence of the event which in this case is equal to the stopping time of the event. For example, the command

[input (from 1 thru 100) (purkinje-neurons N37) 1.0]

causes two input events (rather than 100 input events) to occur. The first event, which occurs at tick 1, turns on input to node N37. Then the event description, labeled to occur at tick 100, is reinserted on the input event queue according to the next time-of-occurrence of the event. When the second event occurs at tick 100, it turns off input to node N37. This is more efficient than an external influence event which occurs at every iteration, indicating that the external influence is still to be applied. Nonconstant inputs and outputs can be accommodated using a user-defined event.

The *learn* event is used when one wants to change the performance of the connectionist network over time. Generally this is done by changing the weights on connections between nodes. The *learn* event enables one to use unsupervised, reinforcement, and supervised learning as desired. MIRRORS/II provides some learning methods in the system library, and advanced users can develop their own learning methods.

The syntax for the system-defined learn *EventType*-command is:

[learn *When Sets LearnRate*]

When indicates the starting and stopping time of the event. Learning can only be done on a set-wide basis; the parameter *Sets* indicates the sets of nodes to which the *learn* event applies. *LearnRate* is a real number used to control the rate at which learning takes place.

The *learn* command is similar to external influence commands in that each *learn* command actually causes two "events" to occur. The first event turns learning "on" at the appropriate time, and it stays on until the second event turns learning "off" at the appropriate time. Learning may be turned on and off any number of times during the course of a single simulation.

The system-defined *nextstate* event saves the current activation value of each node in a temporary location so that it can be used in the calculation of the new activation value without being overwritten by the new activation value. The syntax for a system-defined nextstate command is:

[nextstate *When*]

where *When* indicates the starting time, stopping time, and frequency of the nextstate event. The nextstate event queue processing is handled just like the display event.

The *distribute* system-defined event is used to apply a function defined in a method file to various nodes in the connectionist network. A method file, indicated by the *method*-statement in a *set*-descriptor, typically contains three functions named Output, Update, and Learn. These will be discussed in more detail in the following section. The syntax for a system-defined distribute *EventType*-command is:

[distribute*Methfcnname When Sets*] or
[*Methfcnname When* Sets].

where *When* indicates the starting time, stopping time, and frequency of the event, and *Sets* indicates to which sets of nodes and in which order the distribute event will apply the *Methfcnname* function. The *Sets* argument is optional. If it is omitted, the distribute event will apply *Methfcnname* to the nodes in all of the sets in the network in the order in which the sets are specified in the network specification. (There is no space between the words distribute and *Methfcnname* for implementation reasons.) An example distribute event command

[distributeOutput ? (hidden treatment)]

indicates that the distribute event will apply the Output function throughout the entire simulation (the "?") to the nodes in the hidden set and then to nodes in the treatment set. The distribute event queue processing is also handled in the same manner as the processing for the display event.

5.2. Additional Control Information

Commands other than those concerning events also appear in a control specification. One command which must appear is a *run*-command. The general form of a *run*-command is:

[run *Iterations*]

where *Iterations* is an integer indicating the number of iterations to run the simulation. The number of iterations is cumulative such that if a subsequent *run*-command is encountered, the simulation will continue from its current state and run *Iterations* more iterations of the simulation.

Another control command is one which causes a user to exit from the simulation. Any one of the commands [exit], [quit], or [stop] can be used to terminate a simulation. If none of these commands appears in a control specification, then, when the specified simulation is completed, MIRRORS/II defaults to asking the user directly for additional commands. In this situation the user has access to all of the control commands described above except those *EventType*-commands not included in an *events*-command. The user could thus terminate the simulation with [exit], or indicate that it should continue longer (e.g., [run 100]), or take a variety of more sophisticated steps involving advanced commands not discussed here (e.g., review simulation output so far and decide whether to terminate or continue the simulation).

Other control commands can be used to further customize the running of a simulation. The *delta*-command allows a user to set the time quantization value for a simulation. For example, if a user includes the statement [delta 0.05] in the control specification, then one iteration of a simulation corresponds to 0.05 units of "real time." The *transcript*-command allows a user to enter the name of a file which will store a transcript of the user's session with the MIRRORS/II system and resultant simulations. The *trace*-command allows the user to specify a number which indicates a level of tracing information that the user wishes to see. Tracing simply allows the user to see more detailed information during MIRRORS/II processing.

Sometimes it may be desirable to integrate MIRRORS/II with other software, for example more traditional AI programs. This can be accomplished using the *function*-command. This command takes two arguments: the name of the function/program to be executed, and the file in which the function is located. This function/program must be written in LISP.

6. LIBRARY

An important feature of the MIRRORS/II system that makes it both powerful and easy-to-use is an indexed library of interchangeable system resources. The library includes spreading activation methods, learning methods, event parsers and handlers, example networks, and system components. Example spreading activation methods currently provided with the MIRRORS/II system include linear methods, linear threshold methods, sigmoidal activation methods, a cellular automata "Game of Life" method, and various competition-based spreading activation methods. Hebbian learning, competitive learning, and error back-propogation are among the learning rules supplied with the MIRRORS/II system. These and other system resources are supplied as user defaults, so that a user does not actually have to program any part of some desired connectionist models. However, a user can choose to override any of these system defaults by developing his or her own library of methods and other system resources. Both system and user libraries have an index which records the file locations of named resources. For example, when MIRRORS/II encounters a statement like (method COMP2) in a *set*-descriptor in a network specification, it uses the keyword COMP2 to locate the program code for the indicated method of spreading activation in the library index. MIRRORS/II takes the appropriate method code from the library to use in assembling a connectionist model.

The spreading activation methods, learning methods, and control strategies supplied with the MIRRORS/II system are currently written in LISP. A spreading activation method as implemented in MIRRORS/II typically consists of three parts, each of which is implemented as a single function. The first part, typically called the Output function, is a local rule which determines how a node sends activity to its neighboring nodes. The second part, typically called the Update function, is a local rule which describes how a single node updates its activation value based on the input it receives from neighboring nodes and external sources. Finally, the third part, generally called the Learn function, is a learning rule which typically describes how the weight on a connection should be altered based on the activation values of the nodes to which it connects. Each of the functions performs a *local* calculation. Generally each network node n_i transmits its activation level $a_i(t)$ at time t to neighboring nodes via weighted links, and these neighboring nodes update their own activation level based on activations received in this fashion. Then, the learning method uses the newly calculated activation levels to determine any changes in node connection weights.

A control strategy is used to determine which node(s) in a network have their activation values updated during a single iteration. MIRRORS/II currently provides a synchronous control strategy, implemented via the distribute event, which updates activation values of all the nodes in the network during each iteration, and an asynchronous control strategy where only one randomly chosen node has it's activity updated during a single iteration. Users can also implement their own control strategies.

A function named Control typically works in conjunction with the distribute event to implement the control strategy. The distribute event is responsible for applying the method functions, typically Output, Update, and Learn, to various node(s) in the network. The Control function is responsible for making sure that all events scheduled for a given iteration are handled properly. The Control function is called by the MIRRORS/II system when a *run*-command is encountered in the control specification and it returns control to the MIRRORS/II system once the number of iterations specified in the *run*-command has been completed.

The program code for event parsers and handlers is also part of the MIRRORS/II library. The system-defined events for which these parsers and handlers exist are distribute, nextstate, input, output, clamp, learn, and display. An event parser is used to parse event-specific arguments when an *EventType*-command is found in the control specification. It is also responsible for putting the initial event description(s) on the queue. An event handler is responsible for taking appropriate action(s) when an event occurs and reinserting the event description on the queue if appropriate.

Another component of the MIRRORS/II library is sample networks. A number of networks are included in the library for users of MIRRORS/II to examine and try using to run simulations. This extendable collection of networks demonstrates many of the features of the MIRRORS/II language. Each example network provided utilizes one of the example methods found in the system library.

The last type of system resource stored in the MIRRORS/II library consists of components of MIRRORS/II itself. Currently, the system components found in the library are the constructor and various control strategies, one of which serves as the default control strategy. The system components stored in the system library are available for general use or advanced users can supply their own system components, thereby modifying even the MIRRORS/II system.

7. AN EXAMPLE

The following connectionist model provides a simple example that was implemented and run using MIRRORS/II. An error back propagation learning method (Rumelhart, Hinton, & McClelland, 1986; Stornetta & Huberman, 1987) was used to teach a network to associate a group of manifestations (symptoms) observed in a patient with the proper medical treatment. A local representation of the problem was used: each manifestation and treatment corresponds to a single node in the connectionist network.

An error back propagation learning method is generally used to do associative learning, i.e., associating given inputs to a system with desired outputs of the system. The ultimate goal is to minimize the difference between the desired outputs of the system and the actual outputs generated by the system for all of the given sets of input patterns. The method basically works as follows: a set of inputs is presented to the system; the actual output of the system is compared to the desired output of the system; the difference between the two output terms is considered the "error"; this error is then propagated backward (from the output layer to the input layer), and each weight in the network is changed such that the change decreases the contribution of that weight to the total "error."

A network used with error backpropagation learning typically has three sets of nodes: *input* nodes, which receive external input; *hidden* units, which are not visible outside of the network; and *output* nodes. The connections in the network are strictly feedforward (e.g., from the input units to the hidden units); there are no intraset connections. The input set may also contain a threshold unit which has feedforward connections to all of the nodes in the hidden and output sets. This threshold unit enables the network to learn more general associations.

A complete specification file of a connectionist model for the manifestations/treatment association problem in a form suitable for MIRRORS/II is shown in Figure 9.3. This specification file was written and used to create a connectionist model in less than an hour without any programming in the conventional sense. In other words, for this example using MIRRORS/II qualitatively reduced the effort that might have been expended to implement the desired connectionist model "from scratch."

The specification file shown in Figure 9.3 consists of a sequence of descriptors, each enclosed in square brackets ("[" and "]"). The first three descriptors, lines 4 through 14, describe the three sets of nodes in the model. For example, the first descriptor

[set manifestations . . . .]

declares the existence of a set of nodes named "manifestations." This descriptor lists the names of all nine nodes in the manifestations set (fever, cough, . . ., threshold), the values of attributes for nodes in the set, and the method of

```
;------------------------------------------- ERROR BACK PROPAGATION EXAMPLE -------------------------
;-------------------------------------------------------- Network Specification ---------------------------------------
[transcript ebp2]
[set manifestations
        (contains fever cough nausea stiff-neck headache chest-pain stomach-pain coma threshold)
        (method GDELTAIN) (minact -1.0)(maxact 1.0) (minwt -0.1)(maxwt 0.1)
        (connects (hidden oto (random 3))(treatment oto optional))]
[set hidden
        (contains h1 h2)
        (method GDELTAHID) (minact -1.0)(maxact 1.0) (minwt -0.1)(maxwt 0.1) (initinterms 0.0 single)
        (connects (treatment oto random))]
[set treatment
        (contains pneumocillin neuromycin propranolol antacid)
        (method GDELTAOUT) (minact -1.0)(maxact 1.0) (initinterms 0.0 single)]
[implicit (member manifestations)]
[node threshold (treatment (/ (pneumocillin -0.01) (neuromycin -0.05) (propranolol -0.07) (antacid 0.09)))]

;-------------------------------------------------------- Control Specification ---------------------------------------
;--- setting up parameters and events
[constructor CONSTRUCTOR zerowts]
[events (display)(clamp)(output)(learn)(nextstate)(distributeOutput)(distributeUpdate)(distributeLearn)]
[nextstate ?]
[distributeOutput ? (hidden treatment)]
[distributeUpdate ? (manifestations hidden treatment)]
[distributeLearn ? (treatment hidden manifestations)]
[learn (from 0 thru 671) ? 0.1]

;--- presentation of patterns to be learned
[clamp (from 0 thru ? every 4) (manifestations (& cough fever chest-pain threshold)) 1.0 -1.0]
[output (from 0 thru 668 every 4)(treatment (& pneumocillin)) 1.0 -1.0]
[clamp (from 1 thru ? every 4) (manifestations (& fever stiff-neck headache coma threshold)) 1.0 -1.0]
[output (from 1 thru 669 every 4)(treatment (& neuromycin)) 1.0 -1.0]
[clamp (from 2 thru ? every 4) (manifestations (& headache nausea threshold)) 1.0 -1.0]
[output (from 2 thru 670 every 4)(treatment (& propranolol)) 1.0 -1.0]
[clamp (from 3 thru ? every 4) (manifestations (& stomach-pain nausea threshold)) 1.0 -1.0]
[output (from 3 thru 671 every 4)(treatment (& antacid)) 1.0 -1.0]

;--- display activation values during simulation
[display now ? act ebp2_act ((perline 9)(template))]
[display (from 97 thru 597 every 100) ? act ebp2_act ((string (%s "tick = ")(%d *tick*))(format %8.6f %1d))]
[display (from 98 thru 598 every 100) ? act ebp2_act ((string (%s "tick = ")(%d *tick*))(format %8.6f %1d))]
[display (from 99 thru 599 every 100) ? act ebp2_act ((string (%s "tick = ")(%d *tick*))(format %8.6f %1d))]
[display (from 100 thru 600 every 100) ? act ebp2_act ((string (%s "tick = ")(%d *tick*))(format %8.6f %1d))]
[display (from 601 thru ?) ? act ebp2_act ((string (%s "tick = ")(%d *tick*))(format %8.6f %1d))]

;--- display weight values during simulation
[display now ((manifestations hidden)) linkweight ebp2_wts ((perline 4)(template))]
[display (from 0 thru 0) ((manifestations hidden)) linkweight ebp2_wts
      ((string (%s "tick = ")(%d *tick*))(format %8.6f %1d))]
[display (from 672 thru 672) ((manifestations hidden)) linkweight ebp2_wts
      ((string (%s "tick = ")(%d *tick*))(format %8.6f %1d))]
[run 677]
```

Figure 9.3. A specification file for a localized connectionist model. Anything on a line following a semicolon is ignored by the MIRRORS/II parser.

spreading activation, GDELTAIN. GDELTAIN is taken from the existing library of methods. Similarly, the second and third *set*-descriptors describe attributes of the nodes in the hidden and disorders sets, respectively. The manifestations and disorders sets correspond to the input and output sets, as discussed above.

Immediately following the three *set*-descriptors is a single *node*-descriptor for the threshold node in the manifestations set. This descriptor specifies that the threshold node is connected to all four treatment nodes: pneumocillin, neuromycin, propranolol, and antacid. The numbers in these descriptors, such as −0.01 and 0.09, are used as weights on the connections in the model. All of the other node connections from manifestations nodes to hidden nodes and from hidden nodes to output nodes will be generated automatically by MIRRORS/II when it parses the specification file. This is due to the word *random* in the *connects*-statement in the *set*-descriptors. The weight on each connection will be a random value between the minimum weight and maximum weight of each set. Only the threshold node connections to the treatment nodes need to be specified explicitly.

Approximately the last half of the specification file forms the control specification. The commands here describe the specific simulation that is to be run with this connectionist model. In particular, the network goes through a learning phase (iterations 0 thru 671) and then a testing phase (iterations 672–677). During the learning phase pairs of manifestations and treatments are presented repeatedly to the network, and the network eventually learns the associations between the elements in each pair. For example, the following pair of commands:

```
[clamp (from 0 thru ? every 4)(manifestations (& cough fever chest-pain threshold)) 1.0
    -1.0]
[output (from 0 thru 668 every 4)(treatment (& pneumocillin)) 1.0 -1.0]
```

are used to teach the network the association between the manifestations cough, fever, and chest-pain and the treatment pneumocillin. Then, during the testing phase, just the manifestations are presented as input to the network. If the network activates the corresponding treatment node, the learning method has been successful. The display command is used to describe the format of the output of the simulation. The command [run 677], at the end of the control specification, indicates that the simulation is to run for 677 iterations.

To create and run the simulation specified in Figure 9.3, one activates MIRRORS/II and directs it to read the specification file. MIRRORS/II then parses the descriptors in the file in the order given, checking for errors as it goes. By the time it reaches the last part of the network specification, it has constructed the static network. When it reads the first clamp command, it builds the dynamic network to be used at simulation time by augmenting the static network. This includes constructing the external clamps to the various manifestations nodes. Finally, the run command causes the actual simulation to begin, the output of which is stored in a file for later viewing or post-simulation processing. At the end of 677 iterations, the simulation terminates. Since there are no further control commands following the run command, MIRRORS/II asks the user for additional commands. The user might direct the simulation to run longer, inspect various parts of the connectionist model, or tell MIRRORS/II to stop and return the user to the operating system.

As indicated by some of the *display*-commands (the lines beginning [display . . .) in the control specification, the activation values of nodes in this simulation are placed in a file called ebp2_act, the contents of which are shown in Figure 9.4 (abridged). The first 13 lines summarize information about the simula-

; network = ebp2 delta = 0.1 Wed May 10 09:49:20 1989

; manifestations set - activation level
; method = /mir/new/methods/gdeltarule_input_layer
; fever cough nausea stiff-neck headache chest-pain stomach-pain coma threshold

; hidden set - activation level
; method = /mir/new/methods/gdeltarule_hidden_layer
; h1 h2

; treatment set - activation level
; method = /mir/new/methods/gdeltarule_output_layer
; pneumocillin neuromycin propranolol antacid

0, tick = 97
1.000000 1.000000 -1.000000 -1.000000 -1.000000 1.000000 -1.000000 -1.000000 1.000000
0.941160 0.989527
0.865583 -0.893102 -0.998879 -0.822132

1, tick = 98
1.000000 -1.000000 -1.000000 **1.000000 1.000000** -1.000000 -1.000000 **1.000000 1.000000**
-0.998701 0.845855
-0.821203 **0.876816** -0.810861 -0.998863

2, tick = 99
-1.000000 -1.000000 1.000000 -1.000000 1.000000 -1.000000 -1.000000 -1.000000 1.000000
-0.761798 -0.991236
-0.997637 -0.806411 0.810314 -0.850605

3, tick = 100
-1.000000 -1.000000 1.000000 -1.000000 -1.000000 -1.000000 1.000000 -1.000000 1.000000
0.973606 -0.976193
-0.861497 -0.998919 -0.792458 0.826729

. . .

96, tick = 673
1.000000 1.000000 -1.000000 -1.000000 -1.000000 1.000000 -1.000000 -1.000000 1.000000
0.974626 0.991550
0.944203 -0.945284 -0.999904 -0.941336

97, tick = 674
1.000000 -1.000000 -1.000000 1.000000 1.000000 -1.000000 -1.000000 1.000000 1.000000
-0.999394 0.966521
-0.942843 **0.945051** -0.945245 -0.999959

98, tick = 675
-1.000000 -1.000000 1.000000 -1.000000 1.000000 -1.000000 -1.000000 -1.000000 1.000000
-0.951204 -0.993654
-0.999937 -0.942770 **0.944272** -0.945374

99, tick = 676
-1.000000 -1.000000 1.000000 -1.000000 -1.000000 -1.000000 1.000000 -1.000000 1.000000
0.969940 -0.991032
-0.944128 -0.999948 -0.943419 **0.944032**

Figure 9.4. Output generated by MIRRORS/II based on the simulation specification illustrated in Figure 9.3.

tion. Output frames (tables of activation in this case), numbered 0, 1, 2, 3, etc., show snapshots of activation levels of all nodes in the network. For example, frame 1 is a table of the activation levels of nodes at iteration or "tick" 98. In this frame, the first row of nine numbers is activation values of nodes in the manifestations set, the second row is activation values of nodes in the hidden set, and the third row is activation values of nodes in the treatment set. Each number in the row corresponding to the manifestations set positionally corresponds to the node listed in line 5 of Figure 4 for the manifestations set. In other words, the first number is the activation value for the node fever, the second number is the activation value for the node cough, and so on. Note that the external clamps to the fever, stiff-neck, headache, coma, and threshold nodes have set their activation levels to 1.0 (bold in Figure 9.4) and the rest of the manifestations nodes have their activation values set to −1.0. The third line of frame 1 shows the current activation levels of the four nodes in the treatment set. Node neuromycin has reached an activation level of 0.876816 (bold, last row of frame 1). The other treatment nodes have negative activation levels, reflecting the fact that the neuromycin treatment is the correct treatment for the clamped manifestation nodes. By the time the learning phase ends (at iteration 671), the correct treatment nodes are fully activated, while activity in all other treatment nodes has totally died out. Examination of the hidden unit activation values for ticks 673 through 676 indicates that the hidden units have learned a binary representation of the four possible treatments.

8. IMPLEMENTATION OF MIRRORS/II

As with any general-purpose software tool, trade-offs between generality and power on the one hand and speed on the other, were frequently an issue during the implementation of MIRRORS/II. LISP was chosen as the primary implementation language, because it makes the specification file parsing and manipulation of data structures which occurs in the PARSE and CONSTRUCT phases of processing easy to implement and modify. The RUN phase of MIRRORS/II processing is also currently implemented in LISP. This LISP implementation allows conventional artificial intelligence software to be easily integrated into the MIRRORS environment. Although the use of LISP implies inefficiency to some, MIRRORS/II was designed with efficiency in mind: no list processing is done; structure- or record-like data structures are used; and the LISP code in the system is compiled. As an alternative, the computationally expensive RUN phase code could readily be written in a more computationally efficient language such as C.

The MIRRORS/II system runs on a variety of machines. Specifically, the parts of MIRRORS/II which are written in LISP will run on any machine that supports Franz Lisp and UNIX (e.g., VAX, SUN). MIRRORS/II can be run either interactively or as a batch job.

Ideally, in looking at the performance of a system like MIRRORS/II, one would like to systematically study performance as a function of the number of nodes in a network, the number of connections in a network, the spreading activation and learning methods used for a simulation, etc. We have not undertaken such a study. However, as an example, we can report on simulations of one of the connectionist models implemented using MIRRORS/II (Reggia, Marsland, & Berndt, 1988) which has a network of approximately 2,300 nodes and 12,500 connections. This model has total run times of approximately 35 minutes of processor time for 100 iterations. Approximately 5 minutes is spent in the parse and construct phases of processing, while the simulation itself takes about 30 minutes to run. The run-time figure includes time spent outputting activation values to be used for later analysis. This type of performance makes doing research on connectionist models of this size feasible.

9. DISCUSSION

MIRRORS/II is an experimental general-purpose software environment developed at the University of Maryland. It is currently in use by our research group for a number of research projects. One completed research project involved using MIRRORS/II to build local connectionist models which simulate the process of reading aloud (Reggia et al., 1988). Another involved using MIRRORS/II to implement a diagnostic system for neurologic and psychiatric diseases (Wald et al., 1989). Connectionist models for dynamic resource allocation (Whitfield et al., 1989) and plan execution (D'Autrechy & Reggia, 1989) have been implemented using MIRRORS/II. In addition to being used at the University of Maryland MIRRORS/II is currently licensed to approximately 50 other sites.

Other general simulation systems for automating the construction of connectionist models exist and can conveniently be viewed as falling into two "generations." The first generation of systems, such as NET (Covington, Sampson, & Peddicord, 1978), PABLO (Perkel 1976a,b,c), and BOSS (White, 1978a,b) were developed in the 1970s and are primarily for neurobiologically oriented connectionist modeling. While NET and PABLO model small neural networks, BOSS is used to model "large" networks (approximately 100 nodes). CORETEX is another system proposed as a tool for developing neural network models (Karshmer & Lenherr, 1977).

While cognitively oriented connectionist models using a local representation of information might be developed using neural modelling tools such as these, the application of these tools to cognitive tasks is often not simple or straightforward due to their explicit biological orientation. In contrast, the second generation of simulation systems currently being developed are more general purpose in nature. While using a "neural-modelling style" of computation (massive parallelism, no central control unit, etc.), these more recent systems, like the Rochester Connectionist Simulator (RCS) (Fanty, 1986; Goddard, Lynne, &

Mintz, 1987) and its predecessor ISCON (Small et al., 1983), P3 (Zipser & Rabin, 1986), and MIRRORS/I (Millheim, 1986) are less biologically flavored. For example, each has named units and links or connections. Units have their own methods or functions which must be programmed by the user.

MIRRORS/II, although it differs in a number of specific details, is most similar to RCS, ISCON, and P3. In contrast to these other evolving systems, however, MIRRORS/II is distinguished by the three key features emphasized in this paper: a high-level nonprocedural specification language, a general purpose event mechanism, and an integrated system library. All of these features are user modifiable and extendable. The MIRRORS/II language minimizes and in some cases frees users from the requirements of programming in the traditional sense. The event mechanism allows the user complete control over actions which occur during a simulation. MIRRORS/II is also explicitly intended to serve as a vehicle for maintaining a library of "tools" in the form of previously developed networks, spreading activation methods, learning methods, event parsers and handlers, and system components. These capabilities are achieved without giving up flexibility or extensibility. Any user can specify new properties for nodes, and individuals with programming skills can implement new methods, event parsers and handlers, and system components and add them to the MIRRORS/II library.

The RUN-phase of MIRRORS/II will be expanded in the future. For example, we hope to eventually augment MIRRORS/II to include a "code generation module." Instead of producing a simulation that can only run on a specific serial machine, this module will allow a MIRRORS/II to select a specific parallel target machine and then have MIRRORS/II generate a simulation which will run on the target machine. The goal is to minimize the changes to MIRRORS/II and still allow the user to capitalize on the parallelism of a target machine which lends itself well to the simulation of highly parallel connectionist models.

REFERENCES

Cottrell, G., & Small, S. (1983). A connectionist scheme for modelling word sense disambiguation. *Cognition and Brain Theory, 6,* 89–120.

Covington, Sampson, & Peddicord. (1978). A frequency response neuron model. *Kybernetes, 7,* 45–60.

D'Autrechy, C. L., & Reggia, J. A. (1989). Parallel plan execution with self-processing networks. *Telematics and Informatics, 6,* 145–157.

D'Autrechy, C. L., Reggia, J., Sutton, III, G. G., Goodall, S. M., Tagamets, M. A., & Marsland, P. M. (1988). *MIRRORS/II reference manual* (Tech. Rep. No. UMIACS-TR-88-41, CS-TR-2043). College Park, MD: University of Maryland, Department of Computer Science.

Fanty, M. (1986). *A connectionist simulator for the BBN butterfly multiprocessor* (Tech. Rep. No. TR-164). Rochester, NY: University of Rochester, Department of Computer Science.

Feldman, J., & Ballard, D. (1982). Connectionist models and their properties. *Cognitive Science, 6,* 205–254.

Freeman, A. (1986). *Stabilization time in competition-based spreading activation models* (Tech. Rep. No. TR-1668). College Park, MD: University of Maryland, Department of Computer Science.

Goddard, N., Lynne, K. J., & Mintz, T. (1987). *Rochester connectionist simulator* (Tech. Rep. No. TR-233). Rochester, NY: University of Rochester, Department of Computer Science.

Hebb, S. (1949). *The organization of behavior.* New York: John Wiley & Sons.

Hopfield, J. (1982). Neural networks and physical systems with emergent collective computational abilities. *Proceedings of the National Academy of Science, 79,* 2554–2558.

Karshmer, A., & Lenherr, F. (1977). Some design criteria for the CORETEX language. In J. Metzler (Ed.), *Systems neuroscience.* New York: Academic Press.

McClelland, J., & Rumelhart, D. (1981). An interactive activation model of context effects in letter perception: Part I. An account of the basic findings. *Psychological Review, 88,* 375–407.

Millheim, S. (1986). *Comparative analysis of competition-based spreading activation models* (Tech. Rep. No. TR-1659). College Park, MD: University of Maryland, Department of Computer Science.

Perkel, D. (1976a). A computer program for simulating a network of interacting neurons, I. Organization and physiological assumptions. *Computers and Biomedical Research, 9,* 31–43.

Perkel, D. (1976b). A computer program for simulating a network of interacting neurons, II. Programming aspects. *Computers and Biomedical Research, 9,* 45–66.

Perkel, D. (1976c). A computer program for simulating a network of interacting neurons, III. Applications. *Computers and Biomedical Research, 9,* 67–74.

Reggia, J. (1985). Virtual lateral inhibition in parallel activation models of associative memory. In *Proceedings of the Ninth International Joint Conference on Artificial Intelligence,* pp. 244–248.

Reggia, J. (1989). Methods for deriving competitive activation mechanisms. *Proceedings of the Ninth International Joint Conference on Neural Networks, 1,* 357–363.

Reggia, J., Marsland, P., & Berndt, R. (1988). Competitive dynamics in a dual-route connectionist model of print-to-sound transformation. *Complex Systems, 2,* 509–547.

Reggia, J., & Sutton, G. (1989). Self-processing networks and their biomedical implications. *Proceedings of the IEEE, 76,* 680–692.

Rumelhart, D., Hinton, G., & Williams, R. (1986). Learning interal representations by error propagation. In D. Rumelhart & J. McClelland (Eds.), *Parallel distributed processing* (Vol. 1). Cambridge, MA: MIT Press.

Rumelhart, D. E., & McClelland, J. L. (1982). An interactive activation model of context effects in letter perception: Part 2. The contextual enhancement effect and some tests and extensions of the model. *Psychological Review, 89,* 60–94.

Rumelhart, D. E., & McClelland, J. L. (1986). *Parallel distributed processing* (Vol. 1). Cambridge, MA: MIT Press.

Rumelhart, D. E., & Norman, D. (1981). Introduction. In G. Hinton & J. Anderson (Eds.), *Parallel models of associative networks* (pp. 1–7). Hillsdale, NJ: Erlbaum.

Small, S. L., Shastri, L., Brucks, M. L., Kaufman, S. G., Cottrell, G. W., & Addanki, S. (1983). *ISCON: A network construction aid and simulator for connectionist models* (Tech. Rep. No. TR-109). Rochester, NY: University of Rochester, Department of Computer Science.

Stornetta, W., & Huberman, B. (1987). An improved three-layer, back propagation algorithm. *Proceedings of the First International Conference on Neural Networks, 2,* 637–644.

Wald, J., Farach, M., Tagamets, M., & Reggia, J. (1989). Generating plausible diagnostic hypotheses with self-processing networks. *Journal of Experimental and Theoretical Artificial Intelligence, 1,* 91–112.

Whitfield, K. C., Goodall, S. M., & Reggia, J. A. (1989). A connectionist model for dynamic control. *Telematics and Informatics, 6,* 375–390.

Wittie, L. D. (1978a). Large-scale simulation of brain cortices. *Simulation, 31,* 73–78.

Wittie, L. D. (1978b). Large network models using the brain organization simulation system (BOSS). *Simulation, 31,* 117–122.

Zipser, D., & Rabin, D. (1986). P3: A parallel network simulating system. In D. E. Rumelhart & J. L. McClelland (Eds.), *Parallel distributed processing* (Vol. 1). Cambridge, MA: MIT Press.

10

Neural Network Simulation with Glauber Dynamics on a Generic Multiprocessor

J. M. Cavallo
R. H. Baran
J. B. Restorff
Naval Surface Warfare Center
White Oak
Silver Spring, MD

1. INTRODUCTION

Symmetrically cross-coupled networks of abstract neurons have demonstrated collective computational abilities, giving rise to the expectation that they will find use in future computing systems where associative memory and constrained optimization are important functions. At least three dynamical paradigms are commonly used in simulations: (a) systems of coupled, nonlinear differential equations, corresponding to analog circuit models; (b) synchronous update models, easily implemented in the high-speed digital arrays of present generation neurocomputers; and (c) the asynchronous Glauber dynamics, which, ironically, is ideal for programming on any general purpose computer. The Glauber dynamics specifies the update of the neuron-like units in a random, serial order (Crisanti & Sompolinsky, 1988). Its transparency supports some important innovations, like simulated annealing on "Boltzmann machines," in which the units are influenced by independent sources of additive white noise (Ackley, Hinton, & Sejnowski, 1985, Sejnowski, Kienker, & Hinton, 1986; Coughlin & Baran, 1988).

1.1. Background

Hopfield (1984) portrayed a class of neural networks in terms of an electronic circuit in which high-gain amplifiers (the neurons) feed back to each other through a symmetric array of coupling conductances (the synaptic weights). The circuit exhibits global asymptotic stability, meaning that the electronic variables always settle to fixed points in their state space irrespective of the initial conditions (Cohen & Grossberg, 1983). Each fixed point is then surrounded by a basin of attraction within which the initial state always leads to it in the course of time. Moreover, Hopfield noted that convergence to the fixed points is rapid, typically requiring only a few time constants or rise times of the neuron/amplifiers. The fixed points occur at local minima of the computational energy, which is the Lyapunov function of the system of differential equations describing the ideal circuit.

The practical difficulties involved in the microelectronic fabrication of such networks are the subject of much attention. We suppose that these difficulties will be overcome eventually. Meanwhile, we try to simulate the future applications of these analog neural networks using digital computers. Two considerations lead us away from the differential equations. First, the real circuit, characterized by component variability, parasitics, electronic noise and jitter, may not conform to the model. Second, the differential equations that constitute the model are harder to handle numerically than discrete dynamics. We take the Glauber dynamics as a logical departure, since it guarantees downhill motion in the energy landscape at zero temperature (Van Hemmen, Grensing, Huber, & Kuhn, 1988). In addition, to the extent that simulated annealing will be practiced in the use of the analog hardware, we know that the statistical properties of such physical systems are governed by Glauber's "master equation" (Glauber, 1963). Finally, we recall that Hopfield's original stochastic model (Hopfield, 1982), in which the McCulloch-Pitts neurons were "interrogated at the same mean rate," was implicitly based on these same dynamical assumptions.

While the practical applications that can be addressed by neural network designs will often demand that many kilobits of information be mapped into networks of binary neurons, the speeds and capacities of the best general purpose computers limit the number of units to about a thousand in contemporary research. The pertinent restriction is that the (synaptic) weight matrix, which grows as the square of the number of units, must fit into random access memory, since each step of the Glauber dynamics fetches a single row from this matrix. The random, serial order of the interrogation process means the entire weight matrix must be available for sampling.

When confronted by a symmetrically cross-coupled network in which the number of neurons far exceeds the rank of the largest square array that can be handled with a given computer, the analyst might partition the network into subnets of roughly equal size, each small enough to be treated numerically. We used this technique of "coordinated isolation" in an associative memory model where there was a natural, functional significance attached to each subnet (Baran, 1989). For computational convenience, we can partition any such network into subnets which are then treated one at a time, by updating the units in the selected subnet while clamping all those outside it. Since the fixed point equations are insensitive to the dynamical assumptions, the stable states are unchanged. While the technique places artificial barriers between some adjacent states, it still guarantees that the energy is nonincreasing.

Yet the technique of coordinated isolation does not reduce the number of arithmetic operations required to go from the initial state to the stable state. This number likewise grows at least as fast as the square of the number of neurons, making the digital simulation of large neural network associative memories a tedious process.

1.2. Objective

This chapter studies the feasibility of accelerating the Glauber dynamics on local memory multiprocessor systems. In general, the best that M concurrent processors can do is to reduce the process time by a factor of 1/M. We hope to find that this theoretical limit can be approached in large neural network calculations almost irrespective of the particular problem.

A local memory multiprocessor system is a network of processors, each with its own private memory, that share information via communications channels. In general, there is less than full connectivity. The communications section of a processor can be designed to operate simultaneously with the computation section.

The neural network is partitioned into subnets that are assigned to different processors. The multiprocessor system executes a number of cycles, each consisting of three phases: (a) In the *coordination phase,* each processor computes the net input received by each unit in its subnet from sources outside the subnet. (b) In the *isolated phase* each processor updates the neurons of its own subnet, treating the neurons outside its subnet as if they were clamped. (c) In the *communication phase,* the processors broadcast the updated states of their subnets to one another. These three phases are repeated until a stable state is reached. This multiprocessing scheme does not guarantee that energy is nonincreasing at every step; but the fixed points are invariant and, if the coordination rate is properly adjusted, their basins of attraction may be essentially preserved while convergence is accelerated in proportion to the number of processors used.

2. SYMMETRICALLY CROSS-COUPLED NEURAL NETWORKS WITH GLAUBER DYNAMICS

Let there be N McCulloch-Pitts neurons in a fully connected network described by the symmetric $(N \times N)$ weight matrix $\mathbf{W}$. The initial state (at time $t = 0$) is $\mathbf{x}(0)$, where the components of the network state vector $\mathbf{x}(t) = (x_1(t), \ldots, x_N(t))$ are binary 0–1 variables. The fixed, externally applied inputs to the network are given by $\mathbf{y} = (y_1, \ldots, y_N)$. At zero temperature, the Glauber dynamics consists in updating the neurons in a random, serial order until a stable state is reached.

The dynamical equation is

$$x_i(t+1) = \begin{cases} l\left[\sum_{j=1}^{N} W_{ij}x_j(t) + y_i\right] & \text{if } i = U(t) \\ x_i(t) & \text{otherwise,} \end{cases} \tag{1}$$

where $l[y] = \begin{cases} 1 & \text{if } y > 0 \\ 0 & \text{if } y \leq 0 \end{cases}$

is the unit step and $\{U(t), t = 0, 1, 2, \ldots\}$ is a sequence of independent random variables that are uniformly distributed among the first N integers. The fixed points (stable states), denoted $\mathbf{x}^o$, which satisfy the fixed point equations

$$x_i^o = l\left[\sum_{j=1}^{N} W_{ij}x_j^o + y_i\right], \qquad i = 1, \ldots, N, \tag{2}$$

occur at (local) minima of the computational energy,

$$H(\mathbf{x}) = -\sum_{j=i+1}^{N}\sum_{i=1}^{N-1} W_{ij}x_ix_j - \sum_{i=1}^{N} y_ix_i.$$

N-bit patterns $\mathbf{x}^{(1)}, \ldots, \mathbf{x}^{(L)}$ are stored in the net by setting the weights according to Hopfield's outer product rule,

$$W_{ij} = \sum_{\alpha=1}^{L} [2x_i^{(\alpha)} - 1][2x_j^{(\alpha)} - 1], \qquad i \neq j, \tag{3}$$

$W_{ii} = 0$. When $L \ll N$, this storage prescription will generally create energy minima at the desired locations, so that the pattern set is a (perhaps exhaustive) subset of $\{\mathbf{x}^o\}$.

2.1. The Markov Property

The Glauber dynamics gives rise to a Markov chain, since the probability of having $\mathbf{x}(t+1) = \mathbf{b}$, given the past history up to t, is the same as that conditioned on $\mathbf{x}(t)$ alone. Let $\mathbf{x}(t) = \mathbf{a} \neq \mathbf{b}$. Then the probability of a one-step transition from **a** to **b** is nonzero if and only if the Hamming distance $D(\mathbf{a},\mathbf{b})$ is unity, since the units are updated serially, and only one unit can change at a time.

The transition probabilities are given by the $2^N \times 2^N$ stochastic matrix **P:**

$$P_{\mathbf{ab}} = \Pr\{\mathbf{x}(t+1) = \mathbf{b} \mid \mathbf{x}(t) = \mathbf{a}\}$$

$$= \begin{cases} 0 & \text{if } D(\mathbf{a},\mathbf{b}) > 1 \\ \left.\begin{array}{l} (1/N)l[\mathbf{d_{ab}}(\mathbf{Wa}' + \mathbf{y}')] \\ (1/N)\{1 - l[\mathbf{d_{ab}}(\mathbf{Wa}' + \mathbf{y}')]\} \end{array}\right\} & \text{if } D(\mathbf{a},\mathbf{b}) = 1 \end{cases}, \tag{4a}$$

where $\mathbf{d_{ab}}$ is a vector of N binary digits the ith of which is $d_{\mathbf{ab}i} = |a_i - b_i|$ and the (′) transposes the row vectors (**a** and **y**) into columns. Along the diagonal,

$$P_{\mathbf{aa}} = 1 - \sum_{\mathbf{b}:D(\mathbf{a},\mathbf{b})=1} P_{\mathbf{ab}}. \tag{4b}$$

Note that the nondiagonal elements of **P** are either zero or 1/N; and every **b** that is accessible from **a** has the same probability of being reached in one step. The absorbing states are the solutions of the fixed point equations (2): $\{\mathbf{x}^o\} = \{\mathbf{a}: P_{\mathbf{aa}} = 1\}$. In principle, equations (4) completely describe the network's behavior. In practice, the transition matrix is unmanageably large and the only way to study the network is by programming equation (1).

2.2. Basins of Attraction in the Stochastic Model

The 2^N possible choices of $\mathbf{x}(0)$ lead to a much smaller set $\{\mathbf{x}^o\}$ of stable states. For every $\mathbf{a} \in \{\mathbf{x}(0)\}$ and $\mathbf{z} \in \{\mathbf{x}^o\}$, define

$$q(\mathbf{z}|\mathbf{a}) = \Pr[\mathbf{x}(\infty) = \mathbf{z} \mid \mathbf{x}(0) = \mathbf{a}],$$

the probability that **z** is the endpoint of a dynamical sequence $\{\mathbf{x}(t),\ t = 0, 1, 2, \ldots\}$ starting at the given state **a.** We measure the basin of attraction of **z** as the probability that it is reached when the initial state is random and uniform across the 2^N possibilities:

$$q(\mathbf{z}) = 2^{-N} \sum_{\mathbf{a}} q(\mathbf{z}|\mathbf{a}). \tag{5}$$

Clearly $\sum_{\mathbf{z}} q(\mathbf{z}) = 1$; and the numbers $\{q(\mathbf{z}): \mathbf{z} \in \{\mathbf{x}^o\}\}$ represent a discrete probability density.

2.3. Rate of Convergence

Each time step witnesses the "interrogation" and update of one neuron, in accordance with equation (1), and thus traverses $N - 1 \approx N$ inner product steps (ips), or "interconnects" as they are often called in the context of neural networks, to compute the weighted sum that is the net input to the selected unit. (Each ips involves a multiply-and-add operation.). A *sweep* is defined as the interrogation of N neurons (in any order). Thus each sweep requires N^2 ips.

The mean convergence time for a given symmetric **W** is obtained as an average over many trials leading from $\mathbf{x}(0)$ to $\mathbf{x}^o$, the former being randomly generated. In an ensemble of networks, produced by storing random patterns using (3), the mean convergence time is about 4N time steps, which is 4 sweeps of the Glauber dynamics. A similar result has been obtained by Crisanti and Sompolinsky for networks in which the components of **W** are independent random numbers with symmetry imposed. For a computer that performs 10^5 interconnects per second, the mean convergence time for N = 1,000 is about 40 sec. But if N = 10,000, the time exceeds an hour.

3. GLAUBER DYNAMICS IN COORDINATED ISOLATION ON A LOCAL MEMORY MULTIPROCESSOR

Partition the fully interconnected network of N neurons into subnets in order to distribute the computational burden among a number of parallel processors. Let

M = the number of processors;

n = the number of neurons in the subnet assigned to a processor
= N/M for every processor; and

Ψ_m = a set which contains the indices of all neurons in the mth subnet, so that

$$\bigcup_{m=1}^{M} \Psi_m = \{1,2, \ldots ,N\} \text{ and } \bigcap_{m=1}^{M} \Psi_m = \varnothing.$$

Since every neuron belongs to exactly one subnet, we can also use the notations

m(i) = the subnet to which the ith neuron belongs and

$\psi(i)$ = the set of indices of all neurons sharing the same subnet as the ith neuron
$= \Psi_{m(i)}$.

Recall (section 1.2 above) that the multiprocessor cycles through three distinct phases. Let k = 1,2, . . . count the cycles and consider in detail the events comprising the first cycle, which begins at t = 0.

3.1 The Coordination Phase

With input vector **y** and initial state **x**(0) as before, we compute the net input received by the ith neuron from sources outside its own subnet:

$$\tilde{y}_i(1) = \sum_{j \notin \psi(i)} W_{ij}x_j(0) + y_i. \tag{6}$$

When this computation is carried out for every $i \in \Psi_m$, the mth subnet is initialized. When the N-vector $\tilde{\mathbf{y}}(1) = [\tilde{y}_1(1), \ldots, \tilde{y}_N(1)]$ has been computed, the coordination phase is completed. Since (6) involves N-n ips, the initialization of Ψ_m takes $(N - n)n$ ips. Because the processors work concurrently, the time required to complete the coordination phase is proportional to

$$\tau_1 = (N - n)n \text{ ips}. \tag{7}$$

3.2. The Isolated Phase

Each processor now operates independently, randomly selecting and updating the neurons of its assigned subnet, treating the outside units as if they were clamped to their initial values. The duration of this isolated phase, the same for every processor, is λn time steps, which is λ sweeps of the subnet. We call λ the *coordination period* and assume $\lambda \geq 1/n$. Note that λ is measured in *sweeps per cycle*. Its reciprocal will be called the *coordination rate*. For every $i \in \Psi_m$, the new dynamical equation is

$$x_i(t+1) = \begin{cases} l\left[\sum_{j \in \Psi_m} W_{ij}x_j(t) + \tilde{y}_i(1)\right] & \text{if } i = U_m(t) \\ x_i(t) & \text{otherwise} \end{cases} \tag{1'}$$

where $\{U_m(t), t = 0, 1, \ldots, n - 1\}$ is a sequence of independent random numbers uniformly distributed on Ψ_m. This routine is followed concurrently by every processor and in every subnet. The end result is a new state $\mathbf{x}(\lambda n)$. The duration of the isolated phase is

$$\tau_2 = \lambda n^2 \text{ ips} \tag{8}$$

since each iteration of (1′) requires n interconnects.

3.3. The Communication Phase

The amount of time spent in the communication phase will depend on the details of the multiprocessor. In a rectangular network of processors (such as we made with Inmos Transputers) the communication time can be reduced to an amount that is nearly independent of M by transmitting the states of the subnets in a series of steps. If the communication channels can be kept busy during the entire communication phase, the duration of this phase will be dominated by the time needed to transmit information to the processors which occupy the corners of the network. That there are only two links to these processors requires that half of the message traffic be received through each. Since the processor must receive updates from all others, we have $(M - 1)/2$ messages on each link. Each message will contain at most the information about n neurons. Let r be the ratio of the time to transmit the state of a neuron to the time required by one interconnect. Then

$$\tau_3 = (M - 1)nr/2 \approx Nr/2 \text{ ips} \tag{9}$$

is the duration of the communication phase.

3.4. Cycle Time

The communication phase of the first cycle replaces $\mathbf{x}(0)$ with $\mathbf{x}(\lambda n)$ in the local memory of each processor. Now the second cycle begins with a coordination phase in which $\tilde{\mathbf{y}}(2)$ is computed by substituting the components of $\mathbf{x}(\lambda n)$ for those of $\mathbf{x}(0)$ in the right side of equation (6). In general we have

$$\tilde{y}_i(k) = \sum_{j \notin \psi(i)} W_{ij} x_j[(k - 1)\lambda n] + y_i$$

in the kth cycle, $k = 1, 2, \ldots$; and equation (1′) is generalized by substituting $\tilde{\mathbf{y}}(k)$ for $\tilde{\mathbf{y}}(1)$ with the understanding that $\{U_m, t = (k - 1)\lambda n, \ldots, k\lambda n - 1\}$ is the interrogation sequence in the kth cycle. The duration of a cycle is clearly

$$\tau = \tau_1 + \tau_2 + \tau_3 ,$$

measured in ips. The observable cycle time will be related to this by a scale factor appropriate to a given machine. With reference to (7), (8), and (9), we have

$$\begin{aligned} \tau &= (N - n)n + \lambda n^2 + Nr/2 \\ &= n^2(M + \lambda - 1) + Nr/2 \text{ ips}. \end{aligned} \tag{10}$$

3.5. Convergence Time on the Multiprocessor

Every cycle of the multiprocessing scheme witnesses the interrogation of $(\lambda n)M = \lambda N$ neurons. Defining a sweep as N interrogation steps, essentially as before, this is λ sweeps of the N-unit network. The mean number of sweeps required to converge to a stable state is $\mu(M,\lambda)$ where the dependence on other parameters is suppressed. Since the attainment of a stable state will go untested in the isolated phase, $\mu(M,\lambda)$ will be measured as $\lambda\bar{k}$, where $\bar{k}$ is the observed mean number of *cycles* required for convergence:

$$\mu(M,\lambda) = \lambda\bar{k}(M,\lambda). \tag{11}$$

Note that $\mu(1,1/N) \equiv \mu$ would correspond to the mean convergence time for the pure dynamics described in Section 2 above.

The multiprocessing scheme allows state transitions which go uphill in the energy landscape. Therefore we will need to measure its *inefficiency* as

$$\zeta(M,\lambda) = \mu(M,\lambda)/\mu\ , \tag{12}$$

the ratio of the mean sweeps to convergence on the multiprocessor to that for the pure dynamics (in which the motion is strictly downhill).

3.6. Acceleration of Convergence

It remains to compare the process times on the multiprocessor and the single processor. Let $T(M,\lambda)$ be the mean process time (in ips) for the indicated setup. Then

$$T(M,\lambda) = \tau\bar{k},$$

the number of ips per cycle times the mean number of cycles to convergence. For the single processor,

$$T(1,1/N) = \mu N^2,$$

the mean number of sweeps to convergence times the number of ips per sweep. Then the multiprocessor accelerates convergence by a factor of

$$\begin{aligned} A(M,\lambda) &= T(1,1/N)/T(M,\lambda) \\ &= (\mu N^2)/(\tau\bar{k}) \\ &= (\lambda/\zeta)(N^2/\tau) \end{aligned}$$

with reference to equation (11) for $\bar{k}$ and equation (12) for the inefficiency. Substituting equation (10) for τ then gives

$$A(M,\lambda) = \frac{M\lambda/\zeta}{1 + (\lambda - 1)/M + Mr/2N} \tag{13}$$

after dividing numerator and denominator by n^2M. For $N \gg Mr$ and $M \gg \lambda$, the acceleration increases roughly as λ/ζ times the number of processors. Two questions arise from this result:

- How does the inefficiency vary with the number of processors and the number of sweeps per cycle?
- How slow can the coordination rate be made without incurring an unacceptable loss of fidelity, i.e., without distorting the essential features of the energy landscape?

The next two sections attempt to answer these questions.

4. INEFFICIENCY AND COORDINATION RATE IN A TRANSPUTER-BASED MULTIPROCESSOR SYSTEM

We built a 4 × 4 rectangular network of Inmos T414 Transputers, each with 130 KBytes of local memory, hosted by an IBM AT compatible. Weights and states were represented with integer precision (4 bytes). Using 240 neurons with 2, 4, 8, 12, and 15 processors, our unoptimized multiprocessor system was characterized by a communication parameter r less than unity.

4.1. Test Procedure

The outer product rule (3) was used to create weight matrices from pattern sets of up to $L = 10$ vectors whose 240 components were 0 or 1 equiprobably. Each *trial* consisted in

1. generating a new pattern set,
2. computing the components of **W**,
3. generating an initial state vector with the same statistics as the patterns, and
4. iterating the dynamical equation (1′) until convergence,

which was tested between cycles. In most cases 128 trials were averaged to obtain the mean convergence time for parameter combinations of interest.

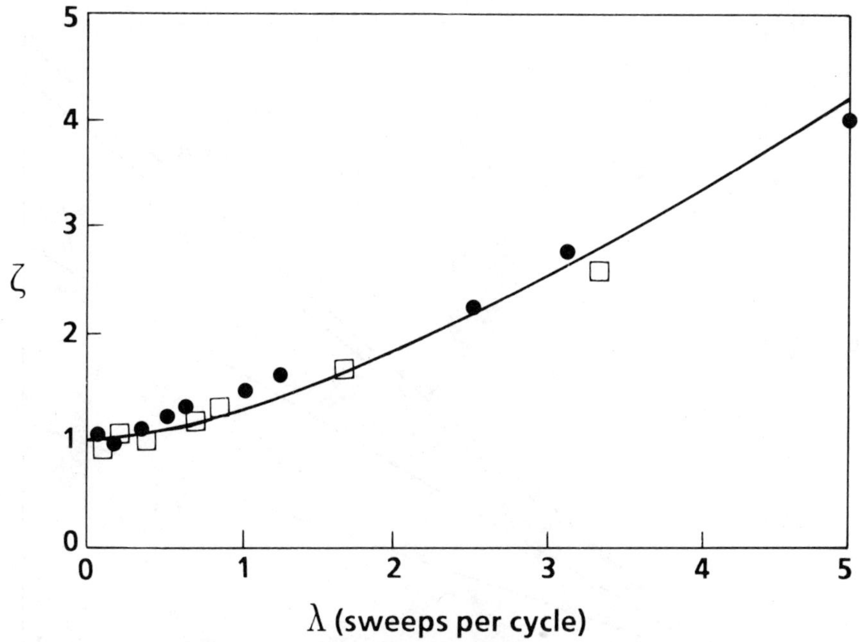

Figure 10.1. Inefficiency (ζ) versus coordination period (λ) using the transputer-based multiprocessor with M = 15 (solid circles) and M = 12 (open squares). Each plotted point represents the mean of approx. 128 trials.

4.2. Results

Figure 1 shows the inefficiency as a function of coordination period with 12 and 15 processors, using the average of all the results for $M \leq 8$ for the baseline mean convergence time. The inefficiency is essentially independent of M, as might be expected from the linear scaling of the mean number of steps to convergence of the pure dynamics. The fitted curve,

$$\zeta(\lambda) = 1 + \lambda^2/(\lambda + 3) , \tag{14}$$

will not receive a rigorous justification here. Note that the inefficiency approaches $1 + \lambda$ in the limit of large λ, as most of the isolated phase is spent updating the stabilized subnets. The inefficiency is close to unity for small λ. Moreover, the inefficiency increases most rapidly as the number sweeps per cycle approaches the mean convergence time.

The convexity of $\zeta(\lambda)$ causes the ratio λ/ζ, which figures so prominently in the acceleration (13), to exceed unity for all $\lambda > 3/2$. Substituting (14) in (13),

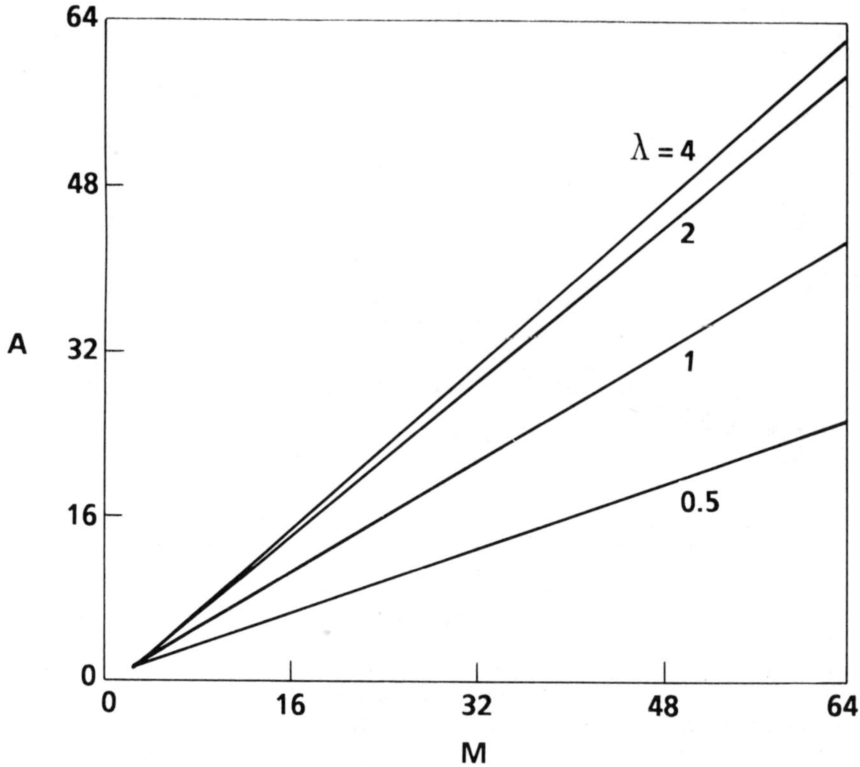

Figure 10.2. Acceleration (A) versus the number of processors (M) for several values of the coordination period (λ).

we obtain the acceleration as a function of M, parameterized by λ, as shown in Figure 10.2.

5. TESTING THE FIDELITY OF THE MULTIPROCESSING DYNAMICS

If the coordination rate is very fast, no subnet will evolve very far without updating the states of the outside units; and the behavior of the network, using the multiprocessing dynamics, will surely be close to that observed with the pure dynamics (1). But if the coordination rate is sufficiently slow, so that most of the subnets have stabilized before the onset of the coordination phase, then the question of fidelity remains open.

Recalling the notation introduced in section 2.2 above, particularly the definition of the probabilities $q(\mathbf{z})$ given in equation (5), let equation (1) be replaced by another dynamical equation (1′) which is guaranteed to converge to the same stable states (and those alone). Then the basins of attraction are located about the same $\{\mathbf{x}^o\}$; but their measures $\{q'(\mathbf{z}) : \mathbf{z} \in \{\mathbf{x}^o\}\}$ might be different. Posit the null hypothesis, that $q(\mathbf{z}) = q'(\mathbf{z})$ for every $\mathbf{z} \in \{\mathbf{x}^o\}$, and perform K independent Monte Carlo trials in which randomly generated $\mathbf{x}(0)$ lead, by (1), to stable states $\mathbf{z}_1, \ldots, \mathbf{z}_K$. The empirical measures of the basins of attraction are

$$\hat{q}(\mathbf{z}) = \#\{i:\mathbf{z}_i = \mathbf{z}\}/K.$$

Now rerun the trials with the alternative dynamics and obtain measure $\hat{q}'(\mathbf{z})$ in the same manner. Under the null hypothesis, $K\hat{q}(\mathbf{z})$ and $K\hat{q}'(\mathbf{z})$ are identically binomial with size K and success parameter $q(\mathbf{z})$.

Let the number of stable states be $L = \#\{\mathbf{x}^o\}$ and index them by superscripts h = 1, 2, . . ., L. Then the sums

$$\hat{Q}(h) = \hat{q}(\mathbf{z}^{(1)} + \ldots + \hat{q}(\mathbf{z}^{(h)})$$

and

$$\hat{Q}'(h) = \hat{q}'(\mathbf{z}^{(1)} + \ldots + \hat{q}'(\mathbf{z}^{(h)})$$

give rise to L absolute differences of the form

$$D(h) = |\hat{Q}(h) - \hat{Q}'(h)|.$$

The largest of these,

$$D = \sup_{1 \le h \le L} D(h),$$

is the Kolmogorov-Smirnov statistic for measuring the dissimilarity of the two distributions (Birnbaum, 1952); and its expected value under the null hypothesis is $0.86/K^{1/2}$.

Monte Carlo trials were performed by simulating the multiprocessing dynamics on an HP-1000 computer. After generating a pattern set and the resulting weight matrix, each baseline trial consisted in selecting a random initial state and iterating (1) until convergence. K = 40 such trials were performed with networks of N = 80 units in which the number of patterns was four and the number of stable states was at least five (since the zero state is always stable). Forty more trials were then conducted with *the same* network, using the alternative dynamics (1′) with M = 4 processors.

Figure 10.3 plots the average D-statistics which resulted at each of the indicated coordination periods. Each plotted value of D is the mean of five sets of trials of the kind just described. These crude results thus summarize the study of only five networks. The dashed, horizontal line marks the criterion level, i.e.,

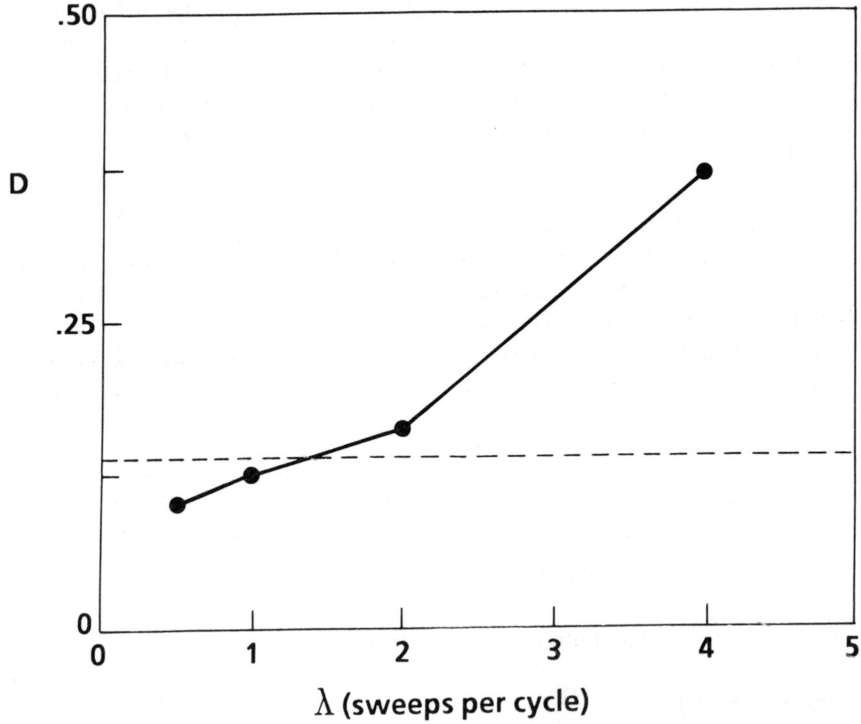

Figure 10.3. Dissimilarity (D) versus coordination period (λ), averaged over five networks with $N = 80$, $L \approx 5$, and $M = 4$. Each plotted point represents the mean of $5 \times 40 = 200$ trials.

the expected value of D under the null hypothesis. While the sampling error is considerable, the increasing trend in D(λ) is significant.

6. CONCLUSIONS

The notion of putting parallel processors to work on large neural network calculations, to accelerate their convergence to stable states by a factor proportional to the number of processors, finds support in the work just described. It is well known that the Hopfield network usually converges in several sweeps of the Glauber dynamics. We find that this is also true *irrespective of the number of concurrent processors* (so long as the processors are much less numerous than the neurons). The artificial barriers placed in the energy landscape by partitioning the neural network into subnets, and the uphill bridges created by concurrently updating the isolated subnets, influence the network's path through state space only to the extent that they are encountered. If the isolated phase persists for only about a sweep, the frequency of such encounters is diminished.

While the desirability of lengthening the isolated phase—to reduce the "run time" cost of coordinating the subnets—is evident to the multiprocessing system designer, the acceleration gained thereby is not appreciably increased by making more than two or three sweeps per cycle, where the distortion of the energy landscape becomes prominent.

The generality of these results should not be overstated. We have considered only the content-addressable memory described by Hopfield in his first landmark paper on collective computation. Networks designed for optimization, in which neurons signifying mutually exclusive hypotheses are linked by very strong inhibitory weights, might converge more slowly on the multiprocessor for all but the fastest coordination rates. Networks with random, symmetric weights might have statistical properties that are vastly different from networks storing small numbers of random patterns.

The widespread view that collective computation networks are impractical without some kind of temperature control (like simulated annealing) to improve solution quality leads to the unanswered question, whether the multiprocessing scheme preserves the depths of the energy valleys. This question can be tested on the Transputer-based apparatus mentioned in Section 4, by measuring goodness-of-fit to a Boltzmann distribution in the course of sampling the network state intermittently at a constant temperature.

REFERENCES

Ackley, D. H., Hinton, G. E., & Sejnowski, T. J. (1985). A learning algorithm for Boltzmann machines. *Cognitive Science, 9,* 147–169.

Baran, R. H. (1989). A neural network approach to data fusion in automatic target recognition. *International Journal of Neural Networks: Research & Applications, 1,* 68–76.

Birnbaum, Z. W. (1952). Numerical tabulation of the distribution of Kolmogorov's statistic for finite sample size. *American Statistical Association Journal, 47,* 425–441.

Cohen, M. A., & Grossberg, S. (1983). Absolute stability of global pattern formation and parallel memory storage by competitive neural networks. *IEEE Transactions on Systems, Man and Cybernetics, 13,* 815–826.

Coughlin, J. P, & Baran, R. H. (1988). Remarks on neural networks and spin glass models. *American Mathematical Monthly, 95,* 630–633.

Crisanti, A., & Sompolinsky, H. (1988). Dynamics of spin systems with randomly asymmetric bonds. *Physical Review A, 37,* 4865–4874.

Glauber, R. J. (1963). Time-dependent statistics of the Ising model. *Journal of Mathematical Physics, 4,* 294–307.

Hopfield, J. J. (1982). Neural networks and physical systems with emergent collective computational abilities. *Proceedings of the National Academy of Sciences, USA, 79,* 2554–2558.

Hopfield, J. J. (1984). Neurons with graded responses have collective computational properties like those of two-state neurons. *Proceedings of the National Academy of Sciences, USA, 81*, 3088–3092.

Sejnowski, T. J., Kienker, P. K., & Hinton, G. E. (1986). Learning symmetry groups with hidden units. *Physica, 22D*, 260–275.

van Hemmen, J. L., Grensing, D., Huber, A., & Kuhn, R. (1988). Nonlinear neural networks (I): general theory. *Journal of Statistical Physics, 50*, 231–270.

11

Computational Logic of Network Processes*

William P. Coleman
MIEMSS
University of Maryland at Baltimore

Department of Mathematics and Statistics
University of Maryland Baltimore County

1. INTRODUCTION

This chapter presents a formal logic, based on the mathematical theory of categories, for describing the behavior of networks. By analyzing the pattern in which the nodes are connected, we hope to provide information on the flow of processes—on the possible sequences of events in the network—and to define rigorously the sense in which such behavior can be shared between two heterogeneous networks. The networks may perfectly well be either computational or natural, but since our analysis depends in either case on viewing a process as a generalized computation, we use the term *computational logic* to denote the methods herein presented. The ambiguity in the title is deliberate: we mean to describe networks of processes and processes that occur on networks.

In this introduction we shall discuss informally three paradigm examples and use them to motivate the set of questions that computational logic attempts to address. (For more examples, see Coleman, 1989a.)

Example 1: Distributed Computation (Coleman, Sanford, & De Gaetano, 1989a, b)

At 7:35 A.M. a nurse in a hospital's intensive care unit requests a report from a computer workstation at a patient's bedside. The report is to consist of two graphs: one of heart rate versus time, at the top of the screen, and one of mean blood pressure versus time, at the bottom. These graphs are to display data that begin at 7:00 A.M., to go up to the present, and to be continually updated until

---

* Like everyone writing on categorial logic, I am indebted to F. William Lawvere for his persuasive influence in shaping this field, and, like almost all of these people, I am also indebted to him for personal encouragement and advice. Ultimately, I am also indebted to Samuel Eilenberg and Saunders Mac Lane for their individual and collective published work.

stopped. The computer process that does this requires a number of conceptually distinct subprocesses. (These might be subroutines of a single program, but more likely are separate programs, in any of several senses of 'multitasking' or 'multi-processing.') There is a subprocess that interacts with the nurse and establishes which report is wanted. There is a subprocess that formats the screen display, draws it, and plots the current data. Thereafter, two processes cooperate: one (which has been operating in the background all along) that gets new data from the physiological monitor and stores it in a database for general use, and one that retrieves data from the database and updates the screen for this particular report. Yet another subprocess waits for a command from the nurse to terminate the whole network of subprocesses gracefully.

The subprocesses themselves have structure. The subprocess PLOTPTS, shared by several processes, plots a data pair XVAL, YVAL. It first computes the screen coordinates XPLOT, YPLOT actually to be plotted. These are given in terms of the previously established minimum and maximum x and y values XMIN, XMAX, YMIN, YMAX and the physical resolution XPNTS, YPNTS of the screen by the formulae,

$$\text{XPLOT} = \frac{\text{XVAL} - \text{XMIN}}{\text{XMAX} - \text{XMIN}} \times \text{XPTS},$$

$$\text{YPLOT} = \frac{\text{YVAL} - \text{YMIN}}{\text{YMAX} - \text{YMIN}} \times \text{YPTS}.$$

PLOTPTS then plots XPLOT, YPLOT.

One thinks of all information governing the flow of a computational process as being available in records. For PLOTPTS, these are

/MINMAX/ XMIN, XMAX, YMIN, YMAX,

/SCREEN/ XPNTS, YPNTS,

/VALS/ XVAL, YVAL, and

/PLOT/ XPLOT, YPLOT.

Abstractly, PLOTPTS is a function—a black box—for computing /PLOT/ from /MINMAX/, /SCREEN/ and /VALS/.

There is also structure at a larger level. There is a workstation at the bedside of each patient in the intensive care unit and more in the labs and in the physicians' offices. Data for any report may originate by automatic entry from computers in the physiologic monitors or in the labs, or by keyboard entry at the bedside. For any one patient, reports may be required at the bedside or in a physician's office that use overlapping subsets of the data and overlapping computational and plotting algorithms.

To cope with all of this, the computing staff adopt the strategy of linking the computers by a local area network and breaking all programs down into a library of modular, reusable, independent processes distributed across the network. The computing is thus distributed in at least three senses; any computation may require, as above, a system of distinct subprocesses; these subprocesses may be physically distributed across the local area network; and computations, or portions of them, may be replicated across different patients, users, or labs.

The resulting network of processes is very complex, and, as one tries to understand it, certain questions (Coleman et al., 1989b) arise:

- The system is difficult to analyze when taken as a whole. It is easier to try to base analyses on either subsystems or simplifications, although these analyses obviously cannot be exactly correct. One would like to develop formal methods that tell when, and to what degree, an analysis would give correct results, even though based on simplifications.
- As time goes on, the computing staff, or individual users, may want to upgrade some process modules in the library with more sophisticated ones. Different versions may have to exist simultaneously. How can one formulate the requirement that such a replacement not change the previous behavior, but only add new capability?
- The hospital we have been speaking of is not the only one in the world. It will acquire hardware and some software from commercial vendors, probably several of them. How can independent standardization authorities write specifications that ensure the interoperability of heterogeneous software modules?
- Part of the preceding question, one that becomes more pointed when one begins to think of sharing data between hospitals or clinics, is *semantic* (Coleman et al., 1989a). How can a general framework be established that allows heterogeneous computing processes to explain to each other, automatically, what the meaning of their data structures and of their requests for and offers of service are?
- The system designer—trying, for example, to estimate use requirements for various components—needs to predict the values of certain statistics of populations of processes. How can analyses of the logical structure of individual processes help in deriving probabilistic properties of these statistics?
- Given an answer to the preceding question, can we go on to develop rational methods of exerting control over the system of processes?

In a way, the semantic question is central to several of the others. When we think of semantics, we usually think of a relation between a language, at one level, and a universe that it describes, at another. However, in this case, the questions are much more sophisticated: There are many levels, or rather, a system of levels—there are data about data about data. At the lowest level there are representations of the patient: the data records, and also the graphs that the nurse requests, which are, in a different way, a symbolic representation of the patient. Then there is a level above that. When the nurse interacts with the process to set up the report, she is describing the plot that describes the patient. Similarly, the subprocess that retrieves data records and plots the data on the screen must in some sense work in a language that describes the data records and the plot. At a still higher level, some process that coordinates the system of subprocesses must use representations of these representations. In the most general sense, many of the questions just raised can be reformulated as requirements that a data manipulation process intended to describe a process at a lower level do so truly; or conversely, that a process conform correctly to some description of it; or simply that two processes at the same level interoperate coherently to produce a predictable joint behavior.

Example 2: Neural Nets

If we are going to regard sequential computer programs as black boxes computing output states from input states, the difference between them and neural networks becomes smaller. Although the brain operates in continuous time, we can logically think of it, using fast-slow approximations familiar from nonlinear mathematics, as a modular system (DARPA, 1988, sec. 14.8, 16) of neural networks, each producing a series of output states in response to input states furnished by others and sometimes by the outside world. At this level of abstraction the method of implementation obviously makes no difference. What one is concerned with is how the processes of any such system of function compositions can be interpreted as having a meaning.

Some of the questions (Coleman, Sanford, De Gaetano, & Geisler, 1990a, b) from the preceding *Example* arise again. One would like to use simplified models to describe the activity of the brain. One wonders if learning can be understood in terms of replacement of subnets by more sophisticated ones. The semantics of brain states are certainly very obscure compared to the relatively explicit states of sequential programs such as PLOTPTS.

Example 3: Biochemical Kinetics

Consider the biochemical system,

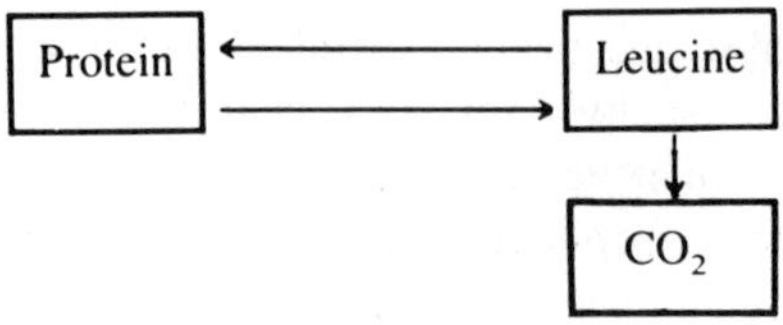

The amino acid leucine may be incorporated into protein, from which it would eventually be recovered when the protein is broken down, or it may itself be broken down, in which case its carbon fragment will be oxidized and eventually expired as carbon dioxide. The biologist is interested in estimating the size of the leucine pool in the body and the relative rates at which leucine is involved in the two processes just mentioned. One way to do so would be to infuse leucine that has been labeled by the substitution of a stable or radioactive isotope for its carbon atom.

The analysis of data from such experiments is made questionable by the fact that the true process is really very much more complicated than the one depicted in the figure. To begin with, there is an intermediate, α-ketoisocaproic acid, in equilibration with leucine and between it and its metabolism into CO_2. Also, on its way to protein, the leucine molecule will spend some time acylated to transfer-RNA. There are many different proteins, each with its own half-life. Next, there is physical compartmentalization in the body; the pools are divided into those in the blood, in the extracellular water, in the cytosol, and in the mitochondria. Finally, the rates of the reactions are different in different organs.

In biological applications one can often expect that, to be practical, a mathematical model will have to be much simpler than reality. It is hard to find simplifications that are based on biological reality rather than on mathematical convenience.

Although arising in a very different way, the structure of the process in this *Example* is similar to that of the previous *Examples*. A biochemical reaction can be looked on as a program that accepts its reactants as inputs and produces its products as outputs. A molecule entering the system enables various possible sequences of reactions to occur. In this case, a carbon atom in a leucine molecule may be incorporated into and then recovered from protein any number of times before it is metabolized and leaves the system as CO_2.

What one observes are population statistics, namely the quantity or concentration of labeled molecules in any of the three pools as a function of time. From these, one wishes to infer other statistics, the relative rates of flow between the pools. These *population processes* are related to the *particle processes*, in which individual molecules traverse the system; for a molecule in any pool, there is a probability distribution on the length of time it takes to leave the pool and on which of the possible reactions will make it do so. The figure is a picture of the path followed by an individual molecule.

The questions that arise are also related to those of the preceding *Examples*. If one attempts to follow a system in which the particle process has many pools and many paths by using a simplified model, is it possible to characterize precisely the extent to which the conclusions drawn are still valid? How are the populations statistics and the particle statistics related? Can one predict the effects of control?

In this chapter we shall give a survey of results, illustrated by examples, and refer the reader to the category theory literature for standard results. Category theory (Mac Lane, 1971) discovered by Eilenberg and Mac Lane, has been used, particularly in work deriving from Lawvere, both explicitly (Lambek & Scott, 1986; Bell, 1988), and implicitly (Barr & Wells, 1985), to provide a foundation for logic. There is an accessible presentation in (Goldblatt, 1984). Of equal importance to the present work are the automata theory books (Eilenberg, 1974, 1976).

2. FORMALIZATION

We remarked above that PLOTPTS can be regarded abstractly as a function that maps inputs in certain sets—namely the sets MINMAX, SCREEN, and VALS containing all possible values of the sequences /MINMAX/, /SCREEN/, and /VALS/—into outputs in the set PLOTS containing the values of /PLOTS/. We refer to such a set comprising the possible values of a specified input or output of a computational process as a *type* and to its elements as *states*.

The inputs to PLOTPTS are themselves established as outputs of other processes: /MINMAX/ is either entered by the nurse or stored as part of the process that interacts with her to define the plot; /SCREEN/ is the output of some system program; and /VALS/ comes from the data retrieval process. These processes, in turn, require inputs that are outputs of still other processes. The structure of these output-input relations determines the synchronization requirements of the system of processes: a process may proceed when it has all the inputs it needs, and it may do so concurrently with any other processes that are similarly enabled. For example, the subprocesses of PLOTPTS may compute the two outputs XPLOT and YPLOT in /PLOT/ in either order, or simultaneously, provided only that preceding processes have furnished appropriate inputs in /MINMAX/, /SCREEN/, and /VALS/.

In general, one sees the computational network as a system of types and processes, or more abstractly as a system of sets and functions, whose structure one wishes to investigate algebraically. A language for doing so is (Coleman, 1989) *category theory*.

Example 4: A Simple, If Artificial, Network And a Model Of It

The real examples described above are, in different ways, too simple or too complex to serve as useful running examples for the mathematics about to be developed. The reader will perhaps excuse us for introducing two artificial examples (numbers 4 and 6) that we shall keep returning to.

Example 4A

Network A has three basic processes f, g, and h. As in *Example 1*, these can be thought of as computer programs, but, as in *Example 3*, they need not be. The possible inputs to f are **a, b** and **c,** which states constitute the type $X = \{\mathbf{a}, \mathbf{b}, \mathbf{c}\}$. The outputs of f are in the type $Y = \{\mathbf{p}, \mathbf{q}, \mathbf{r}\}$. The process g maps Y to X, and h maps Y to $Z = \{\mathbf{s}, \mathbf{t}\}$. These processes are shown in the diagram,

$$X \underset{g}{\overset{f}{\rightleftarrows}} Y \overset{h}{\rightarrow} Z.$$

The actions of f, g, and h are given by the tables,

$\mathbf{x} \in X$	$\mathbf{x}f \in Y$
a	**p**
b	**q**
c	**r**

,

$\mathbf{y} \in Y$	$\mathbf{y}g \in X$	$\mathbf{y}h \in Z$
p	**b**	**s**
q	**b**	**t**
r	**b**	**s**

(Note that we write the argument to the left of the function, with or without parentheses. While this convention is "counterintuitive" at first, it is very helpful when it comes to dealing with extended sequences of processes.) A has not only the basic processes f, g, and h, but also all the sequences that can be gotten by iterating them: fh, fg, gf, $fgfh$, $fgfgfh$, and so on.

Example 4B

Network B is simpler. It has only two types, $I = \{\mathbf{d},\mathbf{e}\}$ and $J = \{\mathbf{u},\mathbf{v}\}$, and two processes $m,n: I \rightarrow J$,

$$I \underset{n}{\overset{m}{\rightrightarrows}} J.$$

These are given by the table,

$\mathbf{i} \in I$	$\mathbf{i}m \in J$	$\mathbf{i}n \in J$
d	**u**	**v**
e	**v**	**v**

B has only the basic processes m and n; they cannot be iterated.

Hidden inside network A is a copy of the structure of network B. To see this, one thinks of the states of B as relabelings of states of A. Let ϕ be the function that does this: it maps X to I by $\mathbf{a}\phi = \mathbf{c}\phi = \mathbf{d}$, $\mathbf{b}\phi = \mathbf{e}$, and it maps Z to J by $\mathbf{s}\phi = \mathbf{u}$, $\mathbf{t}\phi = \mathbf{v}$. With this relabeling, the process *fh* of *A* acts on *X* in the same way that the process *m* of *B* acts on *I*:

$\mathbf{x}\phi m = \mathbf{x}fh\phi$, for $\mathbf{x} \in X$.

Thus *fh covers m*. The same relabeling also allows *fgfh* to cover *n*. More intuitively: to discover the effect of a process in *B* on a state $\mathbf{i} \in I$, find a state $\mathbf{x} \in X$ that $\mathbf{i}$ labels, do the corresponding process in *A*, and then relabel again to find the result in *J*.

Although the network doesn't necessarily carry with it any specification of probabilities, still it seems clear from a probabilistic point of view that, although *A* may iterate *fg* a number of times, eventually all paths will end in *Z*, except in the trivial case that the probability of *h* is zero. For the purpose of giving the final type, and state, of the process, *B* is perfectly adequate. Actually, in this particular example, the relation between *A* and *B* is very close: although *A* has many sequences of processes starting from *X* and ending in *Z*, including (f,h), (f,g,f,h), (f,g,f,g,f,h), and so on, the first of these computes the function *fh*, which covers *m*, and all the rest compute *fgfh*, which covers *n*.

A is in every way more complex than *B*—it has more types, more states, and more processes—yet contained in it is a copy of *B* that does not mislead us as long as we interpret it consistently. As suggested in the introduction, the basic link between networks is semantic. One can think of *B* as a *language*, in a generalized sense, describing *A*, or of *A* as a *model* of *B*. The methods just described give a semantic interpretation of *B* in *A*.

We can apply this in various senses to begin structuring answers to the questions in the introduction. The behavior of *A* can be partially analyzed using the more tractable *B*. In a different application, *B* might be a subnet in a system of networks. A designer could specify that it is permissible for *B* to be replaced by *A* provided that *A* models *B*. Similarly, two heterogeneous processes attempting to join in a distributed computation might explain themselves to each other by explaining that, and how, they are both models of some generally understood process *B*.

With this in mind, we can restate the questions from the introduction in a somewhat more formal way.

- In a relatively simple network *A*, it is intuitively obvious that the behavior of processes starting from *X* and ending in *Z* is $(fg)^*fh$, where $(fg)^*$ denotes zero or more repetitions of *fg*. This way of specifying the behavior of *A* is helpful since it reduces the infinite set of paths to a specification given combinatorially in terms of the finite data *fg* and *fh*. Can one find efficient, or enlightening, methods of stating the behavior of a general network?
- How can one formulate the notion of model in a more general setting?

- Can one state theorems predicting properties of a network based on the fact that it has a model in, or is a model of, some other network?
- How can one extend this machinery to describe not only the abstract schema according to which an individual process might develop but how a population of particles at different stages of the process actually do develop and interact?
- Whenever A is in Y, there is a possibility of g or h, and whenever B is in I there is a possibility of m or n. In cases where a probability distribution can be assigned to such possibilities, can our analysis be extended to help find probabilities describing the development of particles or of populations?
- In cases where control can be used to influence these possibilities, can one help to develop rational strategies?

The mathematics in the remainder of this chapter have been assembled in order to begin answering these questions.

3. SCHEMATA

Although the objects of many categories are abstract algebraic systems, a paradigm example (Mac Lane, 1971, sec. I.3; Goldblatt, 1984, sec. 2.3) of a category is **Set,** the category of sets. It contains *objects,* namely sets, and *arrows* or *morphisms,* namely ordinary functions between sets. An arrow goes from its *domain* to its *codomain.* The objects and arrows are required to display a behavior that is natural to sets and functions. For each object S, there is an *identity arrow* ${}_S1$, and for suitable pairs of arrows $g : R \to S$ and $f : S \to T$ there is the *composition* $gf : R \to T$. That is to say that the following diagram *commutes.*

$$\begin{array}{ccc} R & \xrightarrow{g} & S \\ {\scriptstyle gf}\downarrow & \swarrow {\scriptstyle f} & \\ T & & \end{array}$$

Note again that we write gf for $f \circ g$. These functions obey the obvious rules,

$${}_R1\, g = g = g\, {}_S1,$$

and, for a third function $h : P \to R$,

$$h(gf) = (hg)f.$$

More generally, a *category* **C** is any such system of objects and arrows that obeys these same rules (Mac Lane, 1971, sec. I.3; Goldblatt, 1984, sec. 2.3). The objects might be sets specified to have some structure, and the arrows functions that preserve that structure—for example, the objects might be vector spaces and the arrows linear mappings—or the category might just be a system of letters and arrows.

Sometimes an arrow is invertible, in the sense that there is another arrow that cancels its effect (Mac Lane, 1971, sec. I.5; Goldblatt, 1984, sec. 3.3). In the diagram

$$R \underset{g}{\overset{f}{\rightleftarrows}} S,$$

if $fg = {}_R1$ and $gf = {}_S1$, then f and g are *inverse* to each other, and they are *iso,* or *isomorphisms.* Many times it is only possible or desirable to define an object R up to isomorphism (Goldblatt, 1984, sec. 3.4).

The *product* $R \times S$ of two sets R, S comes with two *projections,* ${}_Rp : R \times S \rightarrow R$ and ${}_Sp : R \times S \rightarrow S$ onto the components R and S (Mac Lane, 1971, sec. III.4; Goldblatt, 1984, sec. 3.8). These have a *universal property,* namely that every other pair of arrows ${}_Rq : T \rightarrow R$ and ${}_Sq : T \rightarrow S$ corresponds uniquely to an arrow ${}_Rq \times {}_Sq : T \rightarrow R \times S$:

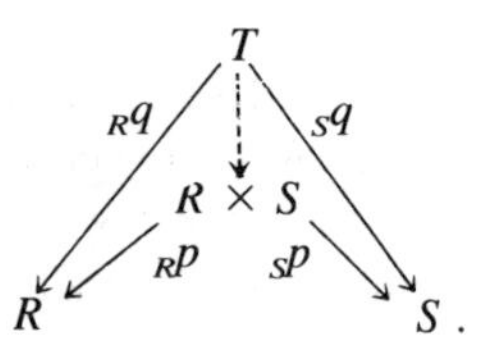

In **Set,** the obvious candidate for $R \times S$ is the set containing all pairs (r,s) of elements $r \in R$ and $s \in S$. Actually any other set isomorphic to this one will enjoy the same universal property (as can be seen by applying the definition of isomorphism) and, in this sense, will do just as well. The usual policy is to speak of any of these isomorphic objects as "the product of R and S." In a category other than **Set,** one lets satisfaction of the universal property be the defining property of the product.

The sets and functions given in *Example 4* constitute a fragment of **Set,** as do those of *Example 1*. To understand *Example 3* in this way, one thinks of the boxes in the figure as sets, each with a single element, and the arrows as the unique functions between those sets. Any of these *Examples* could be made into a subcategory of **Set,** but we shall use a more general method in order to pick out the fragment of **Set** that any network embodies.

A *functor* is an arrow between two categories that preserves their structure (Mac Lane, 1971, sec. I.3; Goldblatt, 1984, sec. 9.1). A functor from a category **C** to a category **D** is a mapping F between them, carrying objects $c \in \mathbf{C}$ to objects $cF \in \mathbf{D}$ and arrows $f \in \mathbf{C}$ to arrows $fF \in \mathbf{D}$. The functor obeys the rules:

$$({}_c1)F = {}_{cF}1,$$

for all $c \in \mathbf{C}$, and

$$(gf)F = (g)F\ (f)F,$$

for all composable $f, g \in \mathbf{C}$.

Example 4 (Continued)

The diagram

$$x \underset{g}{\overset{f}{\rightleftarrows}} y \overset{h}{\rightarrow} z$$

depicts a category **A**, where in all such diagrams it is understood that any identity arrows or compositions needed to make the diagram a category and omitted for legibility are to be supplied. For *Example 4A,* there is a functor $A : \mathbf{A} \rightarrow \mathbf{Set}$ that sends x to X, y to Y, and z to Z, as well as f to f, g to g, and h to h. We call such a functor $C : \mathbf{C} \rightarrow \mathbf{Set}$ a *schema*. The schema shows how a certain structure, embodied in **C**, is realized in **Set**.

Similarly, there is an evident schema B, sending **B**

$$i \underset{n}{\overset{m}{\rightrightarrows}} j$$

to **Set** and defining the network of *Example* 4B.

Example 5: Automata

It may be helpful to insert a word of explanation for the reader familiar with automata theory. Although the diagrams in the previous *Example* look like automata, they are not: the objects are not states, but sets of states, and the set of arrows corresponds bijectively to the set of arrow names. The following figure represents *Example 4A* as an automaton.

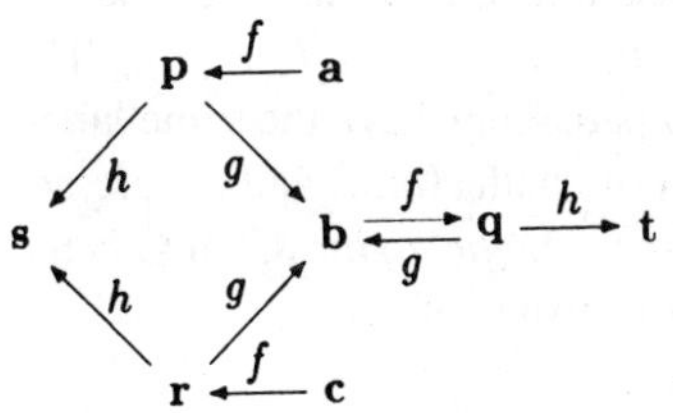

If one were to represent a complete, deterministic automaton—one in which each input gives exactly one output in each state—as a schema, its category would have one object S, corresponding to the set of states, and, for each input of the automaton, an arrow having S as domain and codomain. In an incomplete automaton, if an input α has as its domain a subset ${}_{\alpha}D \subset S$ and as its codomain a subset ${}_{\alpha}C \subset S$ then one uses these sets as the objects. (It may be necessary also to include various *insertion* functions, showing which sets are subsets of which others.) This and other changes in point of view result in a number of differences of detail between the definitions and theorems that Eilenberg gives and the uses that we make of them.

4. THE PATH SPACE AND THE U-P DECOMPOSITION

For a network schema C of even moderate complexity, the path space can be an unwieldy, infinite object. One of our objects is to find a method for producing a finitistic description of the path space, a description that classifies all the paths into a finitely specified system of kinds. Eilenberg (1974, chap. IV) gives such a method for a finite automaton. This method, the *iterated unitary-prefix decomposition,* is easily generalized [8] to a schema with a finite number of types.

Example 6: A Schema and its Path Space

Example 4 is more complex in the internal structure of its types in the connections between them. We now introduce an example in which the opposite is true. Let the category **D** be generated by the diagram

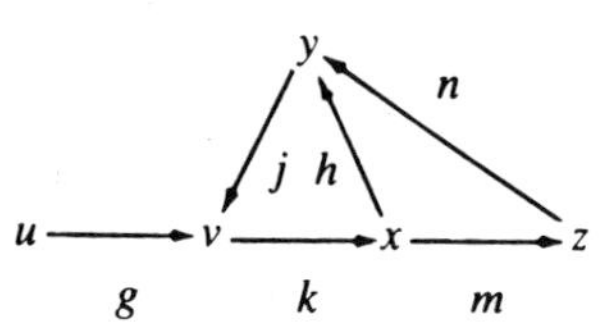

,

and $D : \mathbf{D} \to \mathbf{Set}$ be a schema based on **D.** Some sequences of arrow names, such as *gkh* and *nj,* are names of functions in the category **D,** while others, such as *hm* and *mnk* are nonsense. The general objective of many of the constructions described in this chapter is to characterize the set of names that make sense.

For any schema $C : \mathbf{C} \to \mathbf{Set}$, a *path* in **C** is a sequence $p = (f_1, f_2, \ldots, f_n)$, $n = 0, 1, 2, \ldots$ of nonidentity arrows of **C** such that the domain of f_i is the codomain of f_{i-1}, $i = 2, \ldots, n$. The *label* $|p|$ of p is the arrow $f_1 f_2 \ldots f_n$. The label of the empty path is the identity arrow. Two paths may have the same label; for example, mn may equal h as arrows in **D,** but the paths (m,n) and (h) are not the same. The set of all paths in **C** is the *path space*. The *behavior* $|\mathbf{C}|$ of **C** is the set of all labels of paths in **C.** It is just the set of arrows of **C.**

The schema C shows how the arrows of **C** act on the states. At this point, we are more concerned with an action that the arrows have on each other. In *Example 6,* one can think of n as acting on j, on the left, to form nj and on jk to form njk. Further, hjk acts on m to form $hjkm$ and on hjk to form $hjkhjk = (hjk)^2$. This is the first of several *multiplication* operations that we shall define.

A generic way of looking at multiplication operations is as follows. Let Σ be a finite set of letters. The set Σ^+ of all sequences of one or more letters in Σ, is a semigroup since two words $s,t \in \Sigma$ can be associatively multiplied by concatenating them. Let 1 be the empty sequence of letters. It acts as a unit for the multiplication, so $\Sigma^* = \Sigma^+ \cup \{1\}$ is a monoid, the *free* monoid generated by Σ. For $S,T \subset \Sigma^*$, we write ST for the set of all st with $s \in S$ and $t \in T$. We can use this to restate the problem of *Example 6* by setting $\Sigma = \{f,g,h,j,k,m\}$, letting concatenation represent function composition, and then noting that we are trying to characterize the subset, but not submonoid, $|\mathbf{D}| \subset \Sigma^*$. (To be more precise, we should recognize that $|\mathbf{D}|$ is only a subset of Σ^* after possibly identifying certain elements with others: it is a subset of a *quotient* of Σ^*.)

The most elementary way to begin decomposing a set $|\mathbf{C}|$ is to sort out the arrows in it according to their domain and codomain. For objects d,e of **C,** ${}_d|\mathbf{C}| \subset |\mathbf{C}|$ is the set of all labels of paths starting at d, and $|\mathbf{C}|_e \subset |\mathbf{C}|$ is the set of all labels of paths ending at e. Their intersection ${}_d|\mathbf{C}| \cap |\mathbf{C}|_e$ is ${}_d|\mathbf{C}|_e$. Note that the sets ${}_d|\mathbf{C}|_e$, as d and e range over all the objects of **C,** form a partition of $|\mathbf{C}|$.

Next, it is evident that any $s \in {}_d|\mathbf{C}|_e$ can be uniquely factored (Eilenberg, 1974, chap. IV, p. 3) as $s = pt$, where p labels a path from d to e that only touches e once, and t labels a closed path starting and ending at e and going through it any number of times. In *Example 6,* the path $s = mn(jkh)(jkmn) \in {}_x|\mathbf{D}|_y$ is so decomposed with $p = mn$ and $t = (jkh)(jkmn)$. In general, the set ${}_d|\mathbf{C}|_e$ can be decomposed as

$${}_d|\mathbf{C}|_e = PM,$$

where $M = {}_e|\mathbf{C}|_e$ is an example of what Eilenberg calls (1974, chap. IV, p. 3) a *unitary monoid* and P is a *prefix.* Thus he calls this (1974, chap. IV, p. 4) the *unitary-prefix* or *u-p decomposition.*

The u-p decomposition can (Eilenberg, 1974, chap. IV) be made more useful by further analysis. First, it can be iterated. In *Example 6,* all p in the prefix of ${}_x|\mathbf{D}|_y$ must terminate with h or n. Divide into two cases. The domain of n is z, so perform the u-p decomposition on the part of ${}_x|\mathbf{D}|_z$ that does not go through y. Thus, the part of ${}_x|\mathbf{D}|_y$ whose prefix ends in n is $P_1\ M_1\ n\ M$. Iterating one step further gives a *u-p monomial,*

$$M_2\ m\ M_1\ n\ M.$$

The union of the monomials gotten in this way is (Eilenberg, 1974, chap. IV, p. 6) the *iterated u-p decomposition* of ${}_x|\mathbf{D}|_y$.

Next, the unitary monoids ${}_e|\mathbf{C}|_e$ are freely generated from a *base* (Eilenberg, 1974, chap. IV, p. 5), a subset B such that any element s of ${}_e|\mathbf{C}|_e$ can be decomposed uniquely as $s = b_1 \ldots b_k$ with the $b_i \in B$. In our applications the b_i are just the simple closed paths from e to e. In *Example 6*, ${}_y|\mathbf{D}|_y$ has the base $B = \{jkh, jkmn\}$ and thus

$${}_y|\mathbf{D}|_y = \{jkh, jkmn\}^*.$$

Further,

$${}_z|\mathbf{D}|_z = \{njk(hjk)^*m\}^*.$$

However, all of these paths go through y and so M_1 is empty. Lastly,

$${}_x|\mathbf{D}|_x = \{hjk, mnjk\}^*.$$

However, all of these go through y and some also go through z and so M_2 is also empty. Inserting these values in the iterated u-p decomposition gives,

$${}_x|\mathbf{D}|_y = mn\{jkh, jkmn\}^* \cup h\{jkh, jkmn\}^*.$$

5. MODELS

In *Example 4*, there were two parts to the construction that we gave to make A a model of B: A function ϕ that mapped states of A to states of B, and another function (to which we gave no name) that mapped each process in B to a process in A that covered it. More generally, a model may have either or both of these parts. We now address them, one at a time.

Let $C : \mathbf{C} \to \mathbf{Set}$ be a schema, and let $\mathbf{C}'$ be a category. An *arrow model* is a functor $F : \mathbf{C}' \to \mathbf{C}$. Since functors can be composed, such a model induces a schema $FC : \mathbf{C}' \to \mathbf{Set}$.

$$\begin{array}{ccc} & C & \\ \mathbf{C} & \rightarrow & \mathbf{Set} \\ F \downarrow & \nearrow FC & \\ \mathbf{C}' & & \end{array}$$

In *Example 4*, part of the model was given implicitly by specifying a functor $G : \mathbf{B} \to \mathbf{A}$, sending i to x and j to z, and also m to fh and n to $fgfh$. Using only this part of the model induces a schema GA, different from either A or B, in which i corresponds to $X = \{\mathbf{a},\mathbf{b},\mathbf{c}\}$ and j corresponds to $Z = \{\mathbf{s},\mathbf{t}\}$.

A *natural transformation* is (Mac Lane, 1971, sec. I.4, Goldblatt, 1984, sec. 9.2) a way of converting one functor $F : \mathbf{C} \to \mathbf{D}$ into another one $G : \mathbf{C} \to \mathbf{D}$ between the same categories. The way to do this is by supplying a set of arrows in **D** that drag the image of F across to the image of G. For each $r \in \mathbf{C}$ one gives an arrow ${}_r\alpha$: $rF \to rG$ in **D.** This is to be done in such a way that applying these functions to the images rF and sF of the domain and the range of any arrow $f : r \to s$ of **C** converts fF to fG. Thus, ${}_r\alpha\, fG = fF\, {}_s\alpha$:

$$\begin{array}{ccc} & fF & \\ rF & \rightarrow & sF \\ {}_r\alpha \downarrow & & \downarrow {}_s\alpha \\ rG & \rightarrow & sG \\ & fG & \end{array}$$

One writes this as $\alpha : F \dot{\to} G$.

Let $C : \mathbf{C} \to \mathbf{Set}$ and $C' : \mathbf{C} \to \mathbf{Set}$ be schemata. A *state model* of C' in C is a natural transformation $\alpha : C \dot{\to} C'$,

$$\begin{array}{ccc} & C & \\ \mathbf{C} & \rightarrow & \mathbf{Set} \\ C' & \searrow & \downarrow \alpha \\ & & \mathbf{Set}\ . \end{array}$$

Finally, we combine these two notions of model. A *model* $M = \langle F,\alpha\rangle$ of $C' : \mathbf{C}' \to \mathbf{Set}$ in $C : \mathbf{C} \to \mathbf{Set}$ is given by a functor $F : \mathbf{C}' \to \mathbf{C}$, and a natural transformation $\alpha : FC \dot{\to} C'$,

$$\begin{array}{ccc} & C & \\ \mathbf{C} & \rightarrow & \mathbf{Set} \\ \mathrm{F} \uparrow & & \downarrow \alpha \\ \mathbf{C}' & \rightarrow & \mathbf{Set} \\ & C' & \end{array}$$

In *Example 4,* the model was given by the functor $G : \mathbf{B} \to \mathbf{A}$, sending i to x and j to z, and also m to fh and n to $fgfh$, and by a natural transformation α whose components ${}_x\alpha$ and ${}_z\alpha$ were implicitly given in the function ϕ.

6. CONSTRUCTIONS IN THE PATH SPACE

Thus far, we have formalized the notion of a network of processes by defining 'schema,' we have looked at a tool for characterizing the path space of a schema, and we have formalized the way in which one schema can describe another by defining 'model.' In the next section we shall look more carefully at the semantics of the modeling relationship; as suggested in the introduction, this is the key to answering the questions we raised there. The object of the present section is to build machinery that will prepare us for that work.

To answer the questions before us concerning the schema $C : \mathbf{C} \to \mathbf{Set}$, the individuals populating it, and its relations to other schemata that it models or is modeled by, we shall need to construct some standard representations of the set of sequences of processes that it allows and the set $|\mathbf{C}|$ of functions that it computes.

6.1. The Topos Set$^{\mathbf{C}}$

We first pause to notice that, for a fixed category **C,** the set of all schemata $C : \mathbf{C} \to \mathbf{Set}$ is itself (Mac Lane, 1971, sec. II.4; Goldblatt, 1984, sec. 9.3) the set of objects of a special kind of category with well-known properties, some of which will prove helpful to us. The *functor category* $\mathbf{Set}^{\mathbf{C}}$ has as objects all the functors from **C** to **Set.** The arrows are the natural transformations between the functors. (Thus, a state model, as described above, is just an arrow in this category.) This fits the definition of category, since there is an identity natural transformation $1_C : C \dot{\to} C$, and for any two natural transformations $\alpha : C \dot{\to} C'$ and $\beta : C' \dot{\to} C''$ there is an associative composition $\gamma : C \dot{\to} C''$, given by ${}_c\gamma = {}_c\alpha\, {}_c\beta$ for $c \in \mathbf{C}$.

Such a functor category is (Goldblatt, 1984, sec. 9.3) an example of a *topos,* a type of category specified abstractly by certain axioms (Goldblatt, 1984, sec. 4.3; Johnstone, 1977; Barr & Wells, 1985; Lambek & Scott, 1986; Bell, 1988). (The discovery of topos theory is due to Lawvere and Tierney.) We shall not take the abstract approach, since the only topoi that we shall encounter are the concrete ones $\mathbf{Set}^{\mathbf{C}}$. We shall be using some constructions and results for these that are part of standard topos theory. However, we caution the reader that $\mathbf{Set}^{\mathbf{C}}$ also has some special properties not enjoyed by the general topos.

In the following we shall assume that the schema $C : \mathbf{C} \to \mathbf{Set}$ is based on a finite category **C** given by a diagram like those for *Examples 4 and 6*. The arrows explicitly shown in the diagram have names forming a set $\Sigma_{\mathbf{C}}$, or just Σ, of letters. **C is assumed to be** the free category generated by the diagram (Mac Lane, 1971, sec. II.7). That is, its arrows are assumed to be the smallest subset $|\mathbf{C}|$ of Σ^*, the free monoid on Σ, that would make the diagram a category. In practice, one takes the given arrows, adds in the required identity arrows, and then adds in all legal compositions of arrows. (However, it should be borne in mind that as in *Example 4,* the functor C may cause two arrows not identical in **C** to mapped to the same arrow in **Set,** so that the image of **C** under C need not be free.)

6.2. Multiplication Operations

Our general object is to form standard representations of the schema $C : \mathbf{C} \to \mathbf{Set}$ by picking out certain features of the path space $|\mathbf{C}|$ of $\mathbf{C}$. We have already noted that a path $f : b \to c$ can act on a path $g : a \to b$ by composition to give $gf : a \to c$ and that this action can be represented algebraically as a multiplication operation. We need now to improve our terminology for describing such structures. In particular, we want to be able to talk about a path acting on a set of paths.

Since we have assumed that the arrows of $\mathbf{C}$ are among the words freely generated from the letters in Σ, we can define various operations on the set of arrows by specifying them just on Σ. Indeed, let Q be a set and Σ a finite alphabet, and let a multiplication $Q \times \Sigma \to Q$ be given in which the product of q and σ is written generically as $q\sigma$ for $q \in Q$ and $\sigma \in \Sigma$. This can (Eilenberg, 1974, sec. III.1) be extended algebraically to a multiplication $Q \times \Sigma^* \to Q$ by using the rules

$$q1 = q, \text{ and}$$

$$q(st) = (qs)t,$$

for $q \in Q$ and $s,t \in \Sigma^*$. Thus Q is made into a Σ-*module*. For $q \in Q$ and a subset $S \subset \Sigma^*$, one sets $qS = \{qs;\ s \in S\}$.

We shall be interested in the case where Q equals the set of all subsets of $(\Sigma_{\mathbf{C}})^*$, which set we denote by $\Psi_{\mathbf{C}}$ or Ψ. There are a number of possible multiplications $\Psi \times \Sigma \to \Psi$ aside from the one considered previously. First, we may restrict the product to words in $|\mathbf{C}|$. Define

$$\psi \cdot \sigma = \{s\sigma \in |\mathbf{C}|;\ s \in \psi\},$$

for $\psi \in \Psi$, $\sigma \in \Sigma$. Thus in *Example 4A*,

$$\{gf, gfgf\} \cdot h = \{gfh, gfgfh\},$$

$$\{fg, gf, gg\} \cdot h = \{gfh\}, \text{ and}$$

$$\{fh, hf\} \cdot h = \varnothing.$$

We identify a singleton $\{s\} \in \Psi$ with its element s. Thus, we write $fg \cdot f = fgf$ for $\{fg\} \cdot f = \{fgf\}$.

There is a multiplication that partially reverses the previous one. For $\psi \in \Psi$ and $\sigma \in \Sigma$, we define

$$\sigma^{-1}\psi = \{s \in |\mathbf{C}|;\ \sigma s \in \psi\}.$$

In *Example 4*,

$$f^{-1}\{fh, fgg, fgf, gf\} = \{h, gf\}.$$

This notation is not meant to imply that σ has an inverse in the monoid Σ^*, which it does not. We can use this to define a multiplication $\star$,

$$q \star \sigma = \sigma^{-1} q.$$

(Compare with Eilenberg (1974, sec. III.5) and Goldblatt (1984, sec. 9.3).

6.3. The Action Monoid M_C

The first of three standard representations that we shall give of the path space of the schema $C : \mathbf{C} \rightarrow \mathbf{Set}$ is $M_{\mathbf{C}}$, the action monoid, so called because it is a schema based on a category with a single object.

Extending the multiplication $\star$ to Σ^*, to get a function $\Psi \times \Sigma^* \rightarrow \Psi$, results in a function τ mapping each $s \in \Sigma^*$ to the function $\tau_s : \Psi \rightarrow \Psi$ that sends $\psi \in \Psi$ to $\psi\tau_s = \psi \star s$. We have $\tau_{st} = \tau_s\tau_t$, but if $st \in |\mathbf{C}|$ then $\tau_{st} = \bar{\emptyset}$, where $\bar{\emptyset} : \Psi \rightarrow \Psi$ is the constant function that sends every $\psi \in \Psi$ to the empty set. In the set of all functions $\Psi \rightarrow \Psi$ the image of Σ^* under τ is closed, and is thus a monoid, under function composition, and it equals the image of $|\mathbf{C}|$ together with $\bar{\emptyset}$. This monoid is represented as a category $\mathbf{M}$ with a single object and with an arrow for each element of the monoid. The functor $M : \mathbf{M} \rightarrow \mathbf{Set}$ that sends $\mathbf{M}$ to Ψ defines a schema $M_{\mathbf{C}}$ or M, the *action monoid* (Eilenberg, 1974, sec. III.10) of $C : \mathbf{C} \rightarrow \mathbf{Set}$. In fact, let F be the functor that sends each object $c \in \mathbf{C}$ to $\mathbf{M}$ and each arrow $s \in |\mathbf{C}|$ to τ_s. Then F defines a model of $\mathbf{C}$ in $\mathbf{M}$; it crushes the whole structure of $\mathbf{C}$ into a single-element category with the same behavior (apart from $\bar{\emptyset}$).

6.4. Ideals, Points, and the Topology They Define

The constructions that we shall want to present next involve consideration of the possible ways that a schema $C : \mathbf{C} \rightarrow \mathbf{Set}$ can develop given that it has already computed a particular function s. The set of such paths is $s \cdot |\mathbf{C}|$. More generally, one may not know that the initial segment is some particular function s, but only that it is in some specified set of functions. The set of possible developments is an example of what we shall shortly call an ideal. The structure of the set of all these ideals is intimately connected with the structure of the path space of the schema.

Viewed abstractly, these ideals form the set of open sets of a topology. While this topology is far from the usual examples, the topologies of subpaces of real or complex n-dimensional space, there are a number of advantages to recognizing the connection. First, it helps our intuition; just as the topological structure of a torus represents its geometry, the topological structure of a schema shows the degree to which its paths are related to, and can be transformed into, each other. Second, it happens that the ideals $s \cdot |\mathbf{C}|$ form a basis for the topology; this means that one can specify a transformation between schemata by specifying it on the basis. Third, in some applications one wants to attach probabilities, and even costs and rewards, to sets of paths; it is useful to recognize these functions as continuous maps between topological spaces.

Let $c \in \mathbf{C}$. A subset $S \subset {}_c|\mathbf{C}|$ is (Goldblatt, 1984, sec. 9.3) a *sieve* or *co-crible* or *right ideal* if $S \cdot |\mathbf{C}| = S$, so that S is closed under right composition with any arrow of $\mathbf{C}$. Thus, any path belonging to S, followed by any path in $\mathbf{C}$ that it can be followed by, results again in a path in S. We shall call such a set simply an *ideal* or, for emphasis, a *c-ideal*. In particular, ${}_c|\mathbf{C}|$ is a c-ideal, as is the empty set. For any $s \in |\mathbf{C}|$ whose domain is c, the set

$$\langle s \rangle = s \cdot |\mathbf{C}|$$

is the *principal c-ideal generated by s*. The ideal $\langle {}_c 1 \rangle = {}_c|\mathbf{C}|$. In *Example 6*, $\langle kh \rangle = kh_y|\mathbf{D}|$ is a principal v-ideal, containing kh, khj, $khjkh$, and so on.

Let $s,t \in {}_c|\mathbf{C}|$. If $t = sr$ for some r then we write $s < t$. This gives a partial order on ${}_c|\mathbf{C}|$. Note that

$$\langle t \rangle \subset \langle s \rangle \leftrightarrow s < t.$$

The union of two c-ideals, or of any set of c-ideals, is a c-ideal. In *Example 6*, $\langle kh \rangle \cup \langle km \rangle$ is a v-ideal, although it is not principal. The intersection of two c-ideals is a c-ideal. In *Example 6*, $\langle k \rangle \cap \langle km \rangle = \langle km \rangle$, while $\langle kh \rangle \cap \langle km \rangle = \emptyset$. For principal ideals, if $s < t$ then $\langle s \rangle \cap \langle t \rangle = \langle t \rangle$, but if neither s nor t is an initial segment of the other, then $\langle s \rangle \cap \langle t \rangle = \emptyset$. Arbitrary intersections are more subtle. In *Example* 6, for any finite p,

$$\bigcap_{i=0}^{p} jk((hjk)(hjmn))^i = \langle jk((hjk)(hjmn))^p \rangle,$$

but

$$\bigcap_{i=0}^{\infty} jk((hjk)(hjmn))^i = \emptyset.$$

There is no path $jk((hjk)(hjmn))^\infty$ whose principal ideal is the limit of the right-hand side.

The preceding two paragraphs suggest the following construction. Let I be some index set and let $x = \{x_i\}_{i \in I}$ be a subset of $_c|\mathbf{C}|$ that is totally ordered by the relation $<$ and further is maximal in the sense that it is a proper subset of no totally ordered set. We call such an x a *point* of $_c|\mathbf{C}|$. For *Example,* the point

$$y = \{j_k((hjk)(hjmn))^i\}_{i=0}^{\infty}$$

is the "missing path" of the last paragraph. (Actually, y does not, as given, define a point. There are many other y_i that would need to be included to make it do so, including 1_y, j, jkh, $jkhj$, . . ., $jk(hjk)(hjmn)j$ and so on. However there is only one point containing the given sequence, and we trust the reader to supply the rest of it.) Some points are finite—in *Example 4,* let

$$z = \{1_x, f, fg, fgf, fgfh\}.$$

Let X be the set of points of $_c|\mathbf{C}|$. For an ideal S of $_c|\mathbf{C}|$, we define S° to be the set of points that are consistent with it, the set of $x \in X$ such that for some $x_i \in x$ we have $\langle x_i \rangle \subset S$. For *Example*, $z \in \langle fg \rangle^\circ$, and y is in any of the $\langle jk((hjk)(hjmn))^p \rangle^\circ$. For convenience, we often ignore the distinction between S and S°, and we sloppily write $z \in \langle fg \rangle$, or $y \in \langle jk((hjk)(hjmn))^p \rangle$.

The results of the preceding three paragraphs can now be seen (Johnstone, 1982) as stating that the ideals of $_c|\mathbf{C}|$ are the open sets of a topology for the set X of points of $_c|\mathbf{C}|$, and that the principal c-ideals form a basis for that topology. (In *Example 4,* note that z is an isolated point, since there is an open set, $\langle fgfh \rangle$ containing it and no other point.) One can take this one step further by regarding the $_c|\mathbf{C}|$, for $c \in \mathbf{C}$, as components of a single topological space $|\mathbf{C}|$.

6.5. The Truth-Values Object $\Omega_\mathbf{C}$

The schema M gives a standard representation of the path space of the schema $C : \mathbf{C} \to \mathbf{Set}$ in a category with a single object. For other purposes, it is also useful to have a representation of the path space of C in $\mathbf{C}$. One defines (Goldblatt, 1984, sec. 9.3) the *truth-values object* to be a functor $\Omega_\mathbf{C}$ or $\Omega : \mathbf{C} \to \mathbf{Set}$; for each $c \in \mathbf{C}$, $c\Omega$ is the set of all c-ideals, and for each arrow $f : c \to d$, $f\Omega$ is the arrow that takes $S \in c\Omega$ to $S \star f = f^{-1}S \in d\Omega$. The truth-values object is closely involved in the structure of the topos $\mathbf{Set}^\mathbf{C}$.

Example 4 (Continued)

The schema $A : \mathbf{A} \to \mathbf{Set}$ is based on the category $\mathbf{A}$ whose objects are x, y and z. For x, the truth-values object $x\Omega$ contains principal ideals which we can list by using the iterated u-p decomposition to find their generators: for $p = 0, 1, \ldots,$ all the $\langle (fg)^p \rangle$, $\langle f(gf)^p \rangle$ and $\langle f(gf)^p h \rangle$. It also contains all unions of these and the empty set. (Note that $\langle {}_x 1 \rangle = \langle (fg)^0 \rangle$.)

For y, the truth-values object $y\Omega$ contains the principal ideals: for $p = 0, 1, \ldots,$ all the $\langle (gf)^p \rangle$, $\langle g(fg)^p \rangle$ and $\langle (gf)^p h \rangle$. It also contains all unions of these and the empty set.

For z, the truth-values object $z\Omega$ contains only $\langle {}_z 1 \rangle$ and the empty set.

These three sets $x\Omega$, $y\Omega$, and $z\Omega$, connected by the functions f, g and h constitute the image of the schema $\Omega_{\mathbf{A}} : \mathbf{A} \to \mathbf{Set},$

$$x\Omega \underset{g}{\overset{f}{\rightleftarrows}} y\Omega \overset{h}{\rightarrow} z\Omega\,.$$

Next we work towards explaining the terminology 'truth-values object.' Each topos has (Goldblatt, 1984, sec. 4.3) a *terminal object* 1, defined by the property that, for any object t in the topos, there is a unique arrow $!{:}t \to 1$. An arrow going in the other direction $1 \to t$ is [13, 4.2] an *element* of t. Indeed, although t may not be set, these elements behave in many ways like the elements of an ordinary set. For a topos that is a functor category $\mathbf{Set^C}$, the terminal object $1_{\mathbf{C}}$ is [13, 9.3] the functor that assigns to each $c \in \mathbf{C}$ a one-element set ${}_c 1$ and assigns to each arrow $f : c \to d$ *in* $\mathbf{C}$ the only possible function between the sets ${}_c 1$ and ${}_d 1$. For any schema $C : \mathbf{C} \to \mathbf{Set}$, a topos-theoretic element of C is an arrow $1 \to C$, a natural transformation $\alpha : 1 \dot{\to} C$. This amounts to a choice, for each $c \in \mathbf{C}$, of one set-theoretic element in cC. An element of $\Omega_{\mathbf{C}}$ is called a *truth-value*. For example, the truth-value *true* or $\top : 1 \to \Omega$ assigns (Goldblatt, 1984, secs. 4.5, 9.3) to each $c \in \mathbf{C}$ the ideal $\langle {}_c 1 \rangle = {}_c|\mathbf{C}|$. There are (Goldblatt, 1984, sec. 5.4) other possible truth-values, including *false* or $\bot$, and sometimes others.

Example 4 (Continued)

$\mathbf{Set^A}$ has three truth-values.

$\top$ has	${}_x\top = \langle {}_x 1 \rangle,$	${}_y\top = \langle {}_y 1 \rangle,$	and	${}_z\top = \langle {}_z 1 \rangle.$
$\bot$ has	${}_x\bot = \varnothing,$	${}_y\bot = \varnothing,$	and	${}_z\bot = \varnothing.$
¿ has	${}_x¿ = f(gf)^*h,$	${}_y¿ = (gf)^*h,$	and	${}_z¿ = \langle {}_z 1 \rangle.$

The reason that these are called "truth-values" has to do with the structure of the subobjects of a schema. Let $C : \mathbf{C} \to \mathbf{Set}$ and $C' : \mathbf{C} \to \mathbf{Set}$ be two schemata based on $\mathbf{C}$. C and C' are two elements of the functor category $\mathbf{Set^C}$, and a natural transformation between them is just an arrow $f : C' \to C$ of the category. This is illustrated by the special case in which $\mathbf{C}$ is the category • that has just a single object $*$ with an identity arrow. A functor $C : \bullet \to \mathbf{Set}$ is just a choice of a set $*C$ to be the image of $*$. For practical purposes the functor just is the set. A natural transformation from a second such functor $C' : \bullet \rightarrow$ **Set** to C is just an ordinary function f from the set $*C'$ to the set $*C$. Thus, in this special case, the functor category **Set**$^{\bullet}$ is essentially the same as **Set.** It is easier to understand many constructions in a general topos, by first seeing how they work in **Set**$^{\bullet}$.

In any category **C** an arrow $f : c \rightarrow d$ is *monic* (Mac Lane, 1971, sec. I.5; Goldblatt, 1984, sec. 3.1) if for any arrows $g,h : b \rightarrow c$ one has that $gf = hf \implies g = h$. In particular, in **Set** = **Set**$^{\bullet}$ an arrow is monic if and only if it is 1 : 1, and thus the domain of a monic arrow can be identified with the subset of its codomain that it maps to—one speaks loosely of a monic arrow as actually being a subset of its codomain. More generally, in the topos **Set**$^{\mathbf{C}}$ one calls a monic arrow f from $C' : \mathbf{C} \rightarrow$ **Set** to $C : \mathbf{C} \rightarrow$ **Set** a *subobject* (Mac Lane, 1971, sec. V.7; Goldblatt, 1984, sec. 4.1) of C. One sometimes refers to the domain of the monic arrow as the subobject, when the arrow itself is clear from context.

Example 4 (Continued)

Two examples of subobjects of the schema A are the schemata,

$$A' : \mathbf{A} \rightarrow \mathbf{Set} \quad \text{with } xA' = \emptyset,\ yA' = \emptyset, \quad \text{and } zA' = \{\mathrm{s}\},$$

$$A'' : \mathbf{A} \rightarrow \mathbf{Set} \quad \text{with } xA'' = \emptyset,\ yA'' = \emptyset, \quad \text{and } zA'' = \{\mathrm{t}\}.$$

The arrow $\top : 1 \rightarrow \Omega_{\mathrm{C}}$ is (Goldblatt, 1984, sec. 4.2) the *subobject classifier* of **Set**^{C}. In **Set** = **Set**$^{\bullet}$, any monic arrow $f: C' \rightarrow C$ is associated with a unique characteristic function $\chi_f: C \rightarrow \{0,1\}$. Any $x \in C$ either is or is not in the image of f, and χ_f maps x accordingly either to 1 or to 0. Similarly, in **Set**^{C}, the topos axioms guarantee (Goldblatt, 1984, sec. 4.3) that any monic arrow $f: C' \rightarrow C$ is associated with [13, 4.2] a characteristic function $\chi_f: C \rightarrow \Omega_{\mathrm{C}}$,

$$\begin{array}{ccc} & f & \\ C' & \rightarrow & C \\ !\downarrow & & \downarrow \chi_f \\ 1 & \rightarrow & \Omega \\ & \top & \end{array}$$

This function ${}_{\chi}f$ is actually a natural transformation from $C : \mathrm{C} \rightarrow$ Set to $\Omega : \mathbf{C} \rightarrow$ **Set.** For each object c of **C** the component of ${}_{\chi}f$ at c must specify a function from the set cC to the set $c\Omega$. For any element $x \in cC$ there are various possibilities: x may itself be in the image of the subobject C' under the arrow f, and thus any future evolution within the schema C will keep the descendants of x in the image of f; or x may not be in the image of f but it is possible for C to evolve in ways that will bring a descendant of x into the image of f; or no evolution of C can ever bring any descendant of x into the image of f. Thus ${}_X f$ sends $x \in cC$ to the ideal consisting of all arrows $g : c \to d$ in ${}_c|\mathbf{C}|$ whose working in C sends x into the image of f.

Example 4 (Continued)

The subobject A' of A induces a characteristic function $X' : A \dashrightarrow \Omega$. It has component functions ${}_xX'$, ${}_yX'$ and ${}_zX'$, as given by the tables,

$\mathbf{x} \in X$	$\mathbf{x}_x\chi' \in x\Omega$
a	$\{fh\}$
b	$\varnothing$
c	$\{fh\}$

$\mathbf{y} \in Y$	$\mathbf{y}_y\chi' \in y\Omega$
p	$\{h\}$
q	$\varnothing$
r	$\{h\}$

$\mathbf{z} \in Z$	$\mathbf{z}_z\chi' \in z\Omega$
s	$\langle_z 1\rangle$
t	$\varnothing$

is a natural transformation

In comparison, the subobject A'' of A induces a characteristic function χ' that has component functions ${}_x\chi''$, ${}_y\chi''$ and ${}_z\chi''$, as given by the tables,

$\mathbf{x} \in X$	$\mathbf{x}_x\chi'' \in x\Omega$
a	$f(gf)^+h$
b	$f(gf)^*h$
c	$f(gf)^+h$

$\mathbf{y} \in Y$	$\mathbf{y}_y\chi'' \in y\Omega$
p	$(gf)^+h$
q	$(gf)^*h$
r	$(gf)^+h$

$\mathbf{z} \in Z$	$\mathbf{z}_z\chi'' \in z\Omega$
s	$\varnothing$
t	$\langle_z 1\rangle$

This example illustrates two points: not only does $\mathbf{x}_x X$ show us, as always, what it would take to bring $\mathbf{x}$ into the corresponding subobject; but in this particular example the subobjects A' and A'' represent the two possible terminal states of the schema A, and thus their characteristic functions "partition" the path space $|\mathbf{A}|$ accordingly. Note that, for example, $\mathbf{a}_x X' \cup \mathbf{a}_x X'' = {}_x|\mathbf{A}|$. The fact that this is literally true is due to peculiarities of the example; the fact that it is figuratively true has a much more general meaning.

6.6. The Frame $E_\mathbf{C}$

To each schema $C : \mathbf{C} \to \mathbf{Set}$ we have associated two further schemata, the action monoid $M_\mathbf{C} : \mathbf{M_C} \to \mathbf{Set}$ and the truth-values object $\Omega_\mathbf{C} : \mathbf{C} \to \mathbf{Set}.$ We now introduce a third such schema, the *frame* $E_\mathbf{C} : \mathbf{E_C} \to \mathbf{Set}.$ Intuitively, this schema is to represent all the possible arrows of $\mathbf{C},$ with an arrow g between two arrows f and h if and only if $h = fg$. Thus E spreads out the path space of $\mathbf{C}$ in a schema that has arrows showing how one path is turned into another.

Example 4 (Continued)

The diagram

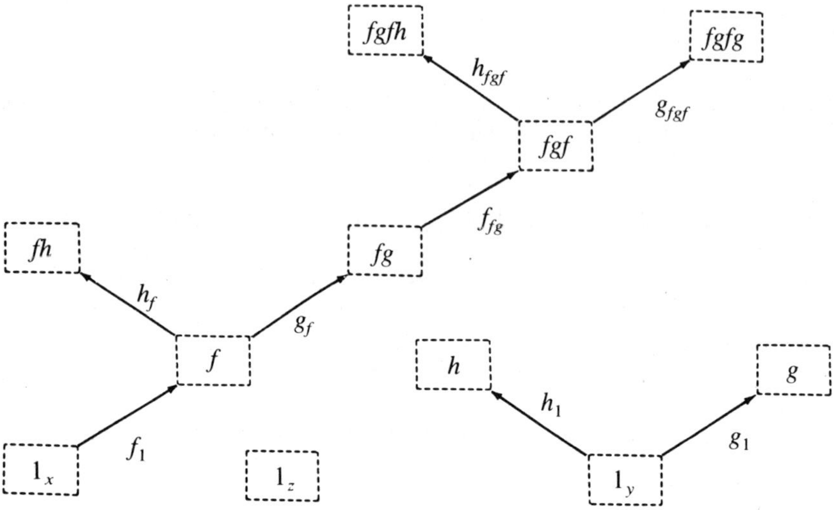

shows part of $\mathbf{E_A}$—the rest of it continues branching indefinitely from g and $fgfg$ toward the upper right.

The underlying set of **E** is $|\mathbf{C}|$. For each arrow $f : c \to d$ in $|\mathbf{C}|$ make a distinct copy f_g for each arrow $g \in |\mathbf{C}|_c$, and take it as an arrow $f_g : g \to gf$ of **E**. Then **E** is the free category generated by these arrows.

Next, we must define the functor $E : \mathbf{E} \to \mathbf{Set}$. For each object f of **E** let $(f)E = \{f\}$, and for an arrow $g_f : f \to fg$ of **E** let $(g_f)E$ be the only possible mapping between the singletons $\{f\}$ and $\{g\}$.

There is at most one arrow between any two objects of **E**, and in fact there is an arrow $f \to h$ if and only if $f < h$. Thus, **E** is partially ordered, and it inherits the whole structure of $|\mathbf{C}|$.

There is also a functor $H : \mathbf{E} \to \mathbf{C}$ that folds the whole frame back up into **C**. For each object $f : c \to d$ in **E**, let $(f)H = d$. For each arrow $g_f : f \to fg$ of **E**, let $(g_f)H = g$.

6.7. The Sequel C_x of the State x

We have looked at a number of constructions designed to represent the paths in the schema $C : \mathbf{C} \to \mathbf{Set}$. Most of them have depended on the category **C** rather than the functor C that embeds **C** in **Set**. Let c be an object of **C** and let $\mathbf{x} \in cC$.

We want to look at the possible sequences of states that the schema can visit starting from the state **x.**

For many of the examples we have looked at, **C** is a free category with infinitely many arrows, but C sends them into finitely many arrows in **Set.** In fact, if the number of states is finite it must do so. One obtains different pictures of this, depending on the starting state. We define the *sequel* of **x** to be the category $\mathbf{C_x}$ that is obtained from **C** by deleting all objects d for which there are no arrows $h : c \to d$, and then identifying two arrows $f,g : d \to e$ if $\mathbf{x}(hf)C = \mathbf{x}(hg)C$ for all $h : c \to d$.

Example 4 (Continued)

In the category **A,** the only arrows that can be iterated are f and g. However, $(gfg)A = gA$, and so the complete set of arrows in the image of A is $\{{}_x1, {}_y1, {}_z1, f, g, h, fg, gf, fh, gfh, fgf, fgfh\}$. These, or their preimages, are the arrows of $\mathbf{A_a} = \mathbf{A_c}$. Somewhat smaller is $\mathbf{A_p} = \mathbf{A_r}$, in which $fg = {}_x1$, and so $fgf = f$ and $fgfh = fh$. In $\mathbf{A_b} = \mathbf{A_q}$, one has further that $gf = {}_y1$, and so $gfh = h$. Finally $\mathbf{A_s} = \mathbf{A_t}$ has only ${}_z1$.

These four categories can be modeled in preorder categories, ones that have (Mac Lane, 1971, sec. I.2; Goldblatt, 1984, sec. 2.5) for objects c,c' at most one arrow $c \to c'$. First, the category

$$\begin{array}{ccccccccc} & & \mathbf{s} & & & & & & \\ & & h_1 \uparrow & & & f_2 & & & \\ \mathbf{a} & \to & \mathbf{p} & \to & \mathbf{b} & \rightleftarrows & \mathbf{q} & \to & \mathbf{t} \\ & f_1 & & g_1 & & g_2 & & h_2 & \end{array}$$

can be mapped into $\mathbf{A_a}$ by the functor that sends a state into its type and forgets the subscripts of arrows. Similarly, the three categories

$$\begin{array}{ccccccc} \mathbf{s} & & & & & & \\ h_1 \uparrow & & & f_2 & & & \\ \mathbf{p} & \to & \mathbf{b} & \rightleftarrows & \mathbf{q} & \to & \mathbf{t} \\ & g_1 & & g_2 & & h_2 & \end{array} \qquad \begin{array}{ccccc} & f_2 & & & \\ \mathbf{b} & \rightleftarrows & \mathbf{q} & \to & \mathbf{t} \\ & g_2 & & h_2 & \end{array} \qquad \mathbf{t}$$

can be mapped into $\mathbf{A_p}$, $\mathbf{A_b}$, and $\mathbf{A_s}$, respectively.

All this can be taken one step further. There is a functor from the partial order

$$\mathbf{A_a} \xrightarrow{f} \mathbf{A_p} \xrightarrow{gf} \mathbf{A_b} \xrightarrow{h} \mathbf{A_s}$$

to **A**. It sends $\mathbf{A_a}$ to x; $\mathbf{A_p}, \mathbf{A_b}$ to y; and $\mathbf{A_s}$ to z.

6.8. Developments

We shall assume in all that follows that infinitely many transitions cannot take place in finite time. Thus if a schema starts in a certain state and one observes it for a finite time, one finds that it has developed more or less. One may then observe it for some further time to find out more of its history. Let $C:\mathbf{C} \to \mathbf{Set}$ be a schema with $\mathbf{C}$ a free category on a set $\Sigma_{\mathbf{C}}$ of basis arrows. A *development* of $\mathbf{C}$ is a functor (and thus an arrow model) from a finite totally ordered category $C_1:\mathbf{C_1} \to \mathbf{C}$ that maps basis arrows in $\Sigma_{\mathbf{C}_1}$ to basis arrows in $\Sigma_{\mathbf{C}}$. The development induces a schema $C_1C:\mathbf{C_1} \to \mathbf{Set}$.

Example 4 (continued)

The categories $\mathbf{A_1}$,

$$x_1 \xrightarrow{f_1} y_1 \xrightarrow{g_1} x_2 \xrightarrow{f_2} y_2 \xrightarrow{g_2} x_3\,,$$

and $\mathbf{A_2}$,

$$y_1 \xrightarrow{g_1} x_1 \xrightarrow{f_1} y_2 \xrightarrow{h_1} z_1\,.$$

are both developments of $\mathbf{A}$. The functors A_1 and A_2 are the obvious ones that just forget the subscripts.

It is evident that a development of C corresponds to a unique path of C and thus to a unique object in $\mathbf{E_C}$. In fact, if one identifies two developments that differ from each other solely by the insertion or deletion of identity arrows, then this correspondence is bijective. In a sense, the set of developments just is $\mathbf{E}$, complete with arrows, and we shall sometimes so speak. But there is a difference. $\mathbf{C}_1$ is a category, and thus one can perform the same constructions on it as on $\mathbf{C}$. In particular, the schemata C_lC and $\Omega_{\mathbf{C}}1$ are important.

7. SEMANTICS

Example 7: The Trolley Company

We now begin to assemble these ideas into a formal logic of processes in a network. To do so, we need an example (Coleman, 1990a) that is not yet completely realistic, but more complex and more realistic than *Examples 4* and *6*. The reader is encouraged to see it as a kind of antique, and certainly non-electronic, version of *Example 1*.

The International Railway Company (IRC) provides trolley service in Buffalo, New York. Its route map can be represented by a schema $R : \mathbf{R} \rightarrow \mathbf{Set}$, where $\mathbf{R}$ is depicted in the diagram,

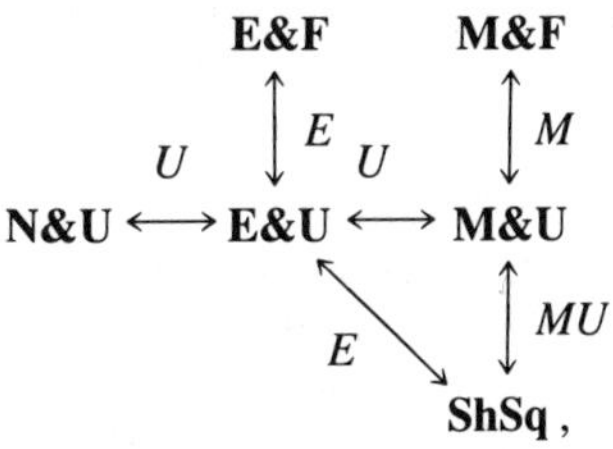

and R maps the objects of $\mathbf{R}$ to singleton sets consisting of certain intersections of Main, Elmwood, Niagara, Utica, and Ferry streets, and also Shelton Square, where the IRC's headquarters are and where all routes start. The arrows of $\mathbf{R}$ fall into families, corresponding to three routes, Main, Elmwood, and Utica, whose categories are,

$$\mathrm{R}_M: \quad \mathbf{ShSq} \underset{M_{i1}}{\overset{M_{o0}}{\rightleftarrows}} \mathbf{M\&U} \underset{M_{i0}}{\overset{M_{o1}}{\rightleftarrows}} \mathbf{M\&F} \quad ,$$

$$\mathbf{R}_E: \quad \mathbf{ShSq} \underset{E_{i1}}{\overset{E_{o0}}{\rightleftarrows}} \mathbf{E\&U} \underset{E_{i0}}{\overset{E_{o1}}{\rightleftarrows}} \mathbf{E\&F} \quad ,$$

$$\mathbf{R}_U: \quad \mathbf{ShSq} \underset{U_{i2}}{\overset{U_{o0}}{\rightleftarrows}} \mathbf{M\&U} \underset{U_{i1}}{\overset{U_{o1}}{\rightleftarrows}} \mathbf{E\&U} \underset{U_{i0}}{\overset{U_{o2}}{\rightleftarrows}} \mathbf{N\&U}$$

Arrows are classified as outbound(o) or inbound(i), according as they are going from or returning to Shelton Square.

The operation of the IRC is simple, at least in our version. It has several departments: SCHEDULING, PERSONNEL, GARAGE, DISPATCHER, and a PRESIDENT The PRESIDENT has issued a memorandum requiring SCHEDULING to make up a schedule monthly. A schedule consists of a list of elements of type /TRIP/ TRIPNUM, ROUTE, where the TRIPNUMS are consecutive integers and ROUTE is Main, Elmwood, or Utica. He has also issued memoranda requiring that each morning PERSONNEL make up a list /DRIVER/ NAME of drivers, and the GARAGE make up a list /TROLLEY/ TROLLEYID of trolleys, and that these lists be sent to the DISPATCHER, who is to use these lists to make up an initial list /RUN/ TRIP, DRIVER, TROLLEY of runs. There are more trips than drivers, so the DISPATCHER initially only sends out as many as he can cover. Later, when drivers and trolleys return, he assigns them to another trip, if any are left, or sends them home.

The passengers are self-dispatching. They appear at an intersection and board their trolley when it appears. At each stop, they continue, or transfer, or get off.

Aside from sending memoranda, the PRESIDENT also receives report. SCHEDULING sends a copy of the schedule each month. PERSONNEL and GARAGE send daily summaries indicating how many drivers and trolleys were available. The DISPATCHER is required to keep a running record of all operations. To do this, each driver is required at each stop to get off the trolley and telephone the dispatcher telling him what stop the trolley is at and how many passengers are on it. The DISPATCHER uses this to update a run sheet with entries /STATUS/ RUN, STOP, NUMABOARD. At the end of the day, he sends the PRESIDENT a summary telling the total number of passengers carried each trip. On the basis of these reports, the president issues policy memoranda telling SCHEDULING how many runs of each kind to schedule, telling PERSONNEL how many drivers to hire and telling the GARAGE how many trolleys to buy.

In Example 1, we raised a number of questions and argued that the key to beginning to answer them was to see them as problems in semantics. We can use this example to try to state more precisely some features that an adequate theory of formal semantics would have to take account of. In the remainder of the section we shall use the mathematics that we have developed to begin work on such a theory.

- The DISPATCHER's run sheets are a paper record describing certain real events involving trolleys and passengers. That they are linguistically capable of doing so is due to the fact that the schema of the run sheets is a model of the schema of the actual trolley runs. They are both based on the category **R.** A particular run sheet at a particular stage of development is associated with a particular trolley at a particular stage of development, and the description it gives of its run may be true or false.
- The passengers and the drivers have different views of the route map. A passenger can develop on any path in **R,** whereas the drivers can only develop on paths in $\mathbf{R}_M$, $\mathbf{R}_E$, or $\mathbf{R}_U$. Yet these two views of the system harmonize because there is a *conceptual schema* (*Information,* 1987) namely *R,* which is simultaneously a model of both the drivers' and the passengers' schemata.
- The run sheets themselves are a sequence of events described linguistically by various memoranda from the PRESIDENT, as completed by the schedule, the driver list, and the trolley list, which are themselves described by memoranda. There is a complex structure of linguistic items talking about other linguistic items. Actually, there is a larger conceptual schema encompassing the different views of these parts of the system as well as the drivers' and passengers'.
- Modeled in the conceptual schema there is also a linguistic schema (Coleman et al., 1989a) showing how the structures TRIPNUM, ROUTE, NAME, TROL-

LEYID, STOP, NUMABOARD, /TRIP/, /DRIVER/, /TROLLEY/, /RUN/, and /STATUS/ fit together into a lattice.

- The PRESIDENT's memoranda not only assert that reality is a certain way, they cause it to be so. However, they do so in general terms—they prescribe schemata, but not developments. The schedule partially develops the DISPATCHER's schema, but the rest is left undetermined.
- Some of the reports do not give a full account of the developments they describe, but only a statistical summary.

7.1. Processes

A *process* is a *conceptual schema* $C : \mathbf{C} \to \mathbf{Set}$ together with a set $\{C_i : \mathbf{C}_i \to \mathbf{C}\}$ of models of C. A *development* of a process is a development of one of the schemata $C_iC : \mathbf{C}_i \to \mathbf{Set}$. A *history of* C is a set of developments of C.

A history shows the state of the process at a given time. It is understood that the process can be reinspected at a later time, and its developments may have developed further. In *Example 7,* each time one inspects, each of the runs, drivers and trolleys will have developed to a stage at least as advanced as before. Without formally introducing notation, we understand a *particle* to be a coherent series of developments, such as the series that belongs to some one particular driver or passenger, that maintains its identity as history goes on. So that the process is a *population* of particles, and a history of the process gives the current development of each particle. Also, the histories themselves develop, on a larger scale.

To speak of realizing a schema as a particle in a population, one has to be able to take account of synchronization restrictions, and this is part of the task of the conceptual schema. In *Example 3,* it is clear that, under normal circumstances, the progress of any one molecule through the schema is entirely independent of the progress of any other molecule. In *Example 1,* the opposite is true—a subprocess within a process usually cannot start without input from some other subprocess and may have to pause in the middle for further input. A protocol for a communications network is likely to have very sophisticated synchronization requirements—one kind of message may have to halt at a certain point until its predecessors have stopped using resources, but other kinds may be able to go through the bottleneck.

7.2. Interpretation

Let $C : \mathbf{C} \to \mathbf{Set}$ and $C' : \mathbf{C}' \to \mathbf{Set}$ be the conceptual schemata of two processes. An *interpretation of* C' *in* C is a model $M = \langle F, \alpha \rangle$, given by a functor $F : \mathbf{C}' \to \mathbf{C}$ and a natural transformation $\alpha : FC \dashrightarrow C'$, together with some extra data. For each schema $C'_i : \mathbf{C}'_i \rightarrow \mathbf{C}'$ of C there must be given a schema $C_i : \mathbf{C}_i \rightarrow \mathbf{C}$ such that $\langle C'_i F, \alpha \rangle$ restricts to a model of $C'_i C'$ in $C_i C$, and there must be a function assigning to each particle of C'_i of particle C_i.

Example 7 (Continued)

The run sheets can be interpreted in the runs. The run sheets have a conceptual schema S that maps $\mathbf{R}$ to the set of possible values of /STATUS/. The runs have a conceptual schema R that maps $\mathbf{R}$ to the product of the set of trolley stops with the set of sets of possible passengers. There is a natural transformation α that forgets all information about a trolley except the name of the stop that it is at and the number of people aboard. Together with the identity functor on $\mathbf{R}$, it constitutes a model of S in R. Similarly, the subschemata of both S and R are based on $\mathbf{R_M}$, $\mathbf{R_E}$, and $\mathbf{R_U}$ and thus are related by identity functors. To make an interpretation of S in R, all that remains is the date and run number at the top of each run sheet that assigns that sheet to its run, along with the sequence number for each /STATUS/ entry on the sheet that makes that stage of development of the sheet correspond to a stage of development of the run.

7.3. Valuation

Let C and C' be conceptual schemata and F and interpretation of C' in C, as in the previous subsection. An *event* S in C is a hereditary subset of the partial order $\mathbf{E_C}$, i.e., a subobject of $E_\mathbf{C}$. Thus S is (Goldblatt, 1984, sec. 10.3) a subset of $\mathbf{E_C}$ such that $s \in S$ and $s < t$ imply $t \in S$. For example, S might be the subobject generated by all the developments that, before a certain stopping time, have reached a certain state $\mathbf{x}$ once, or five times. S might be empty. Corresponding to S is a subobject S' of $E_{\mathbf{C}'}$ consisting of all the developments of C' that the interpretation sends to S.

Conversely, starting with a subobject S' of $E_{\mathbf{C}'}$, there corresponds a subobject S of $E_\mathbf{C}$. S may or may not occur, depending on developments. Formally, let χ_s : $E_\mathbf{C} \rightarrow \Omega_{\mathbf{E_C}}$ be the characteristic function of the subobject S. We call χ_s the *valuation* of S'. χ_s gives a value to S' at each possible stage of development s, namely it assigns to s the set of possible further paths t such that $st \in S$, so that the particle would be in S. The value expresses how far S is at that stage from occurring. Since $E_\mathbf{C}$ is isomorphic to $1_{\mathbf{E_C}}$, we have that χ_s is a truth-value in the sense defined above. (Let $i : 1_{\mathbf{E_C}} \rightarrow E_\mathbf{C}$ be an isomorphism. Then $i\chi_s : 1_{\mathbf{E_C}} \rightarrow \Omega_{\mathbf{E_C}}$ is a truth-value.)

Now suppose that some other event T is known to have in fact occurred. The occurrence of T makes T' true. The events in $\mathbf{E_{C'}}$ that do not correspond to sets containing T are not true, but some of them may become so with further development. In particular, S may now be more, or less, possible than before. It is no longer the case that any member of $\mathbf{E_C}$ can occur: the only possible realities now are those events in T. As we judged the truth value of S before by how large was the set of paths in $\mathbf{E_C}$ that would bring a particle into S, so now we judge by how large is the set of paths in T that bring the particle to S. T corresponds to a subobject $|T$ of $\Omega_{\mathbf{E_C}}$. For each s in $\mathbf{E_C}$, if $s \in T$, let $s|T = \emptyset$; otherwise let $s|T = s\Omega_{\mathbf{E_C}}$. Then the characteristic function $\chi_{|T}$ maps $\Omega_{\mathbf{E_C}}$ to $\Omega_{\mathbf{E_C}}$. The *conditional valuation of S' given T* in the development s of C is the map $\chi_{S|T} : E_{\mathbf{C}} \dashrightarrow \Omega_{\mathbf{E_C}}$ given by $\chi_{S|T} = \chi_S \chi_T$. This map is also a truth-value. We count S' as true given T if $\chi_{S|T} = \top\chi_T$.

8. STOCHASTIC PROCESSES

There are two kinds of stochastic processes associated with a process. A sequence wherein a particle develops within a schema is a *particle process*. A sequence wherein a set of particles enters and develops within the various schemata of a process, subject to the synchronization restrictions provided by the conceptual schema, is a *population process*.

Example 3 (Continued)

A labeled carbon atom introduced to the body in a leucine molecule may, along with the rest of the leucine molecule, be incorporated into and broken down from several proteins before decarboxylation and eventual appearance as CO_2. In the course of an infusion of such molecules, a large number of such particles will enter the body and follow different paths. In this particular example, there are no synchronization restrictions, and in fact, under normal conditions, the particles are stochastically independent. The vector statistic indicating the total number of particles in each of the three states is a statistic of the population process. It is a basic objective of our analysis to relate these processes.

The particle process may take place in discrete or continuous time. Let $C : \mathbf{C} \rightarrow \mathbf{Set}$ be a schema. We use standard notation as set out in Çinlar (1975), who discusses well many of the concepts that our analysis aims to explain. In discrete time, let N be the set of natural numbers, let X_n; $n \in \mathbf{N}$ be the state of the particle after the nth transition. $X = \{X_n\}$ is an indexed set of random variables.

Let a starting value x_0 be fixed. Let s_n be an element of $\mathbf{E} = \mathbf{E_C}$ that takes n steps. These determine an initial segment $x_{(n)} = (x_0, x_1, \ldots, x_n)$ of values of X. $X_{(n)} = (X_1, X_2, \ldots, X_n)$, the set of all possible $x_{(n)}$, corresponds to the event consisting of all such s_n. For integers $m > n$, $s_n \chi_{X_{(m)}}$ is the set of arrows that start from the development s_n and take the process $(m - n)$ steps further.

The closed interval [0,1] can be taken to be a category whose one object is [0,1] and whose arrows are the numbers in [0,1], acting by multiplication.

A *probability distribution on* X is a functor P from $\mathbf{E_C}$ to $\mathbf{E}_{[0,1]}$, such that, for each $n < m \in \mathbf{N}$, the sum over the arrows of $s_n\chi_{X_{(m)}}$ equals 1. A special case is the *stationary Markov chain* in which P is induced by a functor from $\mathbf{C}$ to [0,1].

Example 3 (Continued)

The schema is based on a category **L**,

$$\mathbf{p} \underset{g}{\overset{f}{\rightleftarrows}} \mathbf{1} \overset{h}{\rightarrow} \mathbf{c},$$

that is reminiscent of **A.** In fact, $\mathbf{E_L}$ looks like the picture of $\mathbf{E_A}$ given above. A Markov probability distribution can be given by assigning $f \mapsto 1$, $g \mapsto 3/4$ and $h \mapsto 1/4$. These data induce a functor from all of $\mathbf{E_L}$ to $\mathbf{E}_{[0,1]}$. For example, *gfg* maps to $(3/4)(1)(3/4) = 3/4 \times 1 \times 3/4 = 9/16$.

The conditional truth-values then determine conditional probability distributions. Lawvere has pointed out (Lawvere, 1963; Meng, 1987, 1989) the importance of looking at the category of probability distributions and the way that they act upon each other.

The particle process can be embedded in continuous time by considering (Çinlar, 1975, sec. 10.1) stochastic process $(X,T) = \{X_n,T_n; n \in \mathbf{N}\}$, where X_n is the state after the nth transition, and T_n is the amount of time spent in X_n before going on to X_{n+1}. Let us be a bit more precise about T. Just as with [0,1], so also $[0,\infty)$ can be made into a category. T is a functor from $\mathbf{E_C}$ to $\mathbf{E}_{[0,\infty)}$. The embedding of the discrete time process in the continuous time one can be reversed by taking, for each $n \in \mathbf{N}$, the outcomes to be the partition (x_n,T_n) over all the t_n.

One has to give, as before, the probability distribution on X, and now also on T. A *probability distribution on* T is a functor P from $\mathbf{E_C}$ to $\mathbf{E}_{[0,1]}$, such that, for each $n < m \in \mathbf{N}$, the sum over the arrows of $s_n\chi_{X_{(m)}}$ equals 1. A special case is the *Markov renewal process* in which P is induced by a functor from $\mathbf{C}$ to [0,1].

This approach to stochastic processes has several features. First, it separates the underlying logic of the process, as determined by C, $\mathbf{C}$ and χ, from the probabilistic aspects determined by P. Second, in agreement with modern trends in mathematics, it seeks to reduce questions about stochastic processes and their statistics to questions about the existence or factorability of certain mappings. Last, it tends to focus attention on the path space of the process, and thereby also on the potential-theoretic questions emphasized by Çinlar (1975).

9. CONTROL

Let $C : \mathbf{C} \rightarrow \mathbf{Set}$ be a schema and X a stochastic process on C. A functor R from $\mathbf{E_C}$ to $\mathbf{E}_{[0,\infty)}$ defines a *reward* for each development of $\mathbf{C}$. The expected reward at time n is the sum over all the paths in $X_{(n)}$ of the reward for that path times its probability. Sometimes it is possible to *control* the process in the sense that, for each $x_{(n)}$ one can make a *decision* among the conditional probability distributions leading to $x_{(n+1)}$. A consistent method for making such decisions is a *policy*. It seems reasonable to hope that the present methods, by their analysis of the path space, can lead to further clarification of such decision processes. For example, rather than optimizing the expected reward, one might wish to keep the minimum reward or the maximum cost within some bound.

10. SUMMARY

Computational logic is a body of theory centering around the notions of 'schema' and 'process' and the semantic notions of 'model' and 'interpretation,' describing how one process, and its path space, can be related to another. It can be applied to a very diverse set of problems, and its significance is different in each.

- An analysis of a complex system C can be based on a simple system C', provided C' is a model of C.
- The behavior of a system C can be specified conservatively by requiring that it have C' as a model, or liberally by requiring that it be a model of C'.
- Similarly, two computing systems can explain themselves to each other by telling how they model, or are modeled by, some generally known system.
- A stochastic process has an underlying logic. One begins to compare two processes by seeing if one models the other. If so, it is possible to define compatible probability distributions which preserve certain potential-theoretic quantities, and thereby to make quantitively correct predictions of one from the other.
- This leads directly to the possibility of predicting the control of one from the other.

The title of the present volume suggests the importance of trying to develop tools to understand processes that are, in one way or another, diffuse and distributed. This chapter has been a beginning of an attempt to do so.

REFERENCES

DARPA Neural Network Study. (1988). AFCEA International Press, 4400 Fair Lakes Court, Fairfax VA 22033.

Information Processing Systems—Concepts and terminology for the conceptual schema and the information base. (ISO/TR 9007). International Organization for Standardization.

Barr, M., & Wells, C. (1985). *Toposes, triples and theories*. New York: Springer-Verlag.

Bell, J. L. (1988). *Toposes and local set theories: An introduction.* Oxford: Clarendon Press.

Çinlar, E. (1975). *Introduction to stochastic processes.* Englewood Cliffs, NJ: Prentice-Hall.

Coleman, W. P. (1989). Automata and topoi as models of processes. In W. G. Vogt & M. H. Mickle (Eds.), *Modeling and simulation* (Vol. 20, Part 1, pp. 229–235). Instrument Society of America.

Coleman, W. P., Sanford, D. P., & De Gaetano, A. (1989a). Syntax and semantics of languages for medical information processing. In S. Buus (Ed.), *15th Annual Northeast Bioengineering Conference,* pp. 189–190.

Coleman, W. P., Sanford, D. P., & De Gaetano, A. (1989b). Logic of computational processes. *Theoretical Computer Science.* (Submitted).

Coleman, W. P., Sanford, D. P., De Gaetano, A., & Geisler, F. (1990a). Functional models of neurobiological processes. In X. J. R. Avula (Ed.), *Mathematical and computer modeling in science and technology.* New York: Pergamon Press.

Coleman, W. P., Sanford, D. P., De Gaetano, A., & Geisler, F. (1990b). Modularity of neural network architecture. *Proceedings of the International Joint Conference on Neural Networks.* Washington, DC.

Eilenberg, S. (1974). *Automata, languages, and machines* (Vol. A). New York and London: Academic Press.

Eilenberg, S. (1976). *Automata, languages, and machines* (Vol. B). New York and London: Academic Press.

Goldblatt, R. (1984). *Topoi: The categorial analysis of logic* (revised ed.). Amsterdam: North-Holland.

Johnstone, P. (1977). *Topos theory.* New York: Academic Press.

Johnstone, P. (1982). *Stone spaces.* Cambridge: Cambridge University Press.

Lambek, J., & Scott, P. J. (1986). *Introduction to higher order categorical logic.* Cambridge: Cambridge University Press.

Lawvere, F. W. (1963). *The category of probabilistic mappings.* (Preprint).

Mac Lane, S. (1971). *Categories for the working mathematician.* New York: Springer-Verlag.

Meng, X. (1987). *Categories of convex sets and of metric spaces with applications to stochastic programming and related areas.* PhD thesis, State University of New York at Buffalo.

Meng, X. (1989). *The category of random maps and the statistical decision problem.* (Preprint).

12

Information Systems and Neural Networks*

Ruth S. Dare*
George W. Zobrist
Computer Science Department
University of Missouri-Rolla

1. INTRODUCTION

Information systems come in various shapes and sizes, depending on their purpose and the type of information to be accessed. Such a system provides a suitable method of storing, manipulating, and retrieving the particular type of data needed for the information system. With today's ever-increasing amount of data to be processed, and the need to stay abreast of new developments in rapidly evolving areas, information systems are becoming the backbone of every kind of enterprise imaginable. Most conventional information systems today do not exhibit a great deal of intelligent processing abilities. Neural networks are currently showing promise as a means of creating more intelligent information systems.

1.1. Overview of Information Systems

Information systems exist for virtually any information processing task. These systems have been grouped in the following manner: information retrieval systems, database management systems, management information systems, decision support systems, and question-answering systems (Salton & McGill, 1983). A brief description of each follows.

Information retrieval systems are concerned with processing documents whose input often takes the form of natural language text from publications such as newspapers, research articles, and textbooks. An information retrieval system typically produces a set of references it deems applicable to the user's information request, called a *query*.

A group of related bits make a character. A group of related characters make a field. A group of related fields make a record. A group of related records make a file. And a group of related files make a database. For this data to be useful,

* Partial support was provided by the Intelligent Systems Center at the University of Missouri-Rolla.

programs are necessary to extract the needed data elements from all existing data in the database. Together the data and programs comprise the *database management system* (DBMS).

Every operating system contains a file system and various access methods which extract data from files residing within the file system. Certainly, specialized application programs can be written to extract necessary data elements from the file system as it is needed. What then is the advantage of having a database?

A nondatabase approach tends to encourage redundant data storage for easy access of each application program. This duplication of data often creates inconsistency within the file system; a change in one field, for example, may not be replicated as it should be in the corresponding field of the duplicate file. As new information needs develop, an application program must be written to extract the needed data, or, at best, an existing application program must be modified to reflect the additional processing required. A seemingly minor modification in information requirements can thus necessitate additional programming effort, which may be magnified several times due to data being distributed in several different locations throughout the file system.

A database system alleviates these difficulties. Redundancy and its accompanying inconsistency are no longer necessary; data is centralized, stored once, and may be accessed in a multitude of ways. Changing information needs are no longer a problem, since the DBMS contains its own programs to manipulate its data (Korth & Silberschatz, 1986).

Data from a database may be accessed via a user-written application program or a built-in application program called an *interactive query language processor,* where the user may directly request the DBMS to perform such operations as creating existing files in the database, adding data to files, retrieving existing data, updating file contents, deleting data within a file, and deleting entire files from the database (Date, 1986).

The database administrator (DBA) is the individual(s) responsible for the database system. This individual decides, among other items, the storage strategy, access rights, security, backup and recovery techniques, information content of the database, and access strategy, and specifies the database scheme, the overall database design. The DBA specifies the scheme in a *data definition language* (DDL) (Date, 1986).

The DBMS contains a DDL compiler which produces a data dictionary, describing data stored in the database. The data dictionary is itself stored on disk, together with the data files which make up the database. A DBMS also contains a *data manipulation language* (DML) precompiler, which creates normal host language procedure calls from DML statements issued within the application program. A DML provides for such operations as creation, insertion, deletion, and retrieval of data from a database.

An application program containing an embedded database programming language is then compiled and passed to the database manager, which interfaces with the file manager and query processor. The file manager oversees disk storage allocation and implementation details of data storage. The query processor translates a user's request for information from the database and sends it to the database manager (Korth & Silberschatz, 1986).

Data stored in a database is not in the form of natural language, as it is in an information retrieval system, but is rather stored in specified fields corresponding to the attributes of the database. The method by which the various fields are accessed depends on the underlying data model used in designing and implementing the database. Three database models are prevalent, specifically the relational, hierarchical, and network models (Ullman, 1980). These will be discussed later in the chapter.

A database system must provide an efficient mechanism by which its data can be entered, modified, updated, deleted, searched, and retrieved. It contains mechanisms protecting access rights, data integrity, and consistency of the stored data. A database includes ways of indicating low-level details of data storage, relationships between data elements, and database views where a given user sees only a portion of the entire database.

The database management system interfaces the low-level data stored in the database and the users' queries. It interacts with the operating system's file system, performing the indicated data manipulation language statements. In addition to handling integrity and security problems, the DBMS contains modules handling database access by simultaneous users, called *concurrency control,* as well as rollback and recovery routines in the event data has been corrupted in the database.

A *management information system* (MIS) is a special-purpose DBMS specifically designed for use by managers. It integrates data from many different sources, yielding the information needed by managers to facilitate their decision-making process. An MIS contains a DBMS which creates, stores, updates, and performs normal DBMS operations upon the data of the enterprise. It also contains modules responsible for processing the data obtained by its DBMS portion producing information beneficial to its managers (Hicks, 1984).

Decision support systems incorporate many different kinds of information systems into a system capable of enhancing the decision making abilities of a particular group. A decision support system may include an information retrieval system, a DBMS, the ability to view data in a graphical way, and any other system which would aid the decision makers. A decision support system is similar to an MIS in that they both enhance decision making; however, an MIS is specifically tailored toward the management community.

Question-answering systems often contain a natural language interface for user queries. Thus the system may be queried or questioned in the user's natural language. The system possesses common-sense knowledge in addition to facts pertaining to a specialized area. Question-answering systems attempt to extract specific retrieval operations from the user's query and return facts pertaining to the posed question. Advances need to be made in natural language processing and understanding for question-answering systems to achieve their maximum potential. Database management systems are the information system types considered next.

2. DATABASE SYSTEM MODELS

As mentioned previously, the three most prevalent database models are the relational, hierarchical, and network models. Each model is overviewed in turn.

2.1. Relational Model

The relational database model is the youngest of the three main database models. Data in the relational model is typically conceptualized as a group of tables. The idea of a table and that of a relation in mathematics are closely related. A relation is composed of tuples which can be thought of as rows or records. Also associated with relational databases is the notion of attributes. An attribute corresponds to a column or field of a database record. Attributes assume values from a set of possible legal values called the *domain of the attribute*.

Date (1986) defines a *relation* as a heading and a body. The heading is composed of a fixed set of attributes where each attribute corresponds to exactly one domain. The domains, however, are not required to be distinct. The body of a relation is a set of tuples which change with respect to time. Each tuple is made of pairs of attributes and values, one value–attribute pair for each attribute in the heading. The value for each attribute comes from its corresponding domain.

In a relation, no tuples are duplicated. The top-to-bottom order of tuples in a relation is immaterial, which, roughly speaking, indicates that a "row" in the table may appear anywhere. Attributes exist in no particular left-to-right order, although this property is often nonexistent in operational relational database systems. Each attribute value in the relation is atomic; it cannot be broken down further. It consists of a single value, as opposed to a set of values.

In the relational model, relationships between attributes are not explicitly stored; no pointer fields exist, as they do in other database models. Needed attribute relationships have to be determined after a query has been issued. The lack of storage of explicit relationships makes the model theoretically simple but often complex in the amount of processing needed to determine the necessary relationships (Salton & McGill, 1983).

Without the storage of relationships between attributes, how then is data located in a relational database? The database is accessed via some language in which an application program has been written. This language is what was referred to previously as the host language. A nonprogrammer, merely wishing to use the database, will typically issue queries through a query language or through a developed interface such as a menu system. An application programmer accesses the database via a host programming language such as PL/I. The host language performs activities needed to carry out the query which are not provided in the data sublanguage portion of the language dealing specifically with defining the structure and manipulation of the database. These activities include programming language constructs and various computational operations.

The data sublanguage consists of two separate parts. One part, the *data definition language,* describes the creation and deletion of such database entities as tables and views. It also includes statements causing tables to be modified. The second part, the *data manipulation language,* provides a means of performing modification to existing data in the database, deleting data, inserting new data into the database, and performing search and retrieval operations based upon specified conditions.

Specific data items are identified and located by the use of keys. A *primary key* is an attribute which uniquely identifies a tuple. Relationships between tuples may be established by the use of foreign keys. A *foreign key* is an attribute in a relation A that matches exactly with a primary key of a relation B. Thus matching a foreign key of one relation to a primary key of a second relation establishes a relationship between two tuples of different relations. Often, a query involves a complex sequence of searches and inferences to determine the exact relationship between tuples in many different relations in an attempt to find the answer to a query. The above discussion of data sublanguages is consistent with that given by Date (1986).

The overall design of a relation is given by a relation scheme which specifies the attributes in the order they appear in the database. A relational database scheme also exists which lists all the relation schemes present in the data base (Salton & McGill, 1983).

2.2. Relational Algebra

Without referring to a specific implementation of a database system, the manipulation operations needed to locate information requested by a query may be summarized by describing some operations of a relational algebra (Salton & McGill, 1983). A brief description of the five main operations follow.

The *union* of two relations A and B produces a new relation C composed of all tuples in relation A followed by all tuples in relation B. Tuples in B that are identical to tuples in A are not duplicated in C. The *Cartesian product* of two relations A and B, denoted A × B, is a new relation C formed by concatenating every tuple from B with every tuple from A. A duplicate of a tuple is not allowed in the relation. The Cartesian product provides a way of forming one large relation from two smaller ones.

The *difference* of two relations A and B, denoted A − B, consists of all tuples in A that do not appear in relation B. A relation is produced as the result of the difference operation. The *projection* operation performed on a relation A results in a new relation formed from columns chosen from A based upon the columns specified in the projection statement. A projection causes a large relation to be separated into smaller relations, whereas a Cartesian product of two relations does the opposite. The fifth operation, *selection,* causes rows of a relation to be chosen creating a new relation. The choice of rows comprising the new relation is based upon whether the row contains an attribute of a specified value.

Of the five fundamental relational algebra operations described above, the last two, projection and selection, are unary operators, applying only to one relation at a time. Difference, Cartesian product, and union are binary operators and apply to two relations. The union and difference operators require records contained in both relations to be identical in type and number of attributes (Salton & McGill, 1983).

Other operations needed to carry out database manipulations may be constructed from these five basic operations. An intersection of two relations A and B, can be affected by using the difference operator, A − (A − B). Often associated with database operations is the binary join operator. It is accomplished via the Cartesian product operation followed by the select operation. A single relation results. If a join operator is used with a condition specified for some attribute, as in AGE > 45, then only those tuples in the Cartesian product where the AGE attribute value is greater than 45 are included in the resulting relation. This type of join is known as a conditional or restricted join. See Figure 12.1 for examples of the above operations and illustration of terminology.

A natural or unrestricted join of two relations produces a relation formed by taking the Cartesian product of two relations having a common attribute. Only those tuples in the Cartesian product having equal common attribute values are included in the resulting relation.

2.3. Hierarchical Model

A database based on the hierarchical database model is composed of a group of trees. Pointers connect children records to their corresponding parent records. These children-to-parent links in the hierarchical database perform the same service of establishing relationships between various records as primary-to-foreign key matches do in the relational database model. The relational database model provides the conceptual simplicity of requiring understanding of only one data structure, namely, the table. The hierarchical database model employs a much more complicated data structure environment with its pointers to various records but does have the ability to easily navigate through the records as an answer to a query is being formulated.

Student #	Name	Age	Class Level
147	S. Adams	14	9
342	J. Smith	15	10
831	P. Harris	17	12
926	C. Lewis	16	11

Relation Student

Teacher #	Name	Class #
1125	R. Jones	SS107
1187	J. Rork	EL105
1352	H. Cane	MS100
1114	K. Able	SC103

Relation Hs. Teacher

Teacher #	Name	Class #
0124	S. Korpi	SS002
0187	K. Stern	EL015
1352	H. Cane	MS100

Relation Jr High. Teacher

Figure 12.1. Database Operations and Terminology.

Student #	Class #
147	EL105
342	MS100
831	SS107

Relation Enrollment

Teacher #	Name	Class #
0124	S. Korpi	SS002
0187	K. Stern	EL015
1352	H. Cane	MS100
1125	R. Jones	SS107
1187	J. Rork	EL105
1114	K. Able	SC103

Figure 12.1a. Relation Jr High. Teacher UNION Hs. Teacher.

Teacher #	Name	Class #
0124	S. Korpi	SS002
0187	K. Stern	EL015

Figure 12.1b. Relation Jr High. Teacher—Hs. Teacher.

Student #	Class Enrolled	Teacher #	Name	Class #
147	EL105	1125	R. Jones	SS107
147	EL105	1187	J. Rork	EL105
147	EL105	1352	H. Cane	MS100
147	EL105	1114	K. Able	SC103
342	MS100	1125	R. Jones	SS107
342	MS100	1187	J. Rork	EL105
342	MS100	1352	H. Cane	MS100
342	MS100	1114	K. Able	SC103
831	SS107	1125	R. Jones	SS107
831	SS107	1187	J. Rork	EL105
831	SS107	1352	H. Cane	MS100
831	SS107	1114	K. Able	SC103

Figure 12.1c. Relation Enrollment X Hs. Teacher.

Name
S. Adams
J. Smith
P. Harris
C. Lewis

Figure 12.1d. Relation PROJECTION $_{\text{NAME}}$ (Student).

Age
17
16

Figure 12.1e. Relation SELECTION $_{\text{AGE} > 15}$ (Student).

Teacher #	Name	Class #
1352	H. Cane	MS100

Figure 12.1f. Relation Hs. Teacher INTERSECT Jr High. Teacher.

Student #	Class #	Teacher #	Name
147	EL105	0187	K. Stern
342	MS100	1352	H. Cane

Figure 12.1g. Relation Enrollment JOIN Jr High. Teacher (Natural Join).

Teacher #	Teacher Name	Class #	Student #	Student Name	Age	Class Level
0124	S. Korpi	SS002	831	P. Harris	17	12
0124	S. Korpi	SS002	926	C. Lewis	16	11
0187	K. Stern	EL015	831	P. Harris	17	12
0187	K. Stern	EL015	926	C. Lewis	16	11
1352	H. Cane	MS100	831	P. Harris	17	12
1352	H. Cane	MS100	926	C. Lewis	16	11

Figure 121.1h. Relation Jr High. Teacher JOIN $_{\text{Student \# > 350}}$ Jr High. Student (Restricted Join).

Student #, Name, Age, Class Level

Figure 12.1i. Heading for Relation Student.

342 MS100

Figure 12.1j. Tuple of Relation Enrollment.

Age

Figure 12.1k. Attribute of Relation Student.

Consider the tree in Figure 12.2. In the hierarchical model a child record has only one parent. Suppose it is necessary to store data representing the phone number of the governing body of each city. Each city is located in a county. Each county is located in a state. Further suppose there is a need to know the representatives and the senators for each state. There are many counties, representatives, and senators, then, for each state. This upward progression from the bottom of the tree to its top illustrates the many-to-one relationship between the various record types. See Figure 12.3 for an illustration of the many-to-one relationship. As the records described by the record types are filled with actual data, the data records are generally traversed from the root downward until the desired data are located. Each data record corresponds to an occurrence of its record type. As just described, the hierarchical database model has no difficulty representing the many-to-one relationship, but extra steps must be taken to represent more complicated relationships such as the many-to-many relationships (Salton & McGill, 1983).

Data manipulation within a hierarchal database model involves operators dealing with trees. Operators are needed to perform such activities as finding a specific tree, such as the tree containing data for the state of Missouri, and moving from a county occurrence to the senator occurrence corresponding to the same state. An operator is needed to navigate through the entire sequence of a

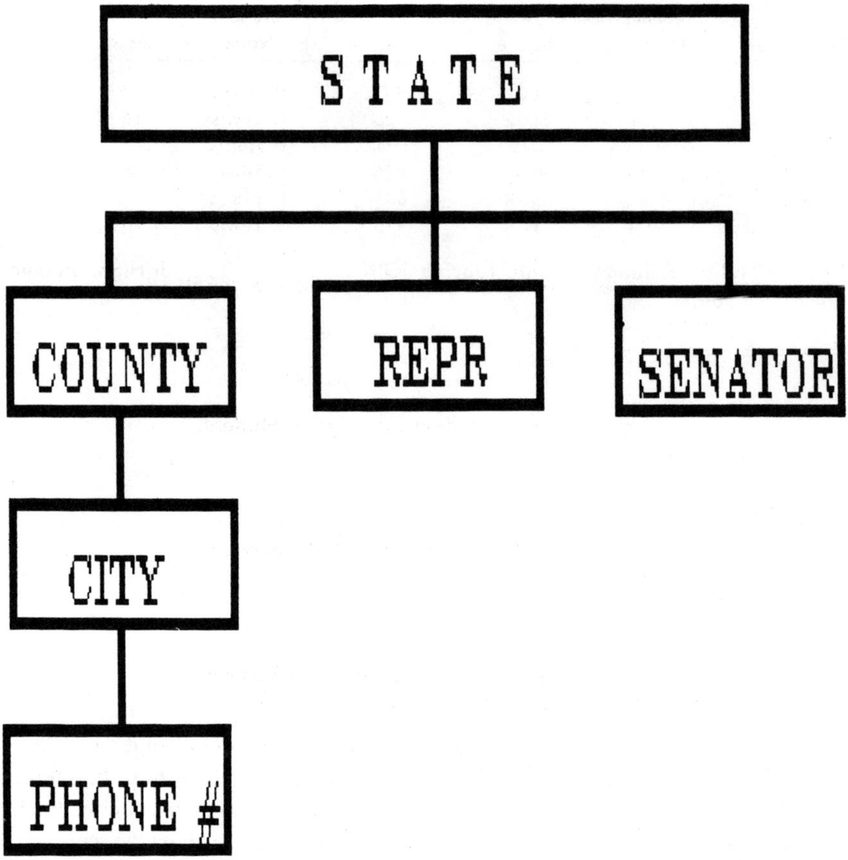

Figure 12.2. Hierarchical relationships.

hierarchy, such as inspecting trees describing all states. Moving down the hierarchy, such as from a county to one of its cities, is an activity for which an operator is needed, as well as operators to insert and delete records within the forest. Most operators of a hierarchical database work at the record level (Date, 1986).

2.4. Network Model

The network database model consists of a group of records with relationships between those records indicated by pointers. The network model is thus similar to the hierarchical database model in using pointers to indicate relationships between records; however, in the hierarchical model, only one parent is allowed

Figure 12.3. Many-to-one relationship.

for a given child record. This restriction is lifted in the network model, which allows a child record to have many parents, or no parents at all.

Data manipulation within the network model necessarily involves operations on records and pointers. These operations include locating a record containing a specified value, moving a record to another location in the network, disconnecting a child from its parent and linking it to another parent, deleting a given record, modifying a specified record, inserting a new record into the network, and stepping through the network in a specified manner, such as to inspect all children occurrences of a specified parent record, etc. (Date, 1986).

3. ARTIFICIAL INTELLIGENCE AND INFORMATION SYSTEMS

There has recently been a great deal of interest in incorporating insights gained from artificial intelligence research with database systems (Brodie, Myopoulous, & Schmidt, 1984; Cohen, 1989). A mutually beneficial interaction is being explored between these two disciplines. Database systems store large amounts of data and are concerned with accessing the data in a convenient and efficient way. Artificial intelligence systems need vast amounts of data from which they can glean common-sense knowledge as well as application-specific information. Current literature indicates users of database systems are clamoring for a simpler, more natural way of interacting with database systems, such as incorporating natural language front-ends allowing queries to be issued in natural language, as opposed to special database access languages, which are often unwieldy for end-users (Chapnick, 1989). Greater emphasis is being placed on user-friendliness in an attempt to conceal the underlying database operations from the user. Interfaces are being sought in which a user can indicate his or her intent, as opposed to specifying the exact database manipulation statements necessary to carry out the task (Salton & McGill, 1983). Thus, artificial intelligence can benefit by using the large amount of data currently existing in database systems as well as insights database researchers have gained with respect to methods of accessing this data in the most convenient and efficient way possible; database systems can benefit from insights obtained by artificial intelligence workers in creating database systems capable of making inferences, having intelligent interfaces, and generally exhibiting more intelligence as needed by the specific database application area. It is suggested that merging techniques of artificial intelligence with those of database systems is a way of achieving the benefits of intelligent processing capabilities and those of large, efficient, long-term memory capabilities (Cohen, 1989).

3.1. Overview of Neural Networks

Neural networks, a subset of artificial intelligence, give promise in many of the ways just mentioned. A neural network, sometimes called a *parallel distributed processing* (PDP) *model,* consists of eight entities (Rumelhart & McClelland, 1986) which will now be described. Computation is accomplished via the interaction of simple computational units called *processing elements* (PEs). As the connection strengths change between the PEs, various input patterns are stored, altered, and eventually retrieved.

An *activation level* exists for each PE which may be 0 (off), or 1 (on), or, in the continuous case, lie within some continuous interval depending on the architecture of the network. An *output function* for each PE maps the current activation level to some output value. Often, the output function serves as a thresholding device where the PE does not affect the PEs to which it is connected unless the activation level is above a specified threshold value. The *pattern of connectivity* between the PEs enables the neural network to store, modify, and retrieve data placed in the network. Various connection schemes exist, depending on the type of task the network is to perform. All programming of a neural network is thus accomplished in determining the connection strengths, or weights, between the PEs. Connection strengths between the PEs are often represented in a connection matrix.

A *propagation rule* exists for a neural network which causes the various input patterns to spread through the network of connections. The network's *activation rule* collects all input values entering the PE from the output function of all PEs to which it is connected and combines these values with the current activation level of the given PE, yielding a new activation level for the PE.

Many networks learn as they process data. Learning in a neural network often takes the form of modification of connection strengths between the various PEs. New connections may be created, connections that have already been established may be deleted, or existing weights may simply be changed depending on the *learning rule* chosen for the network. Learning may be supervised by a "teacher," where the desired output is presented to the network and compared to the network's actual computed output with adjustments made in an attempt to lower the network's error.

Learning in a neural network may be unsupervised. In this instance, the network attempts to discover the appropriate connection strengths between the PEs on its own, without the aid of a teacher. The last item characterizing a neural network is the *environment* in which the net is to operate, involving such considerations as whether or not the input vectors are linearly independent or orthogonal.

3.2. Associative Networks

Neural networks may further be classified as either autoassociative or heteroassociative (Kohonen, 1984). An *autoassociative network* attempts to create connection strengths in either a supervised or an unsupervised manner, whereby an input pattern is associated with itself. This kind of network is useful for applications where the input data may contain errors, may be only partially specified, or may have been corrupted by noise. A neural network may not be of the autoassociative genre but rather classified as a *heteroassociative network.* Here a given input pattern is associated, not with itself, but rather with another specified pattern. Assume A_i and B_i are arbitrary patterns. An autoassociative network then contains the associations (A_i, A_i) and (B_i, B_i). When, in the autoassociative case, a version of A_i is presented to the network, for example, the network's output should be a correct, stored version of A_i. In the heteroassociative case, assuming the association (A_i, B_i) has been previously stored, a presentation of A_i to the network as its input pattern should produce B_i as the network's output (Kosko, 1988).

A small number of information retrieval systems have been prototyped using neural networks. Most of the networks have been autoassociative to achieve retrieval in the event of incorrect or only partially specified retrieval cues.

4. NEURAL NETWORK APPLICATIONS AND INFORMATION SYSTEMS

Some recent work has been done toward applying a neural network approach to the area of information systems. Experiments have been conducted investigating the potential of the Hopfield net (Hopfield, 1982, 1984; Lippman, 1987; Lippman, Gold, & Malpass, 1987) as a bibliographic information retrieval system. Lippman, Gold, and Malpass's experiment consisted of 11 exemplar patterns taken from references in Hopfield's (1982) paper. Lippman et al. discuss their experiments using first a Hopfield net to perform information retrieval and then using a combined Hopfield and Hamming net. After carefully selecting the exemplar patterns (i.e., references from Hopfield's paper) which consisted of the authors' initials, last name, publication name, and two-digit date, the experimenters found that an entire bibliographic exemplar entry was able to be retrieved with the name (with or without initial) and the publication name. For further details see Lippman et al. (1987).

Personnaz, Guyon, and Dreyfus (1986) also describe an implementation of an autoassociative neural network capable of performing information retrieval. Their parallel distributed processing model is a fully connected network of McCulloch and Pitts (1943) neurons. Each PE uses a threshold output function. PEs receive input as either a $+1$ or -1. Their paper examines the problem of designing an autoassociative neural network capable of memorizing exemplars and retrieving this information in the best way possible given possibly incomplete or partially incorrect retrieval cues. They describe a network where the exemplar patterns are stable and function as attractors. Their network has no cycles and contains no unpredictable spurious stable states. They describe a method of storing data that is retrievable even if the input vectors representing the exemplars are not orthogonal. Their network has an "energy" similar to the way Hopfield (1982, 1984) describes the energy of this network. The network of Personnaz et al. has an energy that is an ever-decreasing function which keeps cycles from arising. Learning is accomplished by the generalized Hebb Law (Hebb, 1949; Rumelhart & McClelland, 1986).

Soulie (1986) gives examples of various networks that use a Lyapunov function. The networks described use various iteration modes, including parallel, sequential, block-sequential, and random iteration. Soulie (1986) gives many formal definitions and accompanying corollaries and theorems describing each type of network and its dynamical behavior in the various iteration modes. A necessary and sufficient condition is given, ensuring that input patterns are fixed points, a condition holding even if the input vectors representing the patterns are not linearly independent nor orthogonal, conditions required for correct operation in Hopfield's original network description.

In the example given by Soulie (1986), the network is used for information retrieval. Input patterns used in the experiment were names of authors from the bibliography of their paper. These input patterns were not linearly independent, but results show the system capable of retrieving words, despite the fact that the input pattern contained several bits of error.

Anderson and Murphy (1986) discuss an information retrieval application based upon the brain-state-in-a-box (BSB) model. This neural network was first revealed in Anderson, Silverstein, Ritz, and Jones (1977). Golden (1986) describes the BSB model as an abstract nervous system composed of N highly interconnected neurons with self-feedback. The neural network receives its input as an N-dimensional vector and magnifies the input activation, recycling it via the feedback mechanism until the PEs saturate. The BSB often is used as an autoassociative system.

When considering a BSB model with N = 3, each of the three components is forced to lie in the interval [−1, 1]. Each component of the input vector corresponds to a activation level of one of the PEs. As each PE assumes its maximum and minimum values of 1 and −1, respectively, and is considered as a component of a three-tuple, these eight possible three tuples form the corners of a box and hence the name brain-state-in-a-box. An input vector with N processing elements, when the N components assume their maximum and minimum values, form an N-dimensional hypercube. The BSB model eventually causes the system to go to one of the 2^N corners of the hypercube (Rumelhart & McClelland, 1986).

Anderson and Murphy (1986) describe an autoassociative BSB neural network which employs Widrow-Hoff error correction (Rumelhart & McClelland, 1986). They show how to reconstruct a missing portion of a previously stored pattern by repeatedly passing the current information through a connectivity matrix to reformulate the missing portions.

They also describe an information retrieval system where input vectors are encoded as concatenations of the bytes in their ASCII representation. Here the BSB functions as an autoassociative network. The input vectors consist of 25 characters occupying a 200-dimensional array. They found that approximately 20–30 presentations were needed for the system to store the input patterns. They also conducted a simulation where an ambiguous input pattern is presented and the BSB network attempts to disambiguate the input.

A third simulation reported in Anderson and Murphy (1986) involves learning a concept hierarchy. The neural network was able to make both specific and general inferences based upon the underlying hierarchy. The network could represent and group data items placed in a hierarchy with an extension to their work planned where the network discovers the hierarchical relations on its own in an unsupervised learning paradigm.

Anderson (1986) describes what he terms a "distributed database implemented with the BSB neural network." The BSB was taught a set of related facts about diseases. It appeared to be able to "guess" some treatments for a specified illness, despite the fact that it had never been taught the particular illness–treatment relationship. He notes that no internal record is kept of the line of reasoning used by the system, so difficulty in error correction is greatly magnified. Another feature present in the system described by Anderson is its ability to merge criteria, retrieving data most suitable for two criteria as opposed to finding the best solution for merely one or the other criterion. The number of iterations required by the BSB model to obtain its answer may be interpreted as a certainty measure. Fewer iterations required to arrive at an answer indicates a greater certainty on the part of the system regarding the quality of its answer. The BSB neural network appears to be able to function in a way similar to an expert system.

Information systems need to be developed with capabilities of intuitive reasoning, making intelligent guesses, and acting on hunches. Anderson (1986) notes that information in the real world is not stored in formal propositional form but rather in what he terms "intuitive" form. According to Anderson, traditional AI systems have not succeeded in modeling information of this type. He notes that "intuitive reasoning" is difficult to handle in traditional AI systems due in part to its lack of being well defined. Traditional expert systems, for example, typically require explicit facts, rules, and an inference engine which uses the facts and rules in a clearly specified manner to form inferences. Systems capable of intuitive reasoning are generally not this well defined and thus do not lend themselves well to modeling via traditional AI methods. The PDP models appear to be a step toward creating systems with these capabilities. An idea appears to be emerging that tomorrow's intelligent information systems will contain both PDP models to handle intuitive reasoning and traditional sequential processing systems for the remaining processing tasks.

Storage capacity varies from network to network. Thus, no generic optimal network size exists for the efficient storage of various amounts of information. See the references cited in the discussion of each individual network for further information on optimal neural network size and storage capacity. Peretto and Niez (1986) discuss the long-term memory storage capacity of neural networks. They derive quantitative expressions of storage capacities for complex neural networks with a given topology of connections and discuss the best organization of neurons ensuring a maximum memory storage capacity for a given set of biological constraints.

5. CONCLUSION

Information systems are a vital part of every functioning enterprise both large and small. There are currently several varieties of information systems, including information retrieval systems, database management systems, management information systems, decision support systems, and question-answering systems. This chapter briefly described these systems with emphasis placed on database management systems. The three main database models, relational, hierarchical, and network, were described.

Most conventional information systems in operation today do not exhibit much intelligent processing capabilities. Many researchers are predicting such systems will soon be enhanced with intelligent behaviors. A merge of results gleaned from the area of artificial intelligence with that from the area of database systems is being proposed by some in an attempt to achieve more intelligent database systems. Neural networks appear promising in the endeavor to enhance information systems with more intelligence in such areas as dealing with incomplete data, corrupted retrieval cues, and making inferences from existing data.

REFERENCES

Anderson, J. (1986). Cognitive capabilities of a parallel system. In E. Bienenstock, F. Fogelman Soulié, & G. Weisbuch (Eds.), *Disordered systems and biological organization* (NATO ASI Series, pp. 210–226). Berlin: Springer-Verlag.

Anderson, J., & Murphy, G. (1986). Psychological concepts in a parallel system. *Physica, 22D,* 318–336.

Anderson, J., Silverstein, J., Ritz, S., & Jones, R. (1977). Distinctive features, categorical perception, and probability learning: Some applications of a neural model. *Psychological Review, 84,* 413–451.

Chapnick, P. (1989). Ushering in a new era, *AI Expert, 4*(2), 7–8.

Brodie, M., Mylopoulous, J., & Schmidt, J. (Eds.). (1984). *On conceptual modelling.* New York: Springer-Verlag.

Cohen, B. (1989). Merging expert systems and databases. *AI Expert, 4*(2), 22–31.

Date, C. (1986). *An introduction to database systems, Volume 1* (4th ed.). Reading, MA: Addison-Wesley.

Golden, R. (1986). The "brain-state-in-a-box" neural model is a gradient descent algorithm. *Journal of Mathematical Psychology, 30,* 73–80.

Hebb, D. (1949). *The organization of behavior.* New York: John Wiley and Sons.

Hicks, J. (1984). *Management information systems.* St. Paul, MN: West Publishing.

Hopfield, J. (1982). Neural networks and physical systems with emergent collective computational abilities. *Proceedings of the National Academy of Sciences, USA, 79,* 2554–2558.

Hopfield, J. (1984). Neurons with graded response have collective computational properties like those of two-state neurons. *Proceedings of the National Academy of Sciences, USA, 81,* 3088–3092.

Kohonen, T. (1984). *Self-organization and associative memory.* New York: Springer-Verlag.

Korth, H., & Silberschatz, A. (1986). *Database system concepts.* New York: McGraw-Hill.

Kosko, B. (1988). Bidirectional associative memories. *IEEE Transactions on Systems, Man, and Cybernetics, 18*(1), 49–60.

Lippman, R. (1987, April). An introduction to computing with neural nets. *IEEE ASSP Magazine,* pp. 4–22.

Lippman, R., Gold, B., & Malpass, M. (1987). *A comparison of Hamming and Hopfield neural nets for pattern classification* (Tech. Rep. No. 769). Cambridge, MA: MIT Lincoln Laboratory.

McCulloch, W., & Pitts, W. (1943). A logical calculus of the ideas immanent in nervous activity. *Bulletin of Mathematical Biophysics, 5,* 115–137.

Peretto, P., & Niez, J. (1986). Long term memory storage capacity of multiconnected neural networks. *Biological Cybernetics, 54,* 53–63.

Personnaz, L., Guyon, I., & Dreyfus, G. (1986). Neural network design for efficient information retrieval. In E. Bienenstock, F. Fogelman Soulié, & G. Weisbuch (Eds.), *Disordered systems and biological organization* (NATO ASI Series, Vol. F20, pp. 227–231). Berlin: Springer-Verlag.

Rumelhart, D., & McClelland, J. (1986). *Parallel distributed processing* (Vol. 1). Cambridge, MA: MIT Press.

Salton, G., & McGill, M. (1983). *Introduction to modern information retrieval.* New York: McGraw-Hill.

Soulie, F. (1986). Lyapunov functions and their use in automata networks. In E. Bienenstock, F. Fogelman Soulié, & G. Weisbuch (Eds.), *Disordered systems and biological organization* (NATO ASI Series, Vol. F20, pp. 85–100). Berlin: Springer-Verlag.

Ullman, J. (1980). *Principles of database systems.* Potomac, MD: Computer Science Press.

Author Index

Italics indicate bibliographic citations.

M

N

O

P

R

Subject Index